GERMAN RESISTANCE TO HITLER
Count von Moltke and the Kreisau Circle

'We can only expect to get our people to overthrow this reign of terror and horror if we are able to show a picture beyond the terrifying and hopeless immediate future. A picture which will make it worthwhile for disillusioned people to strive for, to work for, to start again and to believe in. For us Europe after the war is less a problem of frontiers and soldiers, of top-heavy organizations and grand plans, but Europe after the war is a question of how the picture of man can be re-established in the breasts of our fellow citizens. This is a question of religion and education, of ties to work and to family, of the proper relationship of responsibility and rights. I must say that under the incredible pressure under which we have to labour we have made progress, which will be visible one day.'
Helmuth von Moltke, Letter to an English friend (Lionel Curtis), 1942

Portrait of Helmuth James Count von Moltke

GERMAN RESISTANCE TO HITLER

Count von Moltke and the Kreisau Circle

Ger van Roon

Translated by
PETER LUDLOW
Department of History
Queen Mary College
London

VAN NOSTRAND REINHOLD COMPANY
LONDON
NEW YORK CINCINNATI TORONTO MELBOURNE

VAN NOSTRAND REINHOLD COMPANY LTD

Windsor House, 46 Victoria Street, London S.W.1

INTERNATIONAL OFFICES

New York   Cincinnati   Toronto   Melbourne

Translated from *Neuordnung im Widerstand,*
© 1967, R. Oldenbourg, München.

Library of Congress Catalog Card No. 73-125956

SBN 442 08975 9

First published 1971

Paper supplied by
P. F. Bingham Limited, Croydon

Printed in Great Britain by
Butler & Tanner Ltd, Frome and London

Introduction

There are several reasons for welcoming this English version of Dr. van Roon's book about the Kreisau Circle.

The first is that it brings together in a handy form a mass of material which hitherto has only been accessible to those understanding German. Dr. van Roon's diligent researches have explored almost every significant aspect of the Circle's origins, its activities and the lives of its members. As the Circle was one of the main groups in Germany working against Hitler and his Third Reich, this evidence is important to all interested in the history of the period.

Many things about the German Opposition are still controversial. Under what circumstances is assassination justifiable? Was the attempt to kill Hitler, even if justifiable, a mistake? Would it still have been a mistake if it had been successful? Would a successful coup have given Germany, in the long term, a stable democratic government? Were the conspirators putting the interests of humanity above those of Germany—or the reverse? Was their treatment by the British and American Governments fair or wise?

Man may have to go a good way further along his road before he can see either Hitler or the opposition in correct perspective, so that it is likely to be some time before we can give more than provisional answers to these questions. Our immediate task is not to sit in judgement but to make sure that we understand. The information contained in this book will be of great value in assisting us to do so.

This is more than ever the case because the importance of the Group is not primarily due to the contribution which they made to the removal of Hitler. It is true that by July 1944 nearly all of those members who were still at liberty supported the attempt at assassination. Two of them were in the War Ministry on the vital day. But for long many of them, and in particular Helmuth von Moltke, thought that assassination was either wrong or, if justifiable, liable to create more problems than it solved.

The killing of Hitler was not the dominating concern of the Circle and it is a mistake to regard them as a mere appendage to the Stauffenberg plot. They were civilians rather than soldiers

v

(even if some of them may have been temporarily in uniform). Their real object was the regeneration of Germany. They saw that, important as the removal of Hitler and his henchmen might be, it would still be inadequate unless accompanied by clear thinking as to the direction in which a new start should be made. The documents in which they tried to give expression to that thinking are the most important part of this book, for these documents do not merely concern Nazi Germany but in at least three ways provide a challenge to the West today.

When one looks for a common factor between the heterogeneous backgrounds of the Circle's members, one finds it in the importance which one and all attached to the revival and strengthening of moral and spiritual values. The furnace of horror and danger through which they passed gave fresh reality to their religious beliefs and convinced them that, if the rest of the world was to be saved from going in the direction to which Nazism and Communism pointed, it must find again a faith to live by. The paradox of today is that a revulsion from materialism and a bewilderment about values is accompanied by the waning ability of religion—at any rate in any institutional form—to command men's allegiance. The men of Kreisau would have said that this was a recipe for disaster. If they were right, it is urgent for us to find a new way of making religion count, of reinforcing humane instincts by an imperative of belief.

Secondly, the Circle considered that man's ingenuity had brought about a society over which man was in danger of losing control. They regarded Nazism, Fascism and Communism not merely as aberrations in individual countries but as symptoms of a condition into which the whole world was in danger of falling, thanks largely to the unreflecting application of technological discovery. They were deeply concerned with the clashes between efficiency and humanity, between prosperity and welfare, between freedom and authority. They believed that the problem could only be solved by evolving new forms of political, social and economic organization. In particular, they demanded a deliberate return to a society in which the basic unit consisted of simple, small communities giving each individual a chance of participation, so as to end the estrangement of man as ruled from man as ruler.

These ideas can easily be dismissed as the output of people who were out of touch with reality, as the product of élitiste romanticism vainly seeking a return to a past which was in fact anything but golden. One can argue that economic growth demands large units and complex organization, with a consequent diffusion of responsibility, and that men cannot be expected to forego the affluence which economic growth brings. But such a dismissal does not get rid of the problems which they saw and which have grown even more serious in the intervening thirty years. Can we afford to pass over their answers as naïve attempts to put back a clock that moves inexorably forward?

Thirdly although they did their thinking before atomic weapons came into use, they believed that mankind would in due course destroy itself unless national sovereignty could be transcended and the establishment of an effective supranational authority put in hand. They were abreast if not ahead of the resistance groups in German-occupied countries in planning how a post-war Europe could be integrated.

Since those days a number of attempts have been made to move in the direction which they indicated. But success has been limited. The British Commonwealth of Nations, on which Helmuth von Moltke placed high hopes, has ceased to count for much. Even in the Common Market, the Commission, which was intended to provide the germ of a supranational authority, seems to be losing out to the Council of Ministers, representing the national governments.

Many people will think that this is the natural state of things and that attempts to supersede nations are visionary. Those who object to British entry into the Common Market on the ground that it would infringe sovereignty would clearly take this view. But this attitude does nothing to answer the problem faced by the Kreisau Circle as to how a multitude of sovereign states can live together without collisions and how such collisions in a mechanized scientific world can be prevented from becoming lethal to society.

The diagnosis which the Kreisau Circle made may have been mistaken and unnecessarily alarmist. They may have made a correct diagnosis but prescribed an impracticable treatment. There may be other preferable remedies. A further possibility is that neither diagnosis nor prescription is at fault so much as the will of the patient to undertake the cure. What there can be no doubt about is the relevance of their thinking to the present human situation.

M. L. G. BALFOUR, C.B.E.
Professor of European History in the
University of East Anglia

Author's Preface

Until recently there have been so many gaps in the knowledge of one of the most important groups within the German resistance, the Kreisau Circle, that no comprehensive work about it could be written. The author, who has been able to trace many until now unknown documents, and to question many of those involved, hopes that he has succeeded in remedying this situation. In several instances a completely different picture from the accepted one has emerged.

He wishes to express thanks to many individuals for providing material and elucidating it. It is impossible here to mention them all, but their names appear, if not in the course of the book, then in the original German edition, *Neuordnung im Widerstand*. An exception is Countess Dr. Freya von Moltke who has most kindly put all the posthumous papers of her husband at his disposal. He would like to thank her, and all those who have helped him, not least for the friendliness and readiness with which they submitted to his continually renewed questioning.

The author is obliged to the following institutions: the Deutscher Akademischer Austauschdienst, Bonn; the Netherlands Organization for the Advancement of Pure Research (ZWO); the Institute of Contemporary History, Munich; the Political Archives of the Foreign Office, Bonn; The Berlin Document Centre; the Boberhauskreis, the Foundation 'Hilfswerk 20 Juli 1944'; Frankfurt-am-Main; the Militärgeschichtliches Forschungsamt, Freiburg i.Br.; the Upper-German province of the Jesuit Order; the Reichwein Archives, Osnabrück: the Rijksinstituut voor Oorlogsdocumentatie, Amsterdam; the Historical Office of the State Department, Washington; the Adam von Trott Committee; and the World Council of Churches, Geneva.

Much of the apparatus of footnotes which can be found in the original German edition has been omitted; those wishing to work on original sources will need to refer to that. Exceptions are where the author has added footnotes in explanations of passages new to

ix

the English text. The content of many footnotes has, in fact, been taken up with the narrative.

* * *

This English edition, involving considerable rearrangement of the material, and shortening of the text, has been prepared with the assistance of Barry Sullivan, to whom the author and publishers extend their sincere thanks. Grateful acknowledgement is also made of the courtesy of relatives, friends and organizations closely associated with the Kreisau Circle who have made photographs and sketches available for reproduction in this work.

GER VAN ROON

Contents

PART 1

ORIGINS AND COMPOSITION
OF THE KREISAU CIRCLE

CHAPTER 1

Roots of the Kreisau Circle

The word Circle as applied to the main civilian resistance group in Germany during World War II has sometimes been contested. The aim of the Circle was not so much to bring about the end of Hitler—this task was laid on others—as to ensure that when the Nazi tyranny was overthrown a body of men was ready to take over the government of the country and lead it back into the European community of nations. In the conditions of war-time Germany the members could but very rarely meet together, and even then, by no means, all concerned. They were not allowed to know every other person's name for security reasons. At the same time it was a remarkably cohesive group, bound together by sympathy, purpose and danger. Moreover, it undoubtedly had a centre in the person of Count Helmuth von Moltke, who by personal contact and correspondence made himself the pivotal point of the whole enterprise, and at whose family seat at Kreisau in Silesia three important conferences took place. The more research that is done into the clandestine activities of this remarkable far-sighted band of men, the more does the word Circle seem justified—a word which in German is appropriately euphonious—*Kreisauer Kreis*.

The true roots of their achievement lie in the circumstances and trends of the time during and after World War I. The various groups and individuals who were to associate together and whose creative thinking was to find expression in the Kreisau programme were influenced by a number of factors: by the German youth movement as a whole, by the Silesian work camps for students, peasants, and workers, by the young socialist movement and religious socialism, and by the renewal movements in German Catholicism. Here they found their most stimulating experiences while at the same time living through the consequences of World War I, the years of crisis and mass unemployment, the rise and growth of national socialism. There were other trends and traditions, such as conservative thought between the wars, Prussianism, Protestantism, which could have been considered separately, but this would have led to oversimplification. These other influences are traced in the course of the story told in Chapters 2–5. In this chapter we shall consider briefly the main factors one by one.

In no other country did the youth movement develop such a variety of forms or display such marked characteristics as in Germany, and it is significant that many of the most important members of the Kreisau Circle were profoundly influenced by it. Reichwein, for example, belonged to the Wandervögel, Einsiedel was a member of the Akademischer Freischar, and Trotha was a Scout Leader. The last two also worked with Moltke in the Silesian Young Men's Society. Pastor Poelchau had been a member of the Koenger Federation, and von der Gablentz, Haeften and Steltzer belonged to the Berneuchner movement which stemmed from the youth movement. Mierendorff and Haubach were young socialists; Delp and König joined the Jesuit-led 'Neudeutschland' organization.

A crucial event took place in the year 1913, illustrating the strength and militancy of progressive youth. It had been proclaimed that celebrations would take place throughout the country to mark the centenary of the Battle of Leipzig and the German uprising of 1813 against Napoleon. Several groups of young people, however, dissociated themselves from this kind of official patriotism and issued a summons to their own Youth Festival. As a consequence, while the centenary celebrations were being held all over Germany in October 1913, more than a thousand young men assembled on Hohe Meissner, near Kassel. Their manifesto solemnly declared: 'The Free German Youth wish to shape their own lives on the basis of their own decisions and responsibility, and according to their own personal integrity. They are firmly committed to inner freedom in all circumstances.'

Within a year of this meeting on Hohe Meissner, World War I broke out.

The Wandervögel wave was by then at its height. It had started in the eighteen-nineties among grammar-school children from middle-class homes. Despite its expansion, however, it still formed only a small minority of young people, and this may explain why its members behaved like an elite, emphasizing the need for election, venerating their leaders and taking themselves far too seriously. The revolutionary influence of romanticism was still traceable in their movement, and their cultural critique was characterized by protest against the superficiality of materialism and the rigidity of middle-class life. Because the schools themselves were dominated by a bourgeois state of mind, they tried to create their own world outside, and by 'wandering' to escape from the tutelage of parents and teachers. To maintain that this resentment against society and the growth of private communities resulted in a devaluation of the individual is inaccurate, for the protest was intensely personal, and an individual's own conscience decided what style of life he adopted. However, it is true that, as so often in German history, their power of resistance to the spell exercised by the community was limited. Especially after the war, the individual was forced into the background, even in the youth movement. There was also a danger that the private world would come to constitute the entire world, the personal style of life the only permissible one, and the individual communities a model for the State. Basically, however, the youth movement remained one of protest. Links with society or State were little sought for, and for this reason the movement was underestimated by the older generation and its strong points ignored.

However, when the Wandervögel returned home from the war, their numbers reduced from 15,000 to 6000, it was evident that the old times had gone for ever. This consciousness that things had changed was extremely strong, and naturally influenced their thoughts about the future. They had already discussed the problem in the trenches and all assumed that a national renewal was essential, but there were widely differing ideas about the character of that renewal. A significant feature of the Wandervögel who returned from the war was their preoccupation with the Volk.* This was a direct product of their wartime experiences, and they valued it as an idea to be revived under peacetime conditions. A person's private group or social class could not be equated with the Volk; moreover they had also become aware of others who belonged to this same Volk beyond Germany, for instance among the German minorities in the Balkans. Finally, there was the change that had taken place in Germany itself. Instead of a monarchy there was now a republic. The former State, with its strong leadership and aristocratic features—in several cases parelleled in the youth movement—had now been replaced by a State which

* Literally 'people', 'ethnic groups', but sometimes used with racial and even mystical overtones.

was threatened both from within and without. Its republican form was rejected by the romantic elements among German youth. This estrangement of part of the younger generation from the Republic had fateful consequences but the Republic was also to blame for failing to use that generation properly. There was still the same gulf between them and their elders as before the war, but the things protested about and resented were different.

What chiefly caught the imagination of the young were cultural, social and educational ideas, whereas the reaction to economic and political developments was simply one of resentment. This does not mean that the whole of German youth rejected democracy; in a poll taken in 1930, two-thirds of the members of the Berlin groups voted for the democratic parties, and when the independent federations chose a political party—unfortunately too late—they selected the German Staatspartei. Furthermore, their lack of interest in politics was not peculiar to their generation: large sections of the German population had come to expect a solution handed down to them from above.

When the youth groups attempted to preserve their independence after the Nazis seized power, they soon discovered that in a totalitarian state independence so far from being permitted was even regarded as subversive. Some of them made the transition to the Hitler Youth without difficulty, since the latter had assumed many of the external characteristics of the youth movement. Once within it they were gradually corrupted by Nazi ideology, and only a very few, a genuine elite, managed to find the way into resistance. The war-time Munich student group 'The White Rose' (see p. 163) was to be one of them.

In a memorandum drafted in 1933, Theodor Steltzer, later a member of the Kreisau Circle, wrote the following devastating criticism of the youth policy of the new Nazi government: 'Bases of great significance for the building up of the nation already existed in the Christian and Federal Youth Movement, the popular boarding schools and the voluntary work-service (Arbeitsdienst). These had clearly stimulated young people to take a more profound interest in religious and church matters. All these valuable educational foundations, however, have been sacrificed in favour of playing at soldiers.'

Another of the roots of the Kreisau Circle was the Silesian work camps for students, peasants and workers. The experience here showed that it was possible, through the joint efforts of both old and young, to overcome the gap and to discover common solutions to certain specific problems. This work of popular education in the work camps had a decisive influence on several of those who later became members of the Kreisau Circle.

The geographical situation of Silesia meant that it had always been somewhat isolated. It lay midway between the Prussian north and the Austrian south, and between eastern and western Europe, and the character of its people seems to reflect this. They appear to combine an intense devotion to home with a longing for change and distant things. In the Middle Ages, the country acquired its character from the German colonists, while in the fourteenth and fifteenth centuries the influence of Bohemia grew. Later Silesia shared in Austrian Baroque, but after the victories of Frederick the Great in the Seven Years War and his seizure of Silesia, its fate became bound up with the history of Prussia.

The end of World War I meant the beginning of hard times for Silesia. Relations between Germans and Poles had already become more difficult in the late nineteenth century. The German defeat in 1918 was followed by the plebiscite and by the Geneva judgement of 1921 which cut the country in two (see p. 67). The frontiers were drawn right through a thickly populated industrial area which had functioned as a unit for more than a hundred years. The troubles of this post-war period prevented the mutilated country from recovering quickly. Unemployment and refugees increased the difficulties. Towns had been separated from the hinterland and industry had to be built up again, while uncertainty about the economic future provoked political radicalism.

It was against such a background that Eugen Rosenstock, the driving force behind the movement for adult education in the nineteen-twenties, described with some justice as the principal ancestor of the Kreisau Circle, was appointed Professor in Breslau in 1923. He was particularly interested in the problems of man in industrial society. While at Breslau his ideas on popular education were linked with the activities of the Silesian Young Men's Society to which the young Helmuth James von Moltke was later to make his own special contribution.

In the spring of 1926, the Young Men's Society opened the Boberhaus in Löwenberg. Its aim was to develop further the relations with Germans abroad which had existed since 1922. It was also hoped that young people from different and conflicting social groups close at hand would be able to meet. Good intentions were not lacking, but the resources and the necessary insight were. The idea of bringing the communal youth movement face to face with the social, political and ideological problems of the present was insufficiently thought out for the clashes to be overcome. It was here that Rosenstock was able to help. The idea of bringing about co-operation between students of different subjects and members of different social groups was entirely in line with his ideas and aspirations. At the university itself he tried to interest a student group which had formed around him, and which included members of the youth movement, in the ideas of popular education.

The practical take-off was provided by the young Helmuth James von Moltke, who, although only twenty, was extremely mature for his age and viewed the world around him with a critical eye. He was concerned about the human and social needs of the Waldenburg industrial district, an extraordinarily backward area in which centuries of poverty and suffering had sapped all possibility of growth. Moltke began by trying to call the attention of German and foreign journalists to the situation. Later he turned to Rosenstock, whose response was immediate and positive, as he saw a practical opportunity for the development of an effective working party. Rosenstock brought one of his students, Horst von Einsiedel, into the discussions. Later Einsiedel described this first meeting with Moltke and the first impression of his carefree man-of-the-world manner in the following words: 'One day a cousin of Carl Dietrich von Trotha appeared on the scene. He is a man to whom I immediately felt inferior. Although almost two years younger than me and only twenty years old, he knows the Kaiser, Hindenburg and all the European politicians, down to Loebe and Loucheur. He is very clever and astute, able and genuinely impressive. To talk to he is naturally urbane, although this very manner sets a barrier against intimacy. However, as he is not at all pretentious, this causes no offence.' Their meeting marked the beginning of a partnership that continued until Moltke's death.

They first discussed how the problems were to be overcome. It was essential that the work should not be performed as an act of charity but instead be done by able-bodied people in the area itself. For this to be achieved, the co-operation of all was essential. On 14 September 1927 a small group of members of the Silesian Young Men's Society, Professor Rosenstock and other interested persons from the university met at Kreisau, the estate of the von Moltke family. At this meeting the details of a forthcoming conference in the Boberhaus were discussed. At Rosenstock's suggestion, Einsiedel and Moltke called personally on all the people whom they wanted to invite. About ninety people received invitations. A special method was adopted to ensure that the people who attended were the most capable ones. '. . . (I) asked the Catholic which Protestant, and the trade unionist which industrialist he considered most suitable for energetic work of this sort and vice versa. If anyone was mentioned by more than one member of the opposition, we went straight to him and invited him to the conference.' During the conference, in which 68 men and women took part, the Löwenberger Work Centre was founded to do the necessary research, education and publicity.

Einsiedel and Trotha also emphasized the need of a work camp as a place where leaders of the different youth organizations could come together. The work camp was intended, too, to offer an opportunity for leading businessmen and representatives of the German School for Popular Research and Adult Education to meet together for several days. The camp was planned to take place between 14 March and 1 April 1928 in the Boberhaus. The participants were to include, besides members of the Silesian Young Men's Society, representatives of the Christian and Socialist Young Workers, young farmers and students, whether belonging to Fraternities or not. The invitation emphasized that the reason for the work camp was the situation at Löwenberg. Among the young people involved in the preparations for the camp, Einsiedel visited young workers, while Trotha visited the sons of farmers, Moltke's duty being to obtain financial support. Not everybody welcomed the idea of the work camp, some groups indeed viewed it with mistrust. The young workers were rather confused by the idea of the 'National Community', and the young farmers thought the whole enterprise typically urban. Many students also, who were members of Fraternities, had strong reservations about joining in activities of this kind.

In the end one hundred people took part in the camp .The participants were divided into five work groups. There was physical work for four hours in the morning. In the evenings there were songs, music and so forth. There were two lecture courses: the first, by Rosenstock, was historical, and the second, by Adolf Reichwein, was on the dependence of the German economy on the world economy. Four discussion groups considered 'Russia', 'America', 'The problem of age in economic life' and finally 'The use of leisure time'.

The leaders' meeting was held from the eleventh to the fourteenth day of the camp. Rosenstock considered this particularly important and repeatedly emphasized its importance to the youth leaders. The leaders' meeting, a meeting of adults, was held to discuss ways of preventing the young from feeling themselves a separate group over and against the older generation. Eighty prominent men and women from all walks of life took part. The young people listened and contributed some of their own ideas to the discussions of the adults. In particular they urged the need for better educational opportunities and holidays, for care for the unemployed and for the provision of free time and more work camps. The conference agreed on the urgent need to create a new order for industrial and agricultural workers to secure co-operation between employers' and workers' representatives in the education of the new generation and finally to found a new educational centre. They also agreed that plans should be made for another camp.

In retrospect, the three Löwenberg work camps of 1928, 1929 and 1930 form a distinct group; their individual themes were closely related. Under the general heading of 'The depopulation of Silesia' the relationship between town and country was discussed during the second camp. The leaders' meeting was again well attended; the whole administrative hierarchy of the province was present. The third camp, in which women and girls also took part for the first time, discussed the 'position of the graduate in the nation and the State'. Among the lecturers was an English youth leader, Rolf Gardiner.

Work camps were not the only concern of the Löwenberg centre. There was an abundance of plans and ideas, but unfortunately there were often too many obstacles for all these ideas and plans to be developed. The world economic crisis was at its height and its effects made new ventures extremely difficult. Thus, despite the written promise of financial aid, the plan for a bachelor home for mine workers could not be implemented because of the lack of a grant from the State. Despite the difficulties, however, a country home for young town girls was established in Jakobsdorf, where they could receive a thorough two-year training in agricultural domestic science, and general education. The work of this community repeatedly broke down antipathies between different social groups. 'Representatives of the three social groups in the nation were able to achieve a common language that had proved beyond the grasp of the older generation. A group such as this, which formed a cross-section of the community, was capable of rising above class and party interests', was the proud opinion of one of the participants. Work camps and other groups capable of practical work and modelled on the Silesian example were soon formed all over Germany while the idea of the work camps inspired the scheme for voluntary service. After the Nazi seizure of power, Rosenstock, who was of Jewish origin, emigrated to America. (In 1940 President Roosevelt entrusted him with the founding of 'Camp William James': because of this the present day U.S.A. Peace Corps regards the Löwenberg work camps as their fore-runners.) On the whole the Silesian work camps were an interest-ing and welcome experiment. In the period after the Kreisau Circle was established one often comes upon references back to the valuable experience of those days.

The Löwenberg model always excited some mistrust among the young socialists, although these were another root of the Kreisau Circle. The young socialists, as an independent group somewhere between the Young Workers' Society and the Social Democratic Party, made a strong impact on socialist circles. Their aim was a spiritual and intellectual renewal of their movement. Among the influences that stimulated them were the youth movement itself, the new position of the SPD as the ruling party, World War I, the conflict in the Ruhr, and religious socialism.

After 1918 the members of the Workers' Youth Movement could share in the liberal social atmosphere of the youth movement generally. The romanticism of the Wandervögel and the manifesta-tions of the Free Germans had a strong influence on the young socialists. These influences became even stronger as many young men from progressive bourgeois circles joined the Social Demo-cratic movement, but they also created difficulties between the young recruits and the party leadership. These were not the only forces pressing for a fundamental revision of socialist thought. The novel position of the SPD itself did the same. Contemporary prob-lems stimulated a search for contemporary forms of socialist thought. Party members became more accessible to the thoughts and beliefs of others. The majority of young socialists were con-cerned with educational and cultural problems and rejected the one-sidedly materialist emphasis of their elders. The young socialists who later became members of the Kreisau Circle made a vigorous contribution to this general development. Theo Hau-bach, for example, wrote a critical essay entitled *Socialism and the problem of the generations,* and he, like Carlo Mierendorff and Adolf Reichwein, repeatedly expressed the desire to make their ideas more concrete.

The occupation of the Ruhr by the French gave the young socialist movement, which had hitherto been preoccupied with problems of culture and Marxist thought, a political character. At Easter 1923 they staged a conference at the Hofgeismar Winter School. The letter of invitation read: 'Our task is to overcome the strong element of mistrust towards our state and nation which still exists in the socialist movement and to develop a new, positive national awareness along with a clear and definite civic sense.' The participants took the new ideas back to their groups and they were made known to a wider public through further conferences, at which Haubach and Mierendorff were among the speakers. Haubach, who was foreign editor of the *Hamburg Echo*, was also responsible for preparing a study conference on foreign affairs at Whitsun 1924. He himself contributed a paper on the 'Foundations of a Socialist Foreign Policy', which included the following words: 'Just as contemporary political realities have made a rethinking of Marxist socialism compulsory—just as ideas about the take-over of the state (the "capture of social and political power") have had to be supplemented by thought about leadership of the state ("defence and practical justification of that capture") —so the socialist movement is compelled to formulate the objectives and outlines of its own foreign policy.'

The activity of those at Hofgeismar caused a sensation in the party and an opposition group was soon formed in Hanover to expound Marxism and to fight against the 'national romanticism' and the 'concessions to the bourgeoisie' advocated by the Hofgeismar Conference. In 1925 the Jena Reich Conference passed a resolution proposed by the Hanoverians against the Hofgeismar ideas largely with the help of the votes of the centre. At a study conference shortly after the Reich conference the Hofgeismar group adopted a declaration of basic political principles that had been largely written by Haubach. This declaration shows clearly the rightward trend of this group: '. . . , Our political creed is expressed in our devotion to the colours red and black-red-gold. Red is the colour of the socialist idea, while black-red-gold is the flag symbolizing the political activity of German social democracy on German soil with German members. The Hofgeismar Circle sees in the state of today the necessary precondition of the state of tomorrow.' Growing differences led the men of

Hofgeismar to leave the young socialist organization at the beginning of 1926.

Nevertheless, the Hofgeismar group worked vigorously in the party and national organizations and exchanged views among themselves in conferences. Mierendorff and Gustav Dahrendorf were elected to the Reichstag, and, with Kurt Schumacher, leader after 1945 of the West German SPD, and Karl Holtermann, the leader of the 'Reichbanner',* they formed a militant group to fight against reactionary forces. During his imprisonment after 1933 Julius Leber wrote his *Thoughts on the Prohibition of German Social Democracy*, in which he investigated the origins of the party's mistakes: 'When the Social Democratic Party took over the government in 1918 it was already inwardly old. This was disastrous . . .' After 1926 many of those who had been at Hofgeismar linked up with the religious socialism of the theologian and philosopher Paul Tillich; several, including Reichwein, Mierendorff and Haubach, were invited to join the editorial staff and the advisory committee of Tillich's *Neue Blaetter fuer den Sozialismus*.

The importance of religious socialism for several members of the Kreisau Circle can easily be demonstrated. Poelchau was a pupil and friend of Tillich. Von der Gablentz owed much to contact with the circle of Tillich. Reichwein stated quite specifically that he was a religious socialist, while Einsiedel and Trotha were pupils of the religious socialist Loewe. Finally, Adam von Trott zu Solz was introduced to the group responsible for the *Neue Blaetter* shortly before the Nazi seizure of power.

Religious socialism in Germany can be traced back to the nineteenth century, to the work of the Blumhardts and to Swabian Pietism. After World War I a younger generation took over: Dehn and Tillich.† A study group of like-minded people discussed the relationship between religion and socialism. Their intention was not to solve the workers' problem in a nineteenth-century way. For them it was not a question of absorbing the worker into the existing traditional form of society. Tillich and his friends believed

* A paramilitary movement to protect the Weimar Republic against the attacks from the national socialists and from the right.

† Karl Barth belonged to the group of religious socialists for only a few years; soon after this he was stressing the split between God and men. Tillich emigrated in 1933 and became Professor at the Union Theological Seminary in New York, at Harvard, and finally at Chicago University.

that they stood at a turning-point in history, a turning-point in the development of society. To them the revolutionary changes of the preceding years constituted a crisis for middle-class capitalist society. The time had come when a new social order had to be established. In this task they apportioned a decisive role to socialism, or rather to the proletariat. They stressed particularly the religious or prophetic element in socialism. The ideal of social justice, which they found at the core of socialism, became their own ideal, formulated by Tillich as 'the demand for a society in which it is possible for every individual and for every group to live meaningfully and purposefully, a demand for a meaningful society'. In addition to this ethical element in religious socialism, there was also an eschatological one. Tillich introduced into the discussion of the inter-war years the idea of KAIROS. The realization of the new social order ought to be the essence of things to come, it ought to achieve a realized eschatology. In an essay entitled *The Foundations of Religious Socialism* Tillich defined what he meant by this idea. 'It refers to the moment in time which is filled with unlimited significance and unlimited demand. KAIROS is the fulfilled time moment, in which the present and the future, the existing and that which is demanded, coincide, and from the tension of which the new creation emerges. . . .'

It was not, in the first instance, the intention of this movement, which had its roots in the Lutheran church, to effect a synthesis between religion and socialism. Although it had an indirect significance for the church as an apologetic movement the primary intention of religious socialism was to awaken the religious elements in socialism to a new life. Its criticism was directed not only against the church, which had often in its history attached itself to the state, or to specific social groups, but also against socialism because of its materialism and its 'this-worldliness'. The socialism of the future was to be not a movement for workers, but a new ethical ideal for all circles. The object of the movement was the 'theonomous' society, in which 'the autonomous forms of human culture are fulfilled with religious substance, so that all of them point beyond themselves to a final ground of meaning, to a final meaningful objective'.

The ideas of the religious socialists were disseminated through volumes of essays, radio broadcasts, labour weeks, conferences at the universities and in the journals *Blaetter fuer Religiœsen Sozialismus* and *Neue Blaetter fuer den Sozialismus*. The Social Democrats, however, were wary of the very name 'religious socialism' as it aroused suspicions of ecclesiastical propaganda. This led the religious socialists to change the title of their journal, which in the event proved important as they were able to render considerable assistance to the socialist movement. The generation conflict in particular had made it increasingly obvious that socialist cliches needed revision and that the movement as a whole needed renewing.

The importance of religious socialism came to be acknowledged even beyond Protestant and socialist circles. Father Noppel, for example, greeted the venture as something for Catholics to value. 'If it succeeds', he wrote, 'the kingdom of God will profit greatly'. Commenting on the views of the religious socialist economist Heimann, he stressed 'how near this trend in contemporary socialism is to Catholic ideas on social policy'. These quotations are typical of the changes that were taking place at that time in Catholic social ideas. Among those who dedicated themselves to building a new society was the Jesuit Heinrich Pesch, who developed the idea of solidarity in the economic sphere. His aim was not to bring about a compromise between capitalism and socialism so much as to propound a distinctive social principle. 'Man is at one and the same time a person and a member of society. He is a synthesis of the individual and the collective and not a compromise.'

As capitalism considerably strengthened its position after World War I and pressure on the lower classes greatly increased, Catholic views on capitalism became more critical and at the same time a new attitude towards socialism emerged. In spite of their rejection of atheistic Marxism, Catholics in the Weimar period were able to establish contact with the Social Democrats in other spheres for the first time. Catholics recognized the value of some socialist ideas. The need for transforming social structures was constantly reiterated; the trend can be seen in the publications of the various Catholic youth organizations which had come into being soon after World War I. In quick succession there appeared *Quickborn* led by Guardini, *Neudeutschland* under the leadership of the Jesuits and *Neuland*, which united the Catholic youth of Austria in particular. Two future members of the Kreisau Circle, Delp and König, were members of *Neudeutschland*; König, indeed, was a district leader for several years. This Catholic youth movement was to a great extent a movement of social and political emancipation; it provided a sense of national community and of service to the fatherland transcending class conflicts and party divisions. Indeed, one of the most striking features of the Catholic youth movement between the wars was this emphasis on the nation.

The writings of several leading Jesuits show the same trend.* The monthly publication of their Upper German province, *Stimmen der Zeit*, came to occupy a leading place among Catholic journals, as is still does today. Among those who belonged to this province were three men who later became members of the Kreisau Circle: Augustinus Rösch, Delp and König. Rösch was Father Provincial and Delp covered sociological problems on the editorial staff of *Stimmen der Zeit*.

Pope Pius XI's encyclical *Quadragesimo Anno* of 15 May 1931 gave a strong stimulus to new social thinking. The encyclical has had considerable influence on Catholic thought. It refused to place undue emphasis on either individualism or collectivism, since a man must be both an individual and a member of the community. Workers' organizations were held to be essential instruments of social renewal and pioneers of the future order; their work ought, however, to be developed by 'vocational groups' (Berufsstaende). As these 'vocational groups' were described only in general terms, misunderstandings about the term soon arose. The 'vocational groups' were not intended to be a revival of the traditional castes of reactionary romanticism. Neither were they to be regarded as an imitation of fascist ideas, since they were not organs of the state, but, on the contrary, were intended to bring about 'a reduction of the economic role of the state'. They did not signify the dissolution of workers' organizations, which would maintain their special responsibility of acting as corrective forces. As the national socialist party gained power soon afterwards, further definition and application of these ideas was impossible, but they established the guidelines for making fresh starts in the future.

Thus a strong interest existed among Catholics in social problems. But whereas a Jesuit priest was invited to speak at the fifth congress of religious socialists in Stuttgart, a religious socialist was denied the opportunity to speak at the Kirchentag of his own church at Nuremberg in 1930. The Protestant church was gener-

---

* There was a marked spiritual and intellectual renewal in German Catholicism at this time. During the bitter campaign which Bismarck waged against Catholic influence in education and thus in politics the Jesuit order had been banned. But in 1917 the remaining sections of the anti-Jesuit law were repealed, and the Order was once again allowed to establish its houses.

ally more inclined toward the nationalist conservative views of the right than to the socialism of the left. Religious socalism therefore remained the concern of a small minority. Tillich in particular emphasized the danger of political romanticism in Protestant circles and underlined the links between the churches and Judaism in this matter.

This chapter has sought to describe the influences which were decisive on the lives of several members of the Kreisau Circle. Each of the movements depicted had its own distinctive characteristics, but there were also certain common features. Three in particular should be mentioned.

There was an obvious attempt in all of them to break through the rigid demarcation lines between religious, political and social groups in the Germany of that period. 'Class' and 'party' were for many suspect ideas. There was also an increased awareness of the problems of other groups and a desire to know about them and learn from them. As a result there was a growing appreciation of men of different views.

In the second place through contact with members of other groups, individuals were forced to re-examine their own attitudes, and this breathed new life into their own ideas. It produced an hostility to rigidity and conservatism, but also an emphasis among the youth on the significance of the nation.

Thirdly, those who had reformulated their own ideas looked for methods of expression which seemed to them appropriate and contemporary. But although the younger generation were right to insist on making a breakaway, their lack of experience meant that their ideas were bound to be rather impractical. They needed the help of older experts to work out their plans. It is one of the striking features of the Kreisau Circle that it enabled the two groups, the young and the experts, to find a meeting place.

CHAPTER 2

Helmuth James Count von Moltke

Helmuth James von Moltke was born in Kreisau, in Silesia, on 11 March 1907, the first child of Helmuth Count von Moltke and his wife Dorothy, *née* Rose-Innes. Kreisau was a place of historical interest. The estate, 'The Manor of Kreisau, Nieder-Graditz and Wierischau' to give its full title, had been donated to Field-Marshal Helmuth von Moltke, who came from an old Mecklenburg family, as a reward for his famous victories in the service of Prussia. As he had no children himself, Kreisau passed, on his death in 1891, to the son of his eldest brother, the grandfather of Helmuth James. Kreisau, however, was always closely associated with the Field-Marshal, and it contained many momentos of him. His room in the Schloss was left untouched after his death. Two striking pictures hung in the hall: the first showed the entry of the French into Lübeck, with the future Field-Marshal clearly visible among the Lübeck citizens; the other picture showed Moltke with the victorious German armies entering Paris in 1871. Two captured French cannons stood at both sides of the main entrance until the end of World War I, and in the large park, on a small hillock called Kapellenberg, was the much-visited tomb of the Field-Marshal in a chapel containing the graves of the Moltke family.

There were three main houses in Kreisau; the Gatehouse, the Hall (Schloss) and the Hill House (Berghaus). Of the three, the Schloss stood at the centre. For a long time the old Countess Moltke, Helmuth James' grandmother, lived in the Gatehouse. Widely known as Muttel Ella, she was a woman of exceptional astuteness, wit and a charm which allowed her to say and do a great deal that would have been quite out of the question for others. The Hill House, a roomy attractive house with large living rooms and small bedrooms up under the broad gable roof, lay somewhat further away and higher up. It was lived in, at first, by a lady companion of a niece of the Field-Marshal. Later it became the family home of Helmuth James, and it was there that three conferences of the Kreisau Circle took place.

Helmuth James' parents were contrasting in character. His father, although a talented man, had never received a thorough education and many of his gifts were undeveloped or undisciplined. He was a seeker, and in his maturer years was strongly influenced by a firm attachment to Christian Science, through which, as a young man, he had been cured of a chronic heart complaint. An impulsive man, he had a lively mind, at least in things which really interested him, and a considerable influence on, and attraction for, other people. His style of life was simple, though he was rather fastidious in certain respects and unpredictable, which made him sometimes difficult to get on with. He could be extremely affectionate and helpful, but also rather thoughtless. His observations were usually to the point and, as he had all the Moltke reserve, all the more appreciated for being rare. He loved music and had a strong and pleasant singing voice. Now and then in the evenings he would sing Brahms or Schubert or Richard Strauss for which occasions everybody gathered in the great hall up at the top of the wide staircase of the Schloss. To understand this man one had to hear him sing.

Helmuth James' mother was a woman of singular charm. She was the good angel of the Kreisau household, loved on all sides, honoured and cherished. She was on good terms with even the most distant of the Moltke relatives. She took a keen interest in politics, and liked to view problems from all angles. She had a strong and integrated personality, full of warmth and kindness, and a sharp intellect that enabled her to be independent in her thinking and in her actions. She educated her children—after Helmuth James there were three more sons and a daughter—more by example than by any deliberate attempt to direct their activity. On both sides of her family she was Scottish in ancestry, but was South African by birth, being the only daughter of James Rose-Innes, Chief Justice of the South African Union. Her father's attitude, which was liberal in the best sense of the word, had a decisive influence upon his daughter, and through her the children maintained their strong link with South Africa. The Rose-Innes family had first met the Moltkes in the course of a journey made by the mother and daughter to Europe. Wishing to stay in Germany they did not know where to go, so put an advertisement in a German paper which the Countess answered at once, inviting them to Kreisau.

If the atmosphere in the Moltke house was liberal, the style of life was that of the great country seats of Eastern Germany.

Politically, however, the family saw matters very differently from its peers. Their views were neither reactionary nor narrow-minded. British influence, which had already played a part in the history of the Moltkes (the Field-Marshal's wife had been English) can be traced in many aspects of the family life. They read a great deal, and sometimes took part in family play readings—for instance of Shaw's *Back to Methuselah*. They also acted scenes from Hofmanns-thal, and charades. There was plenty of conversation in which the children joined. Countess von Moltke was a Christian Scientist; together with Frau Ulla Oldenbourg she had translated Mary Baker Eddy's *Science and Health* into German. Her involvement in Christian Science meetings meant that she never went to church. Her husband, on the other hand, went occasionally because, as Lord of the manor (Gutsherr), he was also patron of the church. The parents naturally introduced their children to the teachings of Christian Science, but they did not attempt to influence their views in this direction except by example. Although their children respected Christian Science, they did not adopt its teachings. Nevertheless, their relationship with their parents remained very close.

The family were extremely hospitable and the great table in the white dining room was almost always extended to its full length. The Moltke family was indeed so extensive that they almost formed a self-sufficient community within Silesian society. In addition to the relatives, the guests would include certain landed gentry of the neighbourhood, old acquaintances, and new friends introduced by the younger generation. Foreigners who belonged to the Christian Science movement were also frequent visitors at Krei-sau. The mother stood at the centre of this circle, and found her fulfilment in it. It was in this untroubled and liberal atmosphere that Helmuth James grew up, and it guaranteed him a very happy childhood.

World War I brought changes in the family's circumstances. In 1913 the occupants of Kreisau were made aware of the growing international tension when the annual manœuvres ended in the neighbourhood of the estate and the basement was used as a post and telephone depot. War followed and, like other young people of the day, Helmuth James greeted it with flags and war games. While hostilities lasted no English was spoken at Kreisau, though the Countess helped to care for English prisoners of war. The parents' support for Wilson at the time of the Armistice (they were friends of the President's adviser, Colonel House) was the occasion of the first political quarrel in the family that Helmuth James consciously experienced. At the beginning of 1919 their mother took the children abroad to meet their grandparents, who were living in Holland, where for the children the main attraction lay in the abundance of sweets available. On the return of von der Goltz's troops in 1919 from Finland to Silesia, where they were stationed as frontier guards, their staff were quartered in Kreisau. When they were eventually withdrawn, the young Helmuth James wept profusely, as under their presence he had become an enthusiast for the military life.

The war and the immediately succeeding post-war periods were important in the development of Helmuth James. Later, describing his impressions of the post-war years, he wrote 'We then entered the phase of great party struggles, in which everybody criticized everybody else and claimed that his own doctrine was the only one that could heal the people's ills. This period made a great impression upon me because it persuaded me that everybody was false, as I went through an attraction to every side at least once. Indeed I am sure that there is not a party for whose cause I have not fought at some time in my life'.

The most important influence on him was that of his mother. The other children, who were very attached to each other, looked up to Helmuth James, as the eldest; thus from early on he felt himself responsible towards the others. He was very loyal to his family and to Kreisau. After a period of tuition at home and then at the Schweidnitz Gymnasium, his parents sent him in 1922 to a boarding school at Schondorf am Ammersee, in order to harden him. He was, however, very unhappy there and in particular disliked the compulsory drill. He refused to co-operate and resisted the school authorities with others who felt the same way. In the end he and his comrades left voluntarily. He then went to Potsdam where he was schooled up to the stage of Abitur (university entrance), living in the house of his relative, Freiherr von Mirbach. His views appear even then to have been somewhat un-Prussian and, in the opinion of many, hardly in keeping with the Moltke tradition. He cared little for the school. Prince Louis Ferdinand of Prussia, who knew him at the time, has given the following description: 'He was an able speaker and spiced his answers with humorous observations which amused his teachers . . . I used to bike home with him from school, but he was the only student whom I did not address with the familiar "du" form. I liked him because of his witty, rather cynical manner, which made him at times seem almost arrogant.' In the Abitur examination he was, by his own admission, very fortunate, as he had done little work. Even though he was examined by a socialist school inspector who hated the nobility, he managed to write in a short essay so intelligent an analysis of relations between Napoleon and Britain that the school inspector, who was a historian, let him off the rest of the examination. Apart from the little French that he picked up at the Mirbachs, where French was spoken almost exclusively, he learned most in Berlin during the afternoons, when he accompanied an American journalist who could not speak a word of German to his interviews and to the theatre. 'Thus it happened that in effect I lived in Berlin rather than Potsdam and only went to school in the latter.'

Although very fond of the country he did not particularly want to become a farmer, and so decided to study law at the university. As his grandparents were in Germany on a six months' visit, he enrolled to begin with at the local university of Breslau, though he spent most of his time in making long car and motor-cycle journeys. He then moved to Berlin. His favourite subjects were history and politics; he was particularly interested in social history and in the history of socialism. He spent two semesters studying journalism, while his politics were learnt mainly at the Hochschule fuer Politik. His progressive views were confirmed and extended during his student days by many discussions and arguments. He took part in the attempt to improve Franco-German relations, and supported the so-called 'policy of fulfilment' not, however, because he found the Versailles Treaty just, but because in his opinion the government was obliged to observe a Treaty that it had signed. He also supported the Weimar Republic.

While in Berlin he was introduced by a friend to Frau Dr. Eugenie Schwarzwald of Vienna, who became an important influence on him as he developed views. The founder of several progressive girls' schools and director of several welfare organizations, she had set up a number of people's kitchens in Berlin and in other towns during the period of inflation. She visited Berlin frequently, urged the young to help with the work, and formed an international group of young people. Moltke, at the time of his contact with the Circle, already made a mature impression. Like all Moltkes he was taciturn. He was very tall, well over six feet, with somewhat stooping shoulders. His interest in social questions was so marked that he became known as the 'Red Count'. He had a caustic sense of humour and spoke with authority. There was a

Helmuth James Count von Moltke on trial in the People's Court

Moltke's room in the Berghaus at Kreisau

melancholy side to his character that reflected his sensitive nature. He was, nonetheless, popular. As he reckoned that he was physically somewhat weak, he tried to improve his physique in a number of ways. By doing so, he maintained, he would be better able to endure hardships.

Frau Schwarzwald proposed that he should continue his studies in Vienna. He did so. There he was a frequent visitor at the Schwarzwald's house; the couple exercised a strong influence upon him and they themselves were greatly attracted towards him and came to regard him as a son. He was greatly stimulated by many discussions in the Schwarzwald house in Josephstaedterstrasse and in their summer home at Grundlsee in Salzkammergut. Among their wide circle of friends he met numerous people including others of his own age. It was in the house of the playwright Carl Zuckmayer, whose wife was a pupil of Frau Schwarzwald, that he met the young socialists Carlo Mierendorff and Theo Haubach in the summer of 1927. Dr. Schwarzwald was an economist and an Austrian civil servant; later, as President of the Anglo-Austrian bank, he shared responsibility for the stabilization of the Austrian Schilling. He was a clever and highly cultured man of many qualities. After the dissolution of the Anglo-Austrian bank he lived in scholarly retirement among many friends and admirers. His wife was a prominent social worker and her progressive educational methods were much advanced—for example she placed a very strong emphasis on the development of character and personal responsibility. At the University of Vienna, Moltke heard lectures by Verdross on International Law and by Kelsen, whom he met at the Schwarzwald home, on International Civil Law.

It was through the Schwarzwalds that he also came to know Dorothy Thompson, a well-known American writer and journalist. She too was immediately struck by his highly developed social conscience. She, in her turn, introduced him to other American journalists, including the Mowrers. In the course of conversations with these and other friends Moltke showed himself to be very well informed about political developments in Germany. He observed the rise of the new nationalism with growing anxiety and condemned the attitude of the students. He was frequently invited out by the journalists, and occasionally accompanied them to the theatre in which he took a lively interest. When he saw the play '1914', and heard Bethmann-Hollweg's words about 'the scrap of paper', he said to the American foreign correspondent Edgar

G R H—C

Mowrer: 'You see, it's the collapse of political decency that's ultimately the cause of the war'. He had an aversion to literary circles and to the fashionable form of Hegelianism. It was shown in his reaction, for example, to a speaker who claimed that there was neither absolute good nor absolute evil and that it was impossible to define either idea precisely. Moltke suddenly interjected: 'What do you mean when you say that there are no evil things? Indeed there are: to begin with there's sloppy language and bad eggs.' He found the emphasis on the uncertainty principle, on 'becoming', fundamentally uncongenial. He was extremely unconventional in his views and in no way resembled other members of his class. He condemned the financial help given by the government to the great estates. If the landowners had only regarded themselves as farmers and administered their estates rationally, then it would have been unnecessary to subsidize them with taxes. On one occasion he provocatively allowed himself to be photographed with the hammer and the sickle, although he had no particular sympathy with communism.

In his frequent encounters with others, he himself was a source of stimulus and excitement. He made journalists, for example, aware of the problems of the German east. He took them to the disputed Polish–German area in Upper Silesia and showed them the extremely backward conditions in the mining district of Waldenburg. These problems were of particular concern to him at the time, as he was once again a student in Breslau and with others such as Einsiedel, Trotha and Dehmel was helping to organize work camps for workers, farmers and students. Behind the apparently carefree manner of the man-of-the-world, that Einsiedel noted at this period, there lay a strong sense of responsibility and sympathy for the world around him. This characteristic was to determine the whole of his future development.

The interests of the young Moltke come out clearly in a letter to his grandparents in 1928. His grandfather had written rather anxiously to discover what amidst all these other activities was happening to his studies, and to invite him to South Africa. In his reply, Moltke described his experiences of the previous two months. He had resigned from the organization of the work camps and travelled to Kattowitz, where he had informed himself about the minority problem. He was extremely critical of the German groups in Poland who allowed themselves to be managed by Berlin. From Kattowitz he went on via Pless, where the Kaiser had had his headquarters during the war, to Agram, in order to visit the

The family seat of the Counts von Moltke in Kreisau, Silesia, where the three main conferences of the Kreisau Circle took place

Croatian leader Radic,* whom he regarded as the man of the future, who would solve the problems of agriculture. He mentioned that he had known Radic for two years, perhaps having met him at the Schwarzwald home. A month later Radic was assassinated. Moltke wrote: 'I do not think Europe could have sustained a greater loss.'

From Agram he went on to Heidelberg in order to take part in a discussion about the problems of the German east. In the future, closer relationships should be established between Heidelberg and Silesia, 'to try to bring about a connection between Heidelberg's intellectual spirit and our eastern problems, really needing a lot of spirit and intellect'. In Heidelberg he also visited the democratic party politician, Hellpach, and asked him to contribute an essay to a special 'New Germany' edition of an American newspaper. He also asked others for contributions. From Heidelberg he went on to Grundlsee to the Schwarzwalds, and then on to Marienbad, where for three days he had long discussions with the Minister of Education, Carl Heinrich Becker. From Marienbad he returned to Grundlsee, from where he visited the Salzburg festival, seeing among other things the 'Everyman' of Hofmannsthal. Finally he returned to Kreisau to prepare for his Referendar exam.

In this letter, he also outlined his plans for the coming year. First he wanted to learn some Polish and a Balkan language or two. 'I believe,' he wrote, 'that Silesia and Vienna are the two centres from which Germany and Europe can really take a serious interest in the East and the Balkans, and I believe the whole European crisis between West and East, and the Agrarian crisis in the whole of Eastern Europe spring from the same root, and that it is our duty to work on this problem. Work on this problem is of course not my profession but I think before one starts a profession in East Germany, one ought to know something of these things, so I want first to learn the languages.' After he had given several months to language study, it was his intention in July or August to accept an invitation from the Polish government. In this connection Moltke's mother wrote: 'He gets his wonderful opportunities partly because of himself, but also partly because of his name and the fact that so few of the aristocracy are willing to take a part in the future of republican Germany'. Thereafter he would spend some time in

* The well-known Croatian peasant leader and founder of the federalist Croatian peasant party. Up until 1918 he supported 'Austroslavism', then demanded autonomy for Croatia in the new Yugoslavian state. Under his leadership agrarian reform was achieved in 1919.

Kreisau and Grundlsee. After this he intended to make a journey to the Balkans, which would be paid for by reports on his journeys for a Silesian and a Viennese newspaper. In Athens he would take a ship to South Africa, return via England in May 1930 to Kreisau. In all these remarks Moltke reveals himself very much as the young Silesian country aristocrat with his eyes concentrated on central and eastern Europe. The influence of the meetings at the Schwarzwald's home is also unmistakable. Without a knowledge of this background which did not in any way diminish the English influence upon him, it is impossible to understand his subsequent development. In fact the future did not develop in the way Moltke had envisaged. Following his Referendar exam, he worked for a while, in the autumn of 1929, at the Berlin Trading Company on general economic problems. There he received an urgent call from his father to return to Kreisau because the estate was in extreme financial difficulties. The effort of steering an estate, that was so much loved by the family, through this difficult period, brought with it a host of anxieties. His father was not by profession a farmer but in spite of this had exercised an influence on the agricultural work of the estate. In comparison with other parts of east Germany the estates in this area were relatively small; Kreisau had only about 750 acres under the plough, and the whole estate, including the woodlands, only consisted of about 1000 acres. In the difficult economic circumstances of the time and with inflationary difficulties, many country houses had to begin to take paying guests, and in Kreisau this had happened fairly early. At the same time the estates of Nieder-Graeditz and Wierischau were leased out.

These general difficulties were increased by peculiar circumstances in Kreisau. The agent had died, leaving the administration in complete disarray, and with a number of outstanding debts. Helmuth James had to give up his own plans and concentrate on rescuing Kreisau. With the full approval of his father, he took over all the financial and administrative responsibilities. The family had already moved from the Hall to the Berghaus in 1928. At the time he took over, the estate, which was worth about 500,000 Reichsmark, had debts of about 375,000 RM. (i.e. recorded debts). All this occurred just at the beginning of the economic crisis, which only served to make the task of restoring Kreisau all the more difficult. Moltke set about maintaining Kreisau as a unit; that is, he intended to preserve not only the inner estate of Kreisau itself, but also the outlying estates of Nieder-Graeditz and Wierischau. All three had been given to the Field-Marshal, and they formed a good economic unit, although more than once the idea was propounded of clearing off the debts by selling one of the outlying estates, which had originally been small manors in their own right. Moltke was able to persuade his creditors that it would be better for them if he himself administered the estate. Thus he became the administrator of a special undertaking established by the creditors, in which he was assisted by an agent. With the help of loans and the Osthilfe (government aid for the Eastern Territories) and through the exceptional ability of the twenty-three-year-old Moltke, Kreisau overcame the difficulties. Amidst all this excitement, Moltke revealed quite astonishing self-control. 'I will never succeed,' he wrote in the summer of 1930 to his future wife, Freya Deichmann, 'in making it clear to them [i.e. his colleagues] that for me troubles are already over, immediately they become identified'. New problems to master appeared every day, and he was so overwhelmed by work that he scarcely had time to notice which day it was. In the event he did manage to restore the finances. He gave the agent a free hand, and the latter became so attached to the family and the work that he remained in the service of Moltke after the finances had been put in order. Moltke himself, in keeping with his ideas about property, always regarded himself as the manager of an estate which had been entrusted to him, even when, in 1939, after the death of his father, he became the owner.

These experiences influenced Moltke's character. Although cheerful and full of good humour within the narrow circle of the family, the responsibility that rested on him, young as he was, made him appear serious to those outside. However, his feeling of responsibility was not limited to the private sphere. He was deeply concerned about the consequences of general unemployment. Franz Josef Furtwängler recalls that 'No politician saw behind the millions of unemployed the coming revolution and the horror of war as clearly as did this genial lawyer.' Political developments in Germany caused him great concern. Although aware of the weaknesses of the Weimar Republic, he remained a convinced supporter of democracy and of the republic. He condemned presidential government and the introduction of measures under Article 48, and was critical of the lifting of the ban on Nazi uniforms. 'I really long for decisions which are based on solid foundations, and therefore I am now re-reading the parliamentary work on the first Reichsverfassung in 1848,' he wrote to his grandparents.

His personal situation had, in the meantime, considerably

altered. On 18 October 1931 he married Freya Deichmann. Her father, a Cologne banker, and her mother, who was born von Schnitzler, both belonged to Rhenish families who had come in about the year 1800 from the Bergland to Cologne and who were both rooted in the liberal soil of the Rhineland. Moltke had met his future wife in the Schwarzwald circle. She made an ideal partner for him, and supplemented with her own considerable gifts those of her husband. After the death of his mother in 1935, she took over her work in Kreisau, and became the centre of the family. She also took part in the work of her husband in the Kreisau Circle, and she was often present at the discussions and conferences. They had two sons, Helmuth Casper, born in 1937, and Konrad, born in 1941.

As the situation in Kreisau improved, Moltke could turn once more to his plans for a career. In the autumn of 1932 he moved to Berlin, in order to acquire the necessary experience at solicitor level and at the chief provincial court, the Oberlandesgericht, before he took his professional examination, the Assessorexamen. He worked first in the legal office of the former Justice Minister, Koch-Weser, and then he spent several months at the Appeals Court in Berlin. In October he spent several days in Leipzig at the case *Prussia contra Reich*, which was held before the Supreme Court* reporting on it for an American journal. At the court he renewed his acquaintance with Hans Peters, who was representing the Centre Party deputies in the Prussian Landtag.

In the middle of Moltke's preparation for his professional examinations, Nazis came to power. He had never concealed his antipathy to Nazi views. 'Whoever votes for Hitler votes for war,' was his persistent warning, so this development brought new difficulties and led to a substantial change of plans. During his period at the Supreme Court almost half of the judges were dismissed. At the end of 1933 he, like all other young lawyers in the Third Reich, had to spend a period in an educational camp before completing his professional examination, his work-group being treated indulgently by the Nazis, as he wrote to his wife. After the exam-

---

* The reference is to a law-suit brought by the Socialist Government of Prussia against von Papen's Reich Government after the latter had turned the former out of power in June 1932 by appointing a Reich Commissioner. The affair is now quoted as a copybook example of the unrealistic approach of the socialists to the problems of political power: instead of resisting by force and calling a general strike, they appealed to the Constitutional Court. See also Chapter 4, p. 65.

ination he travelled with his wife to South Africa. It had long been his intention to visit his grandparents, but the journey now became a necessity since the Nazis maintained that the Rose-Innes family had Jewish blood in it, and Moltke needed several documents to disprove this. On the return journey, they spent several weeks in England where, among others, they came into contact with a friend of the Rose-Innes family, Lionel Curtis, who treated Moltke as a member of his own family (see also p. 178). At one stage while abroad, Moltke had to make up his mind whether he should remain in South Africa, or return home. The responsibility that he held towards his family and Germany and his ties with Europe, decided him on the latter course even though he had no illusions about what life in Nazi Germany would be like. Immediately after his return in the autumn of 1934, he had to defend himself against attacks from the local farming community. Once again the threat of a compulsory sale of both the outlying estates raised its head. Then, in June 1935, he suffered a severe loss with the sudden death of his mother. The children, and especially Helmuth James, had been very close to her, as can be seen from a comment that he made to his brothers and sister after her death: 'How terrible this separation would be if one did not believe that one would see her again.'

Since Moltke's anti-national socialist attitude made a public career out of the question (he would very much liked to have become a judge), he decided to become a lawyer specializing in international law and international civil law in Berlin. He established an office in Unter den Linden with a legal colleague, Karl von Lewinski. Once, on the occasion of a visit of Mussolini to Berlin, workers appeared in his office and demanded that he, like everybody else, should hang out Nazi flags. Moltke refused and persuaded the other tenants of the house to do likewise. This was dangerous behaviour in those days, and it could have been immediately reported to the Gestapo. Moltke, who counted among his friends many Jews, had resisted antisemitism from early on. As a lawyer he was able to assist many victims of national socialism, especially after the publication of the Jewish laws. Anywhere he could, he tried to help. He did not shrink from visiting the Gestapo in the interests of his clients, nor from looking after the affairs of emigre Jews. These concerns brought him into difficulties with the Nazi Federation of Lawyers.

Despite his pre-occupation within Germany, Moltke wanted to keep in contact with the free world outside. He was constantly on the lookout for ways to do this and at the beginning of 1935 visited the Secretariat of the League of Nations in Geneva, and in April 1935 the International Court at the Hague. He hoped to write a thesis in the field of international law, and he thought of the minority problem as a possible subject. At the Hague, however, the secretary of the International Court suggested as a possible subject the position of the Privy Council in the British Empire considered from the angle of international law. This was a question of actual significance to the International Court. On the invitation of some friends of his mother he went, in this connection, to England, where on the recommendation of Curtis he approached several people for advice on the basis of which he decided to take the examinations which would qualify him to practise as an English barrister. He became a member of the Inner Temple and in the years that followed was regularly in England. Through Curtis he was introduced to a number of influential Englishmen and to many others of his own age.

These visits made a profound impression on the young Moltke; from then on he regarded Britain and the Empire as dominant factors in world affairs. In London he saw several emigre Germans, for instance the former Reich Chancellor Brüning, whom he had known from the time Brüning was Reichstag Deputy for the Waldenburg in Silesia. He also met Adam von Trott zu Solz (see p. 47) then enjoying his visit period of study at Oxford, and felt an intimate kinship for him. Somewhat later, in the autumn of 1938, he passed his bar finals at the Inner Temple, and was on the point of setting up a legal practice in London with the future Conservative M.P. John Foster when war broke out.

Moltke's many contacts abroad were the chief means by which he kept himself free from contamination by Nazi propaganda. Just as earlier he had made Kreisau a meeting place for young people from different social groups in his own country, so too in the years before the war he invited many foreigners to his home. These included Michael Balfour, a lecturer in history at Oxford and Henry Brooke, later Home Secretary in the Macmillan Government. In Berlin he was in close touch with Wallace Deuel, successor to Edgar Mowrer of the *Chicago Daily News*, and the young American diplomats Alexander Kirk and George F. Kennan.

CHAPTER 3

Other Protestant Members

Another leading member of the Circle was **Peter Count Yorck von Wartenburg,** also a descendant of a famous Prussian family of nobles. The Yorck family seat, Klein-Oels in Silesia, was granted to the Prussian Field-Marshal Yorck von Wartenburg, whose daring decision to sign in 1812 the treaty of Tauroggen with the Russian General von Diebitsch was the spark that set off the war of liberation against Napoleon I. The Tauroggen tradition exercised a strong influence on the family.

Heinrich Yorck, Peter's father, described himself, during the Wilhelminian period in Prussia, as His Majesty's most loyal opposition. When William II dismissed five Prussian Landräte* because they voted against his canal project in the Schleswig-Holstein Provincial Landtag, Heinrich Yorck resigned his own post as Silesian Landrat in protest. He wrote to the King that he did not want to find himself in the embarrassing predicament of being thrown out of his job, just as if he had stolen a silver spoon, because he differed with His Majesty in opinions that he felt in conscience bound to uphold. A certain paternalism in their nature enabled the Yorcks to overcome class differences and to serve and help their fellow men. Peter's father, for example, divided up the little family schloss at Kauern into workers' dwellings.

Three factors determined the spiritual and intellectual life of the Yorck family: Lutheran Christianity, Greek antiquity, and the Prussian State. The family were also particularly interested in art and learning. There was an extensive collection of engravings and wood-cuttings in the house, and the library, which in 1945 had around 150,000 books, was world famous. Every significant artist who came to Breslau hoped for an invitation to the Yorck's house. Listz and Rubinstein played there and Schelling, Hegel and Dilthey were among the family's friends. Many of Dilthey's

---

* Landräte: the senior administrative official in a rural district, roughly equivalent to a Burgermaster in a town; but the district would be much larger than an average English Rural District.

thoughts were formulated on walks in the Great Park at Klein-Oels, and in discussions with Peter's grandfather, Paul Yorck, who was extremely interested in philosophical questions.

Peter Yorck's father inherited his ancestor's interest in learning and politics. He spoke seven languages, was a fully qualified lawyer, and familiar with most academic subjects. An honorary Doctor of Philosophy in the University of Breslau, he was deeply versed in classical learning, and communicated to his children his great love of poetry. Politically, he identified himself very closely with the work and person of Bismarck. Prussia was for him the central pillar on which the Reich was built. In the discussion that followed the Kaiser's promise at Easter 1917 to reform the voting system for the Prussian Parliament, he favoured a reform which would increase the importance of the House of Peers over against the elected House, and under which representatives of industry, of the smaller towns, of the universities and technical high schools would supplement the hereditary and non-hereditary members. He also advocated an organization of society on the basis of vocational groups. He believed that the state needed to be reconstructed from below—a continuation of the work of Stein at the beginning of the nineteenth century. A co-operative structure would be a happy mean between liberalism and state omnipotence. He found World War I and its sequel shattering, was very critical of parliamentarianism and saw signs of disaster all around. Party politics and democracy he found uncongenial. He longed for a great successor to Bismarck, for a return to the old dynasty in a new Reich. After his death in 1923, his widow—née Berlichingen, from Swabia—became the centre of the family. By nature quite un-Prussian she was distinguished by her extraordinary capacity for affection, her strong commitment to truth, and her total devotion to his family.

Peter Yorck was born on 13 November 1904, the second son in a family of six daughters and four sons. As this meant that he would not inherit the estate, he had to be educated to earn his living. After a period of tuition at home he, like his brother before him, was sent to the Klosterschule at Rossleben, an institution founded by Melanchthon. For the young aristocrat there was a striking difference between the affection of the family for ancestors and the past, and the confusing impressions of the world outside. This atmosphere exercised a decisive influence on the development of Peter's character. At home, among his family or with his friends, he was gay, calm and charming, but outside he was distant and cold, and could on occasions be sarcastic. As a shy man, he spoke little about his work to others. After he had finished his studies in Law in Bonn and Breslau, a political career was out of the question, as he was increasingly critical of the Republic. The difficulties of the economy, the persistent unrest, and the cramped conditions of the German isolation after Versailles caused him much concern.

At the beginning of 1928 he met Marion Winter, his future wife, on an estate in Silesia. She was the daughter of a senior civil servant in the Prussian Ministry of Education and a law student at the time. She was a perfect companion and assistant to her husband, and supported him also later in his resistance work. As he found no satisfaction as a solicitor, Peter Yorck became an assistant in the county courts Wansen and Oppeln in Silesia. He also was interested in the Löwenberg work camps.

In 1934 he was appointed to a post in the administrative headquarters at Breslau, and after a year he became Councillor (Regierungsrat) under Joseph Wagner, Oberpräsident* and Gauleiter of the provinces of Lower and Upper Silesia. Although Wagner was a party member, and had been a national socialist for a long time, he enjoyed a considerable reputation as a result of his moderation. On many Sundays he drove with his family in his official car, complete with its standard, to the Cathedral in order to attend Mass; he sent his daughters to school at a Breslau monastic foundation.

Yorck's responsibilities at the Oberpräsidium covered agriculture and prices. He earned a reputation as an outstandingly able administrator with a talent for economic affairs. Even though he had been trained as a lawyer, he was somewhat sceptical of legalism. Social questions, and the application of social ethical principles, appeared much more important to him. When Wagner was appointed Reichskommissar for Prices in 1936, Yorck was one of the members of Wagner's staff to move from Breslau to Berlin where he became the senior administrator in charge of organizational questions. In this capacity he played a decisive part in building up the central offices in Berlin and the subordinate offices responsible for price control and the observation of price movements. He also played an important part in drafting the order freezing prices.

In the discussions, Count Yorck also revealed an extensive knowledge of social questions. Although, given his background, he certainly had considerable sympathy for the demands of agricultural

* Prussia was divided into provinces, each having an administration headed by an *Oberpräsident* who was both the senior civil servant and chairman of the provincial council.

interests, he was extremely reluctant to agree to rises in agricultural prices because of the effect of these on the price of foodstuffs. In considering price questions, he never overlooked the interests of the consumers, who, as an unorganized mass, did not possess the influence of the industrial and commercial organizations. So in spite of the fact that the abolition of departmental stores was a specific point in the Nazi party programme, he convinced Wagner that the departmental stores, with their emphasis on cheapness, performed a price stabilizing function. Confronted with the centralizing tendencies of the Nazi régime, Yorck emphasized again and again the Prussian views of self-government. In 1938 he became a Senior Councillor (*Oberregierungsrat*). An attempt by Wagner to advance him further, however, met with opposition from party quarters because Yorck was not a member of the party. One of his former superiors has given the following assessment: 'His above-average talent, his sound knowledge of the law, and his marked sense of what was administratively and economically obtainable enabled Yorck to present the policy objectives of the Reichskommissar skilfully and clearly in negotiations with the relevant government and economic organizations.'

Yorck's pronounced aversion to national socialism developed gradually in the period following the Nazi seizure of power. It was due, in the first instance, to moral considerations. The lawlessness of the national socialist state and the crimes and arbitrary policies of the Nazi authorities were the chief reasons for a growing opposition. As an aristocrat he found the coarseness of the Nazi leadership offensive to his spirit and made his distaste unmistakably clear. When, on one occasion, a senior civil servant from a good family, a former law student and now a member of the SS, regretted that he had not been able to take an active part in the events of the Jewish pogrom at the *Kristallnacht* in November 1938, Yorck was shattered, vigorously criticized this distressing attitude and voiced his complete disapproval of the Jewish policy. When the first reports of murders of Jews arrived, Yorck expressed his dismay, and his deep moral indignation at these crimes.

An episode of great significance in his personal development was a visit he made in 1938, shortly after the Munich treaty, to the Sudetenland, where he learned even more than he had known before of the actual workings of national socialist policies. On another visit, in the spring of 1939, to German offices in Prague, he was sharply reminded of the driving forces behind Nazi imperialist policy. The Czech officials with whom he had to deal were surprised

by his manner and by the understanding way in which he conducted business. When Yorck returned, he said: 'What is going on
there, is imperialism pure and simple.' With these experiences in
his mind, Yorck took the initiative in arranging meetings of several
friends and relatives in his house in Berlin.

Horst von Einsiedel, in appearance massive and robust, but in
character extremely sensitive, humorous and impulsive, was a man
of brilliant intellect and the leader of the Kreisau study circle on
economic questions. He was born in 1905 in Dresden, where his
father was a government medical officer. As a schoolboy he had no
contact with the youth movement. He went on to study law at
Breslau University. Here in Silesia, he discovered the youth movement, and at the university met Professor Rosenstock. Much
attracted by group life, he joined in the activities of the Young
Men's Society, even though he was an outsider and was introduced
as a guest into the Breslau Akademische Freischar. He also participated in the student work camp at Dassel in April 1926.

At the university, where Rosenstock exercised the most important influence upon him, he was fully in sympathy with the ideal
of popular education and nation building and became one of the
most active members of Rosenstock's student group. He poured
scorn on the traditional forms of society and emphasized again
and again that he rejected feudalism and all that it stood for.
More positively, he tried to establish relations with members of
the working class. To the outsider this sometimes appeared too
much like condescension, but he was popular because of his
cheerful sense of humour and because he was so easy to get on
with.

On Rosenstock's prompting, he became one of the organizers of
the work camps in Löwenberg (see page 7). He threw himself
completely into this work with a touch of idealism, he described
the object of this work as follows: 'We need collaboration even
between groups that are hostile to one another: ecclesiastical, cultural, ethnic and economic differences divide our nation. Party
groups rule today in the nation, in the town and in the village, and
as a result no attention is paid to technical problems that are of
vital importance to our people. The solution lies beyond all the
conflicts in the nation, and yet it is obstructed because, as a result
of these conflicts, men will not work together.' After completing
his legal examination, he studied political economy at Kiel and
Frankfurt-am-Main. In Frankfurt he was a pupil of the religious

socialist Löwe, under whose influence he became a convicted advocate of government direction of the economy.

Among several visits to foreign countries he made a study tour of Poland in 1930 where he also had an opportunity to examine the legal problems of the minorities. Later in the same year he travelled to the United States as an exchange student and remained there until the summer of 1932. He went first, briefly, to Clark University, and then to Harvard where, for a year and a half, he studied economic theory, statistics and international law. He was particularly interested in the problem of unemployment and in the remedy provided through public works. He often discussed these matters, bringing in his Silesian experiences, and later was to take a lively interest in Roosevelt's New Deal policies.

After his stay in the United States, he returned to Frankfurt-am-Main, where, in 1933, he completed a doctorate under Löwe, with a thesis entitled: *Public works as a means of regulating the level of economic activity. Lessons drawn from American experience.* After expounding the obstacles and problems, the pre-conditions of the practical implementation of the policy and the measures that were appropriate, he concluded that public works, given certain conditions, could help towards the reduction of unemployment during a depression. He drew a distinction between public works conceived as an aspect of social policy and therefore not intended to influence the level of activity, as measures of economic policy aimed at eliminating secondary disturbances, and as measures of economic policy which had a deliberate counter-cyclical effect.

In the years that followed, he made further study tours of Norway, Turkey and England, where he also visited Löwe who had had to emigrate in 1933. On each visit his chief interest was to discover what the people of other states regarded as the most important economic and social problems. These journeys also helped him to acquire a supra-national attitude.

The great economic crisis of the years 1929–33, in which almost half the German youth were unemployed for much of the time, was a decisive experience for him as for many others. Einsiedel saw it as a fundamental cause of the growing acceptance of national socialist ideas by young Germans. The experience of these years, he believed, demonstrated the importance of an ordered occupational environment for the spiritual development of each individual. Only if his employment, with its duties and rights, was assured, could the individual gain sufficient peace for spiritual and intellectual reflection. He learned to regard the conscientious organization of human and technical relations in economic and working life as the most important pre-condition of any social order, and this decided him to devote his career to assisting in the development of a responsible system of economic control.

After the war (he was one of the few members of the Kreisau Circle to survive), he set out his thoughts about this period in a review of his life: 'The discovery of how much hatred there is between men was a sad and persistent experience of my last twenty years. Hatred between peoples and races, hatred between the political parties and hatred between the economic classes has again and again defaced the image of man. The valuation of other men has not been based on their actions or their character, but instead on their membership of an economic, political or racial group, and in the process traditional Christian standards have been distorted.' If several of his ideas appear to stem from the youth movement, their economic orientation was the result of personal insights and experiences.

In 1932 he became the Director of the Association of German Exchange Students, but was removed from this post in 1933. He was a member of the SPD from 1930 onwards. During 1933 and 1934 he carried out several economic studies for Harvard University, particularly in social insurance. Once these were completed, he spent six months at the Reich Statistical Office, where he was concerned with the national balance sheets. He had to leave this post for political reasons and, with von der Gablentz, moved to the Reich Chemical Office and the Economic Group for the Chemical Industry.

Einsiedel was a determined opponent of national socialism. When in England he had already discussed with Löwe what he and his friends should do. In his office he organized a group which was always ready for action and which had close relationships with economic experts in other branches of industry. He played a part in several opposition groups, including a Christian one which was in contact with the ecumenical centre in Geneva. His modesty and his conviction of the need for service were his most outstanding qualities; behind all his ideas was firm belief in the Christian way of life.

A close friend of Einsiedel from his seventeenth year onwards, was **Carl Dietrich von Trotha**; together they co-ordinated the discussions on economic questions in the Kreisau Circle. He was born at Kreisau, in 1907, the eldest son of Colonel Dietrich von Trotha and his wife Margaret, who was a von Moltke. This made him a cousin of Helmuth James. His father died when he was only seven years old, and thus the dominant influence in his life was his mother, a clever, beautiful and reticent but intellectually distinguished woman who, like Countess von Moltke, was a leader in the Christian Science movement. She was one of the most striking members of the Kreisau family and was certainly the one who bore the closest family resemblance to the great Field-Marshal. In the liberal intellectual atmosphere of this family, totally different to the normal run of reactionary Silesian–Prussian nobility, Carl Dietrich grew up.

While he was a schoolboy Trotha joined the youth movement, and in Schweidnitz, where his family later lived, formed a scout group, which he led until 1925. In the course of extensive travels in south-east Europe, he formed an early acquaintance with the world outside Germany, and made friends with many Czechs, Bulgarians and other Balkan people. On leaving school, he went to the university of Breslau, where he studied law and political science.

Influenced by Rosenstock, he worked in adult education from his first term onwards. During a study tour in England he was able to familiarize himself with settlement work and workers' education, particularly in Yorkshire, Lancashire and London. With Rosenstock's encouragement he took part in the foundation of the first Silesian Institute for Adult Education and the Löwenberg work community, helping to prepare the three work camps in Löwenberg. This work was enormously important to the young student Trotha; indeed it shaped his life. He believed that physical and intellectual collaboration with members of other classes of society formed an essential counterpart to academic education with its prime emphasis on intellectual rather than moral and physical training. He learned to value the qualities of farmers and workers and always stressed the non-political character of the Löwenberg experiment. 'The reconstruction of a nation,' he wrote, 'that has been maimed by capitalist development, war and inflation, cannot any longer be achieved by political methods alone or by political powers. Just as, in earlier times, other forces such as perhaps the church joined in shaping public life, so today we require a non-political power, a mediating force, whose function it would be to unlock the spiritual and creative forces that are today still stored up in the individual parts of the social body and

Carl Dietrich von Trotha

Horst von Einsiedel

ter Count Yorck von Wartenburg

Adolf Reichwein

Otto Heinrich von der Gablentz

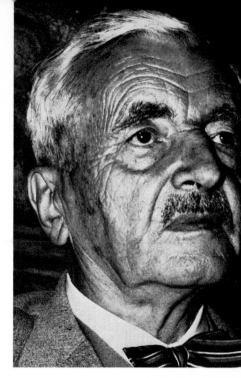

Theodor Steltzer

Hans-Bernd von Haeften

Adam von Trott zu Solz

to enlist their service in the solution of the problems confronting the nation. The work camp fulfills this function in that it creates a sphere where different forms of social life can develop.'

The work camps and the special conferences gave rise to a number of projects which Trotha took some part in. Following the Silesian example, similar work camps were initiated in other European countries and Trotha represented Germany at one of these, organized by the World University Service, in the Grisons. In Switzerland he gave a report on the work camps and on their importance for students. 'The student learns that each person has a responsibility towards the community; he sees what the role of the thinker and the leader is in association with the worker and the farmer.'

In 1929 he became executive director of the Emergency Association for the districts of Landeshut and Waldenburg, where social conditions were extremely harsh. Because Trotha felt baffled by the numerous economic problems of the period, he added economics to his legal studies. In Frankfurt-am-Main he studied as Einsiedel had under Löwe, who had taken part in several of the leaders' meetings at the work camps. At the Kiel Institute for World Economy and Overseas Trade he studied theories of the Trade Cycle, which, together with his own practical experience, made him a convinced supporter of economic planning. After passing his Referendar examination in Frankfurt-am-Main, he continued his academic work in the years 1931–33 at the Frankfurt Institute for Social Research, his studies being again in the sphere of economic planning. In his thesis, completed in 1933 when he was twenty-six years old, he stressed the positive potential of co-operative and agricultural associations in connection with the market relations. In the same year he married the daughter of the Lord Mayor of Wilhelmshaven, Margaret Bartelt, who had been a student in Frankfurt.

Because the national socialists considered it Marxist and unpatriotic, the Institute for Social Research was dissolved in 1933. Trotha then embarked on a legal career, but as the administration of justice came increasingly under national socialist control, he accordingly moved at the end of 1935 to the Reich Economic Ministry, which was still largely free from party influence. Here, as we shall see, he was able, owing to his wide experience, to establish himself solidly, while at the same time working closely with his cousin Helmuth von Moltke. His post was in the section dealing with the leather industry, later to be called 'one of those hibernating holes where plans for opposition and reconstruction were hatched'.

Adolf Reichwein the Kreisauer specialist for education problems, was a born youth leader, able to arouse enthusiasm in all those he met. An incurable optimist, he could enthuse over the achievements of others and be concerned about the cares and anxieties of his fellow men. He was as remarkable for his enterprise and personal dynamism as for his practical turn of mind and his gallantry.

Born in 1898 in Bad Ems, where his father was a primary school teacher, he soon came under the influence of the Wandervögel movement. From its excursions and evening activities he learnt the value of comradeship. When only nineteen he wrote: 'I believe that there are some people who have a solemn and sacred responsibility to play the role of spiritual guardians towards mankind. Everyone who is aware of it has a duty to undertake this responsibility.'

During World War I he gave evidence of the fact that respect for life for him was more important than obedience to a military order. On being posted to an execution squad in Warsaw, he asked for a transfer, as a result of which he received penal confinement. In the trenches the unity of the nation—the unity of the *German* nation—became a living experience to Reichwein, as to many of his colleagues. In quieter moments he and his friends used to discuss what ought to happen after the end of the war. Very seriously he assessed the effects on society: 'The present war has stirred up so many currents and cross-currents, that no political party can come through it without a serious crisis. This crisis, however, automatically contains within it a positive element, in that the war stimulates social reforms as a safety mechanism against its own destructive force. If we wish to salvage anything from this war for the period of peace that will follow, we must secure these reforms.'

Reichwein gave an enthusiastic welcome to the revolution at the end of the war and identified himself entirely with the new Republic. He was prevented from adopting an entirely materialistic interpretation of socialism by his bourgeois upbringing and his experiences in the youth movement. Socialism, like 'the working class', had a somewhat idealistic aura for him. The experiences of war continued to exercise a considerable influence and caused him distress. On one occasion he intervened angrily in a debating discussion of whether it was permissible to employ war as an instrument for achieving justifiable objectives. 'A method that is itself criminal,' he said, 'cannot lead to the achievement of a good objective.'

During his studies, at first at Frankfurt-am-Main, then at Marburg, he urged the younger students not to consider contemporary problems too academically or distantly, but to make themselves available for the tasks that lay ahead. Because he thought it essential that the workers and traditional bourgeois groups should be brought into personal contact with one another, he instituted at the beginning of the twenties a joint camp for students and workers in Bodenrod.

It was one of his Marburg professors, Wolters, who urged Reichwein to devote his doctoral thesis to the influence of China on Europe in the eighteenth century. At that time the younger generation in Germany had a great interest in China. This interest, which derived from a belief in the securer tranquility of eastern wisdom and was itself an expression of personal crisis, should in Reichwein's opinion lead to an inner discovery of the proper way ahead at this turning point in European history. He himself clearly hoped to find help in the truths of ancient China. A letter to his father, after a meeting with some communists, shows in some detail his attitude at the time towards communism and religion; it shows the influence of the youth movement, but also echoes some of his own personal views. 'Even experiences such as these cannot convert me to communism; I cannot believe that it is possible to create a new civilization by simply altering external conditions: on the contrary, I am much more convinced that civilization is a product of traditional values and fresh creative impulses, and I do not believe that knowledge can replace religion, but rather that religion is the earliest and most perfect means of expressing; the possibilities of human experience (I would consider myself most at home among the religious socialists . . .); in addition it seems to me most inappropriate to use force to establish civilization, since civilization can only grow, and the nearest parallels are in the realm of organic nature. There seem to be several points, therefore, that separate me from the communists; nor can I, for example, share their materialistic interpretation of history.' His views about Russia were a mixture of hope and scepticism, in which the scepticism ended by getting the upper hand.

In 1923 Reichwein took over the direction of adult education in Jena, and at the same time founded a home for young workers in the Zeiss factories. He lived with them, developed their self-confidence and sense of responsibility. In April 1925 he, Heinrich Becker and Fritz Klatt were responsible for arranging a gathering of friends of the youth movement, representatives of industry and economists. This particular meeting did not create any basis for further co-operation, because the differences of opinion were still too great. The Löwenberg experiment, where at the first work camp he gave some lectures, was wholly in Reichwein's line; and it was here that he first met several of those who later became members of the Kreisau Circle.

In 1926 Reichwein received a travel scholarship to the U.S.A., in order to collect material for a book on the world supply of raw materials. The award, which was largely due to Becker, then Prussian Minister of Education, was intended to provide him with an opportunity to develop his ideas. He worked very hard at his book, while also seizing the chance to satisfy his thirst for adventure. While still in Jena, he had caused something of a sensation by his ownership of an aeroplane and his skill at flying. Now he could travel the world. In America he bought an old Ford car and drove across the continent, visiting not only the recommended universities, but farms and agricultural workers. He also worked his passage to China and Japan, returning to Germany with a wealth of material, a wide knowledge of men, and a character hardened by many adversities. His book, with 639 pages and numerous charts, appeared in 1928, and two years later he published an account of his adventures.

On his return, he was appointed personal assistant to Becker, who was highly respected because of his policy. He felt teacher training to be specially important and founded a number of teacher training academies intended, in his own words, 'to produce new, integrated men'. When Becker, who had no party affiliation, resigned for party political reasons Reichwein left with him. Trust and loyalty, at times bordering on innocence, were characteristic of him. He too preferred to work with small groups, formed on the basis of loyalty and comradeship and was unable to commit himself to a political party.

Reichwein now became professor of politics and civics in the Teachers Training College at Halle, which he himself had helped to found. Here in Halle he was able to develop a large range of interests, and as the 'flying professor' he was the star of the academy. As elsewhere, the growing influence of the Nazi movement made itself apparent in Halle, and in the Academy. Reichwein took part in many discussions about it. He made his own attitude towards it utterly clear, becoming, towards the end of the Weimar period, a member of the SPD 'in order to help the workers against Fascism'. Shortly after the national socialist seizure of power he was dismissed from his post. After much thought he rejected the idea of emigration and turned down an offer of a professorship in economic geography in Istanbul: he felt he should remain in Germany during the critical time. In the spring of 1933 he married Rosemarie Pallat, a colleague at the Halle Academy and daughter of the German educationalist Ludwig Pallat. In the dark years that lay ahead she was a great support and help. They had four children and Reichwein, widely famed for his understanding of young people, was an ideal father.

At first he waited on events, but when he saw that he could not do any public work, he moved to a single class primary school at Tiefensee, a small village about 40 km east of Berlin. Here he created an island of freedom and an educational model that is still respected and followed today. In the meantime, his attitude towards religion was changing. Earlier in his life he had been sceptical about the Church—because of its outmoded attitudes. Later he came to see in Christianity a possible basis for the development of social justice; his attitude had always been strongly influenced by social and ethical concerns; now the struggle against national socialism deepened his faith. At Tiefensee he could not, however, isolate himself completely from the outside world. He kept himself informed about what was happening and friends visited him. He became clear in his mind that educational work alone could not overcome the powers then at work, and this led him to re-establish his old contacts. The authorities had little notion of the depth of his feelings against the régime.

Otto Heinrich von der Gablentz was introduced to the Kreisau Circle by Horst von Einsiedel, with whom he co-operated at the 'Economic Group for the Chemical Industry'. Although not one of the younger generation among them he had been politically conscious during the lost years of the Wilhelminian era and had become increasingly dissatisfied with it.

Born in 1898 in Berlin and the son of a Prussian officer, he got to know many different parts of Germany by an early age because of the frequent transfers of his father; from him he inherited the Protestant tradition of Pomeranian Pietism while from his mother, who came from a Berlin Huguenot family, he derived a somewhat Calvinistic outlook mixed with a national liberal attitude. In World

War I his father was killed and he himself, after a short period at the front, was severely wounded. After this, as a lieutenant at the Deputy General Staff in Berlin, it soon became clear to him that the war was lost; at this time, too, he began with his law and political science studies first in Berlin, later in Freiburg.

Four things strongly influenced von der Gablentz: the youth movement, the conservative socialism of Wichard von Moellendorf, the religious socialism of Paul Tillich and the liturgical movement in the Protestant Church. Contact with the youth movement strengthened his views that society needed radical reform. Wichard von Moellendorf, the son of a diplomat, was among the close associates of the industrialist and politician, Walther Rathenau. He favoured a state-socialist type of economic structure and a socialistic non-marxist outlook. Von der Gablentz got to know the theologian Paul Tillich when he was teaching at Berlin University; and owed much to contact with the circle around Tillich's *Neue Blaetter fuer den Sozialismus*, and also to discussions in the Michaels Fraternity, founded in 1931, where Wilhelm Stählin in fact introduced him to Tillich (see p. 11).

After finishing his studies he worked first at the Chamber of Commerce in Solingen under Carl Duisberg, the founder of the I. G. Farben concern. Here he gained experience in the big chemical industry and in its quarrels with the monopolistic aims of the iron and coal industry led by Hugo Stinnes. He summarized his impressions of this in a publication 'Industrial Bureaucracy', as a result of which he was invited to speak to the Löwenberg Work Community, where he got to know Eugen Rosenstock. From 1925 he was in the Reich Statistical Office as a specialist in the problems of balance of payments, and was sent on the staff of the banker Carl Melchior to the Reparations negotiations, at first in Basel, later in Lausanne and London.

In politics, von der Gablentz had high hopes of Brüning. The seizure of power by Hitler on 30 January 1933 he considered the worst moment Germany had lived through since the Thirty Years War. When the Nazis wanted to dismiss him, friends in the ministries sent him to the World Economic Conference in London. For a short time he was as an exchange expert in the Reich Economic Ministry, but on protests from the Nazi Party was dismissed. He thereupon moved to the 'Economic Group for the Chemical Industry'.

Together with his friend Theodor Steltzer, von der Gablentz organized ecumenical discussion groups, which brought him into contact with Hans Schönfeld in Geneva (see p. 188). During his stay in England in 1933 he had visited, with introductions from Rosenstock and Stählin, George Bell, the Bishop of Chichester. Appointed as a German delegate to the Life and Work Conference in Oxford in 1939, for which he had written preparatory contributions, he failed to get governmental consent to travel to England. In July 1939 he took part, together with Max Huber and John Foster Dulles, in an ecumenical conference in Geneva on the problems arising out of the war. At a subsequent conference in October 1939 at Copenhagen, Schönfeld gave William Paton (the English ecumenical theologian) some notes by Gablentz and his friends on a just and peaceful European order—beginning with a free Poland and a free Czechoslovakia. It was through Horst von Einsiedel that he came in contact with Count Moltke and the Kreisau Circle.

Theodor Steltzer, a close friend of von der Gablentz, was one of the elder members of the Circle. At the time of his birth in 1885 in Trittau (Holstein) where his father was a district judge, the Bismarckian Reich was in its heyday. In Schleswig-Holstein itself, however, there could be little enthusiasm for the Hohenzollerns. Since the Prussian annexation in the sixties, it had been transformed from an independent state with close ties with Denmark into a Prussian frontier province, and a large part of the population were never able to develop any strong sympathy for the new state. Prussian centralization and the Prussian bureaucracy showed too little understanding for the traditions and problems of the newly acquired territory. This was to avenge itself in later years.

The Steltzer family belonged to the old ruling class, and there was no need to worry about providing for the children. Theodor was a somewhat dreamy boy. He was introduced to the world of music at an early age, and learnt to play both the violin and the viola. His stepmother—his own mother died early—used to take the journal *Die Hilfe*, edited by Friedrich Naumann, through which Steltzer discovered something of the world beyond his own circle. It was through this journal, for example, that he first became aware of the poverty of other children and the existence of social problems. Reviews in it prompted him to read Constantin Frantz, and this turned his antipathy towards Prussia into an interest in Austria. Through his reading of the novelist Adalbert Stifter, and in particular of his *Witiko*, set in Bohemia, he was deeply impressed by the harmony between the individual, the community and culture, and by the beauty of the natural world.

After school at Göttingen, where his father had been transferred, he entered, at his father's request, the 82nd Göttingen Infantry Regiment as a cadet officer. After three years he made up his mind to resign and study economics at Munich University; here he became acquainted with the academic socialist Lujo Brentano, whose work he had hitherto only known through *Die Hilfe*. After his first semester he became one of Brentano's assistants, and the relationship between them was an important influence in Steltzer's life. The life in South Germany, quite different from life in the North, appealed to him, and he found the friendliness and unconventionality congenial. Politically he established contact with the Naumann supporters and the group represented by the *Sozialistische Monatshefte*. During one semester he helped with the workers' education organized by the Freie Studentenschaft, and the experience brought home to him how strong the working class desire for education was. For two semesters he was president of the Social Science Association at the University, which organized lectures and discussions.

Seeing better opportunities now in the army, Steltzer returned there. James Jaurès' views about the educational opportunities offered by a militia and the prospect of a commission in the Far East, with the chance of learning about the culture and society of that region, played a decisive part. The kind of arguments used by Steltzer illustrate the prevalent mood of despair among the younger generation in Germany which led to a great fascination with 'the East' and Russia as a way out of the boredom and sameness of bourgeois European society. In 1912 Steltzer entered the Military Academy in Berlin. One of the youngest of the 1500 candidates, he was nonetheless awarded almost the highest marks. At the very moment when he had been offered a three year commission in Japan, war broke out.

He was sent to the eastern front, and there severely wounded. He asked for further employment and was posted to the Deputy General Staff. One of his responsibilities was to give lectures to the officers on the military situation, and while working on these he became aware of the essential relationship between operational leadership, the uses of weapons and the constitution of the Army. He also recognized that Germany's pre-war preparations had been inadequate and that outdated ideas were dominant. Shortly afterwards he was ordered to a post under the Chief of the Military Railway Organization, Gröner, with whom he established a close relationship. He thus became an expert in transport matters. After the failure of the offensive of March 1918 Steltzer asked for a transfer to a Berlin division. He was on his way there when the revolution occurred. On Gröner's* orders he was made the Army High Command's Liaison Officer with the Armistice Commission in Berlin under the State Secretary and Centre Party politician, Erzberger.

Steltzer was now able to make himself familiar with the political situation. He was invited to discussions by Friedrich Naumann, was still in touch with the group of the *Sozialistische Monatshefte*, and also came in contact with the group of young conservatives. In an article for the *Sozialistische Monatshefte*, in 1919, Steltzer pleaded for an abandonment of power politics and the adoption of a constructive and enlightened policy based on new principles. He called for reconciliation with Germany's neighbours, especially France. There was no cause for indignation. The Peace of Versailles was the logical consequence of the principle of power politics that had been dominant until now. 'It cannot be clearly enough emphasized,' he wrote, while still on Gröner's staff, ' that we were defeated, and that any thoughts of advancing our position by military means is nonsense. This holds true even in the East.' The defeat of the old system of power politics in international relations would lead to the establishment of the principle of self determination for all nations and free international co-operation in building a united and coherent economic system. He felt strongly, however, that there should be no co-operation with Russian Bolshevism, which abused the idea of communism. 'By doing so we would in advance destroy the possibility of establishing a worthwhile and very desirable friendship with the Russia of the future—the real Russia, a nation with a peculiar sensitivity towards socialist ideals.'

On Gröner's advice, Steltzer, who belonged to no political party, became a District Magistrate at Rendsburg Lyme in the heart of Schleswig-Holstein. Rendsburg had a population of 75,000, mostly farmers, and was also his mother's birthplace. As there appeared to his disappointment little chance of establishing a new order from above, Steltzer's hope was to help towards developing new structures from below. In the post-war period, a district magistrate was much more than a civil servant. He was leader of the local government and a patriarchal figure with a great deal of responsibility. Steltzer's experience of leadership as an officer served him

* Gröner was, among the military men, a key figure in the Weimar Republic, as he co-operated with the Berlin Social Democrats under Ebert.

well in these circumstances. His own special interests lay in adult education, problems of work on the frontiers (where he co-operated with the Danes), and housing questions. With the help of colleagues he was able to found a residential adult education centre at Rendsburg, on the Danish pattern, its aim being to train young people to take an independent and responsible part in public life. Steltzer considered public participation in local affairs an absolute necessity; he therefore resented the efforts of Berlin to limit the degree of self-government. He gave active support to adult education and to the work camps. He familiarized himself with all the problems of this difficult agricultural area, encouraged experimentation and called in outside experts to whom he gave a considerable degree of freedom. He also attached great importance to meeting the farmers. When, however, the crisis broke, the deflationary measures taken by the government to meet it made it difficult to appease the growing discontent of the population.

The central authorities continually frustrated his projects, for instance the creation of credit for productive undertakings in the domestic economy. When he succeeded in creating more credit on a local basis, and thereby improving both the objective situation and public morale, a Reich law, initiated by the Reichsbank, forbade any further initiatives of this kind. Steltzer was frequently attacked by the Nazis in the press; in April 1933 he was sent on leave. Thereupon he began working for the 'Verein für das Deutschtum im Ausland', a nationalist association primarily concerned with cultural matters. He was all too aware that Hitler's work for and with Germans abroad was aimed at false objectives. He therefore tried to interest Austria and in particular Schuschnigg, the Minister of Justice, in this work. He travelled to Czechoslovakia and Austria several times in this connection. In the meantime he was falsely charged with embezzling public funds, and he was also in trouble because the authorities had discovered a memorandum written by him under the title 'Fundamental thoughts about the German leadership', in which he was strongly critical of the measures taken by the government so far, and of their behaviour towards the churches, youth and the Jews. After a short period in custody in Czechoslovakia, he voluntarily returned to Germany and was once again arrested, but proceedings against him were suspended. He joined the evangelical Michaels Fraternity and from 1936 acted as Vicar of the Elders. He also visited a number of Church conferences, and passed on ecumenical documents, brought to Germany from Geneva by Hans Schönfeld, to suitable persons. He formed a number of small groups, largely consisting of laymen, to discuss ecumenical literature.

There was no more vivid personality in the Kreisau Circle than **Adam von Trott zu Solz**,* who became its chief foreign policy expert. Like Moltke, Trott was immensely tall and slim, with a high imposing forehead. But where Moltke was inclined to be stern and cautious, Trott had an ardent and restive temperament and was much the more complicated character. Both these brilliant aristocrats had a strong-minded grandmother from the English-speaking world.

The Trott family had lived in Kurhessen since the Middle Ages and over many generations had served first the landgraves of Hessen-Kassel and, after 1866, the Prussian state. Trott's father, August von Trott, after a successful civil service career ending as Ober-präsident of Brandenburg became Kultusminister in the govern-ment in Berlin in 1909, the year when his fourth son, Adam, was born at Potsdam. Eight years later he retired and the young Trott spent the rest of his boyhood at the family seat at Imshausen, near Bibra, where he grew up close to nature and lived the usual life of the landed aristocracy. Trott's mother, Eleonore, came from Silesia and was the daughter of Lothar von Schweinitz, who was Ambas-sador in Vienna and St Petersburg in Bismarck's time. He had married Anna Jay, who was descended from Chief Justice William Jay, the friend of George Washington and a name famous in the history of American liberty. She combined the two sides of her inheritance in a remarkable personality which influenced her son strongly, though he has said that his early years would have been emotionally starved had it not been for his English nurse Louisa Barrett, a splendid example of her kind, whom he kept up with in later life. Trott's schooldays seem to have been dogged by ill-health and somewhat gloomy, except for his contact with the Wander-vögel movement; but once at the university he woke up intellec-tually in the exhilarating atmosphere of Weimar Germany. In order to please his father, whom he revered as an embodiment of the

* This section has been completely rewritten in the light of the recent publication of Christopher Sykes: *Troubled Loyalty—a Biography of Adam von Trott*, London, 1969. The author, however, considers that Sykes over-stressed the nationalist and conservative side of Trott, one of whose striking characteristics is that at a time when most young Germans were choosing a strong national brand of socialism, he turned to international socialism. The isolation of his country, however, brought out his patriotism and often led him to speak with a nationalist accent.

traditional virtues, he studied law with a political career as his ultimate objective. He attended Munich, Göttingen, and Berlin Universities, and finally Oxford. He studied English hard, and soon became virtually bilingual.

In 1928 Trott made his first journey abroad, to Geneva, where he met Visser 't Hooft. The following year he was at a religious conference in Liverpool, which led to an invitation to spend a term as a guest-student at the Congregational Mansfield College—an experience which started off his long emotional attraction to Oxford and the English way of life.

Trott returned to take his Referendarexamen in Göttingen, for which he wrote a doctoral thesis on *Hegel's Philosophy of State and International Law* which is analysed at some length in Sykes.* Later Trott was impressed by the Hegel criticism of Marx and Lenin.

But it is his later study of *The Political and Journalistic Writings of Heinrich von Kleist,* that is the most attractive of his published writings. In it he drew a well-disguised parallel between the resistance of Prussia to Napoleon, which Kleist embodied, and current events. One can almost see a programme for Trott's own future behaviour in this judgement on Kleist. 'There is no trace of collaboration in any of his words, though at times we can see a deliberate and strategic self-restraint.'

In 1931 Trott was awarded a three-year Rhodes Scholarship to Oxford where he became a member of Balliol College. Now began in earnest what Sykes calls his love-affair with Oxford, which went through many vicissitudes. He charmed many people, not least women, and joined in the activities of several clubs and societies, including the Labour Club, and developed a network of friendships, some of which were to become tense, with Englishmen mostly of his own generation, including David Astor, A. L. Rowse, Isaiah Berlin, John Cripps, Richard Crossman, Maurice Bowra, and Christopher Hill.

Trott recognized 30 January 1933 as a disaster for his country, but this did not make him less sensitive of foreign criticism of his country. In the summer of that year he returned home, and was continually exercised with the problem of reconciling his patriotism with opposition to the régime. He embarked on the normal stages of a legal career, being posted to the small provincial court at Rothenburg, where he was the only junior member without a Nazi Party badge. Later he held a post at Kassel where again

* op cit., p. 47.

he was up against the authorities, which did not prevent him taking considerable risks in befriending anti-Nazi defendants and prisoners, including the communist Hans Siebert, who was to become a prominent supporter of the East German régime after the war. Trott was always very positive in his attitude to the courage and sacrifices of the communist opposition, until the great Russian purges of 1935. One day in the spring of 1935—he was by then a member of the legal firm of Paul Leverkühn in Berlin—Trott and his friend, Helmut Conrad, discussed matters with an official of the illegal Communist Party. Thirty years later Conrad still remembered how energetically Trott attacked the primitive egalitarianism of the Russian brand of Marxism, its authoritarian organization of work, the suppression of all intellectual enquiry that was of no use to the Party, and the inadequate appreciation of the distinctive value of the law and the need to cultivate its independence. It was also made absolutely clear for both of them that the failure of the doctrinaire Marxist loyalists before 1933 to understand the fascist movement and its roots in the masses, and to assess the efficiency of its organization and its potential threat to the world, had played into the hands of Fascism.

Like Reichwein, Trott had long been drawn to the wisdom of the East. A study of Confucius and the political system of China would, he believed, complement his work on Hegel. The third 'open' year of his English scholarship was still to be used, and he was allowed by the Rhodes Trust to spend it in the Far East. His passage money was paid for by friends, as a mark of gratitude for his help in escaping from Nazi persecution, and also by Sir Stafford Cripps. The twenty-one months spent abroad led to a great enlargement of Trott's perspectives and to a deepening of his nature. On his way to China via the United States he met Reinhold Niebuhr, through an introduction from Visser 't Hooft. The famous theologian was impressed by Trott as a 'rare spirit', and was later to stand up for him in difficult times. In the Far East, although the Sino-Japanese war had intensified, Trott was able to travel through the 'model' province of Kwangsi, in Manchuria, and to Japan. His friend, the Sinologist Gustav Ecke, has described how deeply he pondered the future of his country, and how he was influenced by what he found in China: the idea of the individual's responsibility towards his fellow men, and of the mutual responsibility of nation and government 'towards heaven' became a guiding principle for the paternalist-popular reconstruction that he longed for.

The reason for Trott's presence in the Far East and his true attitude to his own country puzzled both local Germans and members of the British Embassy in Tokyo. His arrival there happened to coincide with that of Hitler's new Ambassador to Japan, General Ott; and shortly after this he went to Manchuria. Consequently a secret dossier was building up about him which suggested that if he was not a crypto-Nazi, he was at least an ambiguous person. Later on this was to have the most unfortunate results when Trott became the chief foreign contact man of the Kreisau Circle.

When in Hongkong he heard of his father's death and hurried home to his family at Imshausen. During 1939 Trott began to pick up his old friendships, and to make new contacts with anti-Nazis. It seems clear that he considered that if war could be prevented Hitler would fall, and that he believed himself in the words of Christopher Sykes 'to be in the midst of a great and unexpressed secret opposition, a movement covering all Germany, and of which foreign opinion was unaware'. He became one of several unofficial emissaries who visited England to this end, but as he had to play a double game and could not declare his opposition openly, he at once aroused suspicion. He was unaware of the degree to which the whole of the political atmosphere of England had hardened against Germany after, first, the *Kristallnacht* and then the March invasion of the rest of Czechoslovakia. Again and again his arguments for some kind of accommodation designed to avoid the horror of war and to gain time for the opposition to strike were misinterpreted. Nearly all his old friends rejected him. Richard Crossman, then deputy editor of the *New Statesman*, was one of the few who never doubted his real motives. The many moves he made during two visits to England in that last summer of peace do not concern us here, except in so far as they show that the dossier against him was building up still further, and also that he remained unrepentently a *Grossdeutscher*—in other words, he wished to see not only Austria retained in a united Germany, but also the Sudetenland, although it had been won by aggressive means. This alone was often a cause of mistrust.

The question of career raised itself once again on his return. He tried to re-establish his contacts with old friends, among them Helmuth von Moltke who was, however, in England at the time. In 1939 he was abroad twice again, in England in June and after the outbreak of war in America.* On his return he married the daughter of a Hamburg lawyer, Clarita Tiefenbacher, whom he had known since 1935.

* See pp. 184–86.

The other foreign specialist in the Kreisau Circle was **Hans-Bernd von Haeften**, who had been several years in the foreign service. He was a slim, indeed almost haggard man, and made a strong and firm impression on those whom he met, largely because of a special harmony and charm in his personality.

The Haeftens were a long-established family from the Lower Rhine. His father, Hans von Haeften, who influenced him strongly, was on the General Staff, and his mother, Agnes, a von Brauchitsch by birth. In World War I his father, who in the early days was somewhat out of favour because of his strong support for an Eastern policy, was representative of the German military command at the Foreign Office—a post that gave him a key position between the military and political leadership. He was also Director of propaganda to neutral countries. He tried to assess the situation objectively and an idea of his attitude can be gained from the slogan he coined: 'The sharper the German sword the cleaner it is'. At the end of the war he supported the efforts of Prince Max von Baden to set a new political course.

After the war he was able to pursue one of his passions as Director, and later, President of the Military History Section of the national archives, contributing prominently to the writing of the history of the war. During the last years of his life he was also a member of the Prussian Academy of Sciences. At his death in 1938, the famous historian, Friedrich Meinecke, gave the memorial address to the Academy. He praised his intellectual liveliness, his thirst for the sources of the intellectual life—'he was not simply a military specialist'—his idealistic verve and the unusual charm of his personality, which reflected his fundamental need for a balanced life. All he did was founded upon a strong religious belief.

The father's qualities reappeared in his son. Hans-Bernd, born in 1905, was well educated and very intelligent; he too combined an unusually strong sense of duty with a profound and loving humanity. He is remembered more as father and friend than as diplomat. From his youth he was interested in politics, and he was passionately involved both in the war and the revolution. He used to act Reichstag sessions with his brother, three years his junior, his sister and playmates. After leaving the classical Bismarck gymnasium in Berlin he studied Law. In 1928–29 he was an exchange student at Trinity College, Cambridge.

In 1930 he married Barbara Curtius, the daughter of the foreign minister of that name. Haeften wanted to enter the Foreign Office, but opportunities were rather limited at the time. He therefore worked as General Secretary of the Stresemann Foundation, accompanied the lawyer Erich Kaufmann to the sessions of the International Court at The Hague, studied languages and began his referendar work. At the end of 1932 he attended an Anglo-German Conference at Oxford.

He was also on friendly terms with Kurt Hahn, the founder and head of the famous boarding school at Salem (and later of Gordonstoun in Scotland), who had worked with Haeften's father in World War I. Until Hahn's departure for England in 1933—he was of Jewish origin—he and Haeften worked together against Hitler's assumption of power. Haeften set at the head of the collection of their work-papers 'The times are coming when the noble will plot together and the unworthy will fall into their nets'. On 30 January 1933 he wrote an indignant letter to his wife in which he expressed his irritation at the granting of power to 'this Hitler with his robber-chieftain morality'.

In 1933 he entered the Foreign Office. He was soon given a post in the Embassy at Copenhagen, which was followed by appointments in Berlin, Vienna, Bucharest, and finally, from the end of 1940 onwards, in Berlin again. In Copenhagen, in 1934, he had refused to become a member of the Party. In Vienna it was soon apparent that Haeften dissociated himself from the violent methods the Nazis were using against Austria at the time. He joined forces with those who represented the true character of Austria. He did not shrink from unmasking as an imposter a 'golden party member' (i.e., with a membership number below ten), who enjoyed personal access to Hitler. The Party could never forgive him for coming out on top, and from then on there was a permanent black mark against him in his dossier. A watch was kept on his activities and his personal relations. As the official in the Vienna Embassy responsible for cultural questions, he also met the second pastor in the Vienna Protestant 'Stadtkirche'. Their relationship developed into a friendship and they had frequent discussions in which he vented his growing alarm and dismay at the development of the Nazi movement and its criminal policies which were of such fateful consequence for Germany. He was extremely critical of his professional colleagues and it pained him to have to work as a civil servant for the national socialists.

After two and a half years he was sent to take charge of cultural affairs at the Bucharest Embassy. Here, too, he did not confine his attention to cultural matters, but took an interest in political affairs as well. He did stalwart work on behalf of the Saxon Church, and was able to avert several calamities, at considerable personal risk. He shared in their life and their misfortunes, which was very unusual for a German in an official position. He could see that the old and venerable forms had become rigid or withered, and he hoped for a renewal of German life in Transsylvania through the impact of the Michaels Fraternity which had been introduced there by Pastor Möckel, who became a friend of his. He could see only too clearly that Nazi ideas had confused and blinded the German national group. At the end of 1940, he was transferred back to Berlin, an official report noting that he had rendered distinguished service in all his post appointments. He became deputy director of the Cultural Department.

Haeften's opposition to the national socialist regime was fundamental. It stemmed from his strong faith, which he maintained in public just as obviously as it dominated his personal life; and in all he did he received the tireless help of his wife in what otherwise would have been a very lonely struggle. 'Basically,' he wrote, 'we are all defending "lost" outposts. Today more than ever a Diaspora situation is the fate of the Christian community in the world. What a marvellous assurance it is to know that this tiny lost band is least of all lost.' He showed early on which side he stood in the Church Struggle; he was a member of the Confessing Church from the beginning, and he had close relations with Bonhoeffer who had been confirmed at the same time as he, in 1921. When Bonhoeffer proposed that an ecumenical office should be formed by the Confessing Church in 1935, he made the following comment on Haeften: 'Welcome as a close collaborator Legationsrat von Haeften, who is interested in this matter, ready to give up a great deal of time to it, and completely on our side.' Later Haeften was to assist Bonhoeffer with his travels (see p. 192). He was also a friend of Martin Niemöller and the latter baptized his second son, Dirk, in 1934. He therefore took a lively interest in the renewal of the Church, and he was a supporter of the Berneuchener Movement which aimed at achieving liturgical reforms within the Evangelical Church. As an ecumenical Christian he revealed a warm sympathy towards the life of the Orthodox Churches of south-eastern Europe. He kept his confirmation text constantly in mind: Watch, stand in the Faith, be manly, be strong. He was particularly disturbed by the Church's response to the persecution of the Jews. 'The passive attitude of the Church on this matter,' he wrote, 'seems to me to resemble a parson who, while reading piously in the Gospel, loses his way and,

G R H—E

immersed in the text, walks on; or as if suffering was so near to his feet that he stumbles over it, and on seeing it retreats to a psalm of comfort to fortify himself.' He helped many who were persecuted and nobody in need appealed to him in vain. His State Secretary at the Foreign Office, von Weizsäcker, who provided cover for such actions by his subordinates, gave Haeften numerous opportunities. When Müller, the Saxon bishop from Transsylvania, who had long been a thorn in the side of the Nazi authorities, had his passport confiscated on arrival in Berlin for a visit to the Central Office for German nationals, Haeften intervened on his behalf and, after difficult negotiations, managed to have the document returned. They had known each other before, and Haeften who had already on other occasions given Müller confidential advice, warned him against dangerous people and discussed possible measures to be taken by the Church leadership.

Haeften not infrequently criticized German submissiveness and the lack of courage to intervene publicly on matters of conscience. As a believing Christian, he was also intensely concerned with the relationship between the Church and the world. He wrestled continually with the implications of his faith for his day-by-day professional life. In particular he could not help censuring the Evangelical Church for failing to provide its laity with clear directives in the professional sphere. 'Lutheranism's (not Luther's) resigned acceptance of the fact that the world is of the devil has in fact allowed the world to fall into the hands of the devil. Allowed to slip away by the Church, the world has made itself independent and derives its order of values from itself.' Although, in his opinion, the Church should not itself be concerned with the problem of World Order, a situation could arise, for example, in times of disorder and deception, in which the Church and the State found themselves at cross-purposes, and in such situations 'the episcopal office of the Church forbids it to remain silent like a dumb dog'. How difficult it was to see in this period of untold suffering, divine providence or guidance in history! 'Hegel's comment on Napoleon, "I have seen the world's reason (*Weltvernunft*) riding" is a repulsive reminder of how cheaply previous generations thought they could discover an immanent purpose at work in history. The only meaning that we can really discover is the lesson that is always fresh, namely that all human effort is vain, that all human arrogance is doomed and that all the roots of human independence are insubstantial.' In the struggle between Good and Evil upon earth, which he conceived of very concretely, he saw the archangel

Michael fighting against the dragon, Michael, the angel of German history. 'As far as the future of our nation is concerned, everything hangs on whether or not we become increasingly aware of the figure of Michael and his opponent in and above the ruins of the great battlefield.'

In foreign policy Haeften saw the establishment of universal peace as the major objective. Germany should accept all the consequences of its central geographical position. Above all Germany should help to integrate Russia into Europe by at last offering her security, based on friendship and guarantees, against attack from either western or central Europe. He made a sharp and fundamental distinction between the Stalinist régime, which he detested, and the Russian people. He was convinced that intellectually the Russia of the great philosophers belonged to Europe. Further, Russia too had a fighting church, and according to the most recent census, over eighty million people still called themselves Christians, in spite of the terror and the execution of priests. 'Christianity lives, lives again, almost entirely without a clergy or an institutional church; an invisible church.'

Such was the man who in 1940, with the help of Gottfried von Nostitz, came into contact with the group of friends around Counts Yorck and Moltke. He in turn introduced Moltke to **Harald Poelchau**, when the former was looking for Christians of both confessions with links with the working class. Poelchau, a religious socialist, with his home in a working-class district, was born in 1903. Since the Reformation the head of the family, which came from the Baltic region, had always been a pastor. Harald's own father was a pastor in Brauchitschdorf in Silesia. He thus grew up in the country as a member of a family that lay socially somewhere between the nobility and the peasants and was alien to both. The social distinctions that dominated the village were particularly striking to a family that was detached in this way. No unity or organic community was possible.

The pattern of Poelchau's life greatly changed when his parents sent him at the early age of ten to the Ritterakademie at Liegnitz. A school originally intended for the children of noble families, it brought him into contact with town life. He soon joined the school Bible study groups and thus the youth movement. The group to which he belonged had adopted the formula proclaimed at the Hohe Meissner: 'The Free German Youth wish to shape their own lives on the basis of their own decisions and responsibility and according to their own personal integrity.' This set them somewhat apart from Pietist circles and brought them nearer to the Free Germans, although the group was never actually part of the latter movement. Instead they had a distinctive character of their own and developed quite independently. The group provided Poelchau with the communal life for which he was looking and he derived much pleasure from the life together and the discussions. He was critical of the church because he opposed the form in which he had known it at home, where he felt that inwardness had been stressed too much and 'discipleship in action' too little.

He went on to study theology, first as his father wished, at Bethel near Bielefeld, where Friedrich von Bodelschwingh, the founder of the Innere Mission and a pioneer of the 'Christian Social' movement, had established a theological college in 1905. Here he encountered the church in action, the church that helped where there was need. His fellow-students included several who fought in the war; their serious approach to study had an influence on the younger generation. After a year at Bethel he moved on to Tübingen where he became the leader of the 'Köngener Federation', a group belonging to the youth movement that included both Christian and Free German elements. In addition to the Indian mysticism that he learnt about from the Indian expert J. W. Hauer, he discovered two books during this period to which he felt especially attracted: *The Idea of the Holy* by Rudolf Otto, and Karl Barth's commentary on the Epistle to the Romans.

Two journeys abroad extended his intellectual horizons. In 1923, the year of the inflation, he went with a group of students to Latvia, his father's home country, hoping to earn some money for term-time. He was very struck by, and very critical of, the antipathy between Germans and Latvians. In 1924, the year of the Mussolini elections, he went on a tour of Italy, which increased his knowledge of both art and politics. A short period at the famous Robert Bosch factory in Stuttgart gave him some contact, if only briefly, with the world of workers. From Tübingen he went to Marburg, where he became a pupil of the theologian and philosopher, Paul Tillich, who gave him an insight into society and a more positive answer to the question of the purpose of social order than he had found elsewhere.

Tillich, with whom he quickly struck a close friendship, was a religious socialist, and Poelchau became one too. During one semester he joined in discussions in a group of industrial workers that the former pastor Carl Mennicke had assembled in Berlin. The experience helped him towards a greater understanding of industrial society, in which he was very interested. While preparing for his examinations, he attended the welfare school organized by Mennicke, where he trained to be a social worker. He finished his training with an examination in welfare at the social policy seminar at the 'Hochschule für Politik' in Berlin. Offered a post as assistant with Tillich in Frankfurt-am-Main, he was able to complete his doctoral thesis there on *The social philosophical foundations of German welfare legislation*; in it he stressed the necessity of social work alongside insurance and public assistance, but it should be social work in the strictest sense, where the whole personality was committed. Awareness that all are essentially equal because all are the children of God, could help the social worker to rebuild the sufferer's life in solidarity with him.

Poelchau had already emphasized the significance of the social workers' basic philosophy of life in an earlier article. Unlike the Catholic and socialist social welfare organizations, whose approach he considered somewhat ambiguous, the government and humanitarian agencies adopted an unambiguous and constructive attitude towards their work, because they were not hemmed in by ideological considerations. It was of course true that a person's basic philosophy provided a stimulus to take up social work, but in actual practice Poelchau insisted upon neutrality. 'There should, in practice,' he wrote, 'be no difference between Protestant and socialist welfare work.'

The situation in the Protestant Church caused him deep concern. 'The church,' he maintained, 'is not a living, nor is it seen as an essential element in the life of the individual.' He welcomed attempts to make theology more relevant to the contemporary world, but he had to admit that 'conservative tendencies are predominant and the emphasis is so much upon nation and race, instead of on the economic system or the class struggle, that it is almost as if the authors had deliberately closed their eyes and applied themselves to the more "relevant" problems of the day'. Protestantism would have to summon up all its strength to fight against the 'positive Christianity' that pressed in upon it on all sides, if it was in any way to justify its existence apart from Catholicism. Poelchau's warning against the menace of paganism within the church anticipates the subsequent church struggle. He commented sadly: 'The SPD made a mistake in the past when it did not—as the national socialists are doing now—go into the church, and with its more closely related ideology shape the life of the church and give meaning to protestantism.' If this had happened, the church would have been a much more effective counterweight to national socialism.

This leads on to the subject of the responsibility of the Christian in the world, and the relation between the Church and the world. In a review of Gogarten's *Politische Ethik*, in which the author placed the Law before the Gospel, instead of seeing the two in a dialectical relationship, Poelchau asked: 'How can Gogarten as legislator evade the demand by which he is bound as a Christian? Is he not compelled to seek legal redress for what cannot be achieved in our non-Christian world simply on the basis of morality. Is he not bound, for example, to use the instrument of law when fighting for the rights of an underprivileged class, if there are no other means available to guarantee that their demands are heard?' The authorities, Poelchau held, could not remain neutral in the face of these demands. God's mercy must be made known in politics as well, and there is, to adopt Tillich's expression, an 'affinity' between the Christian understanding of God and certain forms of society. 'If individuals retain the freedom to obey—even simply to hear—then specific political decisions must be made in such a way that through them or behind them God's character can be perceived—the God who not only makes men aware of their limits, but who reveals himself as the Father of mercy.'

In the final sentence of his work, *Die Christchen sozialethischen Gesichtspunkte für evangelische Wohlfahrtspflege* he wrote: 'The task of the Church is . . . to make it possible for all classes of society to be obedient to God's demand.' After the completion of his second examination he applied unsuccessfully for a post as a graduate prison welfare officer; instead he became prison chaplain at the Tegel prison—the first prison chaplain to be appointed under the Nazi régime. The fact that his appointment was confirmed by the new National Socialist Minister of Justice shortly after the transfer of power was often a help subsequently, when he was in difficulty. He was twenty-nine when he embarked on this difficult career. Later, looking back on this period of his life in his memoirs, he laid particular stress upon the educational aspect of prison work. It was important that prisoners should no longer be looked upon as people who had done something in the past, 'but as those who now, in prison, must not be harmed and who on release, ought to be fit to take up a position in society'. These words refer only to the universal problems of pastoral work in prisons, and not to the special complications that confronted a prison chaplain during the Nazi period. The first political prisoners, communists and socialists, had appeared very quickly; they often had to be prepared for death and accompanied to the gallows rather than trained for release. The increase in the number of capital offences and his own experience in preparing men to face execution made Poelchau an opponent of capital punishment, on principle. 'I arrived at the conviction that only God has the right to extinguish a life, and that not even the worst offence can justify eliminating the possibility of developing and maturing.' During his chaplaincy at Tegel he had to counsel over a thousand men sentenced to death. It meant a great deal that in the midst of such trying work he was able to establish links with others who shared his views. Especially in the first years of the Nazi régime the ideas and the friendship of the Quakers were a great support to him.

Eugen Gerstenmaier, who was to become speaker in the West German Parliament in 1954, came in contact with the Kreisau Circle through the foreign specialists, Trott and Haeften. A native of Württemberg, he was born in Kirchheim/Teck in Swabia in 1906. He inherited from his father, who was an artisan, a profound interest in public affairs and from his mother a devoutness that was firmly rooted in pietism. On leaving school he worked first as a salesman in various concerns, thus gaining experience of the world of industry. The Protestant youth movement taught him the importance of communal life and he too came to regard the declaration on Hohe Meissner as a legacy. In an effort to broaden his education, Gerstenmaier attended the Eberhard Ludwig gymnasium in Stuttgart. From there he went on to study philosophy and theology at the university, first in Tübingen, later in Rostock.

These were eventful years in German history and the church, too, had its conflicting parties. National socialist churchmen engaged in heated controversy with their opponents, while the rift between Barth and Brunner was becoming increasingly obvious in the school of dialectical theology. Gerstenmaier's own position in these theological controversies can be traced in an article he wrote for the *Württemberg Hochschulseitung* under the title: 'Political Messiasship? The relationship between national socialism and Christianity.' The article was provoked by another, of the same title, but without the question mark, by Karwehl, a former pupil of Barth. Gerstenmaier did not agree with either his argument or his theology, but makes a distinction between an acceptance of national socialism and of 'the blood religion of the racialist philosophy'.

In face of the latter—here the ideas of the national socialist theorist Rosenberg were meant—a Christian cannot remain silent. This would, however, be a task for the individual Christian, not for the church. Here too can be seen the influence of the Lutheran doctrine of the two realms. Gerstenmaier was in fact less aware of the dangers of this doctrine (see p. 54) than was Haeften at this time, though he sounded the warning note: 'The everyday business of politics should not prevent a thoroughgoing examination of basic principles and a rigorous consideration of objectives'.

After two semesters at Tübingen, Gerstenmaier moved on in 1932 to Rostock, where he came under the influence particularly of Friedrich Brunstäd and Helmuth Schreiner. A period at the university of Geneva gave him his first contact with the ecumenical movement and in particular with Adolf Keller and Visser 't Hooft, while later at Zürich he formed a friendship with Emil Brunner. Friedrich Brunstäd had turned to systematic theology after a period as a philosopher and student of Hegel; he was intensely interested in politics and especially in the Christian social movement. A conservative with a critical view of the Weimar Republic, he belonged to the leadership of the German National People's Party (the successors of the National Liberals). Stemming as he did from the tradition of Stöcker and Wichern, he could not but be aware of the problems of the industrial era, but rejected the socialist idea of a class struggle and indeed considered socialism a great danger. He favoured, too, a separation of church and state. Helmuth Schreiner, the other great influence on Gerstenmaier during the Rostock years, had been for a long time Director of the Johannesstift in Spandau before he came to Rostock as professor of practical theology.

As one of the senior students at the university of Rostock, Gerstenmaier held a conspicuous position in the student body. In an essay of this period, he again rejects the ideas of Rosenberg. 'What is at issue is not one's attitude towards the cultural and social phenomenon called Christendom, nor one's preference for an indigenous rather than a foreign religion, but one's answer to the Gospel which is the fulfilment of all religions—including German religion.' He took a leading part in the actions at the university against Reichsbishop Müller. After graduation the limits set on chairs of theology prevented his receiving an academic appointment, so after a short period in the Württemberg Landeskirche he was given a post in the Church Foreign Office under Bishop Heckel.

Before we consider Gerstenmaier's work here, we must look at his *Habilitationsschrift* 'The Church and Creation'. In the controversy between Barth and Brunner, argument centred on the relation between Nature and Grace. Barth equated general revelation and natural theology and, with a strong emphasis on the theme of sin and redemption, denied the possibility of Orders of Creation. Brunner, on the other hand, started off from a basis of two distinct revelations. His doctrine of general revelation was closely bound up with his understanding of man. In the theology of the German theologian Althaus, with its emphasis on Nature and History, the idea of general revelation comes even closer to a natural theology than in the theology of Brunner. For Althaus, the importance and reality of a natural knowledge of God are not matters of debate.

If we turn from this background to Gerstenmaier's ideas, it is soon apparent where he stands in the debate. In his view, dialectical theology, by emphasizing the primacy of the Word, has limited itself to redemption and, in doing so, has set itself in opposition to Luther. Though Gerstenmaier rejects the opinion of the German Christians, that 'this or that event is in a special way the revelation of God', he attempts to indicate 'those signs and features in the world', which also 'determine the course of history, the character of periods and peoples, and their common destiny'. According to Gerstenmaier the problem of creation also raises the question of Nation and State. The Nation is an order of creation inaugurated as an 'autonomous entity by the Creator, the Lord of History, to fulfill the purpose decreed by Him'. The State, which is the vehicle for the action of the Nation (Spengler), is also founded upon the creation—creation being here defined as *creatio continua*. Both Church and State are related to the Nation, since each is an instrument of its activity. The individual is addressed by God as a member of all community, 'and hence it is true to speak of Christ as Lord of all, and of his call as addressed in the first instance to nations and communities, and only within them to individuals, who are essentially a part of them'. The need for and justification of a state of this totalitarian character, Gerstenmaier maintains, stems from the role that the state has to play in the reintegration that has followed upon secularization. Here also Gerstenmaier refers to the traditional Lutheran doctrine of the two realms: The Church should concern itself only with the validity and general direction of the process and not with the problems of the limits of the state's authority or the freedom of the individual.

The comprehensive subordination of natural life to the state, understood as the vehicle for the action of the nation, reflects the influence of a certain type of romantic universalism in Gerstenmaier's thinking. His analysis lacks insight into the internal structure and unique character of quite distinct forms of social life. Furthermore, ideas such as these could easily be adopted by national socialism. It is typical for the conservative and nationalist background of Gerstenmaier that during the war, under the ever growing totalitarian tendencies of the Nazi state, he came to a new evangelical ethics, but these were worked out mainly in a social and not also a political sense.

In 1936, probably with the approval of both Bishop Wurm of Württemberg and Professor Brunstäd, Gerstenmaier was appointed assistant in the Church Foreign Office. This branch of the official Reich church was under strong state control. The activities of the office and of its individual members are still somewhat obscure and problematical. It seems to have been, at least during the thirties, more a centre of opposition to the Confessional Church and the Ecumenical Movement than to the Nazi state. What, up until now, has been known about the activities and journeys of Gerstenmaier in his new function, does not contradict this view. His first duty was to co-operate with the future Christian bishop May in preparing the Reich church contribution to the Oxford Life and Work conference of 1937, which he edited in a volume entitled *Church, Nation and State*. With the help of his friend Hans Schönfeld he tried to monopolize the contacts of the ecumenical movement with Germany. He was exempted from military service at the beginning of the war and arranged an appointment to the post of 'scientific adviser' in the Information Department of the Foreign Office. It was in this and other ways he came into contact with opposition circles; by the end of 1942 he had become a member of the Kreisau Circle.

CHAPTER 4

Catholic Members

One of the older experts in the Kreisau Circle was **Hans Peters,** who was already known to Moltke from the work camp period. A brief account of his career will indicate the breadth of experience he was able to bring to the work of the Circle. Son of a senior Prussian civil servant, he was born in Berlin in 1896. He studied law at the university of Münster, his dissertation in 1921 being the first of over three hundred scholarly publications from his hand. Administration, politics and scholarship, these were the three spheres he worked in during his professional life, and he always endeavoured to enrich the first two with the third.

As a civil servant he underwent the normal training for a higher Prussian civil servant, and completed his examination in the year 1923 with outstanding success. In the following eight years he worked in offices at all three levels of the old Prussian administrative structure, spending two of them in the local government section of the Prussian Ministry of Interior and four years, 1928–32, in the Prussian Ministry of Culture, as an official in the department for Higher Education. In the latter period, which coincided with the ministry of Becker (see p. 40), whose reputation was high with representatives of all parties, Peters was especially concerned with the drafting of university constitutions. He gained further experience at the middle level of Prussian administration in the provincial governments at Münster, Potsdam and Breslau, and at the lower levels in the district offices of Siegen/ Westfalen, Niederbarnim, a northern suburb of Berlin, and Templin/Uckermarck. For a few months, he took over interim responsibility for the county of Westprignitz. This period of administration taught him a great deal, and he was able to call upon his thorough understanding of practical problems in the course of his academic career, which took a step forward in 1925 with his habilitation at the university of Breslau. His thesis, *The Limits of Local Self-Government* which is still frequently quoted, is a contribution to the discussion of the relationships between the local community and the State and Reich and also a demand for reform. 'The revolution of 1918,' he wrote, 'created the external conditions in which the most varied reforms could have been introduced. In fact, there have been no real reforms. None of the pre-war or post-war leaders have produced any notably original ideas.'

After a thorough exposition of the development of the idea of self-government, in which he distinguished between the political and juridical aspects, he arrived at the following definition of the juridical concept: 'An activity performed within limits imposed by the Reich and State Laws, by public corporations—excluding the Reich and State—through which these corporations fulfill, on their own initiative, functions which are neither judicial nor legislative.' He emphasized that self-government must always mean real government, and that its roots lie in the idea of an administration independent of the State's administration. The Stein and Hardenberg reforms at the beginning of the nineteenth century took up the idea of self-government 'as a method of arousing an interest in public affairs among the population and of stirring up an official bureaucracy lost in its own papers'. Where self-government is conducted according to the principle of service to the community, and not on the basis of egoistic interests, it is preferable to parliamentary democracy. On the question of the financial relationship between the Reich, the Länder and the Gemeinde (parishes) he observes that the existing financial law covering local self-government—interpreted as 'activity on its own initiative'—laid down too narrow limits. An important advance could be made if the fiscal sources could be classified according to object.

Between 1925 and 1928 Peters was a lecturer (*Privatdozent*) in Breslau. The students there esteemed him highly, it being well known that he had had to contend against early criticisms by the strongly nationalist Professor Helfritz, but that even so he had in the end completed his Habilitation under him. They knew too that he was a democrat and a republican. Among those who heard him was Helmuth James von Moltke. He and several others interested in these problems were much impressed by Peters' lectures on 'Administrative problems in modern industrial areas'. He was helped to a better acquaintance with Moltke by Dr. Ohle, who was at the time an official in the district office in the industrial area of Waldenburg. Peters himself contributed a paper to the meeting at Löwenberg, organized by the Silesian Young Men's

Association (see p. 7), to consider the problems of the Silesian industrial area.

In 1928 Peters was appointed Reader at the University of Berlin —a post which he retained until 1945. In addition, he was in 1932 given an honorary professorship at the Technical High School in Berlin. In the same year he acted as legal representative at the German High Court for the Centre Party deputies in the Prussian Landtags, in the conflict between the Prussian government and the Reich, over the installation of a Reich Commissioner for the Prussian Land. In the course of the dispute he attacked the 'situation-conditioned interpretation of the constitution' of Carl Schmitt: 'If one starts out from a situation-determined interpretation of consitutional law, the State law itself is endangered.' During the proceedings he once again met Moltke, who was acting as a reporter for a foreign newspaper; the Count sent him his visiting card with a short greeting.

The approaching triumph of national socialism, which Peters foresaw all too well, prompted him to stand as a Centre Party candidate for the Prussian Landtag. He was placed second on the party's Berlin list, and was duly elected. He remained a deputy until the compulsory dissolution of the Landtag. In April of 1933, at the invitation of Brüning, Peters read a paper to the Reichstag and Prussian Landtag deputies of his party, on questions and problems of the constitutional state.

Peters was at the beginning of 1933 also elected to the governing body of the Görres Society, becoming in the spring of 1940 its President. The 'Görres Society for the encouragement of the sciences' had been founded in 1876, during the Kulturkampf, to advance scholarship from a Catholic viewpoint.

It is possible to say that with the election of Peters, a Catholic generation came to the fore without a sense of being isolated and abused for its ideological standpoint.

When Peters analysed the idea of the 'totalitarian state' in the light of Catholic teaching on the state, he arrived at the following definition: 'The totalitarian state is founded upon a distinctive theory of the state, whereby the state, in an attempt to identify state and society, lays a claim to omnipotence over all spheres of human activity.' The Church, on the other hand, 'the institution founded by Christ to develop God's kingdom upon earth, a supranational, authoritarian World Church, lays claim to be the sole guide of men towards their highest and ultimate purpose'. For this reason, the Church is obliged to refuse any compromise with secular authorities which in any way infringes upon her essential tasks. 'This, however, makes the fundamental supposition of the totalitarian state untenable, since the latter seeks its justification in the claim that human society outside the sphere of the state is disorganized, and can only derive order from the dictates of the state.' The author closed his essay by commenting that 'the church must reject the totalitarian state as a political principle, because at essential points it infringes upon the church's God-ordained claim to sovereignty'.

Shortly after Hitler's appointment as Chancellor, Moltke visited Peters in Berlin to ask his advice about the choice of career, and during the following years the two men frequently exchanged views. A closer contact was finally established, when at the end of 1940, Peters who was a Captain in the Air Force Reserve, was appointed to the Luftwaffe Headquarters in Berlin.

Even after his dismissal in 1933 **Hans Lukaschek** remained for the people of Silesia, and thus also for the Kreisau Silesians, their Oberpräsident. He was born in Breslau in 1885. His mother, who came from a prosperous Breslau family, was a sensitive and sympathetic woman with a disposition towards the practical life, and his father, a native of the county of Neustadt in Upper Silesia, was an impressive bearded figure, notable for his dignity, self-control and liberal inclinations in politics.

Because of a lung complaint that later healed, Hans Lukaschek had to spend two years in his teens at the famous Davos Fridericianum. He always considered his stay there to have been an important phase in his development, and to have contributed towards the formation of his supra-national views.

He went on to study law at Breslau. A tall man, he made a striking impact with his generous and cheerful personality, and his clear thinking. Although he possessed the Prussian virtues of a sense of duty and responsibility, his ideas were more in keeping with the Habsburg-influenced area from which he came.

Lukaschek was a great lover of nature, and in particular of the Silesian countryside. He was also a humanist, or more precisely a Christian humanist, for whom the love of God and the love of neighbour were fundamental principles in politics as in the rest of his life. What mattered most was the man himself; his beliefs or his party allegiance were of secondary significance. During the years at university he made an acquaintance that was to have a decisive significance for the whole of his subsequent career. In the course of his legal studies he was placed under the supervision of one of the university staff, Dr Hans Schäffer. The relationship established through the tutorials and soon developed into a personal friendship, which was cemented on various walking tours.

Lukaschek began his career in the Breslau office of the solicitor Dr. Arthur Lemberg. On the completion of his assessor examination, however, he moved on to the Imperial Patents Office, in 1914, but only remained at this post for a short period before entering local government in Breslau. Here, in the early years of the war, he was confronted with considerable responsibilities. Two years later he left Breslau to take up an appointment as mayor of Rybnik. In 1919 he was promoted to the office of district magistrate—an indication of the confidence that, in this period of increased tension between Germans and Poles, he enjoyed. In the course of these years he also completed a doctorate on the Reich Bank.

At the end of 1919 he was placed in charge of the German propaganda before the plebiscite on the future of Upper Silesia. He was given this task by the Breslau Council, itself a product of the revolutionary period and composed two-thirds of socialists and one-third of representatives of the middle-class parties. It meant, however, that, according to the regulations laid down by the inter-allied prebiscitary commission, he had to give up his post as district magistrate. He was succeeded by Paul van Husen, who soon became a close friend. At first, Lukaschek was chiefly occupied with making peace among the Germans themselves, being greatly helped in this by winning the confidence of the priests in this predominantly Catholic area. He eschewed any coercion or corruption, and it was largely due to his efforts, and to the work of his cousin, prelate Ulitzka, that 60% of the population voted to remain in Germany.

In spite of the German victory in the plebiscite, the frontier was drawn quite arbitrarily, owing to French determination that Poland should possess the coal supplies. Lukaschek wrote bitterly some time afterwards: 'Does any one still believe that they would have behaved any differently if there had been a Polish majority of even one vote?' Even so, in his opinion, the plebiscite was not entirely profitless. 'The plebiscite was the first great historical national event to occur in this somewhat neglected country.' People saw themselves once again as Germans first, and party members only second.

After the plebiscite Lukaschek became a German member of the

Mixed Commission for Upper Silesia in Kattowitz.* Here he won the respect not only of the Swiss chairman, Calonder, but also of the Polish members. He attempted to weld the German groups left in Polish Upper Silesia together. This, however, irritated the Poles, and after a stormy period in 1926 he resigned his post in the interests of the work itself. He then became Lord Mayor of Hindenburg, a large new industrial town that had been created out of a number of small parishes. It was an exciting opportunity: a new communal life had to be created where none had existed hitherto. In addition he had to cope with refugee problems, a housing shortage, large-scale unemployment, infant mortality and widespread tuberculosis. Though only working at Hindenburg for a short period, he managed to achieve a great deal.

In 1929 he was appointed Oberpräsident of the newly created province of Upper Silesia. He was once again confronted with the minority problem, but on this occasion he was concerned to do for the Poles what in Poland he had attempted to do for the Germans. His aim was to eliminate national conflict. He also achieved a greater degree of unity among the parties, for the protection of German nationality. His impartial and just approach earned him the respect of both the German nationalist magnates and the communist lawyer Lichtenberg, as well as such few workers as were communists. He counted both Protestants and Jews among his friends. He also displayed an exceptional grasp of the political and economic problems of Upper Silesia. When, on one occasion, the Prussian Landkreistag held a session in Upper Silesia, Lukaschek dominated the three or four hundred delegates, with a paper that he read to them. It was a masterly performance.

The world economic crisis created new problems for all the East German provinces, and, therefore, for the Oberpräsident of Upper Silesia. The fundamental problem was to make East Germany viable once again. The work was threatened by pressures from within and outside Germany. With the help of Hans Schaffer, who was by then Under State Secretary in the German Finance Ministry, Lukaschek tried to obtain help for the economically threatened area. 'It is important for us,' he wrote, 'that we should

* The Mixed Commission was a joint German–Polish institution created by the Geneva Convention of 1922 and responsible under the terms of that treaty for safeguarding the rights of minorities in the area of the Upper Silesian plebiscite. The president was the former president of the Swiss Federation, Calonder. The Commission was, thus, a kind of inter-state administrative tribunal.

Eugen Gerstanmaier

Harald Poelchau

Paul van Husen

Lothar König SJ

Hans Peters

Augustin Rösch SJ

be recognized as a colonial area.' In such circumstances more energetic action was required; the conditions that existed in the west of Germany could not be simply transferred to the east. He argued strongly against any attempt at an impossible equalization of conditions. The Silesian population, he maintained, were passing through a transitional phase between medieval traditions and modern ideas. As yet modern ideas had no deep roots and there was therefore a danger of nihilism and political extremism. He added: 'National socialist fantasies are already misleading the young people in this area, and even the middle classes, anxious and uncertain as they are, have begun to turn to these ideas for salvation.' It was essential that vigorous political steps should be taken to meet the situation, but it was also only too obvious, with the continuing cabinet crises, that no such steps were possible. A revolution in Germany would certainly do nothing to alter the German frontiers, and would only incite the Poles. Lukaschek warned against any illusions; they would only lead to the destruction of Germany. 'The eastern problem,' he wrote, 'is not simply of decisive concern for the east itself, but for the whole country, and, in the last resort, for Europe.' The first requirement was to establish an economic and numerical parity in the east. Lukaschek was a wholehearted supporter of Brüning and when the Chancellor was dismissed from his post in May 1932, he regarded it as a serious misfortune for Germany.

Once Hitler was in power, Lukaschek knew that his own days in office were numbered. He had no intention, however, of giving up his position voluntarily. He was still needed, even though he had the swastika removed from his office building. In May 1933, however, he was dismissed, following his refusal to ban the Catholic newspaper *Oberschlesische Volksstimme*—a refusal that he persisted in despite a wheedling and threatening telephone call from Goering. The 'national revolution' that he had opposed destroyed his efforts at reconciliation and appeasement.

Out of office, he became a lawyer attached to the Upper Provincial Court (Oberlandesgericht) at Breslau. He devoted himself to the cause of the persecuted, and acted as counsel for Jews, priests and foreigners. He was not afraid to include them in his circle of friends. He helped those in danger to emigrate, regardless of the possible consequences to himself. He and his wife attended the funeral of Hans Schäffer's Jewish father-in-law, Dr. Adolf Heilberg, at the Jewish cemetery in Breslau, while his legal colleagues, who only two weeks before Hitler's appointment had joined in

celebrations of the dead man's seventy-fifth birthday, were conspicuous by their absence. In 1938 he and his wife spent two weeks
with Hans Schäffer who had emigrated to Sweden. They had a thorough discussion of the situation in Germany, both being convinced
that Hitler was leading the world to war, and that there was little
prospect of any serious opposition from the army.

One day in 1938, Lukaschek received a visit from Helmuth
James von Moltke. They had known each other since the period of
the plebiscite, Lukaschek having worked with von Moltke's cousin,
who was later ambassador to Warsaw and Madrid, both in the
campaign before the plebiscite, and subsequently on the Mixed
Commission. Helmuth James, then still only a student, had
helped, especially by conducting foreign journalists through the
area, his command of foreign languages proving most valuable.
They had also met while Lukaschek was Oberpräsident. Their
relationship now entered upon a new and more important phase.

Paul van Husen a close friend of Lukaschek, was born in 1891
in Horst, Westphalia. His father, a doctor, came from a family of
strict Catholics. After his schooling at Münster, Paul studied Law
and Political Science at Oxford, Geneva, Munich and Münster.
Such a wide experience broadened his intellectual horizons. After
a short period as a junior official in the government of Münster
and at the district magistrate's office at Lüdingshausen, he joined
the army and was a lieutenant in the reserves in the 8th regiment
of the Hussars, Paderborn, throughout the war. On leaving the
army he worked on a remarkably forward-looking doctoral thesis
on *The constitutional organization of the German Reich from the
Revolution of November 1918 until the meeting of the National
Assembly.* Taking as his starting point the concept of the 'organ'
(*Organbegriff*) he adopted a position between the politically unsatisfactory idea of legitimacy and the juridically unsatisfactory
idea of power. He submitted his thesis in 1920 and at the end of
the same year was appointed government assessor at Oppeln in
Silesia, shortly afterwards being given temporary charge of the
District Magistrate's office at Rybnik in Upper Silesia, as successor
to Lukaschek. His close friendship with Lukaschek dated from this
period and lasted until the latter's death.

The decision to divide Upper Silesia between Germany and
Poland caused him great concern. He regarded the arbitrary drawing of the frontier as 'the severest test of law' in that period and
'the profoundest crisis of confidence in the League of Nations'. In

his opinion Germany should never have agreed to these decisions. Van Husen supported the German demands for a revision of the frontiers, but he maintained that this should not be brought about by force, as 'the survival of Poland and good relations between it and Germany are essential to Europe'.

After the district of Rybnik was handed over to Poland at the beginning of July 1922, van Husen worked as the special political adviser to the Regierungspräsident in Oppeln. On 1 January 1923, however, he resigned from official service and took up a much more lucrative post—the inflation was nearing its climax—as commissioner general for Prince Hohenlohe at Koschentin. As a result of the plebiscite, one-third of the huge estate had been left in Germany, while the rest, including the Prince's residence, became a part of Poland. The already difficult task of administering an estate of over 65,000 acres was made more difficult still by the frontier decision. Inflation and legal problems about currency in both countries hindered orderly administration. In addition the Polish authorities tried to ruin large German estates by evading the protective regulations of the Geneva Agreement, particularly through arbitrary taxation. Tenacious in his resistance to injustices, van Husen succeeded in restoring normal relations with the Polish authorities, establishing a basis of trust by his readiness to make formal concessions. From 1927 until the beginning of 1934 he was a German member of the Mixed Commission for Upper Silesia in Kattowicz, once again as Lukaschek's successor.

Towards the end of the 1920's van Husen received a visit from the young Helmuth James von Moltke, armed with a letter of introduction from Ambassador von Moltke, who had himself formerly been a member of the Mixed Commission. Helmuth James wanted material for a doctorate on the minorities problem but there was scarcely any further contact between them until they met again in Berlin in 1940. The law of minorities was the most recent and least studied area of international law. The Geneva convention, until then the most important attempt to put the law into practice, provided local supervisory agencies for the first time. As information about and study of, its results were of the greatest significance for the development of the law of minorities and, therefore also for the maintenance of peace in Europe, van Husen published the judgements of the President of the Mixed Commission, together with a detailed discussion of the Geneva Convention.

In the preface he gave prominence to the general principles. 'Man is first born into a family and as part of this into a nation and it is only through this relationship that he comes into a relationship with the State. The state is not the source of law; it is itself bound by natural and divine law. Positive law that offends against natural law and God's command is wrong.' The state had become an end in itself and that led to exaggerated nationalism and excessive state sovereignty, which was being carried to absurd lengths in the period of disintegration after World War I. In Austria, he believed, they were familiar with a law of nationalities that was much more deeply grounded in natural law than current ideas on this problem, which he found rather feeble by comparison. He was extremely critical of attempts to define a person's nationality by objective criteria, this idea being a remnant of nineteenth century positivist error. There were, he held, no longer any positive anatomical racial characteristics in Europe. Only the individual's subjective feelings and decision could, in his opinion, determine a person's membership of a nation. This subjective theory underlaid the Geneva Convention. In retrospect, he had to admit that all efforts to uphold the law of minorities, towards which he himself had contributed for seven years, had unfortunately failed.

It was not only in Poland, however, that van Husen saw evidence of arbitrary action by the state, but also in his own country. With the onset of anti-semitic persecutions his attitude to the new authorities in Germany soon became critical. As the general agreement on the protection of minorities, that is the protection of all minorities, was firmly imbedded in the Geneva Convention as a basic principle, several Jews in the German part of Upper Silesia raised minority grievances with the Mixed Commission following the outbreak of the persecution of the Jews. Van Husen, who upheld the complaints, tried first, but unsuccessfully, to persuade the Foreign Office and the Prussian Ministry of the Interior to stop the persecutions and to indemnify the complainants. The judgement of the Mixed Commission was given in favour of the Jewish complainants and as the national socialists were still reluctant to raise a hubbub in the League of Nations, the Jews were indemnified. In German Upper Silesia persecution of the Jews virtually came to a halt and many of the Jews who lived there or who had fled there were able to emigrate in peace. It is hardly surprising that van Husen's behaviour provoked the ire of the German authorities. Quite apart from his support for the Jews he also sided with the strongly anti-national socialist Catholic German People's Party in Poland. Thus, at the beginning of 1934 he was sent a notice of dismissal.

With the help of an old acquaintance, van Husen got a post in the Prussian Upper Administrative Tribunal (*Oberverwaltungsgericht*); it meant demotion but it still offered a certain amount of freedom. He went first to the disciplinary Senate. There he received little support from the other judges. As the Ministry of the Interior found him too troublesome in this position, he was transferred first to the Water Senate and later to the Communal Senate. Once, when his Nazi block leader made energetic efforts to recruit him for the Party, he replied that the Party could manage without old men and that he regarded it as undignified for a man of his age to change party; he had always been a member of the Catholic Centre Party in the past. When Vice-President Bach was called up for military service in the spring of 1940, van Husen went in his place. His army post happened to be at the heart of the army communications system.

Augustin Rösch SJ, Father Provincial of the Upper German Province of the Jesuit Order, was during the war considered in Rome the strongest representative of Catholicism in Germany. He was born in 1893, in Schwandorf. His father, an engine driver, hailed from Oberpfalz, his mother from the Salzkammergut. From the latter he inherited a simple and unpretentious faith. He and his seven brothers and sisters had a happy childhood. For the sake of their education the family moved to Rosenheim where the opportunities were better. There, between 1903 and 1909, Augustin attended the gymnasium and then, in 1909, entered the theological seminary at Freising, where he remained till 1912. In the same year, even though he had only shortly before decided not to become a Jesuit—because he valued his freedom too highly— a short pilgrimage he and his mother made to the Lorette chapel in Rosenheim prompted him to go with a friend to Tisis, near Feldkirch in Austria, where there was a Jesuit seminary.

World War I had a decisive influence upon his subsequent career. He was called up before he could begin his studies. Wounded three times, he was decorated with several distinguished medals, including the Iron Cross Class II and Class I and the Bavarian Distinguished Service Medal. By the end of the war, he was a lieutenant in an infantry regiment and company leader. After the war he studied philosophy and theology in Valkenburg in Holland, and was ordained priest in 1925, taking his final vows in 1930. After his studies were completed, he became student chaplain in Zürich, where he was responsible for students at both the technical college and the university. He also preached to members of the university on Sundays. He was next appointed Prefect General and then Rector of the Stella Matutina at Feldkirch.

In 1935, two years after the Nazi assumption of power, he was called by the heads of the Order to be Provincial of the Upper German Province in Munich. He was only 43 years old. Church–State relations were deteriorating and Jesuits, like communists, Jews and Freemasons, were reckoned to be enemies of the Reich. From April 1935 onwards a police regulation laid down that every movement by a Jesuit had to be reported to the Central Headquarters. The Order was defamed and its houses were searched. The conviction of Father Rupert Mayer, who refused to obey a ban on preaching, marked a high point in the struggle, it being Rösch who, as his Superior, had given him the commission to go on preaching. The persecutions increased. Lectures were broken up, and an impressive trial was staged, in which the Jesuits were accused of currency offences. In 1940 all Jesuits, like the Jews before them, were registered on an index. When Father Rösch refused to disclose the field post numbers of the Jesuits in the army, an order came from the Führer that all Jesuits were to be dismissed from the army and declared unfit for military service. Other plans were being made for them.

These extraordinary times demanded extraordinary talents and Father Rösch possessed them. Alongside a simple faith and great warm-heartedness, he had a sharp intellect, a flair for discovering openings and solutions and considerable skill as a negotiator. He was cautious and thoughtful and never moved too fast. He also made big demands on himself. As a true Jesuit his first concern was to serve his Order and his Church, but he was also a strong patriot.

Despite his experiences with the Gestapo—he had over one hundred encounters with them—which made him aware and fearful of the extent of the danger that he was in, his piety and trust in God sustained him. Indeed he enjoyed spinning webs and making alliances. Sometimes on behalf of the bishops, but often also on his own initiative, he would travel through Germany dressed in a variety of disguises, organizing a courier service between the bishops, transmitting warnings, advising on countermeasures and building up a group of like-minded men. It was at the end of 1941 that he came in contact with Count von Moltke.

Alfred Delp SJ was a sociologist and intellectually one of the most important members of the Kreisau Circle. In a series of penetrating studies he analysed modern man and concluded that the type of person that had emerged from the process of secularization was not so much anti-religious as non-religious. The church itself was partly to blame. 'If the church wants to reach modern man with its message, it must take account of the fact that they have become incapable of hearing it.' Delp contrasted the 'tragic' figure of modern man with what man ought to be—someone whose whole life reflects the image of God. This implied that man had a duty to master and develop reality. The church and each individual Christian was obliged to take the contemporary world seriously. The obligation, Delp maintained, extended to his own time just as much as to any other since 'every historical moment can be an opportunity for the kingdom of God'.

Alfred Delp was born in 1907, the eldest of the six children of a Lampertheim cashier. Conditions at home helped him to develop at an early age a strong sense of responsibility and an acute social conscience. At fifteen he was converted to Catholicism. He entered the episcopal theological seminary at Dieburg, where he came under the influence of the Catholic Youth Movement. Indeed he became the driving force in the 'Neudeutschland' group. He was of above average intelligence and at nineteen top in the abitur at the classical gymnasium.

After leaving school he entered the Jesuit Order. He went first as a novice and 'scholastic' to the Stella Matutina at Feldkirch. While there he formed a close friendship with the Latin teacher, Karl Rahner, later the famous theologian. Their friendship continued after Delp left Feldkirch, and Rahner often visited him in Munich and took an interest in his theological work. From Feldkirch Delp went to Pullach near Munich, where for a further three years he studied philosophy.

German Catholic intellectuals, under the influence of J. Maréchal, Lippert and E. Przywara, emerged after World War I from a somewhat tradition-bound and becalmed neo-scholasticism into a closer and more candid relationship with the contemporary intellectual world. This breakthrough had already begun to affect the philosophy and theology taught at the schools by the time Delp was a student. The new movement penetrated philosophy first before it began to exercise an influence over theology in the narrower sense. For Delp's own theological and philosophical development it was a significant influence.

Between 1931 and 1934 he was 'Prefect' in the gymnasium 'Stella Matutina' at Feldkirch. Here, as earlier in the Neudeutschland Group and later in Munich, he exercised a strong influence on young people. We are told how he drew freely on his store of wealth: he could fill people with enthusiasm, sweep them along and convince them. He was always gay and lively and the pleasure that he found in life spread to those around him.' Here, too, he continued his theological work. At the request of his former teacher, Bernhard Jansen, he wrote a chapter on existentialist philosophy for the latter's book *Aufstiege zur Metaphysik*. The book was generally well received and was translated into French. This chapter became the basis of Delp's own first book, *Tragische Existenz. Zur Philosophie Martin Heideggers*.

Delp considered existentialist philosophy against the background of the contemporary situation, and especially the German position. The problems and the slogans of the time were an expression of profound need. 'Everywhere today,' he wrote, 'existence is in some way endangered and pure, authentic life is threatened.' Without trying to relativize philosophy Delp emphasized its close association with the period. The philosophy of Heidegger has its origins in the spiritual homelessness of contemporary Europeans and, more particularly, contemporary Germans. In the first instance, therefore, the problem of writing the history of this philosophy is identical with the problem of discovering the roots of the homelessness, estrangement and uprootedness of modern man.

Luther and Kant, Delp believed, had been responsible for the total disintegration of human personality and existence. Kierkegaard and Nietzsche, on the other hand, had prepared the way for new developments. They had fought against the threat to human existence, but their ideas of man and his character were radically different. Existentialist philosophy also owed much to other philosophers. Delp's positive assessment of these new initiatives and his attempt to understand them is striking. He began by giving a straightforward account of Heidegger's ideas to date and then attempted to examine the inner meaning of his philosophy. He welcomed the investigation of the totality and meaning of 'being'. He welcomed the links between philosophy and reality, between understanding and daily life. In addition, Heidegger offered support to modern men. 'The person menaced by matter and machine is told that he is the lord and not the servant and slave of these things.' Even so Delp rejected this philosophy—chiefly because it spoke of the utter and total finiteness of men. This was the path that led to hubris and 'titanic finiteness'. It also placed enormous limitations upon men, both horizontally and vertically. 'Existentialist philosophy has a great and solemn purpose: to tie down the guiding thread wherever it breaks loose or wherever it is loosened —in human life, in its undistorted entirety.' The philosopher is always concerned to arrive at a proper understanding of man. Thus Heidegger's philosophy was for Delp a 'summons to tragic existence, because it is a summons to one-sided existence and therefore a summons to dying and declining and hopeless and therefore also purposeless existence'. It was characteristic of an age that 'does not find man because it does not see God and does not see God because it has no men'. It was a 'theology without God'.

The final chapter entitled *Tragic Destiny* contains an important idea that was to play a prominent role in Delp's subsequent thinking: the idea of the 'missing centre'. Human life appears to develop in the form of movement and counter-movement, thesis and antithesis. Defence against danger is exaggerated and itself becomes a new source of danger, which lies hidden in protest and reaction. The reaction against universalism leads to individualism while the reaction against idealism turns to materialism. What is lacking is the 'power to unite the opposites, to weld them into a higher unity, a creative synthesis'. This 'missing centre' is the secret of Heidegger as it is of German life. At the end the author expresses a doubt as to whether this tragedy can ever be overcome and the hope that such an outcome may yet be possible. 'There is today a longing for this country of the centre, the homeland of all men. The work of guiding this inclination and this longing ought to engage the very best so that men are once more free to view existence in its entirety with all its commitments and obligations and components.' Delp saw his own work in these terms.

He studied theology at Valkenburg in Holland in 1935, was ordained priest in 1938 and from 1939 onwards worked as a sociologist on the editorial staff of *Stimmen der Zeit*. He wrote several articles for this journal all of them dedicated to the theme of 'man and his orders'. The idea of 'working through to the centre' soon reappeared. It was true that the individual had a 'personal life', but he also had an existence 'under law'. These external orders are given to man; he is integrated into a totality (*ein Ganzes*) that already exists without him. We can detect here a characteristic that Lutz has attributed to the whole of the younger generation of

Catholics in this period, that is, that in contrast to the older generation, they were not so very interested in 'formal democracy' or parties. What concerned them more was the idea of the orders of state and society and the nation as a whole. Even though their ideas were often vague and confused, they were searching for something new. Delp too reveals this strong emphasis upon the orders. 'God did not only call individuals into existence, he also called peoples and nations and humanity as a whole.' Just how much Delp emphasized the obligation to the nation can be seen in his article, *Das Volk als Ordnungswirklichkeit*. After a thorough exposition of the idea of the nation, he developed his own thoughts on the nation as an order. The nation was an autonomous entity in the natural order. Revelation was not opposed to it. Instead both revelation and the nation had their origins in the creative word of God. The article closed with the words: 'The nation possesses the dignity of the mother, of the homeland of life. What makes the nations most sacred and gives them the greatest dignity, however, is that they are thoughts of God and originate in eternity. They are meant to be special. They ought to represent God in their own way and according to their own character, parts of and contributors to the revelation of his greatness and his lordship. There is a touch of the eternal about them and whoever helps them towards a just order and proper dignity honours God in his work.' Nonetheless in another article he warned against a 'primitivization of life', against a 'flight into the collective'. Here too the centre was his aim. It is as if he is discovering a new world and as if he and others have, for the first time, become conscious of their membership of the nation. He also tried to give the idea of the homeland a new foundation in religion. The ideas expressed in an article of 1939 about 'war as a spiritual activity' are somewhat remarkable: 'It is not our way to glorify war as an ideal state in human life, but as it is a reality we must and will be found ready to come to terms with it and master it.' Each situation that is genuinely mastered 'is a gate and a way directly into the homeland of God— whether we ourselves witness the victory of our nation, or whether we—like our fallen heroes—dedicate our lives to God'. His treatment of the problem of war was decisively influenced by his idea of the relation between the individual and the nation. 'In the last resort what a person does spiritually with regard to war is conditioned by the relationship of the individual and Christian to his nation.' Even here, however, he tries to arrive at the centre, in that he repudiates Jünger's and Scheler's ideas and, with Clausewitz, describes the individual's decision about his attitude towards war as his and his alone.

One very remarkable article that Delp wrote was entitled: *The Christian and the Present Day*. The tension between these two ideas leads him on to the consideration of the generation problem. There are people in every period who are satisfied with the existing state of affairs and there is always a small group 'that is quite aware of what is distinctive about their own epoch and that thoughtfully works to develop these characteristics and to communicate to others what they have discovered'. He defines generation in the first instance not in biological terms but as a fact of 'intellectual and spiritual history'. The preceding generation has to pass on leadership to the next, 'whose responsibility is today'. This brings Delp once more to the problem of the relationship between man and order. The individual is the point of intersection between personal reality and general order, but he is also 'the meeting place between the things of this world, the historical and the transcendent, the unhistorical'. Man is charged with the responsibility of being the image of God; this ought to appear in his relation with the present day. 'The Christian has to be the redeemed of his age. Men must see that we are redeemed today.' In accordance with the '*vox temporis*' which ought to be listened to as the '*vox Dei*', Christians should concentrate on the most fundamental and important aspects of reality. In this, however, history should not exercise a restrictive influence. 'The individual person is always an historical representation of the entire idea of man but he is at the same time a personally responsible being dependent upon his own decisions. He is taken up into the supernatural sphere of the order of Christ and yet remains imprisoned in his historical existence. All the existing orders governing historical development come under the sway of the absolute obligation to the divine Lord and the Crucified Redeemer, who links every historical situation with the world above and, as the point of intersection with the horizontal of the historical process, makes complete existence possible for the first time.'

From 1940 onwards Delp was a regular participant in the 'Mission to Men' conferences, and soon became one of the leading members. His clear and acute grasp of what was needed at the time and his extensive knowledge quickly gained him a considerable reputation among the leading figures at the conferences. People began to look upon him as an important figure in German Catholicism. Professor Donders, for example, who was Cathedral preacher at Münster at the time, commented after hearing a paper by Delp: 'How exhilarating!' These conferences were held at Fulda where a study circle of those interested in pastoral problems had formed around Bishop Dietz. It provided an impetus to a reform of the 'Mission to Men'.

When the national socialists placed a ban on *Stimmen der Zeit* in 1941 Delp, in order to avoid military service, became rector in the small parish of St. Georg in Munich-Bogenhausen. He built this community up in difficult years through his preaching and exercised considerable influence on young people. He preached every Sunday and was always under Gestapo observation. He had an extraordinarily subtle, adroit daring way of giving every problem its name and revealing all the crimes committed by the régime without running into difficulties. People immediately understood what he meant. In the evenings he used to give talks to the parents and teenagers. The problems that he had to solve in these lectures were of immediate relevance, as what the young people heard at home was almost quite different from what they heard in the Hitler Youth or at school. He dedicated a small book to the parish, *Der Mensch und die Geschichte*. After stressing that history was an order and an elemental necessity he expounded the creative freedom of man. 'If history or one of the moments within it is corrupted, then, in that hour, men, though bound not to betray their relationship with history, are equally bound not to surrender their freedom or the immediacy of their relationship with God.' Thus this book, unlike its predecessors, places man at the centre.

If we review Delp's spiritual and intellectual development we can, I believe, detect a shift in emphasis. It can be best seen in the altered relations between man and the orders. In his earliest writings these orders are over-emphasized. The 'people', the 'nation' and the 'homeland' are expressions of a profound longing for security and commitment that Delp shared with the whole of his generation. Reacting against the threat to their lives, they developed a religious and mythological-national emphasis; man as a person and human freedom fell into the background. Man had to adjust himself to the orders that determined his existence and governed him. Nonetheless, even at the beginning, Delp is not entirely lacking in the biblical understanding of man; it is there, but it is in the background or on one side. A man of humble origins, Delp was keenly aware of the importance of the social problem. His over-emphasis on the orders, however, restricted him in his thinking about it. The Nazi abuse of these orders and the discussion in the Kreisau Circle led him to place man as the image of God at the centre of his thought. The orders, the nations still remain but they are subordinated to man. Delp's attempt 'to work through to the centre' was not in vain.

Lothar König SJ had a reputation as organizer and acted as secretary to Father Rösch. He was exceedingly reticent and reluctant to talk about himself or what concerned him. Nevertheless, behind this reserved exterior there lurked a person who was the right-hand man of his Jesuit Superior, who was able to forge innumerable links and who performed his duties with considerable skill and much courage.

König was born on 3 January 1906 in Stuttgart, the son of a tradesman and the eldest child of his mother's second marriage. His father was killed shortly after the outbreak of World War I, the bereavement making him, as is often the case, mature and serious from an early age. After his father's death King William of Württemberg sponsored him, while Lothar König's grandfather, who was a well-known personality in Ulm, arranged that after finishing his studies at the modern secondary school in Stuttgart, and as preparation for a career as an engineer, he should go to the technical college in Esslingen; physics and chemistry had always been his favourite subjects. His career, however, took another turn. From an early age he had been actively involved in the youth movement, first, for a short time in Jung-Deutschland and later in Neudeutschland, throwing himself into the latter Jesuit-led youth organization with boyish enthusiasm. The first meetings of his ND group were held at his home. He was one of the Federation's most energetic and independent young leaders and was Gaugraf (district leader) of Württemberg between 1922 and 1924. He took an active part in the preparation of a basic rule for the Federation at its castle of Normannstein. The influence of the youth movement is evident in the way in which he expressed his thoughts on liturgical worship: 'The holy mass is a community sacrifice. The participation of each individual is profounder and more fervent and the appeal of a service greater and more immediate, the more a community's worship expresses the community spirit. This has been given expression in the communal hymn of the German-sung mass, in the antiphonal singing of the high office and in the antiphonal prayers of the liturgical service.'

König was extremely pushing, and always ready to take up the cudgels on behalf of any cause that seemed to him worth while.

His remark 'There is no such thing as I cannot' is characteristic. For him there were no impossibilities; difficulties only increased his perseverance. From the outside he seemed astonishingly calm; in fact he was not so at all.

Contrary to his grandfather's plans he decided to enter the Jesuit Order. His decision reflected to a large extent the influence exercised upon him by a Jesuit priest called Manuwald, a fiery preacher, with a strong following among the young. After his Abitur he became a novice in Tisis in September 1924. Between 1926 and 1929 he studied philosophy in Berchmanskolleg at Pullach near Munich, but was then ordered by his Provincial to study at the University. He was confused by the order and his fellow brothers were surprised. He had always been highly regarded as an organizer; but König as a Professor, that was hardly conceivable.

König took natural sciences at the University of Munich, leading to the state examination for Junior Teachers (Studienreferendar). After the assessor examination in 1934 he studied theology in Valkenburg in Holland and at the Theologische Hochschule in Frankfurt-am-Main. He was ordained priest by Cardinal Faulhaber in 1936. In the following year he was awarded his doctorate *magna cum laude* for a very detailed and penetrating work: *Die Deutschtuminsel an der Wolga. Deutschtum und Ausland,* a study of the conditions of the German peasantry on the Volga who had maintained their identity in alien surroundings for almost two centuries. These Volga Germans were now, however, seriously menaced by the Bolsheviks. The author does not conceal his anti-Bolshevik attitude. 'It is in German civilization and German life on the Volga, that we can see the most radical antithesis to the Bolshevik maxims against which the western world is rightly called to fight. Claims of isolated achievements in economic transformation and industrialization ought on no account to be represented as general successes. We can observe here not only the threat presented to the national distinctiveness and peasant character of the German settlers by Bolshevik aims, but also the sapping of this national individuality from outside by inorganic and forced industrialization.' The comments at the end of this quotation bear traces of the romantic revival brought by the youth movement.

König also stressed the threat to individuality, and the depreciation of the dignity of human personality. 'Moral norms and ethos, science and technology, education and art are all employed to depersonalize, to drive into the mass and breed collective men.

It is only from this viewpoint that we can regard life in contemporary Soviet Russia. There everything is thoroughly socialized, even thought itself. There are to be no more individual personalities, only soulless machines who grow together in the involution and multiplication of mechanical, external functions and abilities into the united force and activity of the collective and are exposed to the impersonal organization of the collective without any will of their own. Man and personality are in fact set at a minimum in the Soviet State and that is certainly one of the main reasons why the achievements of the Soviet Reich are, in terms of quality, so inferior.'

In July 1939 König was appointed Professor of Cosmology at the Order's Berchmanskolleg in Pullach. The war, however, gave him little opportunity to carry out his teaching duties. He therefore redoubled his efforts on behalf of the Order, which was very much at the centre of the Church Struggle. As one would expect it was Rösch who brought König into contact with the Kreisau Circle.

CHAPTER 5

Socialist Members

Carlo Mierendorff was the most important political figure in the Kreisau Circle. Literature was his first passion, but he later devoted himself entirely to politics, to the construction and defence of the Republic of Weimar and the realization of social democratic ideals in Germany. With these ends in view, he worked for the mobilization of the electors and the defeat of conservatism within the party. He was enthusiastically acclaimed at mass meetings, which only added to the dislike felt towards him by his opponents. He was powerfully built and his personality exuded courage and benevolence. Wherever he went, he made a striking impression. 'A prophet who was strong, simple and convincing—a born tribune of the people. In the ancient world he would have been acclaimed leader,' was the judgement of the dramatist Gerhart Hauptmann on him. Reichwein looked upon him as the representative of the Germany of the future.

A man of bustling strength and abundant vitality, he had an almost baroque feeling for life combined with a revolutionary elan. If ever an idea possessed him it was extremely difficult to hold him back. His intelligence, his sense of balance and his humanity prevented him, however, from becoming a fanatic. He fought strenuously and loved whole-heartedly whether it was his fellow men, art, women or music. He felt most of all, however, for those who were economically and socially weak and always took the part of the underdog. His pamphlets and articles made war on all indifference, apathy and restrictiveness, and on the platform he fought for the forerunners of Nazism and the Nazis themselves.

He was born in 1897 in Grossenhain in Saxony. As his mother was Hessian by birth, the family moved to Darmstadt while he was still a child. There his father worked as a textile salesman, while he went to school at the Ludwig–George Gymnasium with Theo Haubach. Both volunteered with enthusiasm at the outbreak of war. Mierendorff was wounded and taken to a military hospital where again he met Haubach and also Kasimir Edschmid. After a

Alfred Delp SJ

Hans Lukaschek

Julius Leber

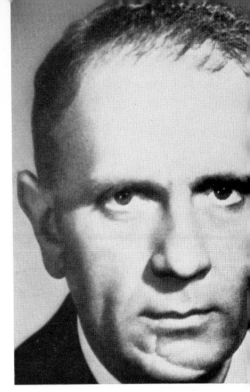

Theo Haubach

Carlo Mierendorff

long illness he returned as a junior officer to the front, where he was decorated by the Emperor in person for bravery in recovering some field guns under enemy fire. But he never fell into false romanticism about the war; it was a decisive experience for him, and it was as a revolutionary that he returned from it.

In August 1915, five fifth-form pupils of the Ludwig–George Gymnasium founded a literary and artistic group that they called the 'Garret' after the place in which the meeting was held in the house of one of the pupils, Joseph Wurth. They were later joined by other friends from both school and the youth movement, and in the attic they discussed art and literature, held readings of classical and modern plays, and tried out some of their own artistic efforts on one another. Being without older and maturer friends, they had to find their own way out of the current confusion. They produced pamphlets, first by hand and then later on a copying machine. Mierendorff and Haubach could not be present at their meetings, but maintained contact with them and others from the front, exercising a strong influence upon them from a distance. They sent in articles, sought out new members, and became the spiritual and intellectual leaders of the group. They also published small volumes—such as *The Gnome* by Carlo Mierendorff. Critics consider there is no style so concentrated or precise as Mierendorff's in the whole of the expressionist prose literature. When the sixty-fifth and last pamphlet appeared in November 1918 its leading article proclaimed: 'The epoch summons us. We can no longer remain inactive. We are free, and monstrous things are happening. Let us now spring into the stream of history, do our utmost and be torn away by nothing.'

In the troubled post-war period, with its numerous groups and journals and its 'Renaissance atmosphere', Mierendorff became editor of a new Hessian journal *Das Tribunal-Hessische Radikale Blaetter*. The new journal supported the revolution and had as its running themes: 'Against the gutter', 'For justice', 'Against indifference', 'For renewal', 'World conscience rather than party loyalty'. Among the many radical journals in this period, *Das Tribunal* was one of the most advanced. Already before it came out, some former officers of the Hessian Leib-Garde-Regiment threatened both the publisher and the editor with physical violence. Denunciations and attacks increased after it had appeared, and the group associated with the journal themselves produced an 'anti-tribunal' in which they gave voice to the antipathies of the respectable citizens and fervent nationalists. Among the contributors were Kasimir Edschmid, Theodor Haubach, and the dramatist Carl Zuckmayer.

In the first number, Mierendorff pilloried the indifference and hostility of young people towards the new situation. 'The balance sheet of grandfathers, fathers and sons will be there to see—nothing will be omitted—and they will be asked, "what have you done for mankind?" The revolution is concerned with humanity. It is therefore a struggle against the press which slanders it, against the state that tried to put it in chains, against the educated who hold it in contempt. It is not over in a day. It begins, and goes on for ever. The youth are the revolutionaries. The conquering idea of socialism and human dignity is sweeping through eastern Europe. It is so incandescent that it annihilates. Born of the hatred of the outcast, Christ and Tolstoy rise again.' The radicalism of their opinons can also be seen in the following quotations from Mierendorff: 'A mixture of adroitness and the wrong deductions from the Russian example have made communism the bogy man. It is time to make this purest of all ideas absolutely clear to a public opinion which has been driven into a corner.' Lenin, Liebknecht, the German communist leader, Eisner, leader of the 1918 revolution in Bavaria, and President Wilson were praised, and there was an enthusiastic awareness that they lived in a revolutionary period rich in possibilities. 'Our feelings and thoughts must be reversed. We must begin with ourselves, since with us the world begins. Whoever wishes to rise up is always "Canaille". We were in 1789—proletariat is in 1919.' Personal commitment was of great importance: 'We must give ourselves to the present. Rather labour under a delusion, but in our actions for the good. Let us hold up the superhuman ideal of the brotherhood of all men. Let us take from Eisner that mixture of fierce determination and generous kindness which Germany can never lose, and with which we can perform the task that the world expects from us: to reveal the new society without delay.' There were great things to be done. 'The challenge that the political poet recognized, namely that humanity, justice and love have still not been realized. Even the state is a step on the way.'

In July 1919 an appeal for solidarity and co-operation was sent to the revolutionary students in France. It was drafted by Kasimir Edschmid, and signed by numerous Germans, including a number of war veterans—among them Mierendorff and Haubach. It was given an enthusiastic welcome in France and also elsewhere. During its third year *Das Tribunal* was discontinued. It had served its purpose and Mierendorff had already seen possibilities for getting specific ideas over to the masses. For example his essay *Hätte ich das Kino* points at the cinema as a means of reaching the masses, since they form the cinema public, the classless public, or, as he described it, 'the class that exists without books'. What opportunities it offered! 'The cinema is an indispensable element of life. It is not a tennis ball for capitalist interests.'

Mierendorff studied at Frankfurt, Heidelberg, Munich and Freiburg. He went to Munich for a semester in order to hear the great sociologist Max Weber, of whom he later wrote an outstanding obituary. At Heidelburg his teachers were Alfred Weber and Emil Lederer. He completed his doctorate in 1922 with a study on 'The Economic Policy of the German Communist Party', in which he pointed to a transformation that was then occurring in the policy of the Party, and to the cleavage between long-standing party members and new recruits and the restrictive influence exercised by Marxist doctrines.

With Haubach he was one of the leaders of a student group working towards a reconstruction of German society and the republic. With his nickname 'Mr Big Noise' (*'Herr Vielgeschrey'*) he was the driving force and among the young political radicals at the university and an outstanding debater. At the time of the attempted putsch by the ultra-conservative Kapp in 1920 he addressed the strikers in the factories and called them out to march on the barracks. He came into prominence again after the murder of the far-sighted, internationally-minded Foreign Minister, Walter Rathenau in 1922 by right wing hot-heads. On the official day of mourning, when the university was closed, Mierendorff led a column of workers and students to the institute of a nationalist professor, Philipp Lenard, who, in defiance of the government order, was continuing to work because they were only mourning a dead Jew. It was typical of Mierendorff's nature that when the crowd stormed the institute, he even protected this anti-republican professor in the name of the German Republic. Tried for his part in the affair by the university disciplinary court, he was acquitted, after a passionate defence by his friend Haubach. It was an incident that the nationalists never forgot. For it was these encounters with the nationalists and national socialists that decided him to take up an active political career.

Within the SPD, however, he was very conscious of the rigidity of party doctrine, the power of the party bureaucracy, and the tension between the generations. He was, nonetheless, devoted to his party and worked for it in the conviction that this party alone, if only it were ready to become a national party,* was capable of providing the mass of people with the political education that they needed. He was prepared, however, to submit to the views of the SPD leadership so as to gain party experience and be able to rise to the leadership himself. He became secretary of the transport workers, the editor of the *Hessisscher Volksfreund* and a member of the Reichstag party secretariat. In 1928 he was appointed Leuschner's press officer in Hessen, and in 1930 he became a Reichstag deputy. He published the notorious Boxheimer documents belonging to the national socialist leader, Dr. Best, which gave the names of those democratic leaders who were to be shot after the Nazi seizure of power. He called out to Goebbels from the speaker's rostrum in the Reichstag: 'Stay in the pub, Herr Goebbels, if you have to look a front-line fighter in the eyes.' But the time available to him was all too short.

He favoured a reform of the electoral system, because it would rejuvenate politics and enliven democracy. 'The longer the proportional system is allowed to continue,'—he wrote in *Neue Blätter für den Sozialismus*—'the more its harmful effects will become apparent. It hinders the democratic process at two vital points: in the selection of leaders and in the expression of political wishes from below: that is, at precisely the central points of the whole parliamentary democratic system.' He turned a searching light on the failings of the system; the drop in voting figures and the war of attrition that passed for political struggle, the fragmentation of parties and the emergence of parties that represented sectional interests, the gulf between the electorate and the elected, the fact that deputies placed at the top of the list of candidates were almost irremovable, the over-abundance of specialists and the shortage of real political leaders, and the habit of making announcements that were not preceded by discussion and made a mockery of democracy. The electoral system—Mierendorff held—only increased the influence of the strong and emotional anti-parliamentary movements. Indeed, he himself was most at home during elections. Once he addressed twelve mass meetings in different parts of the Reich in the course of a single week. Well aware that the struggle to win the non-voters would determine the fate of democracy, he concentrated on improving electoral propaganda techniques. He drew upon the findings of modern mass psychology and, as a counter-

* The SPD, being Marxist, was essentially a class party. Mierendorff was anticipating the development which the party underwent during the fifteen years before 1970.

stroke to Nazi methods, employed a freedom call, freedom symbols and a freedom greeting. Results in Hessen showed how successful his methods were. The symbols were the work of Haubach, but the original impulse was Mierendorff's. He fought for a socialist policy. He was, from early on, a determined opponent of rearmament, whether illegal or legal. It would only provide the nationalists with an opportunity for counter measures. A policy of toleration could do nothing but harm to the party and its ideas. It suggested that the SPD had no other solutions of its own.

Even though he opposed Brüning's policies, he warned that Brüning must not be taken as the main opponent for 'the real danger lies in the national socialists'. He pointed to the economic, ideological and psychological roots of Fascism. The economic roots lay in the social emergency, the ideological, in nationalism and anti-parliamentarianism, and the psychological in youth. National socialism was not simply a social movement for peasants, middle-class and salaried workers, but also a freedom and youth movement. It had anti-capitalist, anti-proletarian, anti-democratic and anti-semitic tendencies. Following a perceptive analysis of the roots of national socialism, he listed what would have to be done if the movement was to be successfully opposed. 1. The conquering of the crisis. 2. The defeat of nationalism. 3. The defeat of anti-democratic trends. Of these the second was the most difficult, and would require 'the clear and sober application of socialist world policies to the actual problems of the present Europe'.

It was hardly surprising that no socialist leader was more hated by the Nazis than Mierendorff. He had power over the masses, even though he was still confined for the most part to Hessen. His enemies were waiting for their opportunity. In 1932 with the socialist electoral successes in Hessen fresh in his mind, he wrote: 'Whoever has seen the masses that we have been able to mobilize with the help of new techniques, will be bound to agree that they will not voluntarily submit to a Nazi dictatorship.' He was a firm believer in the loyalty of the socialist voters and after the defeats of 1930 could comment: 'It is not the soldiers but the leaders who have lost this battle.' Social democracy was too little prepared for a duel with the major opponents, the national socialists.

Just as his influence within the party was on the increase, the Nazis came to power. The first wave of arrests occurred, and the first concentration camps were opened. Mierendorff rejected all opportunities of emigrating. 'What are the workers to make of us,' he said, 'if we leave them in the lurch? They can't all go off to the Riviera!'

He went under cover in Berlin, where he was less in danger than in Hessen. However, after the Gestapo managed to tap a telephone conversation in which he arranged a meeting in an inn with a Darmstadt lawyer, he was arrested. The national socialist papers reported the event triumphantly. His friends were able to establish his whereabouts in the course of the following night so that the possibility of his simply 'disappearing' was precluded. He was taken from Frankfurt to Darmstadt where he was driven by the SA through the streets like an animal. Thus the gates of the concentration camp, 'this world of silence', opened for Mierendorff at a time when many people both in Germany and abroad praised Hitler as the statesman Germany needed, and with whom one could reasonably make compromises.

At first he was kept at Osthofen, where some communist prisoners, to whom he was handed over, half killed the feared adversary. Later he was transferred to Börger Moor in Westphalia together with the former Minister of the Interior of Hessen, Leuschner, then to Buchenwald and finally to Lichtenburg. Everywhere he was given the heaviest work. It seems that their aim was to break him once and for all by forcing him to attempt an escape: he could then be shot. He remained, however, unbroken and unbending—and, furthermore, a source of encouragement to his companions. Finally, in 1938, at a time when the Nazis felt sufficiently secure in power, his friends were able to obtain his release. It seemed like a miracle; he was not, however, allowed to use his own name, so feared was it by the Gestapo; instead he took a pseudonym from Goethe 'Willemer'. He was made to work at the Braunkohlen-Benzin Co. where former inmates of the concentration camps still being kept under observation were employed by the SS. Although forbidden to renew his links with his political friends, he in fact soon did so, beginning by re-establishing contact with former trade union and SPD associates, such as Haubach, Leuschner, Maass and Leber. Through Brundert he renewed the acquaintance of Reichwein. It was an important link because it led to Count von Moltke, to whom he had originally been introduced in 1927 by Zuckmayer, but with whom he was now able to establish a close and co-operative friendship.

Theo Haubach, a close friend of Mierendorff, was a thinker, a philosopher, who liked to express what he felt by quotations from the great German poets. Poetry was for him far more than the mere writing of lyrics: it provided an interpretation of life. As a politician he was particularly interested in problems of political organization, and his work in this sphere retained a certain military flavour. Thin, and with a refined face, he was to be called the 'general' by his friends. He was a talented and compelling speaker. His speeches would sweep his audiences off their feet by their fluent composition, their wealth of ideas, their terseness, passion and objectivity. He was particularly admired by young people.

Haubach was born on 15 September 1896 in Frankfurt and lost his father at a very early age. His mother, who was a Jewess, was devoted to him, her only son. In the last few years of her life—she died in 1939—her son was able to protect her from the successive wave of anti-semitic persecution. His guardian made it possible for him to study and he attended the Ludwig–George Gymnasium at Darmstadt, where he met Mierendorff and several others who became lifelong friends. In World War I he proved himself as a patrol leader on the western front and returned, much decorated, as a lieutenant. From the front he sent his contributions to the 'garret' group in Darmstadt, and once home again became more and more involved in politics. During the revolution he joined the workers' and soldiers' council at Butzbach, where he happened to be stationed at the time, but as an intellectual he soon ran into trouble with them.

Unlike his friend Mierendorff—'a revolutionary who never hesitated, an optimist because of his immense vitality, and someone always in danger of burning up his surroundings by his own fieriness'—Haubach was a man 'who spread warmth and light, a person who weighed everything up and acted only after thorough deliberation'. 'The wise man', he was jestingly described by Mierendorff. The two of them, often referred to as the *Dioscuri*, worked together on the journal *Das Tribunal*. Here Haubach used to develop his ideas very clearly and forthrightly. In an article entitled *Against politics* he considered the ideal and its transmission. 'Men should long ago have recognized that in the mind's eye there is only one constitutional form—the best—and that in the final analysis the whole of political life only serves to conceal this ultimate objective.' Yet it was precisely at this time that politics were achieving a fantastic dominance over the masses. Politics having been trivialized, they had become a business, a machine, a façade, and were helping towards impairing the ideal itself. New style politics, a new façade would not, Haubach held, suffice. 'To put it bluntly: revolutions that are directed against constitutional forms, economic and spiritual organizations—in other words against the mechanical bits and pieces rather than the real driving forces—might just as well never have happened. What is needed is not so much new style politics as a new religion, which summons up the spirits and revolutionizes men's thoughts. This is the most profound and burning message of the time in which we live; this is its lesson: the dictatorship of the bold, of those who believe in the future, the domination of perfect men whose bodies are entirely of this world and whose spirits are infinite.'

Mierendorff replied to this article with another, entitled: *Politics notwithstanding. A defence of activist idealism*. Haubach then further elucidated his ideas. 'My essay preaches a devaluation of the machine in favour of men.' He did not intend to eliminate politics so much as reveal its secondary importance. 'The most important thing is man and not the institution in which he lives.'

Like others he was critical of conditions in Hessen–Darmstadt where so many people still lived in and on the past, and obstructed new developments. When the radical artists of Darmstadt and its neighbourhood decided upon secession and 'carried out the long-needed removal of bourgeois dirt', Haubach was among them. He had a sharp eye for what was going on about him and noticed how the revolution—which he still looked upon as 'the transformation of a political situation *by force*'—was faltering. This pointed to shortcomings in the idea and to deficiencies in the machinery. The main reason for the stagnation lay, for him, in the economic situation. The specific characteristic of the revolutionary movement in Europe, however, was precisely that it had developed from economic conflicts. And what was really wrong with the machinery in all this? It was 'the inability of the economic system to guarantee the basic necessities of existence for every person through production and distribution'. The failure of revolutionary thinking in this direction was due to the inconsistency and lifelessness of the movement. The Marxists went on blindly bandying about outdated quotations from the highly responsible and, in nineteenth-century conditions, extremely important thoughts of Karl Marx. Their devotion to him, however, brutally shattered the possible centres of spiritual and intellectual energy in the socialist movement and therefore also its ability to act politically. Now only one thing was important: 'the creation of a comprehensive theory (systematic) of revolution, providing precise formulations down to the final detail'.

In other words an extension and reconstruction of the whole socialist approach, economic affairs included.

In the meantime Haubach had begun his studies under Karl Jaspers at Heidelberg. He took part in the seminar, and under him wrote a doctoral thesis on aesthetic problems; he also heard Alfred Weber's lectures on sociology. At the university he continued to fight for the new democratic and socialist republic. When Mierendorff ran into trouble over his actions on the day of Rathenau's funeral, it was Haubach who defended him before the Rector and the Senate of the university as a 'militant representative of socialism, distinguished for his soldierliness, intelligence and sense of responsibility, not entirely free of romanticism and influenced by the youth movement'.

He was politically active from early on. The subject of the first political meeting that he spoke at in Darmstadt in 1919 was 'The stabbing of the front-line from behind'. The young front-line officer presented the monarchists and reactionaries with decisive proof that the front had collapsed for military reasons. During the Kapp putsch of 1920 he was placed in command of the defence forces in Darmstadt. In 1923 he and his mother moved to Hamburg, where he soon felt at home. After a year as assistant at the Institute for Foreign Policy he became foreign editor of the social democratic paper *Hamburger Echo*—a position that he held from 1924 to 1929. During these Hamburg years he was extremely busy, particularly as a frequent and successful speaker. He played an important role in the life and work of the young socialist Hofgeismarkreis (see p. 10). He was also in at the birth of the 'Reichsbanner Schwarz-Rot-Gold', an organization dedicated to the defence of the Republic. German socialists, he believed, would have to accept the republic and defend it as the most viable constitutional form for future social democracy. His work in organizing the Reichsbanner gave him a practical experience which helped him to appear rather less exclusively intellectual. He was particularly interested in the technical training of the Reichsbanner groups. With his assistance it became a mass organization in the struggle against the growing forces of nationalism.

What were his views at the time? Foreign policy was his special concern and one need not be surprised to find that he advocated a distinctive socialist approach. His ideas can be seen in an essay entitled: *Revision of the Peace Treaties? Foundations of a socialist policy for Europe.* The occasion for the article was the decision at the Vienna Congress of the Socialist Workers' International to campaign for a revision of the Peace Treaties. He thought it important that a start should be made in reorganizing Europe out of the anarchy created by Versailles. To begin with, however, it was essential to isolate the explosive points and deal with them systematically. No demands should be made for revision of Germany's western frontiers. The problem of Polish–German relations—'If there is a danger of war in Europe, it is here'—was the key to the whole European situation. An agreement between Germany and France would contribute towards a solution of this problem. The Corridor should not be removed but the ills that it caused could be eliminated—including its divisive effect. 'To us socialists a Franco–German and Polish–German understanding is much more than a temporary solution of certain difficulties. It constitutes the stable and permanent foundation for the future Europe. The socialist revisionist programme must aim at a reconstruction of Europe.' He favoured Anschluss with Austria. He regarded Britain as an essential part of Europe, but 'Russia had become an asiatic power'. Bolshevism was for him the asiatic form of revolution, socialism the European.

As an expert on military questions Haubach was appointed to the SPD commission on Defence in 1927. He regarded Julius Deutsch, the organizer of the Austrian Federal Army, as a model. He opposed the Reichswehr and favoured either a voluntary militia or the loosest possible form of conscription. In 1929 Haubach became Press Officer to the Reich Minister of the Interior, Karl Severing. His main enemy was fascism, and he fought against it in articles and public meetings. Everywhere he tried to strengthen the democratic organizations. From 1930 onwards he was on the advisory board to the *Neue Blätter für den Sozialismus*.

At the beginning of 1930, the socialists left the government and Severing returned to his post as Prussian Minister of the Interior. Haubach now became press officer at the Berlin police headquarters, where the socialists had installed the former Prussian Minister of the Interior, Grzeszinski. In this post Haubach worked day and night, touching upon matters far beyond the normal concerns of the police, to protect the republic. 'As long as I have an opportunity to use my sword, I will stay in Berlin like a soldier—the only right thing to do.'

When Papen took over the Prussian ministries in July 1932, Haubach was dismissed from his post. 30 January 1933 came soon afterwards. Haubach's proposals for a vigorous attack on the Nazis —Reichsbanner detachments stood at the ready—were turned down by the party leaders, who did not want civil war or a general strike. Nurtured as they had been in quieter times were they capable of coping in the new conditions? Haubach himself did not hesitate to describe the Hitler government as a disaster and the consequence of a deeply rooted malady in an article that he contributed to *Das Reichsbanner,* fourteen days after the Nazi seizure of power and shortly before the journal was banned.

Shortly after this he was arrested and put in temporary custody. He was soon released, but he was kept under observation. On 24 November 1934 he was arrested again and finally sent to the concentration camp Esterwegen–Börgermoor, from which he was not released until September 1936.

When he did come out it was to a world still more threatening. He would have liked to devote himself to literary studies and was also very fond of music. Compelled to work first as an insurance agent and commercial representative, he finally found a job in 1937 in the firm of a former school friend, Viktor Bausch, working on problems connected with raw materials. He found plenty of scope for illegal activities; tried all possible means to get Mierendorff released. In 1939, following the occupation of Czechoslovakia, some letters of his attacking German Fascism were found there and led to a brief imprisonment. Free once more, he was able to continue his opposition against national socialism. It was Mierendorff who introduced him to Count von Moltke and the Kreisau Circle.

Julius Leber was for the Kreisau Circle the coming man. Although himself more pragmatic and activist in politics, he was friendly disposed towards the Circle and shared their views. He gave an impression of peasant-like strength; his huge vitality could radiate to others and exercise a magnetic influence upon them. Brought up amidst the tension of the class struggle and the battles of day-to-day politics, he felt deeply involved in the aims of the working class movement. As native of a frontier area, he could see that difficult international problems would finally be resolved not through war but through adjustment and agreement.

Born in 1891 in Bisheim in Upper Alsace he had to break off his education at the secondary school in order to earn his living. With the help of a scholarship he was later able to go to the senior modern school (Oberrealschule) in Freiburg. Subsequently he took economics and history at the universities of Freiburg and Strasburg until World War I, for which he volunteered, interrupted his studies. In 1913 he had joined the SPD, the party of the

'Fellows without a Fatherland', as it was called in imperial Germany.

He endured the world war like so many others of his generation and was moulded by the experience. 'The lies and frivolity, passions and fears of diplomats, princes and generals transformed millions of peaceful people into murderers, robbers and incendiaries for four years, all for "reasons of state"; only to leave behind at the end a continent brutalized, contaminated and impoverished. No nation made any lasting gains. All lost what decades could not recover. The people of Europe paid the price with nine million corpses. For my generation 1 August 1914 was the great curse, from which manifestly it was never to recover.' He quickly became an officer and was decorated many times. He spent two years after the war as a frontier guard and in 1920 took part in the suppression of the Kapp putsch. After this he left the forces and worked for a doctorate in politics at Freiburg.

When his studies were completed he moved to Lübeck where he joined the staff of the *Lübecker Volksboten* and became editor-in-chief. He quickly established himself in the Lübeck City Assembly and became the leader of the Lübeck Social Democrats.

In domestic policy he devoted much of his attention to the housing shortage and unemployment. He described currency policies as an enormous swindle perpetrated on the workers, who had to pay the bills. He was enraged that wage negotiations with industrialists usually produced absolutely nothing, while at the same time the industrial associations, under the leadership of the heavy industry of the Ruhr, declared their readiness to present fifty marks to every participant in the Berlin Stahlhelm Congress to be held on 8 May 1927. Leber fought against totalitarianism of both the right and the left and could write proudly on one occasion: 'The present state . . . is the state of the German people, it is the republic, subject to constant democratic control. The German working class laid the foundations for this state.' He was at the same time all too aware of the republic's defects.

In Lübeck he met Annedore, the daughter of a headmaster, who was to be an essential partner for the rest of his life. After World War II, in addition to political activities, she also carried on her husband's coal business which she used to finance a publishing house; she also produced two pioneering portrait volumes of the men of the resistance.

In 1924 Leber was elected to the Reichstag and became a member of the Budget and Defence Committees. As the SPD specialist on defence questions, his attitude was positive and his discernment considerable. The experience was later to prove useful when he needed to establish contact with politically interested officers in the course of his opposition work. He took a considerable interest in the negotiations between the Social Democrats and the government about a reform designed to make the Reichswehr non-political. He called upon his party to accept the necessity of an army and to draw the necessary conclusions from their own position in the republic and from the realities of international tension. The Reichswehr was an instrument of executive power. It belonged to the republic and the republic belonged to the people. Social democracy represented the people. They did not need the senseless cultivation of tradition but they did need democratically organized and convinced republican armed forces. In the battleship debate he took a different position from that of the majority of his party. Sadly he perceived the slim basis upon which the republic rested and the difficulties in forming governments. On this he wrote: 'The German approaches everything, even the most practical matter, by the roundabout way of theory. That is why it is so difficult in Germany to unite different parties or movements on a common platform.'

In foreign policy he was emphatically pro-European. He considered the Versailles Treaty maladroit; it had increased international tension. 'Europe is ill with the peace of Versailles, ill with a malady that no longer has a place in the world; nationalism.' He regarded the partition of Upper Silesia as a central point in European politics. 'Reparations could be altered,' he wrote, 'but frontiers are things that remain.' He pointed out the danger of allowing a new Alsace–Lorraine to emerge in the East. The Germans ought to admit, however, that the voices raised against them were often provoked by what the Germans themselves had done. This led him to demand that Germany herself should be ready to come to an agreement and should not give way to nationalist hatred. The way of agreement was the way of freedom. Although Germany and Russia seemed to be natural allies, Germany also needed agreement with the West—a point he made very early and very emphatically. Consequently he regarded the friendliness of the Reichswehr towards Russia with suspicion. For Leber the Locarno Treaty was a turning point in European history. But he anxiously questioned whether the 'common sense of Locarno' would lead to common sense in the political life of the German people. Politics ought to begin, as the economy with its cartels was already doing, to throw nationalism overboard. It was high time for this to happen. 'Europe,' he predicted, 'will have to fight for its economic existence in the coming decades. Only united has it any prospect of maintaining itself.'

Increasingly, however, the growing totalitarian currents in Germany claimed his attention. Already in the first years after the war he had looked anxiously at Bavaria and the activities of the secret societies. At the other extreme he fought against the terrorist endeavours and objectives of communism. He charged the governments with lack of determination. Why was nothing being done? Leber demanded action to protect the republic. 'The political murders have smeared and degraded the German name in the eyes of the whole world.' He was particularly concerned about the rootlessness of the young people who had rushed to the front in 1914, fired with devotion to their fatherland and had returned disillusioned and embittered. These young people, he warned, offer rich soil for all the enemies of the state to plant and nurture their seeds; they were young people who can see no future and are aware only of the past.

As a speaker Leber was feared by his enemies and loved, even revered by the workers. Hitler did not dare to come to Lübeck, and there were only a few communists there. At rallies, election meetings, in the press, in the Burherschaft and in the Reichstag, Leber was to be found wherever he could give political impetus to his friends and defy his opponents. When Hitler became Chancellor Leber wrote: 'We are not afraid of these gentlemen; we are resolved to take up the gauntlet.' A fortnight earlier he had called to the Lübeck workers: 'Whether there is victory or not, when it comes to fighting for liberty one does not ask what tomorrow brings.'

On the night after Hitler's appointment as Chancellor, Leber was attacked by five Nazis. Reichsbanner members came to his help, but, severely injured, he was arrested. The Lübeck workers demonstrated and called for a general protest strike to force Leber's release. By the middle of February he was free once again and the Lübeck Labour organizations arranged a huge demonstration in Leber's honour, in which fifteen thousand took part. Leber's only cry was: 'Freedom!'

For a short time he went to Bavaria. His friends advised him to go abroad but out of a sense of responsibility towards the Lübeck workers he refused. On entering the Reichstag on 23 March 1933 he was re-arrested and, a few months later, convicted by a Nazi influenced court. After the judgement he wrote to his wife: 'I know that I now have only one major task: not to lose my belief in myself.' The national socialists tried to break him but his will remained strong. He was kept in darkness for a long time and spent several years in concentration camps.

During the period of interrogations, Leber wrote his *Thoughts on the Ban on German Social Democracy, June 1933*. In it he set out to explain, in retrospect, why German Social Democracy had failed. He regarded the Marxist ideas of an earlier age as obsolete. They had only hampered the SPD as it tackled the growing problems that confronted it after 1918. The Party had achieved no genuine reforms and had settled all too frequently for a compromise. As a result its liveliness and its enthusiasm had vanished. The electoral lists and the dominance of the party bureaucracy had led to rule by the mediocre. The antiquated leadership had been unaware of what was at stake and of which were the important decisions. All the members of the parliamentary party's executive committee had been fifty or over and yet they were regularly re-elected. They had remained passive, waiting on events. The leadership had crumbled from within. There were hardly any popular speakers left and the party had lost its firm roots in the nation. Only the loyalists remained. History, Leber believed, would not honour the leaders so much as the unknown soldiers of the republic. Leber emerged from the concentration camp unbroken. His friend Gustav Dahrendorf (father of Ralf Dahrendorf) helped him to acquire a coal business in Berlin–Schoneberg. Here, in the office of the firm Bruno Mayer, hidden behind mountains of coal, he took up his old contacts. Many members of the resistance movement visited him and he was in the remaining years of his life to forge a great many links with both socialists and non-socialists.

PART 2
UNDERGROUND ACTIVITIES OF THE
KREISAU CIRCLE INSIDE GERMANY

CHAPTER 6

Origins

The roots of the Kreisau Circle and the members of the 'inner circle' with their personal backgrounds have been the theme so far. We now turn to the activity of the Kreisau Circle within Germany, seen as a common effort. In spite of all the differences between the members their solidarity was unquestionable and it would be quite misleading to discuss the significance of individual members in isolation. The number of members and associates of the group increased as a result of discussion and common action. In a period in which Nazi propaganda undermined personal relationships and destroyed mutual trust, new relationships could only be established on a basis of friendship and loyalty. For each one of them the knowledge that his efforts were supported by friends was an enormous source of strength.

This chapter will deal with the origins of the Circle, and particular attention will be paid to the original nuclei out of which the Circle was formed. Broadly speaking two distinct groups existed in this preliminary phase, one led by Moltke and the other by Yorck. The former was particularly interested in sociological and economic problems, while the latter was more concerned with administrative questions.

When Moltke decided to return to Germany while on his tour abroad in 1933–34, he was well aware that the overthrow of the régime could only be accomplished from within Germany, and in this he wished to be involved. This called, however, for a much more exacting kind of resistance and new revolutionary methods. With its control over communications and its terrible apparatus of oppression, the régime seemed secure, and organized opposition seemed both spiritually and physically impossible. All that civilians like Moltke could do in these circumstances was to keep themselves informed about developments through contacts within the army and the ministries, and meanwhile wait and keep in touch with those who shared their views. Added to this, von Moltke could in the early years only observe developments from a distance. He was occupied with restoring Kreisau and with pursuing his studies in England. Of course he helped victims of persecution where he could, but he was still too young and too isolated to play a decisive part in affairs. Because of his youth, he turned to his seniors in an attempt to discover their ideas. For example, he took part in several meetings of the so-called Schifferkreis, in which former deputies from the middle-class parties, state secretaries, bank directors and others joined together. The founder was the former Minister of Justice, Schiffer. Among other things, Moltke listened to a paper on the Jewish question and on one occasion he himself spoke. In addition he was in touch with people whom he knew from work camp days. His cousin Carl Dietrich von Trotha, and von Trotha's friend Horst von Einsiedel, both of whom had been intimately involved in the youth movement and the organization of the work camps, brought him into contact with old friends and new acquaintances. Von Trotha worked at the Reich Economic Ministry in the section of the leather industry. Later, at the beginning of the war, he was given responsibility for the comprehensive planning of civilian production, his work bringing him an understanding of economic problems that was valuable in other spheres. From within the general office of the State Secretary he watched the attempts of the Third Reich to introduce economic co-operation throughout the European continent, and the failure of these efforts. When, still later, Albert Speer merged civilian planning with military economic planning, Trotha left his post to take over responsibility for the planning of the coal and energy supply, managing to establish a basic ration for the civilian population. His friend Horst von Einsiedel worked at the Reich Chemical Office. The economic crisis had made Einsiedel favour government intervention in the management of the economy. His strong emphasis on human freedom, on the other hand, was a result of his experience under national socialism. Events in this period showed how dangerous an excess or abuse of government power in the economic sphere could be. Together with von Trotha, Einsiedel was in contact with several opposition groups, for example with the group inside the Economics Ministry led by Arvid Harnack (who later became leader of the Rote Kapelle, a pro-Russian group in the resistance). It was through Einsiedel that Moltke re-established contact with Reichwein who, from 1933 till 1939 had lived in

Tiefensee, but in 1939 was asked by the national socialists, who recognized his talents, to build up the school section of the German Folklore Museum, at the Prinzessinenpalais in Unter den Linden, by adapting museum material for educational purposes. He did not, however, confine his activities to the educational sphere: immediately after his arrival in Berlin he sought out both old and new friends. While he was there, the Prinzessinenpalais rapidly developed into a centre of resistance.

The relations between Moltke, Einsiedel, Trotha and Reichwein became even closer in the course of 1938. Both Trotha and Einsiedel assert that the Kreisau Circle grew out of a group led by Moltke, which came into existence in this period. The information from Lukaschek, at that time a lawyer in Breslau, is rather more precise. According to him he was visited shortly before the Munich Agreement by Moltke who told him of the preparations being made for war and of Hitler's plans to attack Czechoslovakia. He also told him that the generals were firmly opposed to war and had made up their minds to overthrow the régime, and also about Beck, Halder and Goerdeler as the leaders of the *coup d'état*. Now was the time, he claimed, for those who had experience and who still enjoyed a public reputation, to join together to consider seriously what the government that followed Hitler's should look like. He stressed that quite new foundations would have to be built, since the old ones had been shattered. For Lukaschek this was the beginning of his Kreisau work.

It is hardly surprising that a coup was planned in 1938. The situation was extremely critical. The armed forces had received orders from Hitler to march against Czechoslovakia and war with the Allies seemed inevitable. On this occasion the opposition could use the widespread dislike of the war that was apparent among the German population as a weapon against the régime. The necessary arrangements were made. This time, they were serious. For Moltke, the decision to launch a coup came as a great relief. He took it for granted that the army would play a decisive part and that experienced men would take over the government.. He felt that his own responsibility was to be on the alert, to stimulate others and, together with like-minded people, to prepare for the new developments. He considered it absolutely vital that the mistakes of the past should not be repeated in the future.

When external developments made it, in the opinion of the opposition, impossible to execute the plan, there was nothing left to do but to wait once again. Discussions were continued and new contacts established. During 1939 Moltke became acquainted with Otto Heinrich von der Gablentz through Einsiedel. Gablentz also worked in the Reich Chemical Office. He took part in ecumenical discussions within Germany and abroad. For example, he was one of the participants of the conference on political and foreign problems in July 1939 in Geneva to work out the results of the Life and Work conference in Oxford (1937) and he made an ecumenical statement about the war problem (see p. 43). Reichwein re-introduced Moltke to Mierendorff and Haubach. They met at Pohl's 'Fluchtburg' in the Riesengebirge in Silesia where both Mierendorff and Haubach after their release stayed on many occasions. Moltke was also in touch with the lawyer Eduard Waetjen. Feelers were thus put out to people on both sides of industry and to government economic experts. Moltke felt that an effort had to be made to bring the different groups together, in order to prepare a new model of economic structure which could be approved by all of them. It was also essential for them to recognize from the beginning that the period of autarchy was over, and that they would have to try to establish European economic co-operation.* Moltke and Einsiedel often discussed these problems together.

When war broke out, Moltke considered this as the beginning of the end of the Third Reich, though it was to take much longer than Moltke expected. Helped by the international lawyer Bruns, he was able to find a post within the international legal department of the 'Ausland-Abwehr', the military counter-intelligence organization headed by Admiral Canaris. Here, Moltke had to try to soften the impact of the war. The work had the sympathy of Canaris, who urged Moltke to pay attention to the positive aspects of the law governing the conduct of war. He provided him with several personal assignments with this in mind and gave him powerful support when he expressed criticisms of illegal or inhumane orders. Moltke soon became the spiritual centre of the group. Despite the limited area in which he could exercise an influence and despite the fact that measures which he appealed against were often implemented on the command of higher authorities, some things could be achieved and some averted. The Allied judges at Nuremberg had to deal with half a dozen memoranda submitted to the department Ausland, but in each case it

* For more particulars about Moltke's work in the Ausland–Abwehr, and his work for prisoners of war and hostages, see van Roon 'Graf Moltke als Volkerrechtler in OKW: *Vierteljahreshefte für Zeitgeschichte, 1970 18 (1)* 12–61.

was minuted in reply that the proposed measures could not be permitted under international law. Most of these were written by Moltke. Moltke was infuriated by the atrocities committed by his fellow countrymen. Few others had his precise knowledge of what was being done, because such a variety of information came through his department; he was very well informed about just those matters that only became generally known after the war and which make this period one of the blackest in human history. These experiences made a strong impact on Moltke, who was only thirty-two at the outbreak of war. His views and statements during this period have to be understood against this background. To Kreisau itself, unfortunately, he could only rarely travel; he could but view it from a distance and look upon it as a safe harbour in the midst of all the storms.

Another group was formed around Yorck von Wartenburg, who was at that time in the office of the Reich Price Commissar. Ever since a journey through the Sudetenland he had regarded opposition as a mission entrusted to him and which he, in keeping with the traditions of his family, had to fulfil. For this reason, the problem of the future structure of Germany interested him too. The earlier social patterns seemed to have become less and less relevant under the impact of national socialism. He therefore assembled a group of friends and acquaintances to discuss these questions in his house. It included Count Fritz von der Schulenburg, Count Nikolaus Uexküll, formerly a colonel in the Austrian army and now in the same office as Yorck, the industrialist Caesar von Hofacker, Albrecht von Kessel, counsellor in the Foreign Office, Otto Ehrensberger, who was a civil servant in the Ministry of Interior, concerned in particular with the organization of administration, but whom Yorck had met previously as District Magistrate in Silesia, and, occasionally, Count Berthold Schenk von Stauffenberg who was at the Institute for International Law in Berlin and whose brother Claus planted the bomb on 20 July 1944. In addition the wives of both Yorck and Schulenburg joined in the discussions. When the group met for the first time they were all under the impact of the anti-semitic pogrom after the 'Kristallnacht' of November 1938. They met frequently in Yorck's house, but they did occasionally go elsewhere, and were always extremely cautious, for instance, parking their cars some distance away and refraining from greeting one another in public. Their major concern was with the constitution of the new Reich. From the very beginning, Yorck made it clear that they were not simply engaged in a theoretical game. Their most important proposals were: a state structure that was clearly democratic which also, however, left room for leadership; a federal state, with a central government whose rights were precisely defined and Lander with wide ranging competence; extensive self-government in the provinces, counties and parishes; economic governing and representative institutions organized on an occasional basis. According to one of the participants, the Reich was only to have power in foreign affairs, foreign trade, defence, finance, food supply, general economic control, transport and communications. The group was also concerned to discover a Reich structure in which, for example, Austria and the Sudetenland would find it easy to decide to remain with Germany. Their discussions continued, interrupted by the Polish campaign, until some time in the spring of 1940.

Yorck took part in the Polish campaign of 1939 as a reserve lieutenant and had the function of adjutant in a tank division. He was well up at that time in the new preparations for a *coup d'état* in Berlin, because he made a report for the Berlin group on the feeling of his regiment.* During the campaign, Yorck lost his younger brother Hans, who had lived with him in Kauern. Whether or not the failure of Germany's enemies to distinguish between the Nazi government and the German people removed the possibility of revolutionary changes was one of the questions that Yorck and his friends had now to grapple with. Despite the war, they decided to continue to give serious thought to a new political order.

In a letter to his wife in January 1940, Moltke wrote that he had had a meal with 'Peter Yorck, the brother of Davy'. Davy was Yorck's sister and was married to von Moltke's cousin, the former ambassador to Poland. It is clear from the way in which he refers to their meeting that the relationship between Yorck and himself was not yet very close. They had occasionally met at family gatherings, but contact between them was infrequent. They knew about each other and were aware of each other's attitude, but it was not until the spring of 1940 that they really became acquainted. Once having started to meet, however, their relationship developed very quickly, and the acquaintance soon grew into a firm friendship that lasted until their deaths. The reason for the January meeting is unknown, but its consequences were significant: 'I think that we understood each other very well,' Moltke's letter continued, 'and I

* Harold C. Deutsch. *The Conspiracy against Hitler in the Twilight War*, p. 257 (Oxford University Press and University of Minnesota Press, 1968).

hope that we will meet more frequently.' This uncharacteristically positive assessment by Moltke suggests that they immediately talked deeply and that their estimates of the situation coincided. After several more meetings in the following months, matters were taken a step further in June. On 4 June, Moltke again spent an evening at Yorck's house, and they were joined by Schulenburg. As on other occasions they discussed current affairs and future prospects. As a result of their conversation Moltke felt that there was a real chance of co-operation, and after the meeting he wrote to Yorck outlining a possible basis for further discussion. He referred to their conversation of the 4th and in particular to some comments that Yorck had made about the State. The discussion had not been merely theoretical, but had been concerned with the specific problem of the structure of the State that would follow Hitler's Germany. To discuss the collapse of the régime at precisely this time indicated an extraordinarily strong faith. Hitler was at the height of his power. The campaign in the west had been victorious, and an invasion of England appeared imminent. It was a moment at which only convinced opponents would have persisted in their opposition. Moltke was one of the very few who continued to believe that there would not be a German victory.

It was against this background that Moltke wrote his letter. He asked Yorck to explain what he had meant when he said that he would place a heavy security against the freedom of the individual. What did Yorck mean by this and what were its practical implications? In the event of a reconstruction of the State, this would clearly be a fundamental problem. He soon received a reply, and the correspondence continued until the end of the year. The earlier letters were written when the Fall of France was very much in their minds. It is interesting to note that both agreed in their diagnosis of the causes of the defeat, but differed when it came to assessing its consequences. Moltke described the German victory as 'the victory of evil' but Yorck, while sharing Moltke's belief in the senselessness of the event, felt that he could see a basis for the creation of Europe in the accomplished facts. 'If, as I hope, we are witnessing the sad end of an epoch, we must also look for the kernel out of which the new life will emerge among the ruins.' Moltke's reaction to this in a following letter was to observe that what the Germans were doing would itself have to be overthrown, and that anyway the demolition contractor could not possibly build the new structure which, admittedly he had made room for 'by destroying the old façade—be it said at the expense of great human suffering'.

On the same day that Moltke wrote to Yorck for the first time, he sent another letter to Einsiedel, in which he continued a discussion that they had been having about future economic problems. They had hoped that some of these problems would have been solved by a change in the general situation, either through a coup or by successful western resistance to Hitler's advance, which would certainly have had domestic consequences. Moltke commented sadly: 'We are still as far from a change as Voltaire was from the French Revolution, when he used to make it his practice to close his letters: écrasez l'infame.'

It was no coincidence that both these letters were written on the same day. Moltke was attempting to link up the discussions on both sides, or at least to see whether such a link was possible. If he succeeded in his attempt a broader basis would be created for the efforts of each. The answers that Moltke received strengthened him in his resolve and in August he invited the Yorcks, Einsiedel and Waetjen to spend a weekend at Kreisau where they could meet in peace. Thus the first 'conference' took place, and at it the plans were laid for the development of what later became known as the 'Kreisau Circle'. The particular topic of discussion at this weekend was the educational system that ought to be introduced after the fall of Hitler. The influence that Nazism exercised over the youth of the day and the surrender of so many parents, teachers and professors, indicated the size of the problem that would have to be overcome if there was to be a genuine New Order. The origins of the catastrophe, and how its recurrence could be prevented were questions thoroughly discussed, and through the discussion each person present became aware of the others' thinking. Afterwards, Einsiedel and Waetjen drove back to Berlin together in Waetjen's car.

Following the weekend, the correspondence with Yorck was continued, and they met frequently. At that time, Moltke also carried on a correspondence* with von der Gablentz. Moltke, who had been greatly stimulated by the discussions, read extensively in Voltaire, Kant, in the letters and papers of Freiherr von Stein, Spinoza, and the educational theories of Goethe. The influence of this reading can be traced in his correspondence with Yorck and Gablentz, and the letters to his wife also contain several reactions to what he had read. He discussed Goethe's ideas on education in the three reverences, for example, and commented at the end that

* Wrongly ascribed in *Neuordnung im Widerstand* to Yorck.

he regarded 'freedom' and 'natural order' as the two poles of the art of statesmanship. 'A man can only be free within the natural order and an order is only natural if it allows a man to be free.' At another point he remarked that Yorck had urged him to read Jünger's '*Arbeiter*'; 'it appears to me to be romantic humbug'.

Further progress was made in the development of their discussions when Moltke wrote the memorandum entitled, *The Foundations of Political Science*, which summed up the results of their conversations to date. He first showed it to Einsiedel and Gablentz and then, later, to Yorck, their comments convincing him that co-operation had now become a real possibility. Thus he wrote to Gablentz; 'on looking at these three points I cannot see any serious material difference between us'. With this observation the period of exploration came to an end. Moltke, Yorck and Gablentz were by now not only in a large measure of agreement, they had also discovered a workable basis for further collaboration.

This began in November 1940. By then a collapse of the régime was inconceivable. Hitler's Reichstag speech of July in which he had proclaimed unbreakable friendship between Germany and Russia and the latter's annexation of Bessarabia and Northern Bukovina, had been followed by an Axis guarantee to Rumania, and, in connection with this, the entry of German troops into that country. Hungary and Rumania had then joined the Three Power Pact, and, already in possession of northern and western Europe, Hitler was now in a position to overrun the Balkans and to extend his advance eastwards. Before the year was over he had given the order to attack the Soviet Union.

The situation was not therefore very propitious for the German opposition. Moltke himself, however, was optimistic because of the discussions that he had had in the past few months. Two letters written late in 1940 ring with a note of expectancy. 'In front of us we have perhaps only one task: to overcome the chaos that exists here at home. If we succeed in this, then we shall have a period of peace, of secure peace which will long survive us. I am certainly not underestimating the difficulties. Nonetheless this is a war in which the crucial issues are being decided. . . . Basically I have only one aim: to get a group of soldiers who are aware of the problems involved in a Peace Treaty and with whom it is possible to work.'

CHAPTER 7

The growth of the Circle and its work

One of the first results of the agreement between Moltke and Yorck was that their friends on both sides were drawn into their work. Thus, at the beginning of 1941, discussions were held with two acquaintances of Yorck, Hermann J. Abs and Albrecht Haushofer. Abs was a banker whom Yorck had known since 1929 through his brother Hans. Since then they had had a number of discussions about political, social and economic problems. By this time the conversations were mostly about economic, and more specifically, financial problems. Albrecht Haushofer was the son of the founder of German 'Geopolitics', Karl Haushofer, professor and general in World War I. Albrecht had been since 1939 professor for political geography and geopolitics in Berlin and held a post in the Foreign Office. Through his father he was in contact with the 'Deputy of the Fuhrer', Rudolf Hess, who had been his father's assistant in 1922. Albrecht played an important role in the preparation of Hess's contacts with England; but had nothing to do with his famous flight in May 1941 to Scotland. At the request of Hess, Albrecht Haushofer had made several attempts after the Fall of France to contact the English about a compromise peace.*

Moltke and Yorck who were well informed about this matter, would have discussed with Haushofer the possibilities of such an attempt as well as other foreign problems. Although these are the only meetings that Moltke mentions in his correspondence with his wife at this period, there were almost certainly others as well. Their general aim was to bring trustworthy people together.

Already in 1940 several new members had entered the Circle. Gablentz, for example, introduced his friend Theodor Steltzer to Moltke (see p. 43). At the outbreak of the war Steltzer had

* A peace plan drafted by Haushofer, and clearly influenced by his talks with Moltke, for instance in its regard for the position of the Commonwealth, and the importance of the Round Table Circle of Lionel Curtis. On one occasion Haushofer delivered a speech at a Kreisau conference. He was arrested after 20 July 1944, and executed shortly before the end of the war. He was the author of the celebrated *Moabiter Sonette*.

been called up for military service. He took part in the invasion of Poland and was later appointed Transport Officer to the Army Commander in Norway. Before he went to Norway, Gablentz suggested that he should get in touch with Moltke, 'since Moltke has a wide knowledge of people who, like us, radically reject national socialism'. As Steltzer was often in Berlin on official duties he soon met Moltke, and the two very quickly understood one another. Through Moltke, Steltzer also came in contact with Hans von Dohnanyi, who worked at the Abwehr, and Canaris.

It was also in 1940 that the Circle gained the support of the agricultural expert Fritz Christiansen-Weniger, who after his return from Turkey met Einsiedel in Berlin. They already knew each other from their work with Rosenstock-Huessy in the work camps, and from a visit that Einsiedel had made to Christiansen in Ankara. Einsiedel told his friend that he knew of an opposition group which was working to alter the present state of affairs in Germany, and preparing foundations for the future. He asked him whether he would like to co-operate. Christiansen agreed to do so as long as their efforts were really serious. A few days later, Einsiedel took him to Moltke and Yorck, both of whom he already knew from an earlier period in Breslau. They discussed the objectives of the Circle. Their task was to overcome national socialism from within, and to create the spiritual foundations on which the communal life of Germany could be rebuilt and on which a new government could base its work. In other words they were preparing to fill the vacuum that would inevitably exist when Nazism collapsed. When Christiansen agreed to collaborate, he was asked to concentrate on questions of food and agriculture, and to take part in the meetings of the Circle at which these problems were discussed. He was also requested to keep in the closest possible touch with Moltke and Yorck, through visits to Berlin—his official work was in Poland. The conversation ended with something like the following exchange. 'If one thing is certain, Count Moltke, it is perhaps that we are now in an even more dangerous predicament than if we were stationed at the most exposed position on the Front.' 'We must be quite clear about that, Christiansen. If I am hanged I will not be the first Moltke to be hanged, and I hope that I will not be the last.'*

* Once before Moltke made a similar remark to his American friend Wallace Deuel: he had read about this case in the family papers and commented: 'There are Moltkes in other countries who can carry on the family.' He must have meant the Danish branch of the family, or two of his brothers who were abroad.

During April or May of 1941, Moltke talked several times with Adam von Trott zu Solz and Hans-Bernd von Haeften; both were members of the Foreign Office. Already in England during the thirties Moltke had met Trott (see p. 50) who now had a post in the Information Department and, in order to be able to continue his anti-Nazi activity untroubled, had joined the Nazi Party on entry into the Foreign Office. Through his work in the Information Department, he was able to come into official contact with various groups, among them the Foreign Department of the German Evangelical Church, where Eugen Gerstenmaier worked (see p. 62). He was also given permission to travel to the neutral countries, and after his appointment as a specialist on Indian affairs, he was able to make further contacts, including some with the military authorities. Haeften had recently returned to Berlin from Bucharest. It was apparently Nostitz who pointed Moltke and Yorck out to him. Haeften, who had a longer experience at the Foreign Office than Trott and was deputy director of the Cultural Department, was extremely angry at the degradation and break-up of the Office under Ribbentrop. He was offended by the undermining of the traditional body of officials through the introduction of ignorant, incompetent and empty headed party loyalists who only succeeded in filling the Foreign Office with Nazi fog. He made life difficult for the protagonists of this nonsense by isolating them, setting them against each other, and above all, exposing their corruption. Official reports and current talk depressed him more and more, and his health, which at the best of times was not robust, suffered correspondingly. Precisely because he was so depressed he found it a great relief to be able to work on plans for reconstruction.

Following a conversation with Trott and Haeften, Moltke wrote: 'It is hard work to get people like this to support the "grand solution", because they are too familiar with routine. If you once succeed, however, they turn out to be very reliable companions.' Their arrival meant that the Circle could now count upon the services of foreign policy experts. It was during this period that Moltke wrote his memorandum, 'Starting point, aims and problems' (see p. 317); the contents must have been considerably influenced by the conversations with Trott and Haeften and also, occasionally, with other foreign office contacts such as Albrecht von Kessel (see p. 105) and Franz Josef Furtwängler whom he had known since the early 1930's. The discussions may well explain the various drafts of the document.

Another person who entered into the Circle about this time was

Hans Peters (see p. 66), a university reader in Constitutional Law, but at that time posted to the Luftwaffe headquarters at Potsdam. Another old acquaintance from the Breslau period, he was told by Moltke about the Circle's aims: the intention was to discuss what should be done when the régime came to an end; how it was to come to an end remained an open question, but there was no doubt that it would. Its opponents must, therefore, not be caught unprepared, but have a programme—both long and short-term—to enable the new rulers to avoid a mere restoration of the conditions prior to 1933. A new welfare state would be founded on a just social order and numerous reforms would be necessary because of the Nazi penetration of almost all levels of society. When Moltke asked Peters whether he would be ready to collaborate in such a programme, he replied in the affirmative. Outside the Kreisau Circle, Peters had links with Catholic trade union leaders such as Jacob Kaiser, Bernhard Letterhaus (see p. 157) and Hermann Josef Schmitt. He was also in touch with Ernst von Harnack and, in addition, belonged to a group led by Ruth Friedrich, which among other things offered protection to Jews. Finally, he knew Harro Schulze-Boysen, who with Arvid Harnack, was the leader of the 'Rote Kapelle' (see p. 102).

Peters and the other newcomers were asked, on joining the Kreisau Circle, to study specific problems, with the result that gradually there began to emerge a compendium of all those things that would have to be attended to most urgently on the overthrow of the régime.

Moltke continued to be introduced to new people by his colleagues and other acquaintances. One of those who played an important part in arranging some of the meetings was Freiherr Karl Ludwig von und zu Guttenberg, a Bavarian landowner who had previously been the editor of the journal *Weisse Blaetter*,* and who was currently employed by the Abwehr. Guttenberg often met Moltke and approved of him personally and of the aims of the Circle. From Moltke's own point of view the link with Guttenberg was especially valuable because it gave him access to Catholics —it was Guttenberg who introduced Moltke to the Lawyer Joseph Müller, another member of the Abwehr. In 1939–40 Müller had been the representative of the German opposition in negotiations with the British ambassador to the Holy See, Osborne.†

* See James Donohoe, *Hitler's Conservative Opponents in Bavaria 1930–1945*, pp. 58, 114 (Leiden, 1961).
† See the invaluable book by Deutsch (op. cit. p. 106) for a full account of resistance activities at the time.

After their first meeting, Moltke visited Müller whenever he was in Munich, and the latter always returned the visits when he was in Berlin. Guttenberg was also responsible for introducing Father Rösch SJ to Moltke, but this particular relationship will be described in more detail at a later point (see p. 128). Finally, Guttenberg brought Moltke and Hans Christoph Freiherr von Stauffenberg together again—the two men having already met in London in 1938. Among others to whom Moltke was introduced during this year were Bishop Preysing of Berlin and Pastor Poelchau. The bishop gave Moltke a quite new perspective, and Poelchau was particularly useful because of his contacts with workers and the information that he was able to give about working class opinion. As we have seen he was a prison chaplain at the Berlin Tegel prison (see p. 58). Among those under his care three groups need special mention: the persecuted, the resistance fighters from the occupied territories, and the men and women who belonged to the political resistance in Germany. The victims of persecution were both inside and outside prison; those outside used to visit him at the times set for consultation, or at his home. With the help of assistants and by others Poelchau was able to aid many and shelter some. Jews were hidden and sent on their way provided with ration cards and papers. Nobody knocked in vain, and no risk was too great. His wife was the greatest help in all his work on behalf of those in need. The persecuted inside the prison included members of the forbidden sects, such as the Jehovah's Witnesses, pastors of the Confessing Church, and individuals who had refused to do military service or to take the oath of loyalty to Hitler. The Church did absolutely nothing for these people. So, Poelchau had to write afterwards: 'The failure of the official Church to do anything, partly because of its dependence upon the régime, partly because of its deafness to the demands of conscience, was a source of shame to Christianity.' In the group of resistance fighters from the occupied territories, Poelchau had most to do with one Dutch and two Norwegian groups. The third group with which he was concerned—men and women of the German political resistance—had begun to form as early as 1934 with the imprisonment of communist and socialist officials.

Moltke discussed with Poelchau the shooting of hostages and the possibilities of reducing the number of incidents in the occupied territories. In the Kreisau Circle itself, Poelchau was asked to consider the question of a cultural policy for the future. Towards the end of the year, Moltke and Yorck believed that they had also succeeded in associating Schulenburg (see pp. 105, 107) rather closely with the Circle.

During 1941 discussions among the members of the Circle advanced so far that a further step could be taken. 'We have now progressed so far,' Moltke wrote at the end of November, 'that we can put the results of our discussions on paper and once that is done we can coach the members on the various topics.' With this in mind, they prepared for a number of weekend meetings where problems could be thoroughly discussed in small groups. In order to make these meetings easier, Yorck approached the Borsigs who had an estate at Gross Behnitz, not far from Berlin. Moltke and Yorck were invited there for a weekend in October, and they were joined by Trott and Wussow. Almost all of them were accompanied by their wives. The normality of weekend parties at the great country houses provided adequate cover for their meeting. Naturally enough, some of the conversation at Gross Behnitz dealt with the further development of the Circle, and after this weekend meeting the house was used for numerous other small gatherings and several of the larger 'conferences'.

As the number of contacts grew, the danger of detection also increased. This was one of the reasons for introducing a strict division of labour. The collaborators were divided into work groups, and this system was also intended to guarantee that the individual member knew as little as possible about other members of the Circle, so that, in the event of arrest, he could only give a little away. A well-known contemporary poster, 'The enemy is listening in', hung in Moltke's tiny flat above a garage in Berlin. Only he and Yorck knew all the aspects of the Circle's work. Their closest associates were familiar with the general outlines, but the knowledge of details and the names of individuals remained extremely restricted. Outside this inner circle, the other collaborators knew only two or three members and even then they sometimes did not know their names. Several of them have commented on the extreme caution that was characteristic of the Circle. All but the most important papers were burnt immediately after the discussion, and those that were kept were hidden away in an absolutely safe place—(in fact, in a bee-hive at Kreisau). No lists of names were ever drawn up and sometimes participants were not even introduced to one another at meetings.

What 'working parties' then were there? In the course of the year a number of topics were discussed and the identity of the participants varied according to which topic was under discussion.

It would be misleading to think of rigidly organized groups. It was much more a case of members of the Circle establishing contact with specialists who were asked to comment on some draft laid before them. Even with this proviso in mind, however, it is possible to detect the existence of the following 'special groups', which are listed here according to subject: State, Culture, Economy, Social Policy, Agriculture, Foreign Policy, and perhaps also Law. It is impossible to be absolutely certain of the membership of the groups. Alongside the regular members there were collaborators who acted as intermediaries or who performed other special functions. Yorck and Moltke always synchronized the discussions and generally held everything together. Most of the meetings were held in the evening, but some of those in which only two or three individuals were involved, took place in daytime. They met in private homes, especially those of Yorck and Moltke, and in certain government buildings. Official business provided a pretext for many secret meetings in the offices of the Commission on Prices, the Foreign Office, the Prinzessinenpalais and the Abwehr.

Moltke's own method of disguising the arrival of so many visitors can be briefly mentioned here. An important part was played by the Committee for the Development of Martial Law. Peters can remember that Moltke told him one day that 'a group of civil servants and officers from a number of departments has been formed, with the approval of the OKW, to work out the demands of the armed forces in the event of victory. In fact, however, they are at the moment using this cloak of legality to work out what should be done in the event of a Nazi collapse.' There seems little doubt that Moltke was referring to the Committee for Martial Law, headed by Admiral Gladisch. It is uncertain how far the other members of the committee were aware of what Moltke was doing, but it is nonetheless clear that Moltke held a number of discussions under this particular cover. Some of the committee's papers have been examined by the author and two quotations will suffice to show how easily the legal work of the committee could merge into the opposition work of the Circle. 'The restoration of peace affords the opportunity, taking into account the new situation created by the peace, to achieve international recognition and universal acceptance of the legal principles governing warfare that we consider to have proved their value in the present war.' With the object of establishing an internationally recognized code of martial law, it was obviously admissible to discuss the problems of the post-war world. The second quotation suggests what far-reaching and comprehensive preparations could be made within the scope of this brief: 'The clarification of German demands for the further development of international law requires a great deal of preliminary study of existing conditions, of the military developments of this war, and of the military and political interests of Germany after the war.'

In the course of this chapter we have studied the growth of the Circle and its work, especially in 1941. By the end of that year plans were already being made for larger gatherings. Before coming to this, however, we shall examine the links that were established with two particular groups, the labour leaders and the representatives of the churches.

The development of the work of the Kreisau Circle in 1941 was overshadowed by the events in Russia. After the Balkan campaign, Hitler began the war against the Soviet Union with powerful, specially selected forces, but preparation had been inadequate and resistance was stronger than expected. To the initiated, among whom was Moltke, this was soon apparent. As early as August 1941, when the war was only two months old and still appeared to be progressing extremely well, Moltke wrote: 'What will happen when the people at large discover that this war is lost and lost in a quite different way than the last? And all this involving such a shedding of life as can never be atoned or forgotten in our life-time, and with an economy that has been totally ruined? Will men emerge capable of refining out of this retribution penitence, remorse, and, gradually, the forces of new life? Or will everything descend into chaos?' An official report that Moltke wrote in October 1942 condemned the entirely false information that was being given about the progress of the war. It closed with these words: 'Viewed from the standpoint of the war economy, the occupation of the Russian territories has, in my opinion, been a complete mistake which has resulted in dissipation of our economic resources and the imposition of unlimited demands for the supply of investments needed to keep the economy of the eastern territories ticking over.' For Moltke, in other words, the turning point came before Stalingrad.

CHAPTER 8

Links with the Labour leaders

It was taken for granted by the members of the Kreisau Circle that the working class would share in reconstruction after the war. The documents made this quite clear. (See First Instructions to the Provincial Commissioners, p. 355.) Among the members of the earlier group led by Moltke the experience of the work camps had been a decisive influence: in the state of the future it was essential that class conflict should no longer endanger common effort. All constructive forces would have to join together. This was a lesson bitterly learned in the Weimar period, though meanwhile some of the intensity of class conflict had been reduced through the compulsory measures of the National Socialist Labour Front. Another important factor in determining the Kreisau attitude, however, was a feeling of guilt. Yorck, for example, was insistent on this point. He once asked Hans Christoph von Stauffenberg whether he had any contacts with working-class groups and when the latter replied, with some surprise, that he had not, Yorck declared: 'This is all that matters. Those who have been most cheated by national socialism are the workers. If we flatter ourselves that we are something like an élite or that we have a responsibility to lead, then we have failed, particularly in relation to the ordinary man, the worker, because if he had not been misled there would never have been a Third Reich. We have a debt that we must repay to the German working man and it is for this reason that we must overthrow the régime. In order to achieve this we must have a response and some support among the working people.' The specific application of this attitude can be seen in the work of the Kreisau Circle. Thus Moltke made special mention of the workers as one group whom it would be necessary to compensate and in the documents working class interests received a great deal of attention (see p. 348).

It was for these reasons that members of the Circle tried to establish contact with working class leaders during the war. Here, Reichwein played an important role. To this day too little has been written about the political side of Reichwein's work; only in the random comments of a few authors can one discover anything about it. Brundert had introduced Reichwein to Mierendorff and Haubach in 1939 (see p. 90). They used to meet regularly in Brundert's flat, or at the home of Emil Henk in Heidelberg or in the Allgau. Reichwein in turn introduced them to Moltke. Both Mierendorff and Haubach were well-known and powerful figures among the workers. As we have seen they had as young labour leaders, a strong influence on the socialist youth before 1933 and had had to put up with their elders' pretensions to leadership (see Chapter 5). Their faith and determination had only been strengthened by their years in concentration camps. In 1933 both men hoped for a working class protest movement and stood prepared with their followers. They were bitterly disappointed when the older leaders refused to take this step. After his release, Mierendorff had resumed contact with his former colleagues, such as Leuschner, and became the centre of a group of prominent young socialists including Dahrendorf, Haubach, Leber, Schwamb, Henk, Maass, Brundert, Sänger and Siegel. Through him this group came into touch with the Kreisau Circle.

At first only Mierendorff was directly involved in the Kreisau work. In the course of 1941 he took part in a number of discussions on the future economic structure with Einsiedel, Abs and Waetjen, among others. Both Moltke and he had much in common in their assessment of the situation and of the way ahead. They also struck a warm personal relationship and, as Moltke said on one occasion, there was a 'spontaneous *Gleichschaltung*' (co-ordination).

During 1942, Moltke also came into closer contact with the Social Democrat Ernst von Harnack, whom he hoped would share in the work of the Circle. Harnack, who was a neighbour of Dahrendorf and Leber, may well have heard of the Kreisau group from these two. Son of a famous theologian, he had been Regierungspräsident of Merseburg until 1933. In the years that followed he was extremely active in a number of spheres. He was, for example, very involved in relief work for both Jewish and Semi-Aryan victims of persecution and for their wives and children. In touch as he was with several generals, including Beck, he often served as a link between civilian and military opposition groups. He was also in touch with Prince Louis Ferdinand: they used to play music together. For Harnack, the most important feature of their meetings was the opportunity that they afforded to discuss the possibility of a constitutional monarchy. It is not clear to what extent he became involved in the work of the Kreisau group.

Lukaschek thought that he took part in some of the small meetings of the Circle.

In 1942 the range of contacts was extended when the Kreisau Circle forged relationships with the churches. Moltke saw here an opportunity to lessen the gap and modify the antipathies that existed between socialists and representatives of the churches. He hoped thereby to create a basis for co-operation in the work of re-construction, for it was precisely these two forces that would have to carry out the task of reconstruction after the collapse of the régime. His efforts in this direction gave him a stronger influence on the labour leaders as a group. In May 1942 Mierendorff came to him with a request to meet Wilhelm Leuschner. On his release from concentration camp, Leuschner, formerly Minister of the Interior in Hessen, had founded a light metal factory where, under the cover of business activity, he continued to advance his illegal political aims. He had worked his way up from worker to minister and, as a former trade unionist, he enjoyed the special confidence of the trade union movement. During the period of resistance he attempted to re-establish links with his former trade union associates. Being convinced that the divisions among the workers had given the national socialists their chance, he strove to create a united trade union for the future. He was also interested, however, in ending the political isolation of the worker and he tried to establish co-operation with representatives of other groups.

A few days later the first meeting between Moltke and Leuschner took place in the former's home. Mierendorff was also present. Moltke put forward his own ideas and proposed that Leuschner should co-operate in the formulation of a basis for post-war reconstruction in which representatives of the churches would also take part. During the conversation, however, difficulties emerged. Leuschner was undoubtedly in agreement with the emphasis upon self-government and he sympathized with their interests in conditions at factory level, but he insisted that the trade unions would have to be maintained as a weapon in the hands of the workers under any circumstances and with his long experience he was extremely sceptical about any other solutions. The Kreisau group, on the other hand, were critical of centralized organizations like the trade unions. They were afraid that their own efforts to overcome class conflict within industries would be endangered by the continued existence of the trade unions. After another meeting with Leuschner, Moltke wrote: 'Yesterday evening was exceedingly strenuous. We had a hard fight, but we advanced far enough to uncover the ground of Uncle's* fundamental mistrust. In the end we pulled him along so far that he gave in. If these elements really are forthcoming, we are in an entirely new situation in which we can achieve quite different results. I have the impression that the decisive breach has been made, but it was only achieved at midnight and we shall have to see whether the opposition will harden again or whether the victory has finally been won. We will be carrying on next Tuesday.' The next meeting achieved its object. 'The evening with Uncle again lasted until midnight, but it produced considerable advances. We got as far as we wanted to, in that Uncle promised to appoint a representative for October. In some questions we have still some way to go, but at least a broad basis for further work has been established. So we have made some very important progress.' Following this agreement another of the Labour leaders, Hermann Maass became associated with the Kreisau work.

Maass was the former General Secretary of the 'Reich Committee of German Youth Associations' and a co-founder of the 'German Youth Radio'. The first of these jobs had given him contacts with military groups. In the years following the Nazi seizure of power he and the publisher Ulrich Wolf edited *'Youth and Education Abroad'* which was intended to provide factual and unprejudiced reports on youth and educational problems outside Germany. Wolf introduced Maass to Lieutenant Colonel Heinz† and the heavy industrial Oscar Henschel. Political conditions in Germany, however, made it increasingly difficult and finally impossible to maintain adequate links abroad and the project had to be terminated in 1938–39. Maass then worked as private secretary to Leuschner. His particular responsibility was to co-ordinate the work of the Circle that had formed round Leuschner. He also established contacts with the military leaders, first with Beck and later with Stauffenberg. Although he had left the church he was not one of those socialists who was fundamentally opposed to it. He allowed his children to attend religious instruction and he had been married in church. He rejected the dogma, however.

Maass' collaboration with Henschel rose partly from Henschel's international contacts which enabled him to pass on consistently useful information. But he was also able to tell Maass, whom he

* Cover name for Leuschner.

† One of the main plotters in the 1938–39 conspiracies against Hitler, he was to have led a commando-type force to arrest the Führer. Later he went underground and survived the war. See footnote†, p. 113.

saw secretly in Berlin every two or three weeks, the names of those who could be really trusted in the German business world and who, if the situation arose, would be suitable for positions of responsibility. Henschel's special function was to act as an agent of the group in Kurhessen; in this connection he was asked by Maass to specify people who could be given responsible positions at short notice. Quite apart from his personal activity, Henschel also provided Maass with considerable sums of money for his work (about 50,000 RM) and promised that the material resources of his concern would be available on day X. Henschel was also one of the few German industrial leaders who was very interested in social problems and responsive to socialist ideas.

Maass was particularly concerned with building up 'the illegal trade unions'. They were intended to gather together opposition elements in the working class and to create a network of reliable strongholds all over Germany, so that when the intended insurrection occurred there would always be a civilian representative of Labour at hand in every district, who could join the representative of the military executive. This plan was painstakingly prepared under appropriate cover. As the German resistance movement was composed of such diverse elements, the Leuschner–Maass group assumed that transition governments after the war would follow upon one another in relatively quick succession and they set their own hopes on the 'third phase'.

Following his meetings with Leuschner, Moltke met Maass for the first time in July 1942. Mierendorff was also present. According to Moltke the discussion went well. 'Maass is somewhat schoolmasterish and a tough person to talk with; he is extremely well versed in his special sphere, very responsible and serious and well prepared. In general political terms he fits well and he will be the ideal representative of Uncle at Kreisau.' In the days that followed Maass was introduced to other members of the Circle who were preparing for the conference and he took part in some of the preliminary discussions. After one of these discussions Moltke wrote that Maass really did have something to say about the working class situation and that there were certain high points in his somewhat long discourses at which he managed to win everybody's close attention. Their conversations enabled them to establish a common starting-point with which both the Labour leaders and the others, including the Jesuits, could associate themselves. They agreed that both sides would prepare some basic themes with the help of their 'chiefs'—for the Labour leaders that meant Leuschner—and then at the end of August they would exchange their theses. Leuschner, Maass and Mierendorff were to take part in this meeting.

Mierendorff was enthusiastic about this opportunity for co-operation. He regretted that real action would have to be left to the generals, but he understood the reasoning behind this and found the development of a common programme and the preparation of post-war co-operation extremely important. For security reasons he only gave his friends very partial information, so that they would be burdened with as little knowledge as possible. In conversation he used to stress that it would not do to rest their hands on the oars and let matters take their frightful course, but that they must prepare for the day of the collapse or of Hitler's disappearance, in the first instance by preparing suitable persons to take over administration and assume political responsibility. Then he would mention that a group had been formed around Count Moltke that included people from both right and left and representatives of both churches. If possible they would prepare actively for an insurrection. But, as Harro Siegel (see p. 119) reports, his hopes were slender. Among the Labour leaders Mierendorff did his best to enlist the support and co-operation of his colleagues. He also took some initiatives of his own within this group, which advanced the general objectives of the Kreisau Circle. 'It's as good as hopeless but one cannot live without trying the impossible.'

After the preparatory discussions Maass took part in the second great conference in Kreisau and in the third one (see pp. 146, 147). When the proceedings were over the results of the discussion were communicated to the others and set out in a definitive form. Shortly afterwards Mierendorff was able to give the pleasant news that Leuschner approved of the main features of 'almost everything'. Moltke and Leuschner were also able to keep up personal contact and when 'a row' broke out between Leuschner and Delp which had its origins in the close relations between Leuschner and Goerdeler (see pp. 124, 158), Moltke was able to secure a continuation of their co-operation in a talk with Leuschner. 'The whole thing was an important test of confidence for me.'

Yet another labour leader was drawn into the preparatory work on the Kreisau economic programme—Otto Stegemann, a friend of Maass who took him twice to discussions with Einsiedel and Trotha. Stegemann had been district magistrate in Osterholz-Scharmbeck until 1933 and, earlier still, a civil servant in the Prussian ministry of Trade and Industry. In 1934 he was appointed to a post on the supervisory panel for the woollen industry which provided him with a vantage point from which he could observe more general economic changes. His experience in economic administration was the most important factor leading to Maass' decision to bring him in to the discussion of economic problems. As far as he can remember the conversations were enjoyable and, by and large, encouraging. They were all agreed that they would have to work together in the immediate future, though Stegemann himself felt the talks were premature. In the spring of 1943 Maass placed before the labour leaders a memorandum on the trades union problem which provoked long discussions. Maass, Mierendorff and others advocated, according to Dahrendorf, the creation of factory based unions. Leuschner, on the other hand, favoured the retention of occupational unions. Even more controversy was caused by the personality and programme of Goerdeler. Unlike the younger socialists who dismissed Goerdeler, Leuschner advocated the acceptance of Goerdeler as provisional chancellor. As a counter-balance to Leuschner whose role some labour leaders considered to be not in politics but in the building of the trade unions, Julius Leber was pushed into prominence.

In spite of difficulties such as these the Kreisau Circle was still able to lay down an economic programme for the period after the collapse of the régime and the guide-lines for its practical realization. Agreement was reached between all the groups involved on all important points. The work was completed by 1943 and its most important findings were committed to writing.

Nonetheless, disagreements within the resistance movement about Goerdeler, about the assassination of Hitler, etc., had increasingly disastrous consequences as 1943 progressed. They also affected relations between the labour leaders and the Kreisau Circle. First, contact with Maass became difficult and then friction increased with Leuschner, who according to van Husen finally decided to follow the Goerdeler line at the beginning of 1943. Mierendorff and other younger socialists held to the Kreisau line. Alongside him Haubach now began to achieve more prominence and there was also now and then talk of Leber who had kept himself in the background for a long time. Reichwein was also a frequent participant in the discussions. Thus the work continued. ' "Frederick"* was in very good form: lucid, determined, clever, tactful, and humorous. During this night session which went on

* Cover name for Mierendorff.

until 5 o'clock in the morning, the gap that the Uncle left was closed, since Frederick had made sure that his colleagues came with us and left Uncle alone. We made a considerable advance in both theoretical and practical matters.' Moltke's letter of 18 October 1943 contains mention of 'Neumann'. This is probably a cover name but it is not clear to whom it refers. As Leber is referred to as 'substitute Uncle' and 'Julius' in the letter, it is doubtful whether Neumann also applies to him. It is nonetheless striking that Neumann's name is sometimes mentioned together with Mierendorff's. Then in December a great blow fell. During a raid on Leipzig, Mierendorff was burned to death in the blazing cellar of his aunt's house. The last word he uttered was 'Madness'. His loss made co-operation between the two groups much more difficult; indeed it was very difficult to continue the work without him. Nonetheless, Haubach and Reichwein remained and Moltke now tried to enlist the closer co-operation of Leber. This was, however, difficult, since his relations with Leber were not as close as those that he had enjoyed with Mierendorff. Leber was quite different from Mierendorff. On 2 January Moltke was writing to his wife: 'He is a compellingly good man but he has a very one-sided interest in the purely practical and attaches much less importance than I do to spiritual and intellectual powers,' wrote Moltke. A week later he said: 'I must, however, try again to bring him along our road. He is much more boorish than Carlo and much less congenial to me. He won't provide the spontaneous corrective that has hitherto guaranteed our stability. I am, nonetheless, very optimistic.' There were also several discussions with the Austrian Gleissner in whose home Haubach lived. 'I hope that the attempt to provide an heir for Carlo intofar as one can be provided, will succeed,' Moltke wrote.

CHAPTER 9

Links with the Churches

The Protocol of the first Kreisau conference in May 1942 proclaims: 'We see in Christianity the most valuable source of strength for the religious-ethical renewal of the nation, for the conquest of hatred and deception, for the reconstruction of the western world and for the peaceful co-operation of the nations' (see p. 329). These words indicate how essential the contribution of the churches would be to the work of reconstruction after the collapse. The Circle included some who had been members of the churches since their youth, but events made religion for them no longer a matter of habit and tradition; it became more personal and it grew in significance as the pressures increased. Yorck could write at the beginning of 1942: 'Is it not perhaps possible that those whose hearts are stirred by a new longing for God, are to be compelled to give this longing fresh and authentic expression and to build their house anew for their God? It almost seems to me as if it is only when we are in the most desperate plight, both externally in the world and inwardly in the innermost depths of our being, that we can push our way past the accumulated impedimenta of history to the basic essentials; as if we are being prevented from making it too easy for ourselves by the fact that the testimony of earlier generations to their faith is being destroyed. We are compelled to bear witness to our own living convictions.' Other members had only come to believe during the period of national socialist rule. Haubach and Mierendorff had found a religious belief in the concentration camps. Mierendorff thought that without a metaphysical dimension, the individual could not live and the nation could not be ruled. Haubach used to read the bible every day. He hoped that Thomist ideas—a picture of St. Thomas Aquinas hung over his desk in this period—would help the masses towards an understanding of God after the fall of the Hitler régime. Moltke's religious views, too, underwent a decisive change in this period. 'The risks and sacrifices that are today demanded of us, require much more than good ethical principles,' he wrote to his English friend Lionel Curtis in 1942 (see p. 377). In order to think and to act, to find comfort and reassuranace, amidst all these reports of brutality, something more, a new dimension, was needed. Moltke observed with horror that men were capable of any atrocity. 'In the past all these things were fables to me, at least the Old Testament, but today they have become contemporary with me. They have a much greater relevance to me than they have ever had,' he wrote to his wife; and at another point, as he thought about the significance of grace at table: 'It has become clearer and clearer to me during these years that the existence of each one of us depends upon the maintenance of the moral principles laid down in the Ten Commandments.'

They all discovered the bracing power of faith in their struggle against the false doctrines of Nazism. Another positive result of this period was that Christians found the way to one another. As the poet Reinhold Schneider was to write afterwards: 'Under the impact of evil, links were established in which there was thrilling promise for the future.' In praying together and fighting together something of the reality of the *Una Sancta* was made visible.

The links between the Kreisau Circle and the bishops require special mention. They began with the first visit of Moltke to the Bishop of Berlin, Count von Preysing, in September 1941. The legal expert in the diocesan office, Happ, was responsible for introducing them to each other. The bishop lived in Behrenstrasse, in a palace built at the time of Frederick the Great. It was occupied by the Prussian General Staff, and it was here in the large room under the stuccoed ceiling that Field-Marshal Moltke had planned his military campaigns. Eventually it became the residence of the Bishop of Berlin. A scion of one of the oldest aristocratic families of Bavaria, Bishop Preysing had been summoned from Eichstatt to the so-called 'Diaspore bishopric' of Berlin in 1935. At Eichstatt he had already shown himself to be one among the episcopate who was fully apprised of the situation and had been an intrepid opponent of the régime. At meetings of the Fulde bishops' conference he had several times pleaded for a stronger stand by the churches, and he had opposed particular policies of the régime in pastoral letters. He had never issued any declarations in support of Hitler's military adventures. The fact that not all his colleagues agreed with him had greatly hampered his efforts.

Moltke's first visit to Preysing followed only a few weeks after the Bishop of Münster, Count von Galen, had preached his famous sermon on euthanasia. It was a high point in the history of the church struggle: a senior representative of the church protested publicly about the killing of the mentally sick. Until then opposition to national socialism had been largely confined to lower clergy and laymen, while the bishops had remained in the background or addressed declarations of loyalty to the régime. The faithful, however, awaited a word from their bishops, and the impact of Galen's sermon was world-wide. It confirmed the faithful in their resistance, gave a warning to the régime and succeeded in obtaining the withdrawal of certain orders. Other examples of the efficacy of protest could be quoted. Moltke was one of those who kept copies of this and other sermons and had them reproduced for distribution. During his visit to Preysing he asked the latter about Galen and declared himself delighted that the bishop, a man of strong patriotic feelings, had decided upon such steps. At the end of the visit Preysing asked Moltke to call again soon, which he did every three or four weeks from then on; they often talked for many hours.

Baron Guttenberg was responsible for introducing Moltke to another important contact, Father Rösch, Provincial of the Upper German Province of the Jesuit Order (see p. 74). Rösch was a determined man, far sighted, with a lucid mind, a dogged will and dauntless courage, stern and yet at the same time full of fatherly kindness. On his shoulders rested the heavy responsibility of leading the Jesuits in Upper Germany in a period of bitter persecution. His first aim was to serve his Order and his church. He combined this with a considerable love for his country. He was always ready for tireless activity in the service of church and nation. When a member of the Order was arrested, Rösch was almost always successful in discovering where he was and visiting him. He dealt with the Gestapo artfully and judiciously, his decorations from World War I proving useful in this connection. He also worked unstintingly to rescue numerous monasteries and safeguard the interests of his Order. He was supported in his work by a circle of helpers which included Delp and König, the lay brother Moser and the lawyer Josef Müller. In October 1941, while in Berlin for negotiations with the OKW, he met Guttenberg on the street. He had just heard a speech by Hitler over the loudspeaker on the street, in which the Fuhrer claimed that the war with Russia was virtually over. Guttenberg approached him suddenly while he was still very much under the impact of what he had just heard. Although Rösch would have been pleased to see the end of the war, he nonetheless knew what would follow: the intensification of the church struggle and a merciless persecution of his Order. As it was impossible to talk on the street, Guttenberg said: 'Follow me; I am going on ahead. On the way we must not show that we know one another. When I stop at a garden gate and light a cigarette, go in through the next garden gate, round the large garage that you come to and up the stairs on the back wall. Upstairs is a flat. Knock there; my name is the password. I will come by a quite different way.' Thus Rösch met Count Moltke. After the greetings Rösch asked him—Guttenberg had also arrived in the meantime—whether he had heard Hitler's speech. Moltke replied that it did not interest him as he had contacts of his own abroad and through them he knew the truth. When Rösch described the contents of the speech, Moltke was horrified at its lies and deception and disclosed what he knew of the Russian reserves from official reports. He then went on to predict how the situation would develop and forecast that in a few years the Russians would be in Berlin unless Hitler was removed from the leadership; that was the job of the generals. If this happened the Russians could be halted, and it would be possible to arrange a tolerable peace and save Europe. Finally they discussed the situation within Germany and their conversation soon came round to the position of the churches. 'We must fight, we must do everything to save what can be saved; the other side is afraid again; if they find resistance they quiver and they hesitate.' While discussing developments within the evangelical church Moltke said suddenly: 'As a Protestant there is one thing I want to say to you: Christianity in Germany can only be saved through the German bishops and the Pope.' That was why it was essential that both confessions stood together and worked together. He then asked Rösch: 'Are you willing to co-operate in this way? We need pastoral letters that are to be sent to thousands and thousands. And on the chance that there is a collapse we as Christians must consider, plan and prepare how we shall rebuild.' Moltke repeated his question: 'Will you co-operate?' Rösch asked for time to think and suggested they continue the discussion in Munich. This meeting marked the beginning of co-operation between the Jesuits and the Kreisau Circle. Of the meeting with Rösch, Moltke wrote: 'A peasant's son with a first-rate brain, clever, educated, solid—I liked him very much. We discussed concrete questions of pastoral care, education and agreement with the Protestants and he seemed reasonable, unbiased and ready to make considerable concessions.'

In November 1941 Moltke again visited Preysing. They discussed the state of the churches; Peters had prepared a dossier for them. Moltke pressed the bishop to oppose the régime vigorously and, for example, to issue a protest against the confiscation of a church. They also discussed the persecution of the Jews. Only that morning the bishop had received several Jews in his palace and confirmed them in the chapel. For several years the Provost of the Lichtenberg Cathedral with his wife Frau Sommer had run a relief agency from his diocesan office devoted to the relief of the Jews. Now Lichtenberg had been denounced by the Nazis because he had prayed for the Jews. He had just been interrogated when Moltke came to see Preysing. When asked by his interrogators where he stood on the race question, Lichtenberg replied: 'I distinguish only between Christians and non-Christians; for the former I pray as my brothers, and for the latter I pray for enlightenment.' When they thereupon threatened him: 'If you don't change your ways we shall send you to your beloved Jews in Litzmannstadt,' he replied: 'That's precisely the request I wanted to make; what could be better for an old clergyman than to stand alongside these Jewish Christians condemned to death.'

In the course of November Moltke went to Munich and while there he and Rösch agreed upon further co-operation. At the beginning of December Rösch was again in Berlin. Among those whom he met was Steltzer, with whom, assisted by Yorck and Guttenberg, he was to prepare for the Kreisau conference. On the same day Steltzer also met Preysing. Moltke was also present. These contacts were further developed in the New Year. Rösch took part in more discussions and Moltke frequently visited Preysing. Among other things he and the bishop discussed the importance, contents and language of pastoral letters and sermons: in the course of the discussion Moltke pleaded that they should have a much greater psychological relevance to the political situation. 'I got the impression that we made good progress in this discussion,' he wrote to his wife; 'Preysing was clearly pleased and so was I. He now wants another and I am anxious to see whether we can repeat the success of this conversation.'

In the May 1942 conference at Kreisau, Rösch (see p. 145) took part. Encouraged by its success, Moltke suggested that they should proceed further along these lines and draw up a complete basic programme. Representatives of the labour leaders were also to be involved. Moltke asked him to suggest a Jesuit sociologist who could help them by giving the Catholic viewpoint on the state and the economy. At Rösch's suggestion Delp (see p. 75) was brought into the work. As we have seen he had been responsible for sociology on the editorial board of *Stimmen der Zeit* for several years, and during the war he had become one of the most influential speakers at the annual conference of the 'Mission for Men'. When conferences were held to prepare guidelines for the spiritual and religious care of soldiers returning home, Delp, in a summary of the discussions, stressed the need to give men after the war an authentic and convincing idea to live by. Now people found themselves in an 'empty space' between two compelling spiritual ideals. 'First there is the idea of individualistic liberalism with its picture of men as unbound and autonomous, with its cheerfully materialistic picture of the world and its naïve, imperial optimism. Opposed to this is the revolutionary idea of collectivist Bolshivism with its entirely functional understanding of man, which regards the world as man's only home and which subordinates him to rational technique, represented as the fundamental order of life.' Very many people were occupying a false position between these two alternatives, either attempting to mix them or passively resigning themselves. In Delp's opinion this was not true for many church people, but a 'purely religious' solution was very often not a solution at all. 'People will not believe our Gospel of Salvation if we do not do all that we can to redeem contemporary life and society.'

We have quoted Delp at some length because he is here working towards a middle position, probably in accordance with the basic ideas expressed in his *Dritte Idee* (Third Idea). It was a paper of between 30 and 60 pages of which there were several copies, none of which have unfortunately turned up yet. In it Delp attempted to develop the idea of a new social order, which was to overthrow and dissolve both capitalism and communism. According to Delp, nineteenth-century attempts to find a solution to the problem adopted too narrow a base with the result that they played off the individual against the community or the community against the individual. In contrast to these attempts or as an extension of them 'it is essential that the individual's right to life, freedom and property should be associated with far-reaching socialization of the economic system. This should not, however, create a system of state capitalism. The social reconstruction must be executed by the participants themselves and protected by government legislation.' He demanded new regulations governing the relations between employers and employees formulated in the light of the 'Justitia Socialis'. Under these both groups would have a share in

the management and in the profits of the undertaking in proportions already beforehand. Although this programme had some
decidedly socialist features—the proposals included, for example,
a wealth tax—the individual still stood at the centre of it. It is
not unlikely that Delp's paper was stimulated by the Kreisau discussions. In fact if one compares the data that we have about it
with the protocol of the second conference in Kreisau and the
'Basic Principles of the Reconstruction' there are many parallels.
Although Delp gave the impression of a strong personality, his
own ideas were still in the process of development. His work in the
Kreisau Circle was enormously important to him from every point
of view, but the Circle too owed a great deal to him. He became
one of its leading thinkers. In touch with Bavarian and other
opposition groups as he was, he was also able to initiate numerous
important contacts for his friends. He was an upright man, averse
to any form of posing, imbued with an immense sense of justice
and full of love for the oppressed and persecuted, for whom he was
always available regardless of self. His parsonage in Munich was a
centre for the help to Jews, whom he helped to hide and if possible
send over the Swiss Frontier.

At Rösch's request another Jesuit, Hans von Galli, took part in
the Circle's discussions on agriculture (see p. 142). Father von
Galli was the administrator of the Jesuit College at Feldkirch and
had some little experience of agricultural work in this connection.
Rösch brought also Lothar König in contact with the Circle. He,
the right hand of Rösch, provided a courier service between the
bishops and used to appear at their homes, sometimes at their
request, sometimes unexpectedly, but always with fresh information. 'Don't ask me where I have come from, don't ask me where I
am going,' he used to say. When attempts were made to requisition
the Jesuit college at Pullach and the SS and the Gestapo indicated
that they wanted to use the college for their own purposes, König
was able, just in time, to offer the house to the Wehrmacht. König
often used a special communications link, because he had to be
reached by the military in the house for his own purpose, for
example for telephone calls with van Husen, at that time a captain
in the Armed Forces Operations Staff in Berlin. Among other
things van Husen was responsible for issuing the authorization reserved to the Chief of the OKW, for the requisitioning of buildings
and he was thus able to prevent army authorization for the requisitioning of church or charitable institutions. König was incredibly
well informed, versatile and resourceful. He once photographed,

with the help of a secretary, several pages containing the names of Polish priests in the official book of the dead at the concentration camp Dachau. The photocopies were intended to form part of a documentation on the atrocities in Dachau for the Pope. König was also one of those responsible for preventing the attack on the monasteries of Alsace-Lorraine. In June 1943 Rösch received the news that on the following Sunday night, on orders from Bormann's office, all monasteries in Alsace-Lorraine were to be dissolved. It was only a quick journey by Rösch and König, first to Strasburg, then to Freiburg; and an agreement with the church authorities there, who then made their knowledge of what was going to happen obvious in telegrams, that prevented the dissolutions being carried out. König took part in many of the discussions in 1942 and 1943 in Berlin and Munich and he also conveyed many reports and documents between Munich and Berlin.

Another contact man was the author Michael Brink, who had been outstanding among his contemporaries in the Catholic youth movement. During the war he was in touch with both the Scholl Circle and the Kreisau Circle. Shortly before the outbreak of war, he wrote the first part of his *Don Quichotte*, a work in the romantic style of the youth movement. 'I have seen him,' he wrote with the approaching disaster in view, 'riding over the stricken, burning land, over the bleeding and fallen; I have seen his face, pale and blood-stained; it was like a shreek, like a vanishing light: Don Quichotte de la Mancha.' In a later work, *Revolutio Humana*, dedicated to his friend Alfred Delp, he treated the autonomy of dominions and powers and their apostasy from the Trinity and the personal idea of man existentially.

The Kreisau members hoped to gain the support of several of the bishops. While Moltke undertook to talk with Bishop Preysing about this, Rösch was to inform the Archbishop of Munich, Cardinal Michael Faulhaber. Faulhaber, very much a prince of the church with strong monarchical sentiments, had opposed several of the measures taken by the régime. As early as 1933 his sermons showed a certain reserve; later he rejected the totalitarian claims of the state and spoke out strongly against euthanasia. As Provincial of the Jesuit Order, Rösch had to deal frequently with him and always found him helpful. At the end of June Rösch and König came to Moltke with the news of Faulhaber's agreement. When Moltke first approached Preysing he ran into difficulties, but with the help of Peters, Rösch and König they were overcome. 'Conrad [the cover name for Preysing] is particularly relieved by the fact that he would not have to take the leading role.' Preysing had suggested Archbishop Gröber of Freiburg as a more suitable man. However, a discussion between Rösch and Gröber led nowhere, as Gröber raised numerous doubts and could not be persuaded to join in. They therefore needed another bishop 'for the leading role', a representative of the Roman Catholic church to join in the task 'of establishing a common position on the aspects of the Christian world view that affect the structure of public life', as the protocol of the first Kreisau conference expressed it (see p. 329). No bishop was willing to take over this important role. Shortly afterwards through the mediation of Delp they established contact with Bishop Dietz von Fulda, while both Preysing and Faulhaber took a close interest in the working out of the 'Kreisau programme'. There is a note among the Moltke papers which indicates that copies of every document were set aside for Preysing via Peters— and Faulhaber via Rösch; these copies were to be destroyed afterwards. It is quite probable that Bishop Dietz saw the copies intended for Faulhaber.

The Circle's work took another step forward when links were established on the Protestant side with Bishop Wurm. Until then Moltke had always discussed Protestant church questions with Yorck and Gablentz. Yorck and Steltzer had represented the Protestant standpoint in the preparations for the first Kreisau conference; they were assisted by Poelchau who, at Moltke's request, studied the reparations question. In June 1942 'a man from Wurm' came to Moltke. The reference was probably to Oberkirchenrat Pressel who visited Berlin about once a month in these years. Since Niemöller's arrest Theophil Wurm, Bishop of the Evangelical–Lutheran Landeskirche in Württemberg had been widely recognized as leader of the church resistance in the German evangelical church. Wurm, who came from the Naumann–Stöcker national Protestant tradition, had revealed a considerable interest in social problems from very early on and had been involved, among other things, in the city mission. After World War I he was for several years a Burgerpartei deputy in the Landtag. He became Land Bishop in 1933. Unlike Niemöller and other members of the Council of Brethren, he tried for a long time to arrive at an arrangement with the new régime and to establish a peaceful relationship between church and state. His action against euthanasia, however, placed him right at the centre of the churches' opposition. In July 1940 he wrote a long and detailed letter to the Minister of the Interior in which he vigorously objected to such policies. Copies of the letter circulated widely and it led many to place great hope in him. Even the Councils of Brethren trusted him and he was therefore able to speak for the whole church. For both ecclesiastical and political reasons, he also established contact with the leading representatives of the political resistance movement who, for their own part, wanted links with him. His associations were mainly with the Goerdeler group and the Kreisau Circle. Gerstenmaier, a Württemberg theologian, who had been summoned by Bishop Heckel to work in the Church Foreign Office, was both personally and professionally in touch with him regularly and was one of his more important informants.*

Moltke was extremely surprised when the 'man from Wurm' sought him out; 'It looks promising,' he wrote to his wife. Wurm himself visited Berlin on 23 and 24 June 1942 and shortly before he called on Moltke on the afternoon of the 24th, the latter was writing: 'This afternoon Wurm is coming. He spent yesterday preparing and all sorts of different people rang me up to ask what was to be discussed with Wurm. I hope therefore that he is well prepared when he comes. I expect Gablentz any minute now. He will tell me about these preliminary discussions. I am very anxious to see how things will turn out.' Later on the same day, following the discussion with Wurm, he wrote: 'The talk with Wurm went well. I am so exhausted, however, by the strain of these two and a half hours that I cannot think any more. . . . The whole thing passed off so smoothly and without disagreement that I feel slightly uneasy about it. But I did take a great deal of trouble about it.'

The talks with Wurm marked an important advance. The Circle could now count on help from bishops of both churches; both confessions had been won over to the Kreisau programme. These contacts also helped to strengthen the bishops in their public statements. Bishops were in a position to say things that nobody else could. Moltke and his friends regarded critical public statements as very important, partly because they encouraged ordinary citizens, but also because, at least to a certain extent, they challenged the régime. The two objectives, of winning the bishops over to the Kreisau programme and of strengthening them in their critical pronouncements, went together. On 19 July Moltke visited Wurm. He also mentions that there were to be talks with 'W.G.F.' on August 10 and 13; he probably refers to Wurm, Gröber and Faulhaber.

From the end of July 1942 onwards Delp was very actively

* See Gerhard Schäfer, *Landesbischof D. Wurm und der nationalsozialistische Staat*, p. 350 (Stuttgart, 1962).

engaged in the work of the Kreisau Circle. On 31 July he and König came straight from the bishop of Fulde to Moltke and handed him 'on behalf of the three bishops, Faulhaber, Preysing and Dietz, an invitation to Friedrich and myself to take part in discussions'. In the next letter to his wife—this correspondence with her enables us to follow events with some clarity—Moltke mentions that on the evening of 23 August, Delp, Mierendorff and he would be going to Bamberg to 'the B.'—probably the three bishops named above. There was also to be a meeting with Wurm on 26 August. Thus the Kreisau Circle gained the approval of the church dignitaries for their programme and the collaboration that they wanted.

Immediately after his arrival Delp took part in several discussions in the Circle, including discussions with representatives of the labour leaders. 'It is a matter of welding the gentlemen from Munich and the men from Uncle [i.e. Mierendorff] together,' Moltke wrote after several meetings: 'I think that sufficient trust has emerged between these people to go further.' It was not, however, simple to bridge the spiritual and intellectual gap between the groups and progress was not always smooth. 'For an hour we could get no further and then suddenly about 6 o'clock everything went at a gallop.' The point that they were looking for as a test of mutual good faith had been found. For ten minutes, Delp and Maass talked the same language, even though the content of what they said differed. Then Delp proposed that they should both briefly formulate the thesis and exchange their respective definitions before they went any further.

Delp and the other Jesuits took as the starting point for their conversations the two social Encyclicals, particularly *Quadragesimo Anno* (see p. 14). In order to make sure that their statements were not simply personal opinions but were the official views of the Catholic church, they arranged for the socialists and other members of the Circle to have discussions with several bishops. Thus Bishop Dietz had talks with Moltke and Mierendorff. The surprise that greeted the Jesuits' ideas can be seen in Henk's comment: 'The drafts and exposés provided by the Jesuits, for example, were so excellent that they demonstrated beyond any measure of doubt the total change that had occurred in the attitude of the leaders of the Catholic church towards socialism. It was an enormously important, historic decision'.

Apart from Moltke, Peters in particular kept up the contact with Preysing and told him about the work, the participants and plans of the Circle and gave him the programme in writing. Van Husen, who had personal links with Bishop Galen—he was a close friend of the bishop's brother—and Bishop Wienken, the bishops' representative in dealings with the Berlin government offices, had discussions with both of them, at Moltke's and Yorck's request, about problems of interest to the Kreisau Circle. They talked not only about school questions, etc., but also about the right of resistance, the taking of the oath and personnel matters. Bishop Wienken provided van Husen with some points from moral theology about the right of resistance and drew attention to Mausbach who had been one of the few to discuss the problem clearly in the nineteenth century. Lukaschek was in touch with Cardinal Adolf Bertram, the bishop of Breslau and the Jesuits went from one bishop to another.

It was also at this time, in September 1942, that Gerstenmaier became more closely associated with the Circle. Moltke hoped that they would succeed in 'integrating him fully' and consulted him on theological and church history problems. Gerstenmaier and Pressel helped Moltke to maintain links with Wurm and also to establish contact with those of similar political views within Württemberg. Thus, for example, the farmers' leader Stoos, who was also a trusted member of the Württemberg Evangelical Synod, was told by Wurm on one occasion that Moltke wanted to meet him. Gerstenmaier took part in preparatory discussions for the second Kreisau conference, held in October 1942. After the conference itself, Gerstenmaier was very satisfied with the way in which it had gone and Moltke talked with him about future plans, commenting at the time: 'Anyhow it's really gratifying to see what a scoop we have made in Gerstenmaier,' and ten days later: 'Gerstenmaier's capacity for crystal-clear thought is an enormous help in every discussion.'

In the meantime Moltke had reminded Preysing of his promise to produce a good pastoral letter. After another conversation with him Moltke wrote: 'He is in splendid form and I have high hopes that his latest product will be a masterpiece. Anyhow I am full of optimism. Wouldn't it be refreshing.' On 13 December 1942 Preysing delivered the address on the Law that has since become famous. 'In its deepest sense the law,' he proclaimed, 'is a value that rests on eternal foundations. It is entirely independent of the arbitrariness of men. Law corresponds to the unchangeable principles, in accordance with which social life ought to be organized and which God has written in the hearts of men. . . . One of these principles is that the life of an innocent individual, whether an unborn child or an old and feeble man, is sacred and the innocent must not be punished with the guilty, or in place of the guilty.'

It is certain that discussions with Moltke lay behind some of the ideas expressed in this pastoral letter. It is possible indeed that the last sentence may be an admonitory reference to the practice of shooting hostages.

On 5 and 6 May 1943 Wurm was once again in Berlin. He took part in an important session of the so-called Church Leaders' Conference. In it both he and Hans Meiser, the Protestant Bishop of Bavaria, strongly urged that a letter ought to be sent to Hitler drawing urgent attention once again to the crimes against the Jews and the renewed intensification of the anti-semitic pogrom. Wurm was asked, and agreed, to compose the letter and send it; it was to be signed by him alone, although it was sent in the name of the opposition church leaders. In the evening Moltke had a lengthy discussion with Wurm, in the presence of Gerstenmaier and Pressel, and subsequently commented: 'Wurm again made a good and wise impression. One cannot avoid the feeling, however, that he has no sufficiently good assistants and that as a result not enough care is taken. That is very stupid. We talked about our and his most recent plans and arrived at some satisfactory conclusions.'

In the course of 1943 Moltke visited Munich several times and had thorough discussions with Rösch, Delp and König. He also met Faulhaber. One of Moltke's letters shows that he was aware of the contents of the Pope's Christmas addresses; he found the 1942 address on the 'Basic Elements of Communal Life' very fine. While he was in Munich he and other members of the Circle also met members of the Bavarian resistance, with whom they had been put in touch by Delp. Delp also forged links with the leaders of the Catholic workers' movement in Cologne during 1943. The contacts with Austria were extended to include Archbishop Rohracher of Salzburg who often visited Munich.

Another high point of this year was the third Kreisau conference, which was held in May and to which van Husen, with his proposals on law (see p. 148), made an important contribution. Preysing added several ideas when these documents were being re-drafted. The conference was followed by months of intense activity in which the Catholic members and the bishops shared. It was during this period that the 'Basic Principles of the Reconstruction', 'the First Instructions to the Provincial Commissioners' and 'The Punishment of Offenders' appeared (see pp. 347–57).

The second objective of the Kreisau Circle in their contacts with the bishops, namely the strengthening of the latter's public pronouncements, was also pursued further. On 7 August 1943 Moltke was again with Preysing. 'Conrad has come back from holiday in good trim. . . . He is much concerned about the meeting with his colleagues which begins in the week after next, because he is afraid that they will take the wrong turn. I put our most recent requests to him and we are going to meet again on 12th to discuss them. It is not unimportant to see what the reaction will be.' Evidently Preysing and Moltke prepared a specific proposal for the Fulda bishops' conference. The result can be seen in another of Moltke's letters. 'Conrad has come back from Fulda cheerful and full of mischief. The worst has been avoided and what we wanted is to come at the end of September, but, said Conrad: "It has been chemically cleaner; all the stains have gone but so has the colour too. Sad, isn't it, but there is nothing new about this." ' The tone of the letter shows that Preysing had not been able to achieve all that he wanted to at the conference and that his colleagues had cut his proposal sharply. The German bishops' pastoral letter following the conference included a statement against the killing of hostages and prisoners of war. Moltke's influence on Preysing's proposal is evident in this section alone. The 'chemical cleaning' was probably not confined to it, however; Moltke and Preysing would have made proposals relating to other problems also. In the following months of 1943 Moltke continued his discussions with Preysing and tried to remain in contact with Munich. The latter became increasingly difficult as a result of the heavy bombardments. Shortly before his arrest in January 1944 he sought out Bishop Wurm in Stuttgart once again. He also had a thorough discussion with Pressel about what should happen in the event of his arrest, which he considered to be imminent.

The Kreisau Circle was in contact not only with the churches within Germany but also with the Christian community in the world outside. The Protestant members of the Circle had links with the ecumenical movement in Geneva and through this with other circles as well; the Catholics were in touch with the Vatican. Several of the Protestant members had been active in ecumenical work. Schönfeld was the main link with Geneva. After Gerstenmaier became involved in the Circle's work, he too played an important role in this respect. In addition, Adam von Trott had a long-standing personal friendship with Visser 't Hooft, General Secretary of the World Council of Churches—then in process of formation. The latter made it possible for the Kreisau Circle to establish contact with the church resistance in Holland (see p. 206) and he also personally conveyed one of the Circle's memoranda for the English government to London (see p. 182) and transmitted other documents.

The Vatican was kept informed of the Kreisau work by the bishops; Josef Müller who had had dealings with the Vatican over many years (see p. 113), was another important link. In spring 1943 Gerstenmaier visited Rome and met the Pope's secretary, Father Leiber, in the Evangelical–Lutheran parsonage. The pastor Dahlgrün, made the arrangements for the meeting and it took place in his study. The two men discussed relations between the confessions in Germany and their co-operation in the political sphere. On his return Gerstenmaier reported the results to Moltke, who noted down: 'Many details, nothing world-shaking. A completely negative attitude of the Vatican to Russia. That interested me greatly as I had expected the opposite.'*

'A great song of praise besides for Rösch—he's the strongest of the Catholics in Germany.'

* Probably Moltke expected that the Vatican, on the basis of reports about a religious revival in Soviet Russia, should change it, up until now, negative attitude against this country.

CHAPTER 10

The Larger Gatherings and Other Organizational Matters

The larger gatherings, at which the whole of the Inner Circle was either present or represented, marked an important stage in the development of the Kreisau work. It was here that the results of the preparatory consultations were discussed and were given a preliminary formulation. The small gatherings took place not only in Berlin but also in Klein-Oels and Kauern, both of which belonged to the Yorck family, in Gross-Behnitz, the Borsigs' estate, and at Kreisau itself. Precise facts such as the date, the participants, or subject of discussion are known about only a few of these smaller gatherings. The first smaller gathering, as already has been described, took place in August 1940 at Kreisau and was attended by Moltke, Yorck, Einsiedel and Waetjen. The subject of the discussion was Education. In the summer of 1941, Yorck, Moltke and their wives, Schmölders, the Kreisau specialist on political economy, and Ernst von Borsig discussed economic problems at Klein-Oels. At another smaller gathering to discuss political economy at Gross-Behnitz, between 18 and 20 July 1942, Moltke and Yorck were joined by Einsiedel, Trotha, Schmölders and Borsig.

Several details are known about some of the meetings of the study group devoted to agricultural problems and we can therefore attempt a partial reconstruction. Christiansen-Weniger, a lecturer in agriculture and a native of Schleswig-Holstein, was asked by Moltke to do some work on agricultural and food supply problems. A possible venue for meetings appeared when Yorck drew Ernst von Borsig, whose estate at Gross-Behnitz was near Berlin, into the discussions during 1941. Yorck, who already knew Borsig from their school days at Rossleben, had first visited Behnitz with his wife in 1941. Borsig agreed immediately to a proposal to hold agricultural and economic discussions at Gross-Behnitz, and to take part in conversations on other themes elsewhere. Gross-Behnitz, being only 44 kilometres on the railway from Berlin, was thus much more convenient as a meeting place for the Kreisau

Circle than the more distant estates of Yorck and Moltke in Silesia. It consisted of six thousand acres of woodland and six thousand of arable land, and had been purchased by the grandfather of Ernst von Borsig. The latter, a man of liberal outlook and a specialist in forestry, was somewhat younger than Yorck. 'The wood is very beautiful and immensely varied,' wrote Moltke after one visit. 'There are almost no two stretches alike. There is hardly any clear felling. Instead the worst trees are struck out and when the density allows new ones are sown and planted underneath. In this way the wood is kept constantly young. . . . I have learnt a very great deal there.'

Shortly after this, Yorck and Moltke discussed the intended week-end on agricultural problems. 'We want to have an agricultural weekend at Borsig's estate, and it ought to be planned. Yorck intends, or at least ought, first to prepare the agenda, while Borsig and somebody else prepare papers. When this has been done then we ought to invite about ten people who represent different regions, different types of enterprise and differing views on agricultural policy.' The first discussion of agricultural problems took place between 13 and 16 March 1942. The participants were Christiansen-Weniger, von Zitzewitz-Muttrin, Margareta von zur Mühlen, Peter Hans von Galli SJ, with Yorck, Moltke, Ernst von Borsig and their wives; there were perhaps one or two others, as only the guests who slept at Gross-Behnitz wrote their names in the guest-book. Friedrich von Zitzewitz-Muttrin was a Pomerian landowner and an acquaintance of Borsig. He was asked by Beck, at about the same time, to make a thorough investigation of the agricultural situation and to put forward proposals for practical measures in the first years. It is not certain whether this was the reason for inviting him. Margareta von zur Mühlen was a Baltic German whose father, von Sokolowski, had been a distinguished authority on law and political science. After her husband's death (he was the social democratic Landrat Ohle and a friend of Moltke) she had married a Herr von zur Mühlen, who owned an estate near her father's, and who had earlier been a landowner in Russia and a captain in the Imperial Russian Cavalry. When the Baltic states entered the Russian sphere of influence and the German inhabitants were forced out, he acquired an estate in the so-called Warthegau. When Moltke asked Rösch to provide somebody for discussions on post-war agriculture, who was familiar with agricultural problems in Southern Germany and Austria, Rösch hit upon the idea of sending Father von Galli to Berlin as an 'agricultural expert'. Rösch went to Feldkirch which belonged to his Province, handed von Galli a sleeping-car ticket to Berlin and simply told him to present himself punctually at 11 o'clock at a certain address—Moltke's Berlin home. He was explicitly forbidden to show himself to the Berlin Jesuits. On his arrival, he was directed by von Moltke to Gross-Behnitz. At the meeting, agricultural problems were thoroughly discussed, starting out from certain general considerations. The central themes were: 'How can the food supply be safeguarded after the military collapse?' and 'What kind of agricultural policy is needed to enable agriculture to play a healthy and constructive part in the reorientation of the German people?'

A second meeting took place about 25 to 27 July 1942. In addition to those who had taken part in the first meeting, Professor Constantin von Dietze, the former State Secretary Hans Krüger, August von Joest and probably Einsiedel were also present. Professor von Dietze was a member of the Freiburg Circle and knew Yorck from his work at the Prices Commission. Krüger had been joint author with Baade of the social democrats' Kiel Agricultural Programme of 1927. August von Joest was a relative of Moltke and was invited to talk about agricultural problems in the Rhineland. Each participant gave a report on the structure and problems of agriculture in his locality. All the reports were followed by thorough discussion and a large measure of understanding was reached. Short reports were made on the conversations and their results. The final protocol, however, was not completed until after the return to Berlin.

A third meeting took place in February 1943. Only Yorck, Moltke, Christiansen-Weniger and Borsig were present. The agricultural programme of the Kreisau Circle may have been formulated on the basis of the previous discussions. At the Klein-Oels discussion of agricultural problems in 1943, mentioned by Steltzer, at which Schmölders was also present, the agricultural programme was fitted into the general economic programme. It was impossible to draft any concrete plans. Only the basic principles of the subsequent reconstruction could be formulated. They were well aware that there would have to be very great changes in this sphere and they dissociated themselves very sharply from national socialist theories. The longer the war went on, the more important the food supply problem became. The importance that Yorck and Moltke attached to this part of the Circle's work can be seen in the following comment by Moltke himself: 'Yesterday afternoon we came along very nicely, I think, and Christiansen-Weniger in particular is now well aware of what he has to do. There is so much to this whole problem of agricultural policy and Peters and I are simply disqualified from talking about it because we are so obviously interested parties.'

Following this survey of one of the small groups, one must now consider the larger gatherings of the Circle. Seen from the centre, there was a plan, a programme linking these gatherings. Individual participants were deliberately chosen. It is therefore quite legitimate to talk of a Circle—or still better a Super-Circle (*Überkreis*) if one remembers the different backgrounds of the members and the underlying intention of linking separate groups by this means. The larger gatherings at Kreisau helped to establish the fundamental spiritual unity of the Circle and, thereby, to create a basis for the future work of the individual participants. Moltke himself sometimes referred to a 'Kreisau Programme' in his letters. In addition to their spiritual and intellectual unity the members were bound to one another by strong ties of personal friendship. Under the totalitarian régime each conversation, each unguarded comment could make the difference between life and death. The individual had to penetrate the feelings of those with whom he was talking in order to make quite sure where he stood with them. In the Circle, the personal affections that bound the individual members together were pitted against the gigantic machinery of the régime. Their collaboration went far beyond earlier types of idealistic friendship and was founded on a very profound and very personal awareness of their solidarity with one another. In spite of the many differences that distinguished them from each other they could still, tacitly, find identity with each other on the important questions: aristocratic landowners, priests of both confessions, officers, classically educated members of the middle class, trades unionists and socialists. Unable to see their way ahead, they found their mutual trust an unerring compass. In the Circle, people who were, on their own, entirely self-reliant but who, together, were entirely in accord, penetrated the domain of an inhumane régime in an utterly personal way. The work of these men would have been impossible, however, had it not been for the tireless assistance that they received from their wives, their relatives and their friends.

Preparations for the first meeting at Kreisau in May 1942 began as early as the end of 1941. In December, Moltke noted: 'Steltzer and Rösch have to prepare the meeting at Kreisau with the help of Yorck and Guttenberg.' Some of the inspiration for the idea came socially, with a meeting with the poet Rudolf Schneider at the home of Yorck's and Moltke's friend Luckner, shortly before. Schneider, who was living in Freiburg at the time, was on a visit to Berlin and joined the discussion at Luckner's request. Their discussion ranged over the opportunities for resistance and problems relating to the future structure of the state. In addition to Schneider and Luckner, Moltke, Yorck and Guttenberg were also present. 'They, like Luckner, were convinced,' wrote Schneider many years later, 'that as aristocrats they had to grapple with the guilt that lay upon the nation that their ancestors had once led. Their responsibility extended far beyond the sins of the fathers to the sins of the whole nation. Those who had once led in action ought now to lead through sacrifice.'

Preparatory discussions took place from the end of December 1941 onwards. To begin with they had no intention of arranging three meetings. The first which was to be only a start, an experiment, took place at Kreisau over Whitsun 1942 between 22 and 25 May. Invitations were given orally, Poelchau for instance receiving his invitation from Gablentz. The guests assembled on the day before, a Thursday, and were housed partly in the Schloss, partly in the Berghaus. The participants were: Yorck and Moltke and their wives, Peters, Poelchau, Rösch, Steltzer and for part of the time Lukaschek and Reichwein. The number of people present at Kreisau was not so very remarkable, as it was quite common, especially at holiday periods, for the owner of a large estate to have numerous guests. They passed as Moltke's colleagues from Berlin, and this seemed sufficient cover for their meeting. In order to feed them all, Moltke's wife had had to save up her ration book tokens over a long period. Guttenberg, who had helped in the preparations, could not be present, partly because the conference coincided with his fortieth birthday and partly because he was not in the best of health and needed a few days of rest.

The discussions themselves took place in the Berghaus. The meetings began with papers, which were followed by discussion and finally by the preparation of a report. Part of the report on the religious and cultural section was composed by Rösch and Steltzer. The topics covered were: the constitution, church–state relations, educational questions and university reform. Steltzer discussed church–state relations from a Protestant standpoint, while Rösch spoke about problems that concerned the Catholic church and Peters read a paper on the concordat. They had a written contribution from Reichwein on school affairs and Moltke read a paper

on the reform of higher education. At the end of the meeting Rösch
gave an account of his encounters with the Gestapo and advised
his colleagues on what they should do if they were ever interrogated. The success of the first conference made them decide to
carry on along the same lines. The subsequent conferences were
prepared in a number of discussions. They hoped to arrange two
gatherings for the autumn: the first, at the end of September, was
to deal with the state and the other, at the end of October, with the
structure of the economic system. An important preliminary discussion took place in August 1942, when the labour leaders,
represented by Leuschner, Maass and Mierendorff and the Jesuit
priests, Rösch, Delp and König arrived at an agreement about the
continuation of the work. This was particularly important since
each group had discussed these problems with other representatives of their Circles, that is with other labour leaders and bishops,
shortly before. Moltke wrote, with a certain amount of gratification: 'What I aimed at at Whitsun has been achieved, after a good
deal of toing and froing.'

In the course of September Moltke and Yorck decided that it
would be better if the meetings were amalgamated and held at the
end of October. 'I am not happy with the preparations; it's not
good enough or ready enough and I will allow myself no rest. In
addition, the whole thing is too dangerous. . . . I intend to suggest
to Peters that we drop the September meeting and instead defer
the discussion of that topic until October when, preferably, we
should discuss both together. That must be possible. Security considerations argue very strongly in favour of an amalgamation of
the two.' Yorck agreed and so they had time for more thorough
preparation.

The second Kreisau conference took place between 16 and 18
October 1942. The theme was the 'structure of the state and the
economy'. The participants were: Steltzer, Gerstenmaier, Delp,
Reichwein, Einsiedel, Maass, Yorck, Moltke, and the Countesses
Yorck and von Moltke. Steltzer and Moltke spoke about the constitutional problem and Einsiedel covered economic problems. The
programme was rather overburdened. The general character of
the constitution, the need for decentralization and the strengthening of self-government were all discussed. Only the preamble to
the economic system was thoroughly considered, however (p. 335).
They talked late into the night about how far the social structure
could be brought into line with federal ideas, Delp and Gerstenmaier being especially prominent in this discussion. It was clear to

all of them that the federal structure would allow no centralized organizations. When Delp quoted the example of the trades unions, Moltke observed that the greatest hope of success lay in factory-based unions. For Maass, who had come as Leuschner's representative to Kreisau, this was somewhat embarrassing. He had come to Kreisau with some misgivings and he often asked himself while he was there: Do they really mean what they say?

Immediately after this second conference, while its conclusions were still being discussed and enlarged, preparations began for a third meeting devoted to 'Foreign Policy' or, as Moltke himself put it, 'The problem of the transition to a European level'. In April Moltke reported that he had had a detailed discussion of foreign policy problems with Trott and Gerstenmaier, that differences between them no longer existed and that they had reached a large measure of agreement, adding, 'We have thus made a great step forward and Whitsun now seems quite probable'.

The third Kreisau conference was held over Whitsun 1943, 12–14 June. Foreign policy, economic structure and the punishment of war criminals were the subjects of discussion. Those who took part were: Trott, Gerstenmaier, van Husen, Reichwein, Einsiedel, Maass, Delp, Yorck, Moltke and the two countesses. Trott gave a paper on foreign policy. At this late stage the only real problems in foreign policy were: how would the Allies react to a *coup d'état*? would they insist on unconditional surrender? would they make any concessions to the new government? would the Russians eventually go further than the Western allies? The West had given the impression that it would make no concessions. The position in the East, however, was not so clear. In addition, Nazi propaganda against the Russians had had quite the opposite effect to that intended upon several of the Kreisau members, in that they were inclined to believe that the Russians were 'more reasonable' than the Nazis claimed. There was not, however, any real tension over these questions, as they were of secondary importance at that particular juncture. It was for this reason that they confined themselves to formulating basic principles. On Whit Monday Trott wrote: 'I'm very busy, but I'm only partly satisfied with myself: I'm very much at the receiving end throughout—something for which Freya Moltke but also he deserve the greatest credit. One can learn a great deal from them. . . .' The also discussed the structure of the economic system and especially economic self-government. The idea of a 'works union' was thoroughly considered.

The third topic for discussion was the treatment of the leading war criminals. Van Husen had prepared a file on the subject. Under the national socialist régime justice also had become an instrument of the totalitarian state. There could be no question of the independence of the judges; law was what suited the régime and illegality what opposed it, and to a large extent justice simply served as a legal anchorage for the Terror. Many judges and public prosecutors were increasingly inclined to give in to the tendency towards inhumanity and cruelty. Basic principles, essential if an independent legal system was to flourish, were treated with contempt. As many opponents and victims of oppression as possible were to be killed. *Ausmerzung* (eradication) and *Ausrottung* (extermination) were words that were frequently employed. A particularly ominous role was played by the so-called 'Special Courts'. The death sentence was passed with increasing flippancy.

It was, therefore, of the highest importance that Law should be restored and that free and independent judges be appointed after the military collapse. 'The Law which has been trampled upon, must be restored and given authority over all orders of human existence,' declared the protocol of the third Kreisau conference. 'Protected by a scrupulous, independent and fearless judge, it is the keystone of any future peace settlement.'

In addition to the restoration of Law, it was essential that criminals should be punished. The matter was thoroughly discussed at Kreisau. Van Husen emphasized the need for a retrospective German decree. He maintained that, in the case of a crime committed under orders, the orders should not be allowed to provide a ground for the suspension of punishment. He also advocated punishment by a general international court—the international court at The Hague was mentioned. Specific warnings were given against punishment by the courts of the victorious powers. The relevant courts should be composed of six judges: three from the victorious powers, two from the neutral states and one from the defeated countries. The Kreisau proposal ended with the following words: 'If this attempt to arrive at a just solution of what is a serious hindrance to peace for all concerned succeeds, a further step will have been taken towards establishing the rule of law between nations and evil will have brought forth good. If, however, a solution is adopted on purely political grounds, outside a court that can be recognized as just, then evil will be answered by evil and force will once again stand threateningly at the beginning of the path into the future' (see pp. 342–43).

After all aspects of the reconstruction had been discussed at the three Kreisau conferences, a summary of their conclusions was prepared in the course of the summer of 1943 under the title of 'Basic Principles of Reconstruction'. In it certain things were altered, and the general observations made at the third conference were inserted at the beginning. As usual, the whole of the Inner Circle was involved in the work of revision. 'There were indeed important differences, but it was pleasant to see how strong the common ties were, and how they made these differences tolerable,' Moltke wrote. With this the programme outlining the most important features of post-war reconstruction was ready, and it had the support of the two groups who, according to the Kreisau Circle, would have to play an important role in the reconstruction, namely the Workers and the Churches.

In addition to the 'Basic Principles', a new version of the 'Punishment of Criminals' was prepared, Bishop Preysing, among others, helping with this. An important distinction between the first and the second version was that in the later one the proposed retrospective decree was rejected and instead the basic principle of *nulla poena sine lege* was elaborated. Specific mention was made of the necessity for compensation to those 'who have been injured and discriminated against through coercive actions against life and limb, property, honour and civil rights (concentration camps, unjust sentences, loss of civil rights, confiscations and dismissal of public servants)'.

The Kreisau Circle tried in the first place to establish fundamental principles and a government programme that the churches and labour leaders could support. They were also concerned to discover other ways in which they could prepare for the moment when the régime collapsed. There was a danger that individual parts of the country would be occupied and isolated. It was vital that the cohesion of the nation should be preserved and the work of reconstruction begin everywhere simultaneously. This meant that it was essential that there should be persons who were ready to take over responsibility for different parts of the country at such a time and until a new government had been formed. These men the Kreisau Circle described as 'Provincial Commissioners'.

The First Instructions to Provincial Commissioners of August 1943 (see p. 354) contained the following words: '. . . we commission you with the heavy responsibility of assuming the office of Provincial Commissioner for the region assigned to you, the territorial limits of which are marked on the accompanying map, and of taking possession of the instruments of power necessary to exercise your authority. The military authorities in the area are under instructions to obey your orders.' The Provincial Commissioner was to be responsible to the Reich and was intended, in conjunction with representatives of the churches and labour, to order arrests and the release of those in prison, to lift discriminatory measures immediately, to work for demobilization and the restoration and reform of the economic system and to ensure that a real reconstruction was attempted.

From the end of 1942, at the latest, the members of the Kreisau Circle occupied themselves with the selection of these Provincial Commissioners, or, as Moltke put it in his letters, with the personnel plan. This was the object behind some of Moltke's journeys during 1943, during which he discussed suitable names with some of those he met. This task had probably been completed by the end of the year, and Provincial Commissioners stood at the ready all over Germany and Austria, Austria being considered as one of the German states. It is difficult to establish today precisely who was consulted and selected by the Kreisau Circle. Some of the names became known through the orders given on 20 July 1944 (see p. 274).

The person envisaged as Provincial Commissioner in Pomerania was Hans Schlange-Schöningen who had previously been Reich Commissioner for the Osthilfe under Brüning. One of Schlange's sons, whom Moltke had met in England during the 'thirties and who had visited Kreisau with Henry Brooke, the future British Home Secretary, at the end of August 1938, had introduced Moltke to his father. Since then Moltke had paid several visits to Schlange. His estate of Schöningen was about two hours by rail away from Berlin, a few kilometres south of Stettin. The need for care made Moltke arrive in the evening and return while it was still dark.

Lukascheck, a member of the Kreisau Circle and Oberpräsident of Upper Silesia until 1933, was intended as Provincial Commissioner of Silesia. When a *coup d'état* was planned in August 1943 (see p. 172), Moltke sent Lukaschek a document in which he was appointed Reich Commissioner for the Eastern Frontier and entrusted with the special responsibility of protecting the German frontier.

Delp established links between the Kreisau Circle and the Bavarian resistance movement led by the former Ambassador Franz Sperr. At a meeting in Munich, Prince Joseph Ernst Fugger was asked to take over the office of Provincial Commissioner.

Although Fugger did not refuse, he expressed the opinion that there were others who were more suitable.

Van Husen established contact with a suitable man in Westphalia. After an unsuccessful attempt to enlist Freiherr von Oer, the latter's cousin, Freiherr von Twickel, declared himself ready to take over the responsibility. He was kept informed about plans for a *coup d'état* through an intermediary from van Husen. He was also told that a map showing the proposed new divisions in Germany was being prepared.

In addition to Steltzer, who was to be Provincial Commissioner of Schleswig-Holstein, there were certainly others who were intended to take over other parts of the country. The difficulty today is that we cannot determine from the kind of contacts made what their object was. Names are only very occasionally mentioned in Moltke's letters.

The Circle was also interested in discovering people to occupy leading posts in the transitional administration. This does not mean that the Kreisau Circle itself formed cabinets and hawked lists around. It was, however, of vital importance to them that there should really be a reconstruction, and it was therefore essential that the right men should get the responsible posts. Their great hope was that Leber would become Chancellor in the second phase. Members of the Kreisau Circle were probably also asked to recommend some of their own men for specific posts in agreement with other groups. For instance they thought of Reichwein for the Ministry of Culture. He had already prepared for the post and had sought out colleagues, asking Sänger, for example, formerly Secretary of the Prussian Association of Teachers, to find a suitable person in every government district who could become personnel adviser in the district government when matters had advanced that far. By these means, an administrative organization for schools was prepared. At Reichwein's request, Bohnenkamp made himself familiar with the problems involved in the training of teachers. Another Kreisau candidate was the Augsburg lawyer Reisert who had come into contact with the Circle through its Bavarian links. He was to be proposed for the Ministry of Justice, and in connection with this Moltke planned a meeting between Reisert and Falkenhausen, the Military Commander in Belgium, with whom Moltke was closely associated. Occasionally, the possibility of making Falkenhausen Chancellor of a transitional administration instead of Goerdeler was discussed.[*]

[*] See Gerhard Ritter, *Carl Goerdeler*, p. 542 (Stuttgart, 1956); also mentioned by Hermann Kaiser in his diary (12.3.1943).

Another Kreisau candidate was probably Christiansen-Weniger, the lecturer in agriculture who took part in the Kreisau agricultural conferences. Yorck and Moltke regarded agricultural questions as of special importance and it was natural that they should recommend one of their own people to take over the relevant post. When Christiansen-Weniger was in Berlin on one occasion, probably in August or September 1943, he visited Moltke who told him that he should make himself available to take over responsibility for food supply and agriculture. When Christiansen asked Moltke what post he himself intended to take, he replied that he did not consider himself suited to this kind of job and that he only wished to take part in constructing the basic committee (*Gremium*) and to act as an intermediary. When Christiansen agreed to the proposal regarding himself, Moltke told him that a meeting was planned for all those who had been recommended. This would give them an opportunity to get to know each other and it would help them to make a final decision about collaboration if they were certain that the essential human preconditions for co-operation were fulfilled. The meeting should have taken place soon afterwards in Berlin in the presence of Moltke. According to Christiansen, Haubach should have taken the Chair, Mierendorff, needless to say, was busy with propaganda preparations. It was he who told Harro Siegel that he wanted a symbol that would be acceptable to Silesian counts, bishops of both churches, trades unionists and workers, that could be easily chalked up on house walls and that

would give a positive twist to the evil and perverted elements in the Nazi swastika. Siegel thereupon proposed the socialist ring linked with the cross, as a token of the unity of all constructive forces. Later Mierendorff told Siegel that everybody involved had approved of this symbol.* It was also mentioned in a call to 'Socialist Action' composed by Mierendorff and others. This latter proclamation was kept among the basic Kreisau documents by Moltke (see p. 378). It contained, in slogan form, the most important points in the Kreisau programme. The following sentences are taken from it: 'Socialist Action is a non-partisan national movement dedicated to the deliverance of

* This symbol is also reproduced on the dust jacket. Harro Siegel also had the Celtic Cross of Ireland in mind. *Ed.*

Germany. It is fighting for the liberation of the German people from the Hitler dictatorship, for the restoration of the nation's honour, trampled under foot by Nazi crimes, and for the freedom of the nation within a socialist order. The Action Committee is composed of representatives of the Christian churches, the socialist movement, the communist movement and the liberal forces and its composition is an expression of its determination and its unity.'

The members of the Kreisau Circle also arranged a kind of warning system. Mierendorff and Reichwein, for example, asked Siegel to note two names—as far as he remembers one was an official in the Bendlerstrasse and the other an official in either the Foreign or Interior Ministry—so that he could pass on instructions from Mierendorff or Reichwein when he heard the password. When Siegel left Berlin at the end of 1943, he was released from this commission.

CHAPTER 11

Links with Other Groups in the Civilian Resistance

It was Father Delp who brought the Kreisau Circle into contact with opposition in Bavaria. Late in the autumn of 1942 he told the Augsburg lawyer, Franz Reisert, about his membership of the Circle, and in the course of several meetings their acquaintance developed into a close friendship. Delp made it clear that he was very impressed by his meetings with Moltke, Yorck and others and especially by the co-operation with socialist trades union leaders, directed towards a social reconstruction of Germany after the fall of the Hitler régime. At the time, he assumed that there would be a revolt of the generals in December 1942, under the leadership of Field-Marshal Kluge, upon which the Kreisau Circle would seize power, and take over political leadership of Germany after the collapse of the régime.

He said nothing further about the more precise plans that were already in existence. He simply indicated that, if the *coup d'état* was successful, Moltke proposed to re-organize the German Reich in such a way that the Länder would reflect ethnic divisions. Thus there would be Lander of Saxony, Rhineland, Silesia, Frankonia, Bavaria, etc. A Provincial Commissioner, armed with extensive powers, would take over the government of each Land. If, in the event of the anticipated collapse of the régime, certain parts of the Reich were occupied by the allies, there would have to be 'Provincial Commissioners' in the occupied areas with far-reaching powers, to conduct the necessary negotiations with the occupying forces in the interests of the population.

Delp asked Reisert whether he would be ready to take over the office of Provincial Commissioner in southern Bavaria. Northern Bavaria was to be treated as a separate Land with its own Provincial Commissioner. Reisert refused and proposed instead that the office should be offered to the former Bavarian envoy to the Reich Government, Franz Sperr, and if he refused, to Prince Joseph-Ernst Fugger von Glött from Kirchheim. The first choice was

Sperr, since Reisert knew him through the so-called Sperr Circle—
a resistance group that had formed under Sperr's leadership in
Bavaria, and of which Reisert himself was a member. Reisert,
whose father had also been a lawyer in Augsburg, had been an
opponent of Hitler since 1923. The Bavarians, who contributed to
the resistance movement by forming little cells of opposition, knew
full well what had given rise to national socialism: their acquaintance with it was of long standing. Sperr himself had been a strong
opponent of the régime from the very beginning, since he could
see what was coming. Convinced that collapse was inevitable and
that chaos threatened, he prepared a kind of rescue operation
which would save Bavaria from a violent civil war and the complete destruction of public order. He made sure that reliable men
were available to take over the administration of the state. As a
former officer it was not difficult for him to establish contact with
dependable commanders of troop units and police detachments.
He also formed an accurate knowledge of the location and strength
of the reserve group units and he was very well informed about
where the SS garrisons and SS units were. He built up a small team
of collaborators, which included men who had been ministers in
the Weimar Republic. On economic matters, for example, he was
advised by the former Economic Minister Hamm. He was also in
close contact with the former Reich War Minister Gessler and
with General Halder.

Reisert was convinced that Sperr, who had such good contacts
and who had already prepared in Bavaria for what had to be done
in the event of a collapse, ought to be associated with the members
of the Kreisau Circle so that both groups, pursuing the same objectives, could enter into a meaningful co-operation. The same consideration persuaded him that Sperr was the best person to fill the
office of Provincial Commissioner, envisaged by Moltke. Moltke
was told about Reisert's proposal in the course of a visit to Munich
in January 1943, and shortly afterwards Delp arranged a meeting
between the two men in Munich. The result of this meeting was
that in the spring of 1943 plans were made for the first thorough
discussion between leading members of the Kreisau Circle and the
Sperr Circle in Munich. The Jesuit priests were to act as mediators.

The meeting took place at Delp's parsonage of St. Georg in
Munich–Bogenhausen, where Delp was Pastoral Director. Present
were Steltzer and Mierendorff—Moltke was prevented from
attending at the last moment—Fugger, Reisert and the Jesuit
priests Rösch, Delp and König. At the very beginning Reisert

proposed that Sperr should also be invited to the discussion. All those present agreed to the proposal. Sperr was therefore asked to attend the conference and did so. The first meeting revealed a large measure of agreement between the two groups in their assessment of the situation and of the problems that it posed to the resistance movement. Steltzer gave an account of the military situation which he considered utterly hopeless. Mierendorff demanded both in this and in subsequent discussions that the Christian character of the future Reich should be acknowledged and that the churches' interests should be safeguarded along the lines indicated in the Concordat. These, he maintained, should be basic preconditions of the reconstruction. Reisert, on the other hand, spoke out against looking upon the resistance movement as a purely Christian pheno-menon, since there were very many non-Christians who, with a European and humanist attitude, agreed with the basic ideas of the resistance movement but who did not want to be tied to any kind of religion or confession. These ideas undoubtedly found an echo among members of the Kreisau Circle, and even Moltke and Yorck were to begin with somewhat critical towards the churches. Sperr refused to take the office of Provincial Commissioner and urged Fugger to accept it. The latter was convinced that there were others who were more suitable but was not, however, averse to the proposal.

There were further meetings in Bogenhausen and one in the Michaelskirche. Moltke was present at this latter, where some differences emerged between him and Sperr. Whereas Moltke had a pronounced leaning towards a liberal form of socialism, Sperr, for all his understanding of social problems, adopted a more liberal and capitalist viewpoint. Another difference arose out of the Kreisau demand that Bavaria should be divided into two parts. Sperr, Fugger and Reisert were fiercely opposed to this suggestion, basing their argument on the fact that Bavaria already had a well-tried administrative system which it would be dangerous to split in such hazardous times. The differences could not be ironed out and no definite decisions were reached. Relations were further complicated by the fact that some generals approached Sperr, through Moltke, with the request that if Bavaria should start an armed revolt, they would use this as the starting point for an attack of their own against the régime. Sperr and Reisert rejected this proposal decisively, since a revolt of this sort would be tanta-mount to the total annihilation of Bavaria.

Following this, Moltke remained in personal contact with

Reisert. At Delp's request the latter prepared proposals for the punishment of criminals, which were probably used in the final drafting of the Kreisau document on this subject. In September Moltke and Reisert discussed the general situation once again in Augsburg and considered what opportunities there were for successful resistance. Moltke was well aware of the danger that his actions brought upon both himself and his friends. When Reisert asked him whether he realized that discussions of this sort were equivalent to treason and what this meant, he replied that the guillotine took eleven seconds and that it therefore wasn't so bad. (Later in Tegel prison, when he knew he was to be hanged, Moltke met Reisert and referred to this conversation.) As already noted it was intended to recommend Reisert for the post of Minister of Justice. The link was maintained until Moltke's arrest. Delp, too, often visited Reisert or sent him reports through messengers. His last visit to Augsburg was at Christmas 1943.

THE COLOGNE CATHOLIC LABOUR LEADERS

The Catholic labour leaders associated with the 'Ketteler-Haus' in Cologne, had been determined opponents of national socialism in the period before the Nazis came to power. They saw how German workers were being misled by Nazi teaching. Their leaders included Joseph Joos, Bernhard Letterhaus, Prelate Müller, Johannes Albers and Nikolaus Gross. The Kreisau Circle came into touch with this group, especially with Letterhaus and Gross, through Delp.

Bernhard Letterhaus was a man of considerable stature. He had become a labour leader and had therefore dedicated his life to what he described as the formation of the workers' estate, but he could equally well have been a captain of industry. In the years immediately before 1933 he had been a deputy in the Prussian Landtag and a close colleague of Brüning. At the time, most Catholic authors and speakers pointed at Bolshevism and socialism as the most serious dangers, but Letterhaus gave insistent warnings against the growing national socialist movement. As Vice-President of the German Katholikentag at Münster in 1930, he said: 'False prophets with a cross on their flag—no sign, however, of the Saviour of the world—march through the towns and villages. They ravage the hearts of the suffering people.' He was, in Brüning's opinion, 'the only person who was capable of giving really effective political leadership.' Always busy and active, with an extraordinarily strong will, he spoke many times on behalf of

Catholic Action. During the war he served as a soldier and at the end of 1942 he joined the 'Ausland Abwehr' in Berlin.

In the course of 1942 Delp approached the leaders of the Catholic Labour Movement and the Christian trade unions on behalf of the Kreisau Circle. They planned to keep each side informed of the other's activities through meetings. Delp visited Letterhaus twice at his Cologne home, and other members of this group took part in the discussions. Their consultations ranged over resistance, the churches, the future state and its citizens. At the end of December 1942 Delp was again in Cologne. At this meeting, at which, as on the previous occasion, others were present, constitutional problems and questions about the Cabinet in the transitional period were discussed. When Letterhaus' home was completely destroyed by a bomb in July 1943 he left Cologne with his family, but met Delp subsequently in Berlin.

In addition to Letterhaus, Nikolaus Gross was also in contact with Delp. He was editor of the *Ketteler-Wacht*. He travelled on several occasions to Munich and he, like the author Michael Brink, acted as an intermediary for Delp and Letterhaus. Delp warned him against Goerdeler's group and this caused some disturbance within the resistance movement, traces of which can still be found in the interrogations after July 20.

THE GOERDELER GROUP

It is not easy to describe the relationship between the Kreisau Circle and the group that formed around Goerdeler, and clarify the differences between them. War-time conditions only increased the obstacles to a mutual understanding; it was also essential that outsiders should know as little as possible, but this led to inaccurate knowledge which in turn provoked inaccurate judgements.

Let us look first at Goerdeler. It must be said that there were few men of the period who were as tireless and energetic as Goerdeler. He never gave up, he weathered many dangers and he constantly swept his friends along with him when they were inclined to surrender to a hopeless situation. He never lost his belief in the ultimate triumph of good. Reason, or good, he said, would inevitably overcome in the end. He did not doubt this even with regard to Hitler himself. Conservative in politics, his economic views were liberal, although even so he believed in some social reform. In his private life he upheld the old Prussian traditions of personal frugality and responsibility, the extravagance of some Nazi leaders making this characteristic all the more apparent.

Goerdeler had made a success of local politics. As Mayor of Leipzig he had succeeded in bringing the most important political groups round to his views, which experience undoubtedly increased his general optimism. His name became known abroad when, in 1937, he resigned the office of Lord Mayor in protest against the removal, in his absence, of a Leipzig memorial to the composer Felix Mendelssohn-Bartholdy. In the last years of the 1930's, the most significant figures in the civilian resistance gathered around him, and saw in him the head of a new government following a successful *coup d'état*. It is important to note that the Goerdeler group bore many similarities to a coalition government, composed of members of different parties. The Kreisau pattern was quite different.

At the beginning of the period of resistance, Goerdeler's group was the only nucleus of opposition that stood above party lines. Subsequently, when the Kreisau Circle emerged, it seemed natural enough that the two groups should work together. Why was it then that the move towards co-operation met with such resistance, and to what extent were their reservations justified? Could the gulf have been easily bridged by compromises? What follows is an attempt to answer these questions.

One of the more important differences between the groups was that they belonged to different generations, though one should remember that there was some overlap. When dealing with the Kreisau Circle, some members of the Goerdeler group, both then and subsequently, contrasted the 'critique by the young theoreticians' with the 'experience of the older men'. However, the antipathies between old and young, or practitioners and theoreticians, are not in themselves sufficient to explain the antagonism between the two groups. Not all the members of the Kreisau Circle were young men. Among the older members or associates there were persons of considerable experience. We have only to remember Steltzer, Rösch, Lukaschek, van Husen, Peters and von der Gablentz. They played an important part in the Circle and especially in the formulation of its views. Even the younger members had considerable practical experience of life, administration and politics, whereas during the war everyone involved, both the young and the old, was forced to be simply a 'theoretician'. Nonetheless the 'generation gap' did become an obstacle; the younger men, who in their previous work had placed little emphasis on it, now felt themselves restricted and this provoked strong reactions.

The Kreisau Circle made two types of criticism of Goerdeler:

they were critical of his method of working and critical of his
views. They had similar objections to other members of the Goerdeler group but their reservations concentrated upon Goerdeler
himself as leader. It is unfortunately true—several vouch for this
—that Goerdeler made an enormous 'hullabaloo' in the course of
his immense activity, and that he was careless. During or after
visits he used to makes notes and prepare lists which could be
fatal in the circumstances of the time and were completely unnecessary risks. For this reason people were warned against
meeting him. General von Falkenhausen, for example, experienced
Goerdeler's carelessness in Dresden and Berlin and as a result
would not allow him to visit Brussels. Abs reports that Goerdeler
began to make notes at the end of a conversation with him, and
that this was sufficient to make him never meet Goerdeler again.
Steltzer tells how he was warned by Canaris against meeting Goerdeler, for the same reason. Peters speaks of the 'dangerous
loquaciousness' of Goerdeler and his group. Yorck often used to
begin conversations with the ironical comment: 'The latest news
going round Berlin opposition groups today is . . .' For the
members of the Kreisau Circle, who were extremely reticent in
their own work, these facts alone provided a justifiable reason for
preserving on security grounds alone a distance between themselves and Goerdeler. To have done otherwise would have been
to endanger their own work.

The second group of criticisms made by the Kreisau Circle concerned Goerdeler's views. There is not much point in making a
thorough analysis of the details of the programmes. No member of
either group had ever read or saw the whole of the programmes of
the other group. It ought also to be remembered that this was
not a confrontation between programmes but between living men
who either got on with one another or differed. If this is clear, then
the differences that undoubtedly existed between the programmes
of the groups become rather more understandable. Goerdeler and
many members of his group came from another epoch, whether or
not they were actually older in years. It is naïve to determine the
epoch to which a man belongs simply on the basis of his age. The
personalities of Goerdeler and several of his friends, both on the
left and on the right, had been moulded by life before World War
I, and their views had been formed in the period before 1914.
That they were nonetheless mostly loyal supporters of the Weimar
State and occupied prominent positions does not make any difference. Many men of this kind were unable to accept the conse-

quences of the terrible breach that World War I had created. The old Europe had disappeared; a new world had to emerge. Inwardly Goerdeler was unable to complete this transformation. When he thought of reintroducing the monarchy, when he spoke of a national state or of the working class, or of the economic system, his words seemed to members of the Kreisau Circle like something out of the past. They were more aware of the enormous break in history. They knew that the world was entirely altered and they wanted to draw the necessary conclusions from this. Whether they succeeded in doing this in their programme is another question, but they did recognize one thing: many of the tensions that had dominated the political life of the Weimar Republic were now superseded and could therefore be overcome. New problems forced themselves forward. They knew, therefore, that they themselves would have to change, and that many prejudices and cliches on all sides would have to disappear. It was precisely this readiness to change that brought representatives of opposing groups together in one circle, and which made them reasonable and willing to make concessions. The Kreisau Circle never regarded its programme as definitive. The emergency building of Weimar, hastily put together in 1918, had succumbed to Hitler. Talk of a return to the Weimar State, of a restoration, was out of the question. Even a simple restoration of the old constitutional state was inadequate. It is here that the real differences between Goerdeler and some of his friends on the one side, and the members of the Kreisau Circle on the other, are apparent. It was on these grounds that the Kreisau Circle considered Goerdeler 'reactionary'. 'I don't understand,' Yorck said to an acquaintance on one occasion, 'why you maintain contact with this arch-reactionary,' when once asked how as a friend he could co-operate with those 'drawing-room Bolsheviks'. A similar attitude to Goerdeler was shown by other members of the group: and when Reichwein read a manuscript by Goerdeler entitled *Die Wirtschaftsfibel*, it was clear to him that the economic reforms outlined in it would be inadequate.

In spite of the antagonisms several individuals tried to bring the two sides together and success here would have meant co-operation between two important groups in the civilian resistance. It was in this connection that the 'row' between Leuschner and Delp occurred. At the end of 1942 members of both the groups pressed energetically for a meeting at which the most important differences would be discussed. Yorck, for example, discussed the matter with the economist Jessen, to whom he had been introduced by

Schmölders, while Hassell and Popitz talked with Gerstenmaier and Trott. Schulenburg also made a contribution. In the end both groups agreed to a discussion.

The meeting took place at Yorck's house on the evening of 8 January 1943. Beck, who was to take the chair, Hassell, Goerdeler and Popitz went to Jessen's home and then on, with him, to Yorck. There they met Yorck himself, Moltke, Trott and Gerstenmaier. Beck, who was recognized by both groups as the leader of the resistance, listened to everything but did not intervene in the discussion. They discussed questions of foreign policy, administrative reform, economic policy and other general problems. Where Moltke wanted a fundamental discussion of the differences between them Goerdeler tried to damp them down and to present them as of only minimal significance. This provoked a sharp reaction from the members of the Kreisau Circle. 'Every attempt to move forward to fundamental questions', Moltke wrote, 'was lightly deflected by the other side'. At one point Moltke allowed his distaste for the proceedings to appear in a reference to the 'Kerensky solution'.*

The differences were not bridged. They were, however, all united in their desire to bring about the *coup d'état* as quickly as possible.

A few days after this meeting Moltke informed the Jesuits about its results. Yorck who had at first campaigned vigorously for the co-operation, seems to have been disappointed by Goerdeler's utterances and to have come to share Moltke's considerable scepticism. In spite of their criticism, the members of the Kreisau Circle were ready to accept that Goerdeler should become Chancellor in the first government, largely because they regarded it only as a transitional government. It is probably true to say that as time passed and the group around Count Stauffenberg grew in influence, the criticisms of a Goerdeler government increased still more.

THE FREIBURG GROUP

In 1938, shortly after the *Kristall Nacht*, a group was formed in Freiburg, composed of university professors and theologians who were members of the Confessing Church, with the aim of considering the problems of resistance from a Christian standpoint. Its members included Professor Gerhard Ritter the historian, as well as von Dietze, Eucken, Lampe. In the course of 1942 these pro-

* Kerensky, the revisionist socialist Prime Minister in defeated Russia of 1917, overthrown by Lenin.

fessors, at the request of the 'Provisional leadership of the Confessing Church' communicated through Dietrich Bonhoeffer, prepared a memorandum that was intended to serve as a basis for post-war discussions, both within the German Protestant churches, and in the first contacts with other churches in the ecumenical movement. After a thorough analysis of the contemporary scene—'the political chaos of our time and its causes'—the memorandum developed the 'basic characteristics of a political community organized on the basis of Christian insight'. At the centre of the analysis stood the idea of personality, the relationship between the individual and the community and the idea of justice.

Some of the ideas that are prominent in the Kreisau documents can be seen here too. The Freiburg memorandum, however, lacks any concrete proposals for university reform, while foreign policy is given a relatively minor place, and there are no suggestions about punishment or war criminals. One must, however, also remember that the composition of the Freiburg Group was quite different from that of the Kreisau Circle, and that it occupied somewhat of a middle position. Reports of meetings at Lampe's house were sent both to Goerdeler, who had taken part in a discussion of the memorandum mentioned above, and to Yorck who was highly thought of by the Freiburg Group, and in particular by Eucken. Doubtless Yorck used this material in the Kreisau discussions of economic problems. On one occasion, probably on an invitation from Yorck, von Dietze took part in one of the agricultural conferences organized by the Kreisau Circle. As far as he remembers the differences between the Goerdeler Group and the Kreisau Circle seemed larger than they really were. Franz Böhm, who was in touch with both Goerdeler and Yorck, was also of the opinion that in time the antagonism between the two groups would have lessened and that, in particular, the Freiburg Group and the Kreisau Circle would have grown closer together.

THE WHITE ROSE

Only indirect relations existed between the Kreisau Circle and the student group led by Professor Hüber in Munich, known as 'The White Rose'. Some members of Delp's group in Munich were in personal contact with members of The White Rose. One of them, the author Michael Brink, tried unsuccessfully to arrange a discussion between Hüber and Delp. 'As a result', he wrote in 1947, 'of the disastrous postponement of a meeting between Professor Hüber and Alfred Delp the action took place at a time at which it could have little political impact and was bound to end violently.' When details about the Scholl case became known in Berlin at the beginning of 1943, both Yorck and Moltke came to the conclusion that there was an organized resistance among the students in all German universities, and they asked their friend Schmölders to come from Cologne immediately to Berlin, so that they could find out what was happening in Cologne. Unfortunately, Schmölders had to disappoint them. Yorck returned from a journey to Munich with a pamphlet by The White Rose. When Moltke made another journey to Norway in March 1943 he took the pamphlet with him. He had it translated into Norwegian by an acquaintance, and the text was then published in the Norwegian underground press. Moltke also arranged for the pamphlet to be sent from Sweden to England, so that people there could be informed and he gave a Swedish acquaintance a memorandum on the matter (see p. 193). Moltke found the participation of young people in the resistance movement very significant and was extremely pleased about it. During a visit to Paris in June 1943, he talked again about 'the importance of the Munich student stories'. After the trial of several members of this group, Ernst von Borsig, who had studied in Munich until 1933 and knew many of the professors and graduates there, went to Munich at Yorck's and Moltke's request to find out whether groups still existed and whether it would be possible eventually to establish contact with them. The visit was fruitless.

THE COMMUNISTS

When, following the arrest of Moltke in January 1944, the possibility of establishing contact with the communists was discussed in the Kreisau Circle, it was not the first time that the question had been raised. It had been considered at least as early as 1943. Several members of the Kreisau Circle had personal links with individual communists. These links, however, had at that time little to do with the Kreisau Circle. It was also well known that there were many informers among the communists. The problem of eventual contact with representatives of the communist resistance seems to have been taken seriously during 1943. In this year there was talk of the growing influence of the pro-Russian group in Germany, and possibly this development had an influence on discussions in the Circle. The Proclamation by Mierendorff and his colleagues of 14 June 1943 speaks of the 'representatives of the communist movement' as well as of other groups. Probably some members of the Circle had already established contact with the communists. Two of the members spoke about the contacts in the course of journeys abroad during the summer of 1943. When Trott was in Turkey in June 1943, he told an acquaintance that communists wanted to make contact with the Circle but this could not be allowed. In the same year, probably in the summer, Haubach too, while on a visit to the Netherlands, expressed concern that there were, unfortunately, people in the Circle who wanted to make a deal with the communists. When Moltke went to Turkey in September 1943 and pleaded there for co-operation with the western allies, he stressed that it was necessary 'to win over rather than to repel as many as possible of the pro-Russian groups in Germany'. In the same connection he said: 'The participation of communists who were personally reasonable and not tied to Russia could well be desirable.'*

It appears that it was Reichwein who was most concerned to establish contact with the communists. It was not only that he was anxious to tell them that a *coup d'état* was planned and that it was hoped that the communists would not attack from behind: he also believed that they would be needed at the time of the collapse. He regarded an alliance with them a matter of some importance at least at the beginning of the new phase. They would provide a counterweight to the conservative forces which might possibly be in the majority. The decision to approach the communists was in fact only taken in 1944 after Moltke's arrest.

FRITZ-DIETLOF VON DER SCHULENBURG

There are always people who are difficult to fit into a group. In a period of contrasts between several groups they could be especially important as contact men. Such a person was Fritz von der Schulenburg (see p. 105). He had considerable administrative experience and, as deputy police president in Berlin between 1937 and 1939, he had taken part in the preparations for several *coups d'état*. Between 1938 and 1939 he had been a member of the 'Counts' Group' led by Yorck. Appointed Regierungspräsident at Breslau in 1939, he visited Moltke several times at Kreisau in the weeks following the outbreak of war, before being called up for military service. When he was again in Berlin at the end of 1941 in connection with a new job, he had a long conversation with Moltke and Yorck. Afterwards Moltke wrote: 'Yorck and I tried to enlist him for our work, and I must now make every effort to create the

* See *Neuordnung im Widerstand*, pp. 375, 585.
G R H—M

preconditions that we discussed . . .' Although Schulenburg thought highly of Moltke and entirely shared the views of the Kreisau Circle, he thought, in his position as an officer, that it was more important to bring about the *coup d'état* as quickly as possible. Since, however, several attempts in this direction failed, he turned up now and again in the Circle.

About September or October 1942 Schulenburg was appointed to a post in the Reich Ministry of Food, and about this time visited Yorck and Moltke on several occasions. At the beginning of September Moltke wrote: 'At 8 o'clock Fritz appeared, in the best of form. I have never had such an interesting and trouble-free conversation with him. We made a survey of the whole territory and discussed the reasons for my measures. On the whole he was not only satisfied, but also convinced of the necessity of certain things that had originally displeased him.' This trend continued in the next few months. In his letters of November, Moltke writes of two conversations with Schulenburg several weeks after the second Kreisau Conference on the constitution and the economic system. After the first of these conversations Moltke wrote: 'Yesterday evening was extremely productive. It will take a long time before Fritzi is entirely integrated, but he is well on the way and I very much hope that we shall soon be successful. He had a whole host of constructive criticisms of the Kreisau documents, but they were concerned with details, or, sometimes, arose out of misunderstandings, or applied to things that we ourselves have never thought very highly of, such as the "Reich Specialist Offices".' In the period that followed, the Kreisau Circle made use of his administrative experience in their discussions. By the end of November, Moltke is writing: 'The slight detachment that Fritzi always adopts towards us has visibly diminished and is well on the way to disappearing.' Schulenburg campaigned especially in this period for co-operation between the Goerdeler group and the Kreisau Circle and gave a great deal of effort to preparing the important discussion of January 1943. In 1943 differences of opinion emerged on the question of assassination, which Schulenburg regarded as absolutely necessary; only some members of the Kreisau Circle agreed with him. He was very active in this period as intermediary between the civilian and military resistance and he was responsible for arranging a large number of meetings. At the end of 1943 Moltke mentioned another discussion: 'Fritzi seems to have slipped back a little again . . . I am anxious to know whether we can again attach him to us more strongly.'

CHAPTER 12

Links with the Armed Forces

As the régime had all the instruments of power at its disposal, the army alone was in a position to effect a change of government. Many people, therefore, set high hopes upon the generals. Even in 1934 Moltke's mother could write to her parents in South Africa: 'People talk of a military dictatorship (the Reichswehr is not at all Nazi), but who knows if there is a personality capable of taking command'. After going into several of the difficulties, she added: 'However it is a great comfort that the Reichswehr are more or less normal people, less infected by this ghastly Nazi doctrine than most others'. (This letter for safety reasons was posted just over the border from Kreisau in Czechoslovakia.)

Could the Reichswehr fulfil the hopes that it would emerge as a champion of freedom and bring about the restoration of democratic and republican government? The fact that the majority of the Reichswehr's leaders had never adopted a positive attitude towards the Republic had fateful consequences. They were as a result far more susceptible to Hitler's seductive powers. Many of them felt able to speak of common interests. They drew no conclusions from either the murder of General von Schleicher, or the new oath introduced after Hindenburg's death, or the anti-semitic legislation, or the Fritsch Affair. Moltke was later to regard the chances of a *coup d'état* then as having been greater; and he held that several good opportunities had been lost in the thirties. The majority of generals were more impressed by the stage-managed meeting between Hitler and Hindenburg held at, as it were, the shrine of Frederic the Great—known as the 'Day of Potsdam', as well as by the reduction in the power of the SA and the proclamation of universal conscription. There were only a few with clear vision and a willingness to take courageous decisions. Serious resistance from the German army was not to be expected.

Nevertheless, hopes rose again in the course of 1938, when at last somebody had the courage to oppose Hitler and to hinder his preparations for war. This was Ludwig Beck, Chief of the General

Staff, who repeatedly warned Hitler against his adventures. He also told his officers in no uncertain terms of the limits of a soldier's obedience. 'Your obedience as soldiers stops where your knowledge, your conscience and your responsibility forbid the execution of an order . . . A senior officer who sees his responsibilities and duties in times such as these only within the limited terms of his military duties, without being aware of his grave responsibility towards the whole nation, lacks greatness and a proper understanding of his duty.' Those upon whom those words had made any impact were unfortunately few in number. Beck was completely deserted by his new superior, General von Brauchitsch. The only possibility left open to him was to resign in protest. On Hitler's orders, his offer of resignation was accepted without publicity. He was a courageous man who dared to say what many thought and who preferred to sacrifice a brilliant career if the alternative was to take part in enterprises of which his conscience could not approve. He was not, however, a natural fighter.

Beck's name was a symbol in this period and the resistance gathered round him. He had been in touch with Goerdeler since 1935 and the latter had kept him informed about the economic situation. The civilian and military resistance were linked through the co-operation of these two men and as Hitler's war planning progressed, preparations were made for a *coup d'état*. Chamberlain's leniency towards Hitler, however, prevented the realization of their plans. Moltke himself had been aware of the preparations and had tried to recruit experienced men for the work of reconstruction. He could write, however, in the spring of 1939 to an acquaintance in England: 'Where there was a chance for a change a year ago, there is nothing now.' He and his friends considered it inevitable and entirely in keeping with the political situation that the decisive action that all the opponents of the régime wanted could and would only be carried out by the army. They frequently counted upon a lead from the generals and tried to make use of their links with them. Yorck had some contacts in the army from his service days. Moltke too had links; he was, for example, directly in touch with Beck's successor, General Halder. He was also regularly in contact with Beck himself and he and Yorck sent numerous letters to Beck. They were also able, on occasions, to discuss matters with him.

With the help of Moltke's letters and some other pieces of evidence, it is possible to reconstruct relations between the Kreisau Circle and the military resistance during one particular episode.

The incidents in question occurred towards the end of 1942. After the high hopes and disappointing experiences of the winter of 1939–40 and of the summer of 1940, intervention only seemed feasible again in 1941. As the war against Russia developed, horrifying reports came back and the situation was viewed very pessimistically by the experts. The murders committed in all the occupied territories shocked many senior officers. Their indignation, however, did not automatically lead to action. Instead, many of the generals allowed themselves to be 'bought' by Hitler with honours, property or money. It was in this period that Moltke wrote: 'What worries me most about the present is the lack of any reaction from the military.' The repeated failures of the military leaders disappointed and infuriated him. He referred to them as 'no proper Generals but military technicians, and the whole is a gigantic crime.' Nevertheless, he and the other opponents of the régime were still dependent on the armed forces to take the lead in any serious action against the régime. The relationship is well illustrated in this episode.

At the end of September 1941 Moltke noted that von Dohnanyi 'has finally done his part and we can now proceed.' Moltke and von Dohnanyi saw one another frequently and kept each other informed about what they were currently doing. Their meeting at the end of September, however, had a special purpose. It was concerned with a piece of work that von Dohnanyi had written for the Kreisau Circle. Moltke had asked him to examine the problem of the oath of loyalty in a dictatorship and the right of resistance, from a legal standpoint. Moltke doubtless wanted to use his paper to apply pressure on the generals. Only two days later a conversation took place at Yorck's home between Beck, Moltke and Yorck. 'It was a successful evening and one can only hope that it helps to forge the iron,' Moltke wrote afterwards. When he met the Jesuit provincial, Rösch, in October and told him about the real situation in Russia, he added: 'Father Provincial, consider what this means if we are still alive; in the spring of 1945 the Russians will be in Berlin, if we do not succeed in wresting the leadership from Hitler.' This remark is one piece of evidence that Moltke and his friends were busy working on the generals at the time.

New signs of activity appear again in Moltke's letters in the second half of November. He reported on a visit that he had paid to General Föhrenbach in Stettin. The letter gives no indication of how he came into contact with him but it may well have come about with Beck's help. About the visit Moltke wrote: 'I was not entirely successful with him. He asked for time to think and then the conversation is to proceed.' In the same letter, Moltke quoted Föhrenbach's farewell words: 'This business is very good. I do not know a better way, but I am not up to it.' Moltke added that Föhrenbach wanted to discuss the whole question again in Berlin with Beck and himself. 'I am convinced,' he wrote, 'that we shall get him then. I am going to Beck on Wednesday afternoon to discuss the problem with him. I have just been to Dohnanyi to prepare this conversation and a discussion with Halder . . . ; I hope we shall now succeed in making two or three big steps forward before Christmas.' This obviously referred to an attempt to rouse the military to take action. There is a further indication in a subsequent letter of Moltke's at the beginning of February 1942: 'A remarkable paralysis of the will seems to have affected everybody again and instead of the "it's too early" that I heard again and again before Christmas, I am now told that it is "too late". It is sad to see how correct Peter and I were in diagnosing 18 December 1941 as "the right day".'

This remark suggests that once again, at a decisive moment, the generals refused their help. In Yorck's and Moltke's view, 18 December was a suitable time because a German defeat before Moscow appeared unavoidable and Hitler, who was furious about the insignificant successes of his troops, was swamping his generals with reproaches, and especially von Brauchitsch, the Supreme Commander of the Army. Tension between them had reached such proportions that the Supreme Commander offered his resignation. What in fact happened was that on 17 December, Hitler told Brauchitsch that he personally was taking over supreme command in order to lead the army to certain victory. Brauchitsch was dismissed on 19 December. Yorck and Moltke wanted to nurture the anger that the senior officers held against Hitler and exploit their indignation so as to provoke them into action. In this way they hoped, like all the opponents of the régime, to put an end to the senseless and bloody killing and to bring about a tolerable peace while there was still time.

Yet another source offers some confirmation of these events. 'About 1941–42 a plan emerged for linking a revolt by the army with a general strike. At the time, Berlin generals were enthusiastic. Leuschner waited for the signal to press the button. Even the day had been arranged. At the last moment, however, the plan was shattered by the cautiousness of the chief of the General Staff, who, as I was told at the time, considered the enterprise too early because it could possibly lead to the emergence of a "stab in the back" legend with all that that would inevitably mean. There was, however, no intention of killing Hitler but only of taking him prisoner. The scheme was much better prepared and more comprehensive than the subsequent attempt on the 20th July.' These remarks confirm what has been described above. It is particularly noteworthy that this writer, like von Moltke, uses the phrase 'too early'; it would seem that it was a phrase employed at the time. The man who was ultimately responsible for the collapse of the plan was the Chief of the General Staff, Halder, with whom Moltke, as we have noted above, had already had discussions. Even if the members of the Kreisau Circle themselves could not intervene—they did not command any soldiers—they did not sit back passively but played a very active part in this attempt to launch an action against the régime.

Their disappointment is understandable. Even so, their hopes that one of the leading front-generals would act, flickered to life again on several occasions in the years that followed. During his official journeys at home and in the occupied territories Moltke discussed the matter with various generals. In the winter of 1942–1943, great hopes were pinned on Kluge, Supreme Commander on the Eastern Front (Centre), but once again they were frustrated. Naturally enough, other civilian leaders also tried to arouse the military leaders to take action. It was at about this time, for example, that the bishops Wurm and Meiser approached a very senior officer. He was a convinced Christian. They eventually managed to talk to him about the untenable situation and to ask him openly whether now at last the military could not take the action needed to put an end to the destruction and murder of hundreds of thousands of lives and desolation of Germany and the occupied territories. Was he not prepared, for the sake of his conscience, to take the risk himself now and to act before it was too late to avert the catastrophe that loomed ahead? The general is supposed to have replied, that although he himself considered the total situation extremely serious, he could not be sure of the support of the junior or non-commissioned officers in the event of an army action against the régime. It could, therefore, provoke a bloody conflict within the army with all its terrible consequences. The bishops were extremely depressed by the outcome of their visit.

As more and more crimes became known—events in the concentration camps, the murder of Jews, crimes in the occupied territories—these problems were discussed again and again in the Circle. It was clear that changes in the régime was not enough. The overthrow—including the spiritual defeat—of national socialism became ever more urgent. They persisted in their efforts to provoke some positive action. The position, however, grew increasingly hopeless. In the depths of depression Moltke wrote on one occasion that he was now certain that nothing could be achieved with the generals; they would have to wait until the bitter end. This tone of extreme depression comes out in other letters of the period. He no longer placed any hope in the generals. When new possibilities were discussed at the beginning of 1943, he wrote: 'They are much more positive in their assessment of the changes than I am.' He was convinced now that the defeat would first have to be endured: 'Why are people unable to show any real patience? This seems to me to be the virtue that is the most difficult to acquire. I too prefer it when everything is going quickly, but I am, nonetheless, relatively patient. Even König and Delp, who must have learned patience through their discipline, are unable to show it, and if an action suffers the inevitable setback they grow impatient and do not see that the valley will be succeeded by a mountain. All these emotions seem so uneconomical to me: they must cost a lot of strength.'

There are, however, some signs that Moltke himself began to regain hope during 1943. Reisert, for example, reports that some generals approached Sperr through Moltke with a proposal that the Bavarians should begin an armed uprising, which they would then use as the basis for an action of their own. Steltzer also remembers that Moltke spoke of the possibility of a Bavarian military action against the Obersalzberg—Hitler's 'eyrie'. At Moltke's request, he discussed the matter in Munich. Moltke asked Lukascheck to come to Berlin on 10 August 1943 and told him that Hitler, Goering and Himmler would be at the Wolf's Lair, the East Prussian headquarters, on 13 August. The tank division responsible for guarding the place was under the command of men who were determined to act. Hitler and his colleagues would be arrested and finally put on trial. Beck was going to make a proclamation, the contents of which he had already read to Moltke. Goerdeler would form a government, etc. As part of the plan, he handed Lukascheck a document appointing him Reich Commissioner for the Eastern Provinces with special responsibility for protecting the German frontier. Hitler did not, however, visit the Wolf's Lair on the 13th August and the tank division was, as usual, replaced. This episode indicates incidentally the co-operation between Moltke and the military resistance, Beck himself was very highly esteemed by the members of the Kreisau Circle.

Yet another indication of the Kreisau Circle's efforts to bring about the overthrow of the régime in this period can be seen in Moltke's visits to Turkey and the discussion that he had there. At the beginning of July 1943, Moltke went to Turkey with a plan which involved the landing of a German Staff Officer in Britain, under the cover of an 'air accident'. Once there, the officer, furnished with all the documents and powers that he needed, would negotiate with the Allies to open the western front to them, while keeping the eastern front blocked against a Russian advance. At least some of the generals were aware of this plan. On another visit in December, Moltke repeated the offer of military and political co-operation with the Allies. They would approve 'the creation of a second front and a sudden and overwhelming attack by the whole of the allied fighting force, aimed at occupying the whole of Germany immediately'. On the German side, the landing would coincide with the formation of a 'provisional anti-Nazi opposition government' which would act in close association with the Allies. This proposal which was put forward in a memorandum and reached the highest American authorities will be considered in more detail at another point in the book (see p. 197). All these examples indicate how energetically the Kreisau Circle worked, with other groups in the opposition, to initiate action against the national socialist régime.

The continued refusal of the military authorities to act, in spite of the insane conduct of the war and the unrelenting efforts by resistance groups to persuade them, gave rise to more and more discussion within these groups about whether or not the assassination of Hitler might be the best means of preventing the deaths of millions. The problem was discussed within the Kreisau Circle from about the end of 1942 onwards. It was, however, always a rather marginal question. The Circle belonged to the civilian resistance and they did not have at their disposal the military resources that were essential if an assassination was to be carried out. Their own immediate responsibility was to prepare for the reconstruction. Even if they had considered the matter as urgently relevant to their own plans, there was little that they could do about it, as Hitler spent most of his time at his headquarters in East Prussia and only a small group had access to him.

Opinions differed about the rights and wrongs of assassination: sometimes, individuals changed their views. Trott, Gerstenmaier and Haeften were the most prominent supporters of this solution. The reservations felt by the other members of the Circle were partly ideological, partly political. The emergence of the 'stab-in-the-back' legend after World War I—in other words that Germany had not been defeated militarily—was a solemn warning of what might happen if this solution were adopted. On no account should it be possible for their opponents to lay the responsibility for the defeat that was already certain upon their shoulders. It was also essential to avoid making Hitler a martyr. The most important objections to an assassination attempt, however, were ideological: the refusal to employ the methods of their opponents. The destruction of life or murder—even if it was the murder of a tyrant—could not be a genuine way out of their dilemma.

When Hans Christoff von Stauffenberg said to him on one occasion: 'Isn't there anybody who will shoot this Hitler down? Is there no-one who will do away with this Bohemian corporal?' Moltke replied: 'You haven't thought about what you are saying. Nobody may do this.' When the other person retorted: 'What do you mean *may* not, somebody *must* do this', Moltke said: 'No. Nobody may do this. Why are we opposed to the Third Reich, why are we opposed to national socialism? Isn't it precisely because it is a lawless system? We cannot set about creating something new, initiating a renewal, by committing a lawless act ourselves. And murder is always unlawful.' Moltke explained his position from both a religious and a legal standpoint. He said much the same to Rösch on another occasion: 'We cannot protest against the daily murder of thousands in the concentration camps or anywhere else, if we ourselves are also going to commit murder. There are other ways. The military authorities ought to arrange an armistice on the western front and make peace.'

Even so, Moltke continued to think about the problem and at a later date had ceased to place assassination in the category of actions that are 'not allowed'. In a talk with Berggrav in March 1943, Moltke stressed that he considered the reconstruction of the administration as his special task, but that he should not shirk his duty, if he was needed absolutely to kill Hitler* (see also p. 210). Steltzer was fundamentally opposed to the use of assassination for political ends. Von der Gablentz shared his views. Rösch, too, rejected the idea and,

---

* Jørgen Glenthøz, *Documente nur Bonhoeffer–Forschung,* p. 264 (Munich, 1969).

unlike the other Jesuits, Delp and König, he was opposed to any form of 'activism'. He maintained that any would-be assassin would have to be absolutely certain that the assassination would bring about a substantial improvement of the situation. Mierendorff was still opposed to assassination in a long conversation that he had shortly before his death at the end of 1943, his main reason being that it would give rise to a new 'stab in the back' legend. Reichwein was another who frequently raised this point as one of the numerous doubts that he had about assassination. 'The cure is dreadful, but it must be completed, or Germany will learn nothing,' he once said to his friend Bohnenkamp. Yorck, on the other hand, changed his mind early on, according to Gerstenmaier. Then in the spring of 1943, he swung back to Moltke's position. After the arrest of Moltke in January and Reichwein and Leber in June 1944, however, he seems to have changed his mind once again and approved of an assassination attempt. Others changed their views at about the same time and for the same reasons. Einsiedel, for example, eventually came to the conclusion that assassination was the only possible solution, even though he never gave up his fundamental rejection of it. Despite all differences of opinion, however, the collaboration of the Circle's members was unimpaired.

Moreover they were in touch with certain junior officers in the army; for example von der Schulenburg and Schwerin von Schwanenfeld who were very close to the Circle indeed. It was their investigations that eventually led them to Count Stauffenberg, and Stauffenberg to the Kreisau Circle. This turning towards the younger generation was in line with an observation of Mierendorff to Otto John: 'We do not need generals and state secretaries in order to construct a new social order and a new state in Germany, so much as majors and junior civil servants'.

PART 3
FOREIGN RELATIONS

CHAPTER 13

Links with the Allies

In wars between nation states a distinction is drawn between citizens of allied, neutral and enemy states. In a period of growing supra-national unity both within and outside Europe, this conventional pattern was already ceasing to have much meaning. People were becoming increasingly aware of a unity which embraced the whole human race. The same trend could also be seen within international totalitarian systems such as communism or fascism which penetrated across existing frontiers; words such at nationalism and treason took on potentially new meanings. Many people were not aware of this change or did not want to be: national states continued to exist, and in them events were still assessed according to the outmoded criteria of who was a patriot and who a traitor.

Moltke and the other members of the Kreisau Circle gradually came to see—some early, others late—that the struggle against Hitler was part of what was essentially an international struggle against fascism and totalitarianism. They believed in the unity of European peoples and supra-national standards of international law. Fascism, a relapse into nationalism, denied this unity. Because this was so, Moltke held that every man had a duty to combat this evil wherever it existed or appeared and to co-operate with those of a like mind. As far as he was concerned, Germany's defeat was terrible, but after all the fearful things that had happened, an unavoidable stage in the fight for this objective. The Kreisau members took supra-national co-operation after the collapse of the régime for granted. Their hopes were often disappointed both within and beyond Germany and they frequently had to fight against a solid wall of misconceptions.

LINKS WITH ENGLAND

Two members of the Kreisau Circle had particularly close relations with Britain, where they had many friends and acquaintances:

177

Moltke and Trott. It has already been noted that the former's family association with England, as we have seen, went back to the Field-Marshal himself. It became still stronger when Dorothy Rose Innes married into the family. She was the only daughter of the Supreme Justice of the Union of South Africa, James Rose Innes, who had been one of the Unionists who had pressed for an understanding between the Boers and the English following the Boer Wars and who, on the basis of this experience of a co-operative effort, saw opportunities for a similar development of co-operation between the different national groups in the British Empire. Dorothy Rose Innes introduced the Moltkes to the world of the Commonwealth. We can still detect her influence in the words of her eldest son, Helmuth James: '. . . She has never for one moment lost touch with Great Britain and with South Africa and through these connections has always felt herself to be one of the members of the Commonwealth of Nations transcending nationalities'. Englishmen were frequent visitors at Kreisau. After their return from a visit to the South African grandparents, Helmuth James and his wife spent some weeks in England at the end of 1934, where they were entertained by Lionel Curtis, a friend of the Rose Innes family.

Curtis was a man of wide-ranging influence. He was a co-founder of the Round Table group and of the Royal Institute of International Affairs, a Fellow of All Souls and a member of the Federal Union. He too had been a Unionist in South Africa, and had subsequently dedicated himself to strengthening the British Empire. He had formed discussion groups in different parts of the Empire and had founded his own journal, *The Round Table*. This movement aimed at counteracting the disintegration of the Empire by achieving an organic unity and the growth of a 'World Commonwealth' through the co-operation of all the groups involved. One of Curtis' closest colleagues was Philip Kerr, after 1930 Lord Lothian. Lothian's biographer describes the relationship between the two men in the following words: 'To Kerr, Curtis was "the Prophet", a noble, almost heroic figure possessed of immense moral strength and moral courage; single-minded and to some extent narrow-minded; doctrinaire but not interested in theory unless it led to action, and capable by his own enthusiasm of inspiring actions in others . . .' On an earlier occasion, Dorothy Moltke has asked him to be as helpful as possible to her son Helmuth James. She felt associated with Curtis' work. 'I have always known', Helmuth James wrote to Curtis on one occasion, 'how my mother believed in you and in your work.'

The meeting with Curtis meant much to the young Moltke and it was followed by a number of subsequent visits in the course of which they quickly established a very close relationship with one another. Particularly after the death of Moltke's mother, Curtis became a fatherly friend who advised him and encouraged him in his career plans. He arranged for him to have discussions with influential Englishmen such as Lord Halifax and Lord Lothian, with whom Moltke frequently talked, and with contemporaries like Michael Balfour, at that time a lecturer in modern politics at Oxford, and an assistant at the Royal Institute of International Affairs. Moltke, as explained earlier, took and passed his Bar examinations; he wanted to retain the link with his new friends and with his mother's spiritual home. On his visits to England, he used to stay with Curtis and was given countless introductions by him.

In the various discussions that Moltke had while he was in England, British foreign policy, especially towards Germany, was a regular topic. For example, he had a conversation with Lothian on this theme in July 1935, and Moltke, who was well aware of the fateful consequences of current British policy, took up a position quite opposite to that of Lothian, especially when presented with the familiar arguments for a policy of appeasement. From his conviction that the external causes of the rise of national socialism had been greatly exaggerated he opposed Lothian's view that the mistakes of British and French post-war policy, especially at Versailles and during the occupation of the Ruhr, were responsible for the emergence of the Nazis.* Lothian's claim that the Nazis were a stable régime and that one revolution was never followed by a second seemed to Moltke to be a product of German propaganda. That after a while the more extreme Nazis would disappear, as Lothian believed, was apparent, according to Moltke, only to foreigners and not to Germans. Lothian thought finally that a policy of concessions would help to change the Nazis. To Moltke this was fallacious; it was erroneous to believe that concessions in the face of a threat of war would make the person who threatened any less eager to try the same thing again. Summing up, he wrote: 'I fear his policy will be successful in England. . . . I fear that it will prove to be misleading for Germany; it will induce our government to believe, that we can count on English

* '. . . that foreign faults are greatly responsible for German national socialism is, I believe, utterly wrong, although it is often used by German people as an excuse.'

neutrality, while in truth, should a European war break out, England would fight on the side of France; this possibility of misleading the others is what I fear most about the English policy of keeping the balance. England is in reality not an arbiter but a party to the struggle; but her lack of a firm policy is just what induces Germans to believe that she is an arbiter.'

It was in England that Moltke met Adam von Trott zu Solz, who had been a Rhodes Scholar at Oxford. They found much common ground, introduced each other to mutual friends and kept in touch. These were years of enormous international tension. Hitler constantly made new demands, and one action was quickly followed by another. Many anxiously asked themselves: 'Will the allies always give in? When will they finally oppose Hitler?' At the Nuremberg Party Rally in 1938 Hitler made yet another of his violent speeches and threatened the use of force if further concessions were not made on the Sudeten question. On the same day, Moltke wrote to his grandparents from London: '. . . he will try to split the English people on the issue involved. His whole technique is over and over again to avoid fighting and to avoid an issue. The long Cabinet meeting here today is not a good indication as it tends to show that the Cabinet are not really united and of one mind.' In conversations with Lothian and others Moltke often harped on the consequences of British policy and gave quite explicit warnings against it. In Germany he had frequently emphasized that the British Empire was not disintegrating and that it would strike back if it was provoked. A few weeks after the Munich Agreement, Moltke wrote to Curtis frankly: 'It is to anyone knowing anything of continental affairs nearly incredible, that Chamberlain seems to have disregarded the important facts. . . . It is the old story of Wilson over again; a man with good intentions and no knowledge of the problem he was dealing with, was duped into agreeing to a solution which was none.'

Within a month of Munich, Hitler ordered the Wehrmacht to prepare for an attack on the rump Czech State. Tension rose once again and German propaganda fabricated stories of numerous Czech atrocities. At the end of 1938, Moltke wrote: 'What we must hope is that public opinion in the world is finally roused to the worldwide threat to the foundations of our civilization and will find means of preventing contagion without going to war over it.'

During this period several Germans visited England, either on missions from German resistance groups or simply because of their own concern, to urge the British to adopt a more determined attitude towards Hitler. Moltke and Trott were among these. Moltke was once again in London at the beginning of 1939 and talked with Lothian, Wheeler-Bennett and others. Shortly afterwards Lothian seems to have finally perceived the threat presented by Hitler, and to have changed his opinions quite openly, as when he wrote to Vansittart: '. . . though if we had tried appeasement more vigorously in the days of the Republic, there might never have been a Hitler at all'. Shortly afterwards he was appointed Ambassador in Washington. Moltke, who hoped that this would lead to closer co-operation between England and the United States, sent him word: 'I need not assure you with what feelings of relief I learned that you have gone to strengthen that public service which from the outside looks your country's weakest spot'. In June, Trott visited England, officially to investigate Anglo-German relations, but unofficially and much more importantly to tell the English government of the intentions of the German opposition. His double role estranged him from some of his friends who could not conceive of the need for such a double game. Trott was able to talk with Neville Chamberlain, Lothian and Halifax, thanks to the Astors, and tried to gain understanding for Germany.

About a week after the outbreak of war, Moltke wrote to his wife: 'It is still true that the French and the English have not yet undertaken anything to assist their allies. I am still trying to explain this away by preparations for an offensive and other considerations. This explanation, however, cannot be maintained for very long, and if it is wrong then they are still sticking to an indescribably stupid policy of allowing their enemies to pick off their opponents one by one.' In this, he was thinking anxiously about those Western European countries of which he had already written to Curtis at the beginning of 1939: 'It seems to me, that now it is not a question of how to continue until the Caesarian régimes fall, but really how to preserve the rest of western Europe from falling either a prey to these régimes or developing such régimes themselves.'

At the beginning of 1940, at the time of the contacts between the British government and the German opposition via the Vatican, the American church leader Roswell Barnes visited von der Gablentz. On this occasion von der Gablentz asked that England should in an official statement distinguish between Hitler and the German people. The German opposition believed that a clear statement to this effect would induce the opposition generals to act.

G R H—N

During the war Moltke tried to maintain contact with his English friends. In July 1940, following Hitler's victorious western offensive, and a few days before Hitler gave orders to prepare for an invasion of England, Moltke wrote to Yorck: 'Throughout my adult life I have worked together with people of other countries, and since 1935 especially I have quite deliberately tried to help "new forces" in England to establish their position against the ruling generation, two above their own. (The generation between the present rulers and the new generation was practically destroyed in World War I.) I did this because I was convinced that only the triumph of this new generation in Great Britain could prevent the war. I remain convinced that the relationship with these men must be re-established as early as possible.' Yorck, like many others, was very much impressed by the German victory. Immediately after the outbreak of war he asked himself whether it did not exclude the possibility of revolutionary changes, as Germany's opponents made no distinction between the government and the German people.

In the period that followed, Moltke's and Trott's personal contacts were linked with the work of the Kreisau Circle. Planning for the future continued in England, just as it did in Germany. Curtis and Kerr were preoccupied with plans for post-war reconstruction and a federalization of Europe. A memorandum prepared by this group reached the Kreisau Circle via Sweden. In April 1940, in anticipation of a German defeat during the western offensive, Moltke wrote to Curtis in an optimistic vein: '. . . . your plans are progressing . . . I suppose that this progress will be badly needed fairly soon.' When Deuel, the American journalist and friend of Moltke, had to leave Germany in December 1940, Moltke gave him an oral report for Lothian and the South African Ambassador in Washington. Its contents were as follows: 1. Moltke's views are still the same as they were before the war and they are shared by others; 2. Moltke is very pessimistic about the opportunities open to him and others who share his views; 3. Moltke is very pessimistic about the favour of active resistance; little reliance can be placed upon the Generals; 4. In the long run Hitler will compromise all Germans and make them responsible for the atrocities in the occupied territories and in Germany. This report was delivered.

In 1942 new efforts to establish contact were made. At the end of April, Trott gave the General Secretary of the World Council of Churches in-process-of-formation, Visser't Hooft, a memorandum, with the request that he should take it with him to London and give it to the English government. This memorandum, written in the first person plural is as to the contents entirely consistent with other memoranda and documents of the Kreisau Circle. At the same time, another document was sent to the USA. Later, Moltke commented that Trott had 'returned from Switzerland with the first English and American reactions to our efforts'. With a strong emphasis on the growing disorder, the memorandum described conditions in the parts of Europe under fascist control. Specific warning was given of the increasing influence of the communist movement, following Russian military successes. Stress was laid on the necessity of political co-operation between the western allies and the German opposition and of a speedy overthrow of the régime. 'We feel justified to appeal to the solidarity and fairness which some responsible groups in the west are extending to those forces in Germany which have consistently fought against nihilism and its national socialist manifestations. . . . We sincerely hope that our still inadequate attempt . . . will be met with frank co-operation in the practical task to face a common future beyond the catastrophe now confronting us all.'

As many people in Britain still harboured some doubts about Trott, the memorandum did not make the impact that he had hoped for. It is true that certain influential people, such as Sir Stafford and Lady Stafford Cripps, whose son was a friend of Trott, and David Astor, another of Trott's friends, pressed Trott's case, but the official reaction appears to have been rather cool. In the same year, in May, Bishop Bell met Pastor Schönfeld in Stockholm.

In the meantime, other ways of establishing contact were tried out. Whenever Moltke visited a neutral country, he sent cards and letters to his English acquaintances. These messages—from a German in wartime—sometimes caused his friends embarrassments. Contacts with resistance groups in the occupied territories also presented opportunities for informing the English government of the existence of the German opposition. Moltke was especially concerned to let the British know that their propaganda was pointless and actually furthered national socialist objectives. It was for this reason that he invited his friend Michael Balfour to meet him at Stockholm in the course of 1942. (Moltke was a frequent visitor to Stockholm.) Balfour was not, however, allowed by the British authorities to make the journey. It is said that von Moltke's cousin, then German Ambassador in Madrid, had also been making secret overtures to the Allies at the same time, and the two approaches got mixed up at a high level.

Moltke found another possibility after the failure of the last meeting. He wrote a detailed message which he did not sign, took it to one of the Circle's contacts in Sweden, Johansson at Sigtuna, and asked him to arrange for its transmission to his friend Lionel Curtis. As Johansson considered it dangerous to send the document itself to England, he asked an American visitor who was to return to the United States via England to learn the contents by heart, and, as he was only intending to stay in England for a short period, to communicate them to Bishop Bell whom he already knew.* This was done. The American subsequently wrote a comprehensive report while he was in England, and this was given to Curtis in September 1943. Moltke had two main objectives in mind in writing this message. In the first place he asked for a trustworthy Englishman to be appointed to the staff of the British Embassy at Stockholm, with special responsibility for making contact with the resistance movement. For security reasons, this person should not belong to an intelligence service. In the second place, it was of the utmost importance that the BBC should receive better information, so that its broadcasts could be better and more successfully adapted to the domestic situation in Europe and Germany. This could be achieved through the proposed contact man in Stockholm. The memorandum also described conditions in Germany and, in particular, the different situation in which the German opposition found itself. The contents were made available to certain important people in Britain. It is possible that some of the contacts that Trott had with members of the British Embassy in Stockholm in the autumn of 1943 were also a result of the request expressed in this memorandum.

THE USA

Political relations between Germany and the USA were not close in the Weimar period. George Kennan, in his study *American Diplomacy 1900–1950*, rightly speaks of 'lost opportunities' in this context. After the USA, under Wilson's leadership, had come to the aid of the Allies in World War I and aroused enormous expectations throughout the world, the country had retreated once more into isolationism. The world economic crisis only strengthened this tendency. Two years after Hitler's appointment as Chancellor, Congress passed the Neutrality Law, a clear indication of its desire not to become involved in a European conflict.

Shortly after the outbreak of World War II, Adam von Trott

* See documents pp. 364–67 and Addendum p. 387.

visited the United States,* his pretext being an invitation to take part in a conference organized at Virginia Beach by the 'Institute of Pacific Relations'. It was difficult to make non-Germans understand that a 'good German' could travel as an official representative, with the permission of the German Foreign Office; throughout his stay in America Trott could not but be aware of the suspicions that his visit aroused, as two FBI officers followed him everywhere. Indeed the FBI believed not only that Trott was a Nazi agent, but Hitler's master-spy. His main plan seems to have been to confirm the neutral position of the Americans and, in this way, to bring home to them their responsibility for mediating during the war and guaranteeing peace after it. From the very beginning, however, it was probable that, in the event of a conflict, the Americans would opt for the British side. To a certain extent their neutrality was a delusion and Trott attached too much importance to it. He used the opportunity offered by his visit to have discussions with the former Reich Chancellor Brüning and other emigrants. He had a secret meeting at the Mayflower Hotel in Washington with the British Ambassador, Lord Lothian. In some quarters he was thought to be too open, and this made him suspect. He was given the chance to speak in some smaller groups, and in these he developed his ideas about how the Germans could get away from the Nazi régime, stressing that the external situation would be of decisive importance for these developments, and that in this connection it would be advisable for the Allies to state their peace aims early on. These ideas can also be seen in a memorandum written by Paul Scheffer, which Trott edited and added to and sent under his own name to a number of leading American statesmen. It is typical of Trott's patriotism that he insisted on striking out the passage that the German opposition would prefer a defeat of Germany to a continuation of the conquering Nazi régime. The memorandum was also given to the Assistant Secretary of State, Messerssmith, and he in turn, encouraged by an initially favourable reaction from Roosevelt, passed it on to several other people. Soon afterwards the President changed his mind on advice of Justice Felix Frankfurter, who had been warned by Maurice Bowra (see p. 50) against trusting Adam. Bowra who had concluded during Trott's last visit to England that he was an ambiguous person, subsequently deeply regretted his mistrust.

* This visit is dealt with in considerable detail in Christopher Sykes' *Troubled Loyalty, A Biography of Adam von Trott*, pp. 286–331. (It appeared after this book was written.)

Trott's mission was doomed. American neutrality, on which Trott still counted, had become more doubtful. The whole enterprise was, from Trott's standpoint, very disappointing.

Nevertheless, during the first years of the war, contacts were maintained between Germans and Americans. Moltke, whose parents had been friends of Wilson's adviser, Colonel House, had several American friends and acquaintances. One need only remember his relations with Dorothy Thompson, the Mowrers and the Deuels (see pp. 21, 28).

In the course of 1939, as the tension in Europe increased, he established contact with the American chargé d'affaires in Berlin, Alexander Kirk. How their association began is unknown but during the rest of 1939 and 1940, Moltke met Kirk frequently. The meetings were of a private character and were kept secret. Conversations ranged over the current situation and future prospects. For Moltke, who was never asked to communicate any military information, these conversations were important because they provided another link with the free world and an opportunity to keep himself informed. From the outset he was convinced that the USA would soon place itself at Britain's side. Thus, for example, he wrote in a letter telling of Kirk's departure on the next day: 'The situation in the USA seems to be unchanged: it is hardly now a question of "whether", so much as "when".' Before Kirk's departure he was recommended to Kennan, who was on the staff of the American Embassy.* Kirk stressed the importance of a continuation of this contact with Moltke for the American government.

At the end of November 1940 Moltke had to take leave of Deuel who was returning to the United States. 'It is extremely painful to me,' he wrote, 'that he will not be returning, because I like him and conversation with him was a great help to me.' In this connection, Moltke mentioned that Deuel 'has taken everything else with him, and we can now only hope that everything works out'. This means probably that Deuel took something in addition to the oral report that he was to transmit to the British and South African Ambassadors to the United States.

When Kennan too had to return to the United States, Moltke took the opportunity to present him with a specific request. Of it he wrote: 'More has come out of these meetings than out of the meetings with Deuel. He has agreed to a proposal of mine to do something quite specific, and at Christmas he will be returning

* See KENNAN, G.: *Memoirs 1925–50.*

home, leaving his service and will devote himself to carrying out this task. He is a good and pleasant person, and I hope that he will be really energetic on our behalf.' The request certainly had something to do with the external contacts of the Kreisau Circle. Precisely what it referred to, however, is not clear. In the same letter, Moltke made some remarks about Kennan's reaction to his proposal: 'I hope by that way to be able to repay my debt of gratitude to Europe for the most important fifteen years of my existence'. Possibly it was Moltke's intention that Kennan should use his influence to induce the British and American governments to co-operate with the German resistance movement. However, Pearl Harbour intervened; Kennan was held for several months in Germany and only returned to the United States in May, 1942. After a great deal of hesitation he decided not to tell the American government about the matter. He was aware that Moltke and his group were already in touch with Britain, and he was afraid that his information might fall into the hands of the Gestapo; that would have had fateful consequences for Moltke and his friends.

Kennan's return to the United States put an end to all direct links between Moltke and the Americans. In the followings years he and his Kreisau colleagues were chiefly dependent upon indirect contacts, which continued until the end. In 1942, Dorothy Thompson gave her radio talks addressed to Moltke, under the title 'Listen Hans!'; but Moltke knew nothing about them, though from the text of the broadcasts, it would appear that Moltke had approached her indirectly. She has said, for example, that a Swedish woman had visited her in May 1942 with information from Moltke. The following words from another part of the broadcasts are also significant: 'I deduced that others of your group have attempted to reach people in England, for almost simultaneously with your report, which reached me by the usual channels, I received a somewhat similar report from Great Britain, though with fewer details'. These remarks would appear to be yet another indication that at about the same time as the memorandum written by Trott was sent to the British government, a report with similar contents was transmitted to the Americans. Mrs. Thompson was close to President Roosevelt.

From the beginning of 1943 onwards, the Kreisau Circle was in touch with Allen Dulles, the representative of the American Intelligence Service in Switzerland, through Trott and Waetjen. Later in 1943 contact with the Americans was also established in Sweden. Finally, reference must briefly here be made to the contacts that

Moltke had in Turkey in the same year (see below p. 196). Behind all of them was the desire to achieve some degree of political co-operation. There was a danger that after the war Europe would be dominated by communism, and this disastrous development could only be avoided if the western Allies, including the USA, co-operated with the German resistance movement in overthrowing the régime and barring the frontier against Russia. All the contacts between the Kreisau Circle and Americans had this objective. There was, however, no response from the other side, except refusal. Under the influence of a crusading spirit, the policy of unconditional surrender was formulated. An idealistic disregard for future developments meant that too much importance was attached to the military requirements of the hour. Political considerations seem to have played little part in the formulation of this policy, and its psychological impact foiled its purpose—as representatives of the German resistance repeatedly pointed out. In the end, Moltke himself, in the hope that he might thereby achieve the co-operation he sought, accepted 'unconditional surrender'. His arrest, however, spared him knowledge of the Morgenthau Plan.

SWITZERLAND

The Secretariat of the World Council of Churches in Geneva and, later, the Berne Office of Allen Dulles, were the contact posts of the Kreisau Circle in Switzerland. Schönfeld, Trott and Gerstenmaier maintained links with the former, and Waetjen and Trott kept in touch with the latter through Gero von Schulze Gaevernitz. Some of those who later became members of the Kreisau Circle such as von der Gablentz, Steltzer and Gerstenmaier were already associated with the Geneva offices of the ecumenical movement before the formation of the Circle. Furthermore, Trott had been put in touch with Visser 't Hooft, the General Secretary of the World Council of Churches, by friends of his mother in the YWCA. These personal contacts were later used in connection with the work of the Kreisau Circle. Visser 't Hooft and his colleagues Schönfeld and Ehrenstrøm gave the Kreisau Circle important help, especially by providing them with introductions to groups interested in church affairs in the occupied and neutral countries. It was by these means that the Kreisau Circle established links with the resistance movements in Norway, and in the Netherlands and made important contacts in Sweden. They also passed on Kreisau documents to representatives of the Allies—probably more frequently than has hitherto been assumed. The memorandum that Visser 't Hooft took with him on a journey to England and communicated to the British government has already been mentioned (see p. 182). The Kreisau Circle also gave Schönfeld a memorandum for his discussions with Bishop Bell in Sweden. At the end of 1942, an essay on economic problems, written by Trotha and Einsiedel on the basis of discussions in the Kreisau Circle, was sent via Geneva to certain church groups in England that were concerned with the preparations of the World Council for the postwar period.

Rather more detailed consideration must be given at this point to a memorandum that was sent to the American churches at the end of 1943 (see p. 364). It is curious that Rothfels, when publishing this document, did not, as in the case of the April 1942 memorandum, point out that it was written in the first person plural, indicating group authorship. Instead, he speaks of 'Trott's observations'. Apart from the first person plural, there are several other internal indications which suggest that it was not drafted by Trott alone. In June of 1943, the year in which it was written, the third Kreisau conference formulated the basic principles of the foreign policy of the Circle and took decisions on international economic policy and the punishment of war criminals. It would thus appear reasonable to conclude that this is a summary of these discussions.

The remarks in the first paragraph of the memorandum are very similar to points 4 and 5 of the *Foundations of Foreign Policy* prepared at the third conference. This is particularly true of the emphasis upon an order that embraces all nations on the basis of self-government. In the second paragraph the words 'Order' and 'Freedom', already familiar from other documents of the Circle, are used in connection with economic problems. The need for a 'limitation' upon the sovereignty of the nation states, mentioned in the third paragraph, bears a striking resemblance to the second part of point 5 of the *Foundations of Foreign Policy*. The fourth paragraph which is concerned with the problem of the minorities cannot, for personal reasons, be attributed to Trott but must stem from other members of the Circle. The first sentence in the fifth paragraph is very similar to Moltke's memorandum of 1941, particularly its comments on 'penitence'. Sentences in the sixth paragraph, and above all in the last, also contain ideas common to the Kreisau Circle. We are therefore of the opinion that this memorandum also should be designated as one of the Kreisau documents.

Moltke's letters make it clear that Trott was still in regular contact with him at the time. Could it be that the comment, 'In addition, Adam has returned with information that he would like to discuss first with me', refers to this? For security reasons Moltke always confined the most important issues to marginal observations. There is further no clear evidence that Switzerland was the country where Trott came across the American document to which the memorandum was a reply. It may have reached the Circle via Sweden or as part of a foreign press report in the Ausland-Abwehr (see p. 104).

At the end of November 1942 Allen Dulles* came to Berne as chief of the American Intelligence Service in Switzerland, with instructions to make contact with groups in the German resistance movement. Formerly a diplomat, working from Berne he was able to provide his government with many important reports. His closest colleague and adviser, particularly in contacts with the German resistance movement and in support for it, was Gero von Schulze-Gaevernitz who was Silesian by birth. Moltke already knew Gaevernitz, as his father, who was a close friend, had been a member of the managing committee of the Löwenburg Work Community. As a colleague of Dulles the younger Gaevernitz was also in contact with several members of the Kreisau Circle, especially with Trott and Waetjen.

On two occasions, Dulles received summaries of Trott's views via Gaevernitz. In the first, Trott complained about the negative attitude of the western Allies towards the German resistance movement, and contrasted it with the Russian attitude which was more positive. He gave warning of a growing 'eastward orientation' in Germany. In the second he emphasized the communist and pro-Russian influence in Germany even more strongly and pleaded for support for the pro-western groups in the working class, through encouraging declarations. If one compares Trott's remarks with the contents of the foreign policy memoranda, it becomes increasingly clear—Moltke's discussions in Turkey in 1943 point in the same direction—that the Kreisau Circle kept on stressing to the western Allies that Russia, both through the radio and through communist agents, was careful to distinguish between the régime and the German people, whereas the western Allies hardly ever made this distinction. This stifled support for a western solution in the resistance movement. Trott's remark that there

* See Allen Welsh Dulles, *Germany's Underground* (New York, 1947), pp. 81, 173.

LINKS WITH THE ALLIES   191

would be an anti-Bolshevist revolution in Russia after the war seems unrealistic and romantic in retrospect; in fact the war itself strengthened the Russian régime. Trott was more critical of the west than others. This, however, was nothing new. His whole thinking clearly proceeded from the centre 'Germany' and from the German position in the world. This was genuine patriotism, but he was insufficiently aware of the dangers of nationalism. He perceived Germany's central position between West and East more strongly than the others. It would, however, be false to talk of communist sympathies, as the statements of several of those who talked with Trott testify. Trott remained in touch with Dulles until the assassination attempt. On each of his visits to Switzerland he also had conversations with Elizabeth Wiskemann, of the Political Intelligence Department of the British Foreign Office.

There was a certain animosity between Trott and Waetjen. Trott was more orientated towards England whereas Waetjen, who was less of a nationalist than Trott, inclined because of his mother more towards America. Trott's distrust of Waetjen went so deep that he let Allen Dulles know that Waetjen could not be considered a spokesman for the Kreisau Circle. Waetjen had, however, been in regular contact with Moltke since 1939 and had at an earlier time taken part in the Kreisau work. In his conversations with Moltke he had spoken about German relations with the United States and about the need for a re-organization of Germany's social structure. In addition, at the request of the Circle, he had drafted a number of memoranda on economic questions which were intended to serve as a basis for the Circle's draft economic constitution and which were then discussed with Einsiedel, Moltke and Yorck. As we have seen (p. 108) he took part in one of the earliest gatherings at the start of the Circle's development, but later he had to move to Switzerland, with only occasional visits to Germany. In Switzerland he was in touch with Gisevius and he also had contacts with Beck and, via von Lukowicz, with the group around Leber and Dahrendorf. He met Trott on two occasions in Switzerland.

SWEDEN

The contacts of the Kreisau Circle in Sweden were aimed at establishing links with Britain. The first feelers were made in 1940. Shortly after the German occupation of Norway, Harry Johansson, Director of the Scandinavian Ecumenical Institute at Sigtuna, received word from Ehrenstrøm, Visser 't Hooft's colleague, that a German called Steltzer, who was well known to the World Council in Geneva, had been appointed to a post in Oslo. Before Johansson could make contact with him, however, Steltzer, who had heard of Sigtuna from his Norwegian friends, and who retained an interest in adult education, visited Sigtuna and was introduced to Johansson by Ehrenstrøm who happened to be there at the same time.

Following this, Steltzer, who had to make frequent official journeys to Sweden in connection with arrangements for military holiday transport, visited Johansson several times, and was introduced by him to other Swedes, including Ivar Anderson, the editor in chief of *Svenska Dagbladet* and a member of the Swedish Upper House, Nils Quensel, a former minister and President of the Court, Hardy Gøransson, Director in chief of the Swedish prisons, and the Bishops Manfred Bjørkquist and John Cullberg. Steltzer also had regular meetings in Stockholm with Werner Dankwort, of the German Embassy, and through his cousin Tamsen, who was resident in Stockholm, he had still more contacts. When Steltzer later told Johansson about the links between the Norwegian resistance movement and the Kreisau Circle, his Swedish contacts began to extend beyond the personal sphere and he had regular meetings with the group mentioned above in Stockholm. The Swedish foreign minister Günther was kept informed about these discussions by Anderson and Quensel, and on one occasion Steltzer was able to meet Günther himself.

In May 1942 Bishop Bell of Chichester met the two German pastors Bonhoeffer and Schönfeld in Stockholm. On hearing of Bell's visit each of them had travelled to Stockholm separately, unaware of the other's journey.* Bishop Bell was one of the few people on the Allied side who dared to speak out in public, during the war, on behalf of the other Germany. He had come to Sweden in connection with an effort to revive Anglo-Swedish cultural relations. The purpose of his visit had long been known and had been announced in the press. Both Bonhoeffer and Schönfeld had made up their minds, independently of one another, to travel to Stockholm to meet Bell. Before his departure for Sweden, Bonhoeffer had had a long conversation with his friend Haeften about his plan and especially about the international situation. He also discussed the results of the visit with him afterwards.

Within the scope of this book, only Schönfeld's visit will be considered. The Kreisau Circle knew about it. It is true that it

* See Eberhard Bethge: *Deitrich Bonhoeffer*, p. 851.

was not initiated by the Circle, but nonetheless, when they heard about it, they prepared a memorandum which was later somewhat altered by Schönfeld. He probably did not take it with him but instead, after his arrival in Stockholm, wrote down several Kreisau ideas from memory and handed them over in the form of a memorandum. It was probably he who named Trott as another contact man and passed on Moltke's greetings to Curtis. Immediately after Schönfeld's return from Sweden, he had a discussion in Berlin with Trott, Haeften and Collmer. Meanwhile, Bell prepared a detailed report of his conversations in Stockholm for the British government, in the person of Eden. The latter expressed himself very interested but was not, however, willing to offer any help. Nonetheless, Bell persisted in his fight for this cause; the German resistance included several of his friends from the ecumenical movement.

In the spring of 1943 Schönfeld, who frequently made courageous journeys through Europe, establishing important contacts and handing on numerous reports, had another opportunity to visit Sweden. While there he met a friend of Bell, Robert Mackie, with whom he had an hour-long conversation and who later gave Bell a detailed oral account of it.

At that time also Moltke spent an entire week in Stockholm, on the return journey from Norway. For the first few days he was alone, but towards the end of the week he was joined by Steltzer. The real purpose of the journey is indicated briefly in one of Moltke's letters: 'I must travel to Stockholm on Saturday, because somebody whom I have to see is leaving on Monday morning.* Steltzer intends to arrive in Stockholm on Wednesday evening. By then I will already have had to fight the main battle. It is a little unfortunate, but in a way perhaps quite good since a new impetus in the struggle will be given on Thursday.' This quotation shows that Moltke, whose journey was an official tour in connection with shipping problems, intended to use this opportunity to establish an official contact between the Kreisau Circle and the Swedish group of friends. It is not entirely clear who it was that Moltke had to see in Stockholm on the Sunday—possibly the person who took 'The White Rose' pamphlet to England (see p. 164). On the following day, Moltke met Anderson in his office. He gave him a memorandum about the action of 'The White Rose' and had a thorough discussion about developments in Germany. Anderson later described the conversation as one of his most memorable

* Perhaps Mackie is meant.

experiences of this period. He remembers Moltke's lucid understanding, his profound seriousness and his unshakeable conviction.
His ideas appeared always clearly thought out. A few days later,
following Steltzer's arrival, a meeting took place between Moltke,
Steltzer, Johansson, Quensel, Gøransson and Anderson. In the
meantime, Moltke no doubt had several other discussions. On the
day before the larger meeting, Moltke and Steltzer had a talk with
Johansson. In the course of it Moltke inquired about the possibility
of making a brief flying visit to England with the help of his
Swedish friends. The scheme turned out to be impracticable.

Following Moltke's visit there were several meetings between
the Swedish group and other members of the Kreisau Circle. The
Kreisau members were chiefly interested to discover whether their
Swedish friends could see any opportunity for sending to England
reports other than those sent by the Intelligence Services. After a
thorough investigation the Swedes concluded that there was no
possibility and their conclusions were supported by Günther in his
conversation with Steltzer. Even so in subsequent discussions the
Germans repeatedly raised the question of how the British could
be informed about the real situation in Germany and about the
significance of the resistance movement and be persuaded to make
a distinction between the Hitler régime and the other Germany.
The Swedes informed the Germans of the British view that a
military defeat of Germany was an unavoidable necessity. Nonetheless, the contents of another memorandum mentioned above
were sent to England via Sweden and the Kreisau Circle itself
received a memorandum from Britain via Sweden (see p. 182).
There were possibly other contacts too. In the same year, 1943,
Lukaschek also paid a brief visit to Sweden where, among others,
he met the banker, Marcus Wallenberg, who promised him that
he would pass on information about the Kreisau Circle to England,
though this was not done.

Trott and Gerstenmaier also visited Sweden and discussed with
their Swedish friends the possibility of establishing contact with
the Allies. In addition, one of the Swedes occasionally visited
Germany. From the autumn of 1943 onwards Trott played a particularly important role in maintaining these contacts. On one of
several visits, at the end of October, he had a discussion with
Anderson, in which he claimed that conditions in Germany were
deteriorating and that there was growing popular discontent. The
possibility of a change of régime, however, was very slight and
Russia in particular was capitalizing upon these developments for

her own purposes. He asked Anderson what the attitude of the Allies would be and whether they could count upon Allied assistance in the event of a *coup d'état*. 'If we can manage to cause a change of régime in Germany, it would be necessary for us to get help from abroad more or less immediately. We are in no position to wait. The risk of a counter-action, maybe a civil war, is too great. Our own power is so weak that we can hope to carry through our aim only if the course of events is favourable and we get help from abroad. What do you think of our chances of getting help?' Anderson replied that in his opinion the likelihood of their receiving help was very small. This provoked Trott to comment: 'In that case there is nothing for us to do but wait and see. This is dangerous, because it may mean that Russia will win the game'. Once again he expressed the wish to establish contact with the west through Sweden. Anderson later arranged a meeting between Trott and Günther. Günther formed a favourable impression of Trott during their discussion and passed on certain information to him. Anderson also arranged for a meeting between Trott and Sir Walter Monkton, Under-Secretary at the Ministry of Information; the discussion, however, was fruitless, as were other contacts with members of the British Embassy. The German Consul-General, Werner Dankwort, arranged for Trott to have talks with foreigners who had recently been in England and the USA. In all these conversations Trott tried to convince his companions that 'unconditional surrender' was the most serious obstacle to ending the war through the formation of a new government in Germany. His arguments were generally rejected and he found it difficult to conceal his personal disappointment. It appears that he had both American and British contacts in Sweden during this period; the British seem to have been readier to renounce 'unconditional surrender', but the Americans were adamant.

After his journeys Trott reported the results to his friends in the Kreisau Circle and together they discussed further possibilities. Moltke, for example, made the following comment after Trott's journey at the end of October: 'In addition Adam has returned with information that he wants first to discuss with me. . . .' In the next letter he wrote: 'Adam came in the afternoon. He had spent some very interesting days in Stockholm and had made some progress.'

TURKEY

'Tomorrow I am going (for the first time) to Turkey which pleases me greatly—the day after tomorrow I should already be on the

Bosphorus. A friend who has just returned gave the most splendid account and I think that I shall find it like the first, a touch of my old and best-loved Chinese homeland.' Trott wrote these expectant and very characteristic words in June 1943. The Kreisau Circle believed it might be possible to establish better contacts with the Allies through Turkey than had hitherto been possible through Sweden and Switzerland. Turkey had been tending towards the Allied side since the beginning of 1943. There were, moreover, emigrants living there who might be able to act as go-betweens, several of those being known to the Kreisau Circle. Trott's journey was intended to sound out the possibilities, and it led directly to Moltke's subsequent visits.

Trott owed the chance to make this journey to the help of his colleague Wilhelm Melchers. Melchers was Director of the section 'Near and Middle East' in the political department of the Foreign Office. Since reports from Turkey about events in the Arab world were of considerable interest to Germany and, particularly after the Conference of Adana where Churchill secretly met Turkish representatives on the Syrian border on 30 January 1943, Trott was given an official commission to collect information on the Turkish attitude, and was able to use this journey as a cover for his illegal purposes. Once in Turkey he spoke to members of the German embassy and emigrants, acquainted friends with the existence of the Circle, gave his opinions on the ideas that were most prominent there and discussed the possibility of drawing von Papen, who was at the time German Ambassador to Turkey, into the work of resistance. Not everybody with whom he spoke agreed with this latter suggestion. In any event, the journey led to Moltke travelling to Turkey at the beginning of July 1943 and Trott may indeed, according to Eberhard, have met Papen. He certainly considered there were real possibilities of establishing the type of contact that they sought.

Moltke's journey was made possible by Canaris. The pretext, that is the official commission, was that Moltke should investigate an affair of certain missing Danube ships. He was accompanied by Wengler, a scientific adviser at the Ausland-Abwehr. They travelled to Vienna by train from there flew to Istanbul, where Wengler attended to the problem of the missing ships while Moltke pursued his own plans. From the German consulate he telephoned an acquaintance, Hans Wilbrandt. The latter had been an accountant at the Annuity Office in Frankfurt-am-Main before 1933 and as such had come into contact with Moltke in connection with the provision of financial help for the Kreisau estate; they had been friends ever since. He had emigrated to Turkey in 1934. Wilbrandt was now invited to meet Moltke at the home of the head of the German Abwehr in Turkey, Paul Leverkuehn. Moltke had been associated with Leverkuehn for a while before the war, but he did not tell him about the real purpose of his journey.

At Moltke's request Wilbrandt arranged a meeting with Alexander Rüstow, who had lived in Turkey since 1934 and had contacts with the American Secret Service. The three of them had an hour's very heated conversation about Moltke's proposed plan to get a German staff officer, provided with all the necessary papers and powers, to Britain under the cover of an air accident, in order to make an agreement with the Western Allies that only the eastern front should be held against Russia and that the western front should be opened to the western allies. In addition Moltke urgently wanted to establish political contact with the western allies through people who were personally known to him—in this connection he mentioned Alexander Kirk, then American Ambassador in Cairo, Dorothy Thompson, who was highly regarded and trusted by President Roosevelt, and General Smuts. He said that he was ready to fly to Cairo for this purpose and thought that he could safely disappear for a few days. Wilbrandt immediately tried to get in touch with Dorothy Thompson through intermediaries and Moltke himself wrote to her. In the course of their conversations, Moltke made a strong attack on the demand for 'unconditional surrender' and his principle aim in the proposed negotiations was to persuade the Allies to withdraw this condition. Rüstow could understand this but told him emphatically that there was no hope of achieving anything in this direction. If conditions had to be laid down now, force of circumstances would doubtless make them much less generous than they would be after the collapse of the régime. If it could be guaranteed that Germany would only be occupied by the Western Allies, all that they wanted would in fact have been achieved. Preliminary negotiations about peace terms would only complicate the situation. For these reasons Rüstow said that he would not be ready to help any longer, if Moltke was not prepared to accept the demand for 'unconditional surrender' as a pre-condition. Although it understandably cost him a great effort Moltke in the end agreed. As time ran out before a final decision could be taken about the execution of the plans, further discussion was postponed until Moltke's next visit. During this same first visit Moltke made a vain attempt to get in touch with

Churchill through the Patriarch of Constantinople and the Church of England.

Before Moltke returned to Germany, he asked Rüstow and Wilbrandt to make contacts and then to inform him in a telegram with a text agreed between them. He was particularly interested in contacting the Americans, emphasizing that preparations would have to be made in the strictest secrecy. With Moltke's agreement his friends prepared a report on the conversations for the Americans and informed the highest authorities. It was proposed that the Americans should send to Istanbul a special envoy with the fullest powers and an introduction from Kirk in order to work with the German resistance movement, to indicate the main outlines of allied post-war planning and to give the Germans certain assurances about the approval of a democratic constitution in Germany after the collapse of the régime.

While Moltke waited anxiously for news from Istanbul, Rüstow arranged a meeting in September between an American diplomat, George Earle, and von Papen. The American was meant to persuade von Papen to join the German resistance movement. Von Papen was undecided, and remained so when, a few days after the first discussion at the Embassy, he arranged for the American to be invited to the Prinkipo summer house of the Director of the Deutsche Orient Bank, Johann Post, where von Papen himself was staying at the time. He said, however, that he would be travelling to Berlin within a few weeks and he promised to have his answer by the time he returned. Von Papen later told Post that he had discussed the American invitation with Weizsacker and that the latter had strongly advised him not to take it up. When von Papen asked Post in March 1944 to try, through Rüstow, to get the American diplomat to Istanbul once again, the answer from the American side was a categorical 'too late'. Although this conversation had nothing at all to do with Moltke's mission it is mentioned here because it indicates a certain willingness on the American side. Against this background Moltke's attempts seem all the more tragic.

In November 1943 the German intermediaries received the news that Kirk was to visit Turkey incognito. Moltke was informed and sent a telegram announcing that he would arrive in the middle of December. At the first conversation Moltke had declared himself ready, if his discussions with Kirk produced a positive result, to secure co-operation between the German General Staff and the High Command of the western powers. He was provided with information and documents. When Moltke arrived in Istanbul, however, Kirk was not there. Why the meeting did not take place is not known. Was Kirk's journey vetoed in high circles as Balfour's had been to Sweden? In order to be prepared for all eventualities several plans had been drawn up. In case Kirk's presence in Istanbul aroused attention, it was proposed that Moltke should fly to Cairo in a military aircraft. All the plans, however, proved to be of no avail, possibly because others might have become suspicious, possibly because Moltke refused to talk with strangers.

Moltke composed a letter to Kirk (p. 379) explaining why he insisted on a first contact with him and emphasized the German readiness to co-operate politically and militarily. He could come to Istanbul whenever he was wanted. This letter was taken to Cairo by the American Secret Service. The American Ambassador in Turkey refused to allow one of Kirk's intermediaries to take the letter personally; he was only ready to pass the letter on if Moltke agreed to a meeting with the American military attaché, Brigadier-General Tindall. The two men met in a private house without anybody else present a few hours before Moltke's return flight; the German intermediaries had secured the agreement of Tindall and Moltke to both the object and the venue of the discussion. It produced no results. Moltke was distrustful, while the American wanted information of a military nature, regarded Moltke as a secret agent and was unready to enter into any political discussion. Even so Moltke did not give up his plan. In the meantime another of the leading German emigrants, Ernst Reuter, had tried in vain to establish contact between Moltke and Kirk through the Dutch Ambassador. When Wilbrandt asked Moltke to stay for a few more days, he refused because he wanted to celebrate one more Christmas with his family. Bitterly disappointed, he left with the words: 'Now all is lost.'

Following this failure, the German contacts felt that the only way by which they could further Moltke's plan was to put it down in writing and to try and get it to Roosevelt through the American Secret Service. Wilbrandt composed a memorandum which Rüstow revised. The German text was translated into English and appears, in fact, to have reached Roosevelt. The latter is supposed to have asked the advice of Felix Frankfurter, who warned him that it was only a double game by the Germans. On the 10 January 1944 the German intermediaries received through the American Secret Service a note to Moltke from Kirk, written in his own hand, but bearing no date and no signature. Its text was as follows: 'I would always be glad to see you, but I do not see that any good purpose would be served by our meeting now as it is my personal conviction that nothing short of the unconditional surrender of the German armed forces will terminate the war in Europe'. There is no point in dwelling upon 'ifs', but a chance of shortening the war had been lost. In spite of all his disappointments it was still Moltke's intention to return within a few months to Turkey, where the American military attache was interested in pursuing the contact further. However, Moltke's arrest put an end to all such possibilities.

CHAPTER 14

Links with the Occupied Territories

The Kreisau Circle quite deliberately based their reflections of post-war foreign policy upon the assumption of European integration. It was therefore natural enough that they also should try, while the war was still on, to establish contact with other European countries. At a time of growing tensions brought about by German coercive measures, this was not so easy. It was indeed a basic presupposition of their collaboration, that all those involved viewed national socialism or fascism as a dangerous phase in European history and not as a movement confined to Germany. The common struggle for the supra-national values of Christianity, humanism and socialism would make a European structure and European co-operation possible and would effectively exorcize the dangers of totalitarianism. A further practical pre-supposition was that there were suitable intermediaries available who could establish these contacts and maintain them. Finally, only those belonging to the resistance movements were looked upon as representatives of these countries. The members of the Kreisau Circle believed that the future governments of these countries would be formed from the ranks of the members of the resistance.

The Kreisau Circle's reasons for co-operation were various. The long-term aim was a European federation of states, the United States of Europe. According to the Circle the autonomous nation state that had provoked tensions with other states no longer had a place—it ought not to be allowed to have a place any longer. In the light of this ultimate objective, all the contacts with other European countries during the war were part of a practical European policy, preparations for the construction of the new Europe. European policy meant for them, however, more than a political issue. 'For us,' Moltke wrote to Lionel Curtis during the war, 'Europe after the war is less a problem of frontiers and soldiers, of top-heavy organizations or grand plans, but Europe after the war is a question of how the picture of man can be re-established in the hearts of our fellow citizens. This is a problem of religion and education, of ties to work and family, of the proper relationship between responsibility and rights' (see p. 377).

Alongside this long-term aim there were also other motives, considerations of both a political and humanitarian nature, at that time no less important. For political reasons, they hoped that the contact would enable members of resistance movements in the occupied countries to give better information about the significance, the work and the difficulties of the German resistance movement to their allied partners and to commend the members of the German resistance as dependable collaborators. On humanitarian grounds, they wanted to find a way of warning the populations of the occupied countries about Gestapo acts of vengeance ordered from Berlin, the so-called penal expeditions (*Strafexpeditionen*). As the resistance movements grew in the occupied countries, so the actions of the Gestapo became more numerous and more atrocious; a well-timed warning could be of some assistance. In individual cases it was also possible to intervene and effect releases from prison and concentration camp.

NORWAY

The first occupied country in which the Kreisau Circle established links was Norway. They were the work of Steltzer, who was transferred to Oslo immediately after the German occupation as Transport Officer on the staff of the Commander of the Armed Forces in Norway. Steltzer had a somewhat independent position there. He was often in Berlin and Sweden where he had discussions with the Swedish railway authorities about the transport of men on leave. He managed to have several of his acquaintances appointed to his own department. Steltzer was on good terms with the Supreme Commander, whose powers were limited: he could do nothing, for instance, to prevent atrocities being committed on the orders of the Reich Commissar and he was even strictly forbidden to inform his military superiors in Germany about such incidents. Steltzer, however, managed to inform Moltke, who passed information on to his chief, Admiral Canaris. This link also had other uses.

Steltzer was soon able to establish contact with Norwegians. On one occasion he met the painter Henrik Sorensen, a close friend of Bishop Berggrav. The two men became friends and Sorensen made arrangements for Steltzer to talk to Berggrav. The bishop had long been interested in the struggle between national socialism and the German church, and he asked Steltzer about the experiences of the Confessing Church and about what could be useful for Norway in this experience. From this initial contact there developed a close personal friendship between Berggrav and Steltzer. As it soon proved necessary for Steltzer to be in touch with a Norwegian who could keep him regularly informed about specific situations and about public opinions, Sørensen introduced him to the sociologist, Arvid Brodersen, who spoke German fluently and who belonged to the leadership of the Norwegian Home Front. Steltzer also took part in discussons in a larger group at the home of Wolfgang Geldmacher, about the post-war situation in Europe and future relations between Norway and Germany.

When the Quisling government tried to extend its totalitarian organization to young people, the church had protested, and when the protest was dismissed, almost all the pastors of the State Church, under Berggrav's leadership, resigned their offices on Easter Sunday, 5 April 1942, gave up their salaries, and left their official residences. With this the tension reached a climax. The Quisling people were furious about this decision and arrested Berggrav, with the intention of treating him as badly as possible. Their plans were foiled, however, just in time. Steltzer had agreed with Moltke on a code word which he would use to report the arrest of Berggrav if and when it occurred. He sent the message, and immediately Moltke informed the highest military authorities. Canaris sent Moltke and Bonhoeffer on an official tour to Norway to assess the situation on the spot and to prepare a report for him. Bonhoeffer, a pastor of the Confessing Church and well-known as a theologian, had for a number of reasons become a civilian member of the Abwehr, and thus could travel as Moltke's companion. Arriving on 12 April they were very warmly received by the Supreme Commander, who had been a guest of Moltke's parents in the past. Several conversations were held and they were agreed in their assessment of the situation. Indeed, Moltke and Bonhoeffer were able to agree with all the military authorities concerned about the contents and objectives of their report to Admiral Canaris. The report, written by Moltke, came to the conclusion that the measures taken by the Reich Commissioner and the government did not coincide with the interests of the Armed Forces and indeed endangered them. Just what a close call it was can be seen from the fact that proceedings against Berggrav were intended to start on 13 April in a 'People's Court'. On the 16th he was released on orders from Berlin, and interned in his small country house at

Asker. As the guards were friendly disposed towards him, he was able, on occasions, to leave his cottage, dressed in the uniform of a policeman, for important discussions.

Apart from this official duty, Moltke also wanted to use his journey for a secret purpose. On the evening of the first day, following the discussions with the military authorities, a meeting took place at the home of the German industrialist Max Krohn, between the Germans, Moltke, Bonhoeffer and Steltzer, and three Norwegians, among them Sørensen and Brodersen. Via Berggrav's lawyer Larsen and Sørensen, Moltke received unsigned greetings from Berggrav, who was in prison. The reception was very warm. They had a thorough discussion about whether the Norwegian resistance movement should send an appeal through Berggrav to the King and more particularly to the Crown Prince, the present King, asking them to intervene with the Allies and propose that contact should be established with the German resistance movement. After extensive discussion this possibility was rejected, at least for the time being. They thought that the time was not yet ripe. Both sides were keen to develop the contact. On the next day, therefore, Moltke and Brodersen discussed further details. Discussions were also held with other Norwegians. Steltzer's adjutant, Schauer, who was a pastor in civilian life, arranged a meeting between Bonhoeffer and Moltke and Rector Alex Johnson, who gave them a pastor's view of the Norwegian situation. On 16 April Moltke and Bonhoeffer left Norway. On both the journey there and on the return home they used the opportunity to have a very wide-ranging discussion about the German situation and about the chances of the resistance movement. When Bethge met Bonhoeffer on his return to Berlin with his father's official car and drove him to Canaris to deliver his report, Bonhoeffer told him about his discussion with Moltke, but added: 'Unfortunately our views differ.'* Moltke, for his part, wrote to his wife that the conversations with Bonhoeffer were satisfactory.

That Moltke had more in mind with these Norwegian contacts than simply an exchange of information, can be seen from the fact that he spent an entire week there in September and that he had with him the notes that had served as the basis for the August discussions at Kreisau. The Norwegians were very surprised by the contents which were thoroughly discussed in their presence; it seemed scarcely credible that Catholics and socialist labour leaders

---

* Bonhoeffer's biographer Eberhard Bethge considers that this refers to the assassination attempt.

should have agreed on a common programme. During his stay in Norway Moltke was also able to meet Berggrav secretly.

In March 1943 Moltke was again in Oslo and once more had material with him, probably a summary of what had been discussed in the Circle in the previous months. He also had with him some broadsheets from the Munich Scholl Group, 'The White Rose'. These were translated into Norwegian by Brodersen and published in almost all the Norwegian resistance papers. On this visit Moltke also had a long talk with Berggrav.

The last time that Moltke was in Oslo was October 1943. Before his arrival he had spent two days in Denmark, warning Steltzer that the persecution of the Jews was about to begin in Norway. The latter arranged, with the help of the Swedish Consul, for the speedy granting of residence permits for Jews in Sweden. Moltke noticed that his Norwegian friends—and even Steltzer himself—were impatient, as the period of waiting had lasted so long. Since he did not receive a visa to travel in Sweden in time, Moltke remained in Norway until the date of his return to Germany. In the meantime he had a discussion with the SD-chief in Norway about the shooting of hostages, which was especially occupying his mind at that time.

THE NETHERLANDS

Fairly soon after the German occupation in May 1940 several sections of the Dutch population showed they were not going to acquiesce in the military defeat and its consequences. A report sent to the Church Foreign Office of the evangelical church in Berlin at the beginning of September 1940, described how a steady increase in passive resistance could be observed among the majority of the Dutch population and how this had already found expression in some sections in open hatred. Dutch officers, politicians and other leading personalities discussed the situation and the outlook. At the prompting of pastor Eykman a group was formed composed of individuals who represented various opinions and in which the lawyer Paul Scholten played a leading role. Some of them, especially Patijn and van Asbeck, helped in the formation of the World Council of Churches.

In connection with the work of this body, Dr. Hans Schönfeld, Director of the Research Section of the Ecumenical Council in Geneva, made regular visits to Holland, sometimes accompanied by Collmer. Officially they came in connection with prisoner-of-war work, but the chief purpose of their visits was to collect information for Geneva about the attitude of the Dutch and particularly of the churches. In spite of Visser 't Hooft's introduction, contact was at first rather difficult to establish. Schönfeld was astonished at the passionate spirit of resistance among the Dutch and thought that Holland's day as an independent state was over. Later he showed more understanding. He used to visit Holland about every four months, taking all sorts of risks upon himself. He also acted as a link between the Dutch and Bishop Berggrav in Norway.

In the summer of 1942 Schönfeld passed on a request from Visser 't Hooft that Patijn should receive a certain von Trott zu Solz who belonged to the East Asia section of the Foreign Office. Patijn agreed and Trott visited Holland from 5 to 9 December. This was clearly a new attempt to get in contact with the English government after the negative result of the memorandum which Visser 't Hooft had taken with him to London. Patijn, who did not want to receive Trott alone, asked van Asbeck, G. J. Scholten* and van Roijen† to join in the discussion at his home. On the day on which the discussion was to be held, Trott, whose arrival had been announced in the *Deutsche Zeitung in den Niederlanden*, had had talks with German officials.

Understandably the Dutch were rather cool at the beginning of the discussion. Trott began by remarking that they ought first to concoct an alibi for their meeting and he proposed, as the official purpose of their conversation, a consultation about Dutch prisoners-of-war in the Japanese camps. Surprised by his candour, the Dutch asked him what the real purpose of his visit was. His intention was, Trott declared, to make contact with reliable Dutchmen from opposition groups, in order to arouse 'good will' in case the group that he represented took over the government of Germany, and in order, secondly, to recommend to the Allies the names of certain reliable Germans. The Dutch agreed and began to trust him. For their own part, however, they asked him to give them, or arrange for them to be given, a sign if anything was going to happen and in addition to intervene with the German authorities on behalf of certain Dutch prisoners, who would be of special importance for the reconstruction of Holland. In this connection some names were mentioned, at which Trott reported that it was

* Son of Paul Scholten, who had met Trott at a Christian students' conference.

† At that time head of the diplomatic affairs department at the Dutch Foreign Office, but dismissed by the Germans; until 1970 ambassador in London.

occasionally possible to propose a person's release. He gave a detailed and sober description of Germany's predicament and described the composition and objectives of the German resistance movement. The contact man between Germany and Holland was to be a Herr von Goerschen who had already applied for Dutch citizenship before the war and who had frequently to make business trips to Berlin from his home in The Hague. He was a friend of Beck and had links with certain Abwehr officers, which made his travelling easier.

At Moltke's request his brother-in-law, Carl Deichmann, who had been Goerschen's secretary for a time, had arranged a meeting between Goerschen and Moltke before Trott's journey, so that Goerschen might take upon himself the responsibility for maintaining contact with the Dutch. The first meeting between Moltke and Goerschen took place in Berlin in the middle of November 1942, and after a brief period of reflection Goerschen agreed to take the part that had been assigned to him. When he was in Berlin he regularly discussed the situation in Holland and the contact with the Dutch with Moltke and Trott. After his first discussion Trott made three more visits to The Hague in August and December 1943 and at the beginning of July 1944, shortly before the attempted assassination. Meetings were usually held in Goerschen's office.

The Dutch never doubted the good will of this group, and were, therefore, all the more disappointed when Trott reported Churchill's negative attitude. Trott named Goerdeler as the head of the future German government, von Hassell as the future Foreign Minister and himself as von Hassell's State Secretary. In the course of a meeting at van Roijen's home, Trott read out a manifesto which was to be published after the *coup d'état* had been carried out. The Dutch were in complete agreement with its basic ideas.

At the beginning of June 1943 Moltke himself visited Holland in the course of his activity against the shooting of hostages. He had discussions with the Commander of the Armed Forces, Christiansen, with his Chief of Staff von Wühlisch and some other staff officers and with the SD General Harster in The Hague. Moltke also had a talk with van Roijen at Goerschen's office. The Dutchman made an extremely favourable impression upon Moltke, was ready to co-operate and, as Moltke observed, was able to distinguish between Germans and Nazis. Moltke expected a great deal from these contacts in the future and hoped that he could help this group by arranging the release of certain Dutchmen. At the end of his stay in Holland, in Brussels Moltke had another conversation with Goerschen about the talks with Harster and about what Goerschen should inform the Dutch about them. In September 1943 Moltke was once more in Holland.

Von Goerschen was in regular contact with the Dutch group and in particular with van Roijen. Discussions used to take place in Goerschen's office, about 5 o'clock in the afternoon. He passed on reports about German troop movements, changes in command, the current situation in Germany and military and economic information that might be useful in the event of transitional government in Holland. He also warned the Dutch about impending German measures, raids, house searches, etc. At the beginning of 1944, in the course of an official journey to Switzerland, he gave Visser 't Hooft a detailed report about the Dutch resistance movement for the government in London. On several business trips to Switzerland he passed on reports from the 'Fatherland Committee', which co-ordinated political resistance, and the 'Scholten Group' for transmission to London. He also offered his services as courier between Switzerland and the Netherlands to Alan Dulles, the representative of the American Secret Service in Switzerland, and his colleague Schulze-Gaevernitz. Goerschen who came from a well-known Aachen family—his father had been Regierungspräsident there—was personally acquainted with several of the German officers in Holland who came from the frontier region. This enabled him to provide his Dutch contacts with information.

Another of Goerschen's activities consisted of trying to arrange for the release of Dutch prisoners or to find out where they were being held. He tried to intervene in many cases and was sometimes successful. The persons concerned were political prisoners, prisoners-of-war and resistance people.

Although they lie somewhat outside the scope of this book, reference ought to be made at this point to the activities of the German Colonel Wilhelm Staehle in the Netherlands during the war, since Staehle appealed to von Trott in connection with his own contacts and knew of some of the Kreisau contacts in Holland through von Trott. Staehle's contacts and the report about these contacts written by members of the Dutch resistance for the exiled government in London, have been described by the author elsewhere.*

* See van Roon, *Wilhelm Staehle*, pp. 46–59 (Munich, 1969).

BELGIUM AND FRANCE

In September 1940 Count Moltke made an official tour to Belgium and France, which brought him into contact with the military commander of Belgium and the North of France, Alexander Freiherr von Falkenhausen. Before the war von Falkenhausen had been Military Adviser to Tschiang Kai-schek, and after its outbreak briefly Commanding-General in Dresden; in May 1940 he became Military Commander in the Netherlands but only for a fortnight, after which he was transferred to Belgium. Among the generals, von Falkenhausen was acknowledged to be a determined opponent of Hitler. In Belgium he was able to help many through his humane military administration and was in touch with the different groups in the resistance movement.

Falkenhausen himself had expressed the wish to meet Count Moltke as he needed his help with problems of international law. Moltke's brother, J. W. von Moltke, was ordnance officer under Falkenhausen and had drawn the general's attention to his brother. During Moltke's stay in Belgium he was able to have a long talk alone with Falkenhausen one night. They discussed the German spoliation of the country and its adverse economic and political consequences, and they assessed the situation very much alike. Falkenhausen told Moltke how he thought he should fulfil his function, and how far he was ready to co-operate. Moltke was very favourably impressed by him, being particularly pleased that the Commander was more concerned about the population than about his own position. Subsequent to these meetings Falkenhausen used to send Moltke the monthly reports on conditions in Belgium prepared by his staff. Moltke, for his part, advised him on several matters and sent him a memorandum on the problem of hostages.

Moltke visited Brussels several times in the following years, and had discussions with Falkenhausen and his staff. In June 1943 he was there again in connection with the shooting of hostages. During his visits Moltke also told Falkenhausen about his Circle. The General was in agreement with many of their ideas, and from then on Moltke kept him regularly informed about Kreisau developments (see also p. 151).

Trott, too, made several journeys to Belgium. He showed Falkenhausen several documents, including the map indicating the new administrative 'divisions' in Germany. As Falkenhausen himself had links with the Belgian resistance movement, it was unnecessary for Moltke to make contact. On one occasion, however, Mierendorff is supposed to have asked incidentally for Belgian help for the German resistance movement.

How much value Moltke attached to Falkenhausen's interest in the development of the Circle can be seen from the fact that Moltke tried to arrange a meeting in Aachen, in October 1943, between him and Franz Reisert, whom Moltke intended to recommend for the post of Justice. The meeting could not, however, take place, in the first instance because Reisert was prevented from coming, and later because Falkenhausen's Chief of Staff von Harbou committed suicide as he was about to be arrested by the Gestapo. Falkenhausen discovered, as a result of this incident, that he himself was being shadowed by the Gestapo. During his last visit to Brussels in September 1943 Moltke, deeply moved, is reported as having told Falkenhausen: 'In spite of all our scruples there is no other choice but to eliminate Hitler physically.' When Falkenhausen thereupon commented that the war must be ended as quickly as possible so that matters could be prevented from becoming still worse, Moltke replied: 'Yes that is true, but I think that the Germans must first go under completely.' At the time Falkenhausen would not admit this.

In 1942 Moltke wrote to Lionel Curtis in England (the full text is on pp. 376–77), 'After considerable difficulties we have established links with Christian groups in the various occupied territories, with the exception of France, where, as far as we can tell, there is no effective opposition based on fundamental principles, but only sporadic activity.' It ought to be remembered in this connection that there was no organized resistance in France before 1942. In the early period communist participation was relatively strong and conditions in the German occupied area were quite different from Vichy France. It is, nonetheless, a matter for regret that Moltke failed to establish sound links with the French resistance movement. We now know that there existed, among other things, a kind of discussion circle and it would have been important if Moltke could have had links with this 'Comité d'Etudes de la Delegation de la France Combattante'.

Moltke paid official visits to France on several occasions during the war. On 1 August 1940, he was still very much under the impression created by France's speedy collapse. It figures in his discussion with Yorck in 1940. Moltke, who in the winter of 1939–1940 had placed high hopes in the military strength of the Allies, was aghast at the failure of the French and their leaders. He observed regretfully that in spite of their superior weapons, the

French were deficient in morale; on his journey he detected this 'lack of backbone' everywhere. His disillusionment with France came out in an untypically extreme remark in a letter to his wife: 'It is impossible to live in a country where men have lost the courage and the will to work and where women have lost any trace of loyalty. This country can only recover under a Bolshevist régime after equality in poverty has prepared the ground for it.' The impressions made by this journey undoubtedly remained with Moltke for a long time.

It was Carlo Schmid* who enabled Moltke to have a fresh contact with France. They met in Berlin in October 1941. Schmid gave a lecture there at the Academy of German Law, during a conference organized by the Committee on International Law, and Moltke was among the audience. Both men felt that they did not really belong to this society and in the course of a conversation Moltke invited Schmid home for a meal. They had a far-reaching discussion and found that they were by and large in agreement. Schmid, a professor at the University of Tübingen, was a senior wartime civil servant and was responsible for the economic administration of the part of Northern France that was under Falkenhausen's authority. His base was Lille. As Moltke knew already he had often attacked the shooting of hostages and, at Schmid's request, Moltke promised to help him in this. A few months later Moltke visited him in Lille and they continued to keep in touch with one another in the years that followed. Schmid talked with Moltke about his relations with the French resistance movement and on one occasion introduced him to a Protestant clergyman who sometimes acted as an intermediary for him. Unfortunately the pastor can no longer remember the meeting.

In June and September 1943, Moltke was again in France in connection with the shooting of hostages. Paris was one of the places that he visited and here he urged several German Commanders to evade orders from the Führer that were contrary to international law. His visits were entirely taken up with these discussions. At one point he refers to 'our man in Paris', but it is impossible to know from this whether he refers to an official liaison officer, a contact man with the German military resistance groups in France, or a contact with the French resistance movement.

DENMARK

On 1 October 1943, on his way to Oslo and Stockholm, Moltke

* After the war the well-known leader of the West German SPD.

landed at Copenhagen. He broke his journey to give warning about an imminent raid on the Jews. An order from the Führer had fixed this for the following night. The Danish Jews had already been warned a few days earlier by the Danish resistance movement, but Moltke now brought official confirmation. During his time in Vienna he had met at the home of the Schwarzalds the Danish journalist, Merete Bonnesen; she was one of the foreign correspondents who had visited Silesia in the twenties at Moltke's instigation, in order to see for themselves the difficult conditions in that part of Germany. On arrival Moltke went straight to her home where he also met her brother Kim, another acquaintance of the Vienna days. He gave them the warning and Kim, who was a senior civil servant in the Ministry of Social Security, went immediately to the Foreign Ministry where he spoke to a senior official, a friend of his and a distant relative of his wife. He could therefore be sure that the latter would accept what he said without any further investigation and would pass on the warning to the highest level. Although the majority of Jews had already been hidden in the homes of friends, in hospitals, in old people's homes or elsewhere, one can assume that Moltke's warning was important. He stated specifically that the raid and deportation stemmed from an order of the Führer, which meant that they could not be circumvented. He also gave the precise time, which must have made an impression.

The warning was followed by a hideous night, during which Gestapo vehicles roared through the city and the sound of the raids could be heard everywhere. For several hours the Germans cut all telephone connections. When Moltke called on Kim early the next morning, the latter, still aghast at what had happened during the night, opened the door and saw a smiling Moltke before him who stretched out his hand and said: 'Kim, what a magnificent achievement. He [Hitler] wanted to get six thousand but he's not even got four hundred.' During his stay in Copenhagen Moltke also had discussions with the military and SD authorities there. When he was told on 1 October that the armed forces were to take part in the raid, because the SS detachment from Berlin was not large enough, Moltke answered the general: 'You must be mad. One day you will have to pay dearly for this. Don't you understand?' Both the Commander of the Armed Forces and the SD chief were well aware that the raid had created a great deal of trouble politically and they waited for a reaction.

POLAND

It was in Poland that Gestapo actions were most numerous and most ghastly. Moltke who had already frequently protested in his official duties against orders in Poland that ran counter to international law, asked Christiansen-Weniger who was responsible for agricultural and food problems in the Kreisau Circle, whether he would take over warning duties in Poland. Christiansen-Weniger was at the time in charge of agricultural research in the occupied areas of Poland, and in particular at the research institute at Pulawy.

As Christiansen, however, was too prominent officially and was regarded as politically unreliable by the Gestapo and kept under special observation, they both agreed that he should establish a link between Moltke and the church leadership in Cracow. He found an opportunity to do this in the Fisheries Institute at Cracow; for it happened that its adjoining fish ponds belonged to the church. Christiansen arranged that he himself should enter into official negotiations about the possible use of this pond for research work, which in turn led to an interview with the Cardinal, Prince Adam Stefan Sapieha. In the course of their conversation, which was very adroitly conducted by the Cardinal, he was able to present the request of the Kreisau Circle and to arrange for a visit by Count von Moltke. Shortly afterwards Moltke visited Cracow and was received by the Cardinal. He subsequently visited the research institute at Pulaway.

Unfortunately nothing more is known about the conversation between Moltke and the Cardinal. Whatever happened, Moltke told Father Rösch about it in Munich. Although the course of the conversation remains unknown we can be almost certain that it led to further contacts in Poland. It is said that Moltke had links with certain Polish groups that were trying to give part of the Polish resistance movement not so much an anti-German as a European and anti-totalitarian character. Moltke also talked about the possibility of providing these people with weapons.

AUSTRIA

Austria, for the Kreisau Circle, was one of the German states. Several individual members of the Circle had personal friends there, and all of them hoped that the Austrian population would declare in favour of a union with Germany after the war. Contacts had always been especially close between Austria and Bavaria, and after the Anschluss the Austrian socialists had declared in favour of co-operation with their German colleagues in bringing about a 'common revolution'. In the course of the war, however, and particularly after the Moscow conference of October 1943, it was clear that the Allies favoured the re-establishment of an independent Austrian state. This fact exercised a considerable influence on relations between the Austrian and the German resistance movements. The Austrians were more reserved in their dealings with the Germans, because they did not want co-operation with resistance groups in Germany to arouse suspicions that they were anxious to preserve a united state after the war. This development increases the difficulties of research today.

Like other German resistance groups, the Kreisau Circle maintained links with Austrians. Lukaschek, for instance, mentions that 'the Circle extended throughout Germany and Austria', and at another point talks of 'small discussion groups scattered over Germany and Austria'. In the remainder of this chapter we shall mention the names of Austrians and their German colleagues, but it is unfortunately impossible to give a comprehensive account of the co-operation that existed, or do more than piece together some of the contacts made.

In Berlin Mierendorff established a link between the Kreisau Circle and the former commissioner of Upper Austria, Gleissner, who, like Mierendorff, was employed by the Gestapo in the Braunkohlen-Benzin AG following their detention in concentration camps. Gleissner in turn introduced them to other Austrians who were living in Berlin, including Karl Gruber and Erich Mair. Of the Kreisau Circle itself, Gleissner knew, in addition to Mierendorff, Haubach, Reichwein, Moltke and Yorck and had numerous discussions with them. Haubach and Mierendorff were to have had a thorough discussion in Leipzig with Mair about Austro-German relations. However, when Mierendorff was killed in a bombing raid shortly before the scheduled date, Moltke asked Gleissner to continue to co-operate with the other members of the Kreisau Circle. Haubach joined in a number of discussions with Austrians at Gleissner's home in Berlin-Grunewald, where he himself lived after his own house had been bombed. He was well informed about conditions in Austria and the state of opinion. At his request Fritz Sänger sought out Heinz Paller in Vienna. It was in the latter's cellar that Goerdeler and Häcker held preparatory talks with Seitz, the Mayor of Vienna.

In addition to these socialist contacts there were also links with Austrian Catholics. Thus, for example, Rösch was in touch with Archbishop Rohracher in Salzburg. Moltke too had conversations with the Archbishop and probably received from him the names of reliable contacts, such as Rehrl, with whom Lukaschek, in particular, was associated. At Moltke's and Yorck's request Husen frequently held discussions with Austrians, including, for example, a former colonel whom van Husen saw probably in the summer of 1942 in Graz. The man in question was perhaps Nikolas Graf Uexküll, a former colonel in the Austrian–Hungarian army, who was a relative of Yorck. Another contact in Graz was the well-known professor of economics Taucher who had also been minister of Trade.

Delp was also in touch with Prelate Karl Rudolf in Vienna with whom von Trott too is said to have had discussions. Wilhelm von Cornides, the son of a publisher whose family were partners in the publishing house of Oldenbourg, approached Delp in May 1943 with an introduction from Rudolf. He was an Austrian and worked as an interpreter in the prisoner-of-war camps in South Germany. He had also numerous contacts in Vienna including links with the Circle round Otto Molden. Cornides planned a European publishing house which would call upon the help of a large circle of leading personalities and would support the work of renewal. A co-operative venture, it would uphold certain central values, and it was in this connection that he approached Delp and asked for introductions to suitable people. In addition to the publishing plans they also discussed the basic problems of post-war renewal. At one of their meetings Delp told him, very cautiously and without mentioning any names, about his links with the Kreisau Circle and he asked Cornides for help in establishing contacts between Austrians and members of the Circle. Cornides, for his part, gave Delp some Allied publications on post-war problems. Delp was very disappointed when he heard the negative reaction of the Austrians, who wanted their own state and thought of themselves as an 'occupied country'.

As relations between Austria and Germany became more tense, Moltke wrote: 'Haubach has greatly improved our reports about Austria. Things there look just about as bad as possible. The only comfort is that we seem to have the best possible man there. . . . Let's hope that the doctor will allow me to travel. . . .' At the end of August 1943 Moltke travelled to Graz via Munich. It is no longer clear whom he visited there. It could have been Uexküll or Taucher or even somebody else. It is by no means also impossible that he was still in touch with Austrian members of the former Schwarzwald group.

PART 4
INTERNAL AND FOREIGN POLICIES

Introduction

We will now describe the practical ideas of the Kreisau Circle, presenting them as answers to the problems posed by the events of the last decades before the forties. In each sphere, the particular answers to particular questions stemmed from essentially the same basic ideas.

At the beginning of 1941 when Moltke was pondering on bases for reconstruction, he attempted to summarize the current situation as follows: 'It is no exaggeration to say that everything that ought to be absolute has become relative. As a result things like the state, race and power which are entirely lacking in absolute value, have become absolute.' As this memorandum was composed at a time when the foundations for further work were being laid and the larger gatherings of the Circle had still to take place, it is not inappropriate to take these words as a starting point and *leitmotiv* for this part of the book.

The state and the other communal institutions had been greatly and increasingly abused, through the accumulation of powers in the hands of the state. Many functions that had been performed by individuals or smaller communities had been taken over; the very existence of a sphere of individual freedom and the value of the individual had been denied. The false absolutism of power, both political and economic, had led to coercion of the individual and the disintegration of his responsibility. The false absolutism of race had led to inconceivable atrocities and breaches of the law. The false absolutism of the state had also made contact with citizens of other states, and a right solution of international problems, more difficult.

The men of Kreisau also stressed in their documents the significance of the community. 'Justice', von der Gablentz wrote, 'does not simply mean to provide men with a sphere of freedom, but to provide men who have been trained in freedom with the possibility of creating a just social and economic life.' Another objective that they set themselves was reconstruction from below. Through decentralization and self-government responsibility ought to be transferred to the smaller communities. 'I think that the best administrative organization', Moltke wrote, 'is the one that allows the individual the greatest possible area in which to exercise his responsibility and to fulfil his urge to do something for others, and I also think that, outside the purely administrative sector, the most desirable order is one in which there is the greatest possible number of the smallest possible communities.'

That these leading ideas had implications for cultural policy, for the state, for the economic system and for foreign policy, will be clear. In the following chapters we will see in more detail what solutions the Kreisau members did propose and in what measure their proposals were really solutions. In their formulations there is not only a reaction to national socialist times; there also is a large amount of culture criticism, not always free from romantic and utopian thinking. Finally, we shall have to bear in mind the differences between the individual members in background and attitude. Naturally, the documents of the Circle show, as in all such cases, the character of a compromise; more important, however, is that Catholics, Protestants and social democrats here came to common solutions, at that time still a rare exception.

The Documents in Part 5 should be read in conjunction with Chapters 15–18.

CHAPTER 15

Cultural Policy

The Kreisau Circle held that each individual needed to be re-awakened to a sense of Christian commitment; only thus could he recover his liberty and sense of responsibility. The only living spiritual force in Germany that remained appeared to be Christian ideas; here was to be found the national starting point of new life in Germany after the period of utter spiritual destruction. The socialists, although not practising members of any church, agreed wholeheartedly with that idea. The first Kreisau conference in 1942 declared: 'We see in Christianity the most valuable source of strength for the religious–ethical renewal of the nation.' With this in view they needed and welcomed the co-operation of the also re-awakened churches. The only signs of opposition against national socialism were to be seen in church circles and in the worker underground. It should be the task of the organized churches to provide fundamental directives of faith for every zone of life; to steer the unfolding of society in the right direction. It was, however, no attempt to 'churchify' all of life and had nothing to do with 'clericalism'. In agreement with the churches the participation of clergymen in the political life was thought of as undesirable and to be avoided. Christian principles meant neither the oppression of other people with diverging ideas nor any infringement on their rights. Moltke made that clear in the following words: 'The state can simply guarantee the church room in which to act, but cannot confer upon it any monopoly or compulsory character, not even compulsory financial powers.' (*Neuordnung im Widerstand*, p. 519.)

The churches were considered extremely important and a healing power for social life. The opposite attitude was for the Kreisau members not possible or no more possible. For the Catholic members a society without the church was still an imperfect society, a society which was robbed of its real meaning and purpose. The Protestant members experienced the fateful consequences of the Lutheran doctrine of the two realms: the church existed all by itself in its own, self-enclosed realm, outside and above the lower realm of the state or society. Within the context of such a dualistic approach the pronouncements of the church were at the very outset prevented from effecting a fresh formulation of the fundamental principles of political life and the rest of society. When Hitler attained power, he began to dictate to churches and church leaders what they could and could not proclaim. Though several theologians tried to re-interpret church–state relations, the churches were in danger of becoming disciples of the state. Opposition assembled around the Pastor's Emergency League, the Confessing Church (of which Pastor Niemöller became a symbol abroad) and the relatively intact Churches of Bavaria and Württemberg under bishops Meiser and Wurm. They felt themselves compelled to wage a struggle both within and beyond the church. Karl Barth played a particularly important part in the work of re-thinking the relationship between church and state. The Bethel confession of 1934 defined church–state relations as follows: 'The secular authorities and the church are both of God. They are divided from one another by insurmountable frontiers and yet they are both entirely dependent upon one another.'

Among the individual members of the Kreisau Circle there was still considerable divergence of view about the nature of the church. Whereas it was, as we have already seen (p. 65), for Peters, the church's claims to lordship that were incompatible with the demands of the totalitarian state, von der Gablentz, at the very beginning of the Moltke–Yorck–Einsiedel–von der Gablentz discussion in 1940, favoured a separate existence for the church. There should be no link with the state—indeed it should be forbidden by law. It is typical of his opinion about the nature of the church, that for him the sacraments, prayer and meditation are essential and that the state in exceptional circumstances should be able to intervene, 'in order to prohibit in the church attitudes and doctrines that it would also prohibit among its ordinary citizens', a judgement which could have dangerous consequences. In a later letter, von der Gablentz stressed more the task of the church towards the state. The church could not withdraw from any sphere of life. The state must submit to the pronouncements of the church. The church is in a sense the natural censor of the state, and it is precisely the authoritarian state that requires such an objective independent authority. Because of fairness he adds: 'The contemporary church, however, is just as inadequate in these respects as the contemporary state.'

The letters exchanged between Moltke, Yorck, Gablentz and Einsiedel in the second half of 1940, prove how the Kreisau members favoured close co-operation between the churches. The hostility between Catholics and Protestants had been submerged by the 'common persecution at the hands of the national socialists'. The first statement of May 1942 welcomed the fact that two bishops representing the two major confessions had declared themselves willing to co-operate with the object of 'establishing a common position on the aspects of the Christian world view that affect the structure of public life'. In order to make Christian influence on public life even more extensive, Reichwein and Poelchau proposed the creation of an ecumenical lay organization. They hoped that this would overcome the differences between the confessions and provide a partner for the civil authorities at every level. The composition would be determined on lines similar to those applying to the civil representative institutions, starting from the parish level and working upwards. Their proposal has been included in the conclusions of the first Kreisau conference.

The churches were assured of autonomy and self-government. The state's oversight was to be adjusted to correspond with the altered circumstances, both in a material and personal sense, on the basis of historical development and established law. Church–state relations were to be governed by the law. Since 1933 a Reich concordat had existed between the Nazi State and the Vatican. Whether or not this was a right decision is still the subject of heated debate. In public life, at least, it gave the totalitarian state more freedom while providing little enough of a defensive line for German Catholics. At the first Kreisau conference Moltke and Yorck seem to have tried to persuade the Catholics to agree to an annulment of the concordat. The latter, however, especially Peters and Rösch, protested against this suggestion; in their opinion a concordat was a kind of international legal agreement and could not be annulled. They therefore decided to take the concordat as a starting point: 'The agreements in the concordat remain unaffected,' declares the protocol. Probably on Peter's proposal a similar agreement was also envisaged for the evangelical church. The status of the other religious and ideological communities was also to be established on a legal basis. Thus the Kreisau ideas on church–state relations went far beyond the 'limping separation' of the Weimar constitution. Taking the churches' distinctive rights as their starting point they aimed at a co-ordination and critical co-operation of church and state in solidarity with the new experiment.

There were significant differences of opinion between von der Gablentz and Moltke in 1940 over the relations of the state to education. Both naturally refused to allow total power to the state in the educational sphere, but Moltke was more positive in his assessment of the importance of the state, which, he declares, 'has to ensure that the people are instructed, that they receive at least a minimum amount of education and that influences contrary to the just order are kept out of popular education'. As for the content of education, the state should determine this only in exceptional circumstances. The Christian humanist von der Gablentz, however, paid particular attention to the responsibility of the churches in just this, though he was afraid that the churches were not awake to this, consequently it could happen that 'the new education which is astonishingly Christian in its results would supersede them'. Such a view seems hard to justify, even at that time.

National socialism had abused and manipulated education so much that it was necessary for the Kreisau Circle to begin again from the beginning. The true meaning and purpose of education was therefore a prominent subject at the first Kreisau conference. Education was to come through the school, the family and the church. Parental rights were to be strongly emphasized. The object of educational work was 'to determine the future attitude of the individual towards God and his active membership of the living and natural communities of family, profession and nation, parish, state and church'. The child should have a right to receive the education that is appropriate to his needs. Special emphasis was to be placed upon the value of learning for character formation. 'Character training produces an upright person of religious conviction who is able to adopt as the guide-lines of his behaviour, good morals and lawfulness, truth and sincerity, love for his neighbour and loyalty to his own conscience.'

The major churches would hardly be in a position to build their own schools in grand style after the wounds that they had received from national socialism, and in order for them to express their spirit of co-operation in the educational field as well, both the report on the conference and the 'Basic Principles' envisaged 'Christian community schools'. 'The state school is a Christian school in which religious instruction by both confessions is a compulsory subject.' The Catholic members of the Circle and the bishops whose advice was sought were evidently in agreement with this solution. The Kreisau Circle never declared the confessional school to be the ideal, although they naturally discussed it. They proposed Christian community schools that were to be really Christian as the highest attainable objective (see p. 330). At the end of 1943, however, Husen and Lukaschek in particular seem to have decided to support the establishment of confessional schools. Their decision was apparently prompted by Husen's last visit to Bishop Galen. It seems unlikely, however, that the Circle as a whole took up this position and if it did there would certainly have been some dissentient voices.

Technical schools and higher schools were to carry on from where the elementary schools left off 'by increasing the share of responsibility given to the pupil'. Existing textbooks were to be banned even if replacements were not yet ready. They were too thoroughly permeated by nationalist spirit. A uniform history book was considered feasible. This was a point to which the socialist members attached special importance as they knew full well what fateful consequences tendentious historical writing had had even before the national socialist period.

A striking feature of the findings of this first Kreisau conference is the determination to re-organize the existing universities into colleges of further education and 'Reich universities' (a term used by Hugo Preuss, father of the Weimar Constitution). The colleges of education which are to preserve the character of the existing universities are responsible for providing technical and academic preparation for the professions. The 'general guide-lines' give a list of the subjects that would be covered at these colleges: law, economics, medicine, arts subjects, natural sciences, education, agriculture, veterinary studies, forestry, engineering and mining. The churches themselves were to be responsible for theological training and there would therefore be no theological faculties. Every teacher at these colleges would be required to have a master's degree which would also mean that he had been at a Reich university. The observations mention that the question of teacher training is left open. The Kreisau members did not agree about whether this belonged to the colleges of further education or to the technical schools. Reichwein in particular advocated special colleges of further education for the training of elementary school teachers. His proposal was intended to guard against the dangers of a return to exclusive teacher training colleges, on the one hand, and complete incorporation into the universities on the other.

The Reich universities were to place the unity of research and teaching, 'the relationship with the whole of scholarship', in the foreground. The researcher–teacher was to be intellectually distinguished and possessed of a universal vision. The student had to produce a certificate of maturity from the classical gymnasium and must have completed his studies at a college of further education. He would thus have already proved himself in his subject. The twin aims of university studies were research and education. Every Reich university ought to include the traditional faculties and their basic disciplines. Over-specialization conflicted with the attempt to arrive at an intellectual synthesis. Specialization had its place in the colleges of further education. Living conditions at the universities were to be modelled on the Anglo-Saxon college pattern with integrated living and study quarters. The most suitable centres for universities were medium-sized towns in 'a lively and historically interesting district'. Autonomy and self-government were to be guaranteed. Only the first rector was to be appointed by the state and the first teachers would also be named by the state following recommendations by the rector. If the student was successful he would receive the master's degree from the university. This degree was to be an essential qualification for 'appointment to leading positions in public service' (see p. 331).

The Circle's ideas look like a compromise. The traditional university was not to be retained; the Circle only proposed a reconstruction. Their universities, however, were not to be devoted to vocational training; instead they made the universities into an upper tier for an élite. Links in personnel between the universities and colleges of further education were not envisaged. The links that did exist were intellectual, in that every teacher at a college of further education was required to have a master's degree. The Reich universities were not organized on the basis of the principle of insularity nor were they purely academic institutions; they possessed considerable significance for the public at large and particularly for the state. Their graduates were intended to be 'the knowledge and conscience of the state' but in a different way. It is legitimate to ask whether the Reich universities' dual function as research institutions and 'political' universities was not too hybrid in the traditional sense. Summing up, however, we may say that the Kreisau Circle attempted to provide a solution to the contradictions existing between the different functions of the universities by entrusting academic–vocational training to the colleges of further education and scientific, humanist and political education to the Reich universities.

The evil influences of national socialism had deeply penetrated everyday life. 'The means of expression', Moltke wrote, 'have been destroyed. Words have lost their unequivocal meaning, symbols no longer arouse a unified response, while works of art have been deprived of their absolute significance and, like all educational values, have been subordinated to expediency. They serve the state and in doing so they have lost their absolute significance and have become relative.' Following this analysis of the existing state of affairs he went on to outline the objectives for which they must strive: 'The individual must be re-awakened to an awareness of his inner commitment to values that are not of this world . . . Yes must again be Yes, and No, No. Good must once more be an absolute and evil likewise.'

In the paper that he read at the Kreisau conference Peters, too, placed strong emphasis on the essential role that cultural work would have to play in the reconstruction. National socialism could only be effectively overcome if it was overcome on the cultural level. Cultural matters and education should be transferred to the private sphere to a much greater extent than they had been hitherto. The state should not have a monopoly of culture. Fragmentation and specialization were the bane of cultural life. They ought to aim at a unified culture on an evolutionary basis. A unified culture would prepare the way for a European civilization and the return of Germany into the family of nations. Any synthesis ought to allow for the five basic elements in western civilization: antiquity and humanism, Christianity, rationalism, romanticism and technology. As Christianity was a constructive force, it was important that Christians and churches should share in the work of reconstruction. In any event, Christians themselves and very many who rejected Christianity as such shared the same basic views on ethical, cultural and spiritual problems. Decentralization and self-government ought to provide the basis for cultural activity.

For the section of his paper that dealt with the Press, Peters asked for help from Professor Emil Dovifat of Berlin University, who outlined a form of provisional Press organization referring back to the last democratic draft law on the Press of 1932. He proposed that the system of professional democratic press chambers envisaged then should become part of the new press law. These were to be independent of the state, with their independence guaranteed by laws similar to the old laws of the estates of the realm, and drafted by the profession itself. A system such as this would make it possible to recruit trustworthy democrats for the work of reconstruction. Dovifat had particularly in mind former journalists in the Catholic press, in the democratic papers, both SPD and middle class and in the so-called 'commonplace press'. This would be the first step towards a free press; and in fact a short press law was drafted, on the lines of 1932, to be included in the provisional regulations.

For broadcasting it was proposed that 'advisory councils' should be appointed composed of representatives of political and cultural groups. They would be responsible for keeping in touch with the public and recruiting voluntary help from among the public. It was hoped to develop the advisory council that had already existed in the regions before 1933. In those days they had been rather inappropriately called 'political supervisory committees'. Their place in the scheme indicated an intention of drawing broad sections of the public into active participation in the reconstruction of the broadcasting services. To guarantee an evolution in this direction, the state should use its influence in cultural matters during the period of transition.

The 'First Instructions to the Provincial Commissioners' included orders to prepare the way, in co-operation with the acknowledged cultural leaders of the country, for a reconstruction of Christian education and, through it, a genuine renewal of spiritual and intellectual life. For this task it was most essential that the land and church should co-operate. The 'Basic Principles' of the reconstruction only repeated the statements on culture in the Kreisau protocol. Mierendorff's action programme shows that the socialist members agreed with this emphasis upon Christian renewal: 'Respect for the foundation of our civilization which is inconceivable without Christianity.'

CHAPTER 16

The State

The rise of national socialism and the Nazi seizure of power brought into prominence an entirely new kind of political theory, the idea of the 'totalitarian state'. Making use of the numerous authoritarian ideas of the period, but going far beyond them, the national socialists subordinated all spheres of life to the state and demanded a complete co-ordination (*Gleichschaltung*) of the life and thought of all citizens. Ideas such as this were incompatible with the preservation of specific rights for individuals.

Experience in the totalitarian state influenced the men of Kreisau in their discussions about the proper role of the state and about the relation between the individual and the state. They did not fall into the equally one-sided approximation of liberalism, but gave an increasingly central position to personal freedom and respect for human dignity, though differences between the individual members of the group remained visible. Surviving traces can be found, however, of earlier attempts at reform, sometimes mixed with examples of 'cultural despair', a continuation of the ideas and plans for giving the state a new face which were propounded by the young conservatives at the end of the Weimar Republic.

When von der Schulenburg, Yorck and Moltke discussed recent developments at the beginning of June 1940, following the victorious western offensive, they wondered how long they would have to endure the national socialist state. Schulenburg was prepared to bet that within ten years there would be a state of which they could completely approve; Moltke could not be so optimistic. They then discussed what would be the most important distinction between such a state and the existing one, and Moltke suggested that its most outstanding characteristic would be justice. But how did justice manifest itself in the state? They agreed on the following definition: 'Justice can be said to exist when each individual is able to develop and express himself fully within the framework of the state as a whole' (see p. 292). Moltke's emphasis here on the freedom of the individual is typical for him, and he stresses it against the background of the dangers of centralization of power in the twentieth-century state. In a somewhat idealistic sketch of European evolution since the Middle Ages, Moltke asserted: 'None of these other ties, however, has had sufficient coherence to make a claim on the whole man in the way that the state finally did and has done in this century. . . . The sense of inner commitment to the state has been replaced on the one hand by something similar to the herd instinct—to mutual association for security—and, on the other hand, by control and coercion of the individual. This process has deprived the individual, who has lost his sense of obligation, of his freedom.' In this quotation two examples of romantic thinking are visible. The past is idealized and all that developed after it condemned. Further the sense of inner commitment to the state—typical of the Prussian upper class families to which Moltke belonged—was not always free from an identification with the state in a bad sense. But, though not always correct in details, Moltke's emphasis on the freedom of the individual is still more important. Moltke was, however, quite certain that this freedom could not be re-established immediately after the collapse of the régime. Though it must be the objective to remedy this lack of freedom as quickly as possible, the state according to Moltke would have to begin with a very heavy 'security'. People must first be educated in freedom. A kindred thought came from the German philosopher Karl Jaspers after the war when he was asked by an American for his views on the plan to set up Land Parliaments. 'You ought not immediately to put such great tasks on men who are politically children or politically deprived. Political education must proceed step by step.' It was a balance that it would be very difficult to secure. Would not those who had been deprived of their freedom by the Nazis think that they were being handed over to a new coercive régime? In stressing that the object of the state was to protect the individual's freedom, Moltke's understanding of men is influenced by idealistic thinking while his repeated emphasis upon reason indicates a secular humanist foundation.

The above-mentioned discussion with Schulenburg and Moltke did not, however, entirely satisfy Yorck, who knew more about the subject of the state administration than Moltke. He felt that the given definition would allow the individual too much freedom and that this could have adverse consequences for the state. Asked by Moltke to work out his point of view, Yorck wrote in a later letter, that these questions were concerned 'with the discovery of the substance of national and state life and the form that is appropriate to the substance'. This discovery, he maintained, assumed 'a knowledge of previous developments' and of the 'spiritual driving forces that have together and in conflict with one another shaped history'. Yorck's first comments reveal already something of his basic position. A representative of the Prussian conservatism, he described historical developments in irrational, Ranke-like terms. He was concerned to clarify the much used term 'freedom' and he stressed the relationship of the individual and the community. His opinion was that freedom ought to be 'freedom for others'. However, just as the individual was limited by law and duty in his relations with the individual he should not be exposed to the arbitrary political will of the all-powerful state. The will of the state must also submit to moral demands. As the state according to Yorck was 'an instrument of divine order', he favoured a positive approach to it.

Moltke, however, doubted whether the state was subordinate to a moral command 'I am inclined to the view that ethics are related to the individual'; for him Kant's words are valid: 'Act in such a way that your action could be taken as a universal standard.' He added in a later letter to Yorck: 'I cannot see any ethical principles that are valid for anything beyond human relations. If we maintain that the state is a moral personality, we are, I believe, on the way that leads via Hegel to a deification of the state.' Moltke also had reservations about the idea of the state 'as an instrument of divine order'. He believed that political science belonged to the sphere of philosophy and not to that of theology, although he later took it for granted that the individual's conception of the state was determined by his basic attitude and that his attitude was itself decisively influenced by his faith, his understanding of history, and his spiritual education. In order to clarify his position, Yorck sent Moltke a paper, *The Image of the Western State*, but it did not convince Moltke; he found it romantic and its ideas obsolete.

The views of Einsiedel's acquaintance, von der Gablentz, were next canvassed. An expert in this field and an exponent of Christian humanism, he held the view that political science could only be substantiated by theology. On the other hand he stressed that there is no theological doctrine directly relating to the state, only to men within the state. According to von der Gablentz the state is amoral because it is abstract; when concerning himself with men one is dealing with the concrete statesman. This special attention paid to the 'statesman' is typical of the discussion; which is not always free from 'élite' thinking.

When the three met face-to-face Moltke and von der Gablentz were able to convince Yorck that the state was not governed by any ethical precepts, that theology and political science were separate disciplines and that there was therefore no such thing as a Christian state. They agreed on the following definition: 'The purpose of the state is to provide men with the freedom that enables them to perceive the natural order and to contribute to its realization'. In this way they were able to indicate that the individual was bound by the somewhat vague and obsolete idea of 'natural order'. Thus, Yorck's insistence upon a 'security' was in fact upheld. In the light of their discussions Moltke produced a treatise *The Foundations of Political Science*, which he discussed with von der Gablentz and Einsiedel and at another time with Yorck. On the basis of their observations he made appropriate changes. It appeared that von der Gablentz when talking about the relation between the state and the individual placed the law more in the foreground, while Moltke emphasized the promotion of education. Typical for Moltke's attitude in this matter is also his remark to von der Gablentz: 'I agree with you that there are such things as minimum human rights but they mainly belong to the sphere of the economy and the others I regard simply as a prerequisite to education.'

A brief analysis of the ideas of Peters and Steltzer is also called for because they too were frequently consulted about these problems. Peters gave a Catholic viewpoint on the totalitarian state in an essay published in 1936. In it he refuted the opinions of the national socialists, and in particular those of Carl Schmitt and his pupil Ernst Forsthoff, but also the ideas that lay behind the liberal constitutional state. If he does not rule out a universalist conception in principle, he affirms that the individual has his own personal sphere and sets the significance of the individual in the foreground. 'If the church too gives precedence to the common good rather than to the individual's interests when a conflict arises between them it nonetheless demands, starting as it does from natural law, that the independence of the individual and therefore his freedom of action must not be set aside. It makes these demands because it is the individual and not the community who has to render an account before God. . . . The complete absorption of the individual into the community and the idea that the individual's right to exist is only derived from the community, leading logically as they do to the completely totalitarian state, contradict the natural order and are rejected by the church.'

Steltzer gave a public statement of his ideas on political theory shortly before the Nazi seizure of power. Here we are confronted by a different set of ideas. He strongly emphasized the role of the nation in contrast to the limited functions of the state. For him it was not the individual who stood at the centre, but the nation and the classes (*Stände*). He recognized the importance of the individual's roots in the nation, but he made them absolute. He rejected liberalism and supported the ideas of Rudolf Smend about integration. For Peters it was the church's claims to lordship that were incompatible with the demands of a totalitarian state, for Steltzer it was the nation's totalitarian demands. 'The state can never be an end in itself. It derives its function, its limits and its justification only in its relationship with the nation which it has to serve. . . . Every nation is a special thought of God.'

As the basis for a renewal of the state had already been clarified in the early years of the Circle's existence, the Kreisau documents themselves mostly contained proposals for the work of reconstruction. Only isolated statements allow us to see that the line laid down at the beginning was still being pursued. The texts of the Kreisau conferences place strong emphasis on the importance of the people participating in and sharing responsibility for the political life of the state. The summary of the third conference speaks of the destruction of the totalitarian hold over the freedom of conscience and the recognition of the inviolable dignity of the human person as the foundation of the legal and international order that they ought to be aiming at. The 'First Instructions to the Provincial Commissioners' stress legal security, personal freedom and a general share in responsibility for all the inhabitants of the land. All laws that discriminate against an individual on account of his membership of a particular nation or race or religion are no longer valid; discriminatory measures based upon these laws are to be abrogated forthwith.

In conclusion, one can say that the political theory of the Kreisau Circle combines elements from both the individualist and universalist traditions.

There are only isolated clues as to the views of the Kreisau members on the constitution of the German state. At several points stress is laid upon the need for strong authority; at the same time their state model is that of a 'basic democracy'. Although fundamentally committed to the political freedom of the individual and of the nation, they wanted, with the help of the selection principle, to place the best in the nation at the head of the state. It is in this light that we should interpret Moltke's remark to Horst von Einsiedel: 'For the purpose of illustration we assumed that state had an aristocratic constitution. . . .' Such thinking was in line with the views of the young conservatives before 1933. A more acceptable starting-point is found in Moltke's *Foundations of Political Science* (p. 310). 'We must first establish what the substance of the state is—what it is from which the state derives its life and that distinguishes it from a large organized group. If this substance is clearly recognized, it can be developed under any form of constitution.' This comment is also in line with the most modern thinking on constitutional problems.

As Moltke and indeed the whole of the Circle believed that the correct solution to the German problem would only be discovered within the context of a European development, and as they regarded the re-introduction of the monarchy as reactionary, we must refute the suggestion made now and then that the Kreisau Circle were very sympathetic towards a restoration of the monarchy. Hassell's notes in his diary on a conversation with Trott indicate that the latter rejected the monarchy because of co-operation with the socialists. It is highly improbable that the socialists as a group would have agreed to a monarchial solution, and it is hard to reconcile such a solution with the contents of Mierendorff's proclamation.

There was at least one point on which anybody reflecting on the Reich–State problem during the war had to be clear: the dominant historical trend since Bismarck's day and particularly in the Weimar and Nazi periods had been in the direction of a unitary solution. There could not fail to be a reaction against this trend, not least because distaste for national socialism included distaste for the measures carried out by the Nazis. For the men of Kreisau in particular, their emphasis upon the importance of the individual and of small communities (see p. 348) was another factor of obvious relevance to their discussions of this problem.

Before the Circle discussed these problems at one of the larger conferences and arrived at a common decision, several individuals were asked to consider them. Lukaschek, for example, mentions that Moltke asked him in the course of 1942 how the federalization that was needed could actually be achieved. How were they to create states that could preserve their own distinctive life while conceding to a federal government at the very top responsibility for foreign affairs, defence and finance? The actual implementation of the basic idea was nevertheless no easy matter. Whereas the Länder west of the Elbe had been independent states in the past, some of those to the east of the river had never developed organically.

The relations between the Reich and the Länder were discussed at the second Kreisau conference in October 1942. The basic principle was that there should arise after the war great economic supernational territories. As a necessary counter-balance the political territories had to remain small. The great national states should delegate their sovereign competences upwards and downwards. This principle meant that anything that could sensibly be done by the Länder ought to be done by them. This principle is also in line with Catholic 'subsidiary' ideas and with ideas of an organic state structure. Although it meant that the centre of gravity would shift to the Länder, the principle also indicates that there was no intention of creating a completely federal state. The Länder would have each between three and five million inhabitants. This arrangement aimed at making each Land capable of effective self-government. It would also make them generally viable. Neither the former states nor the national socialist provinces (*Gaue*) were taken as the basis for determining the size of the Länder, but historical, cultural, economical factors and factors of communication. A maximum of five million inhabitants meant that Prussia, 'an artificial construction', would have to be broken up. A proposal for the dissolution of Prussia, however, would also entail the dissolution of Bavaria, with their 'casual conglomeration of territories'. This met with vigorous protests from the Bavarians (see p. 156). In accordance with the general principle and in contrast to national socialist practice it was decided that the Land government would be responsible for performing the Reich functions within its own territory. As we shall see at another point, the importance of the Länder was also underlined by the increased powers of the Reichstat. That socialist distaste for the Nazi régime made them sympathetic towards the federal system can be seen from Mierendorff's demand for a 'dismantling of Bureaucratic centralization and the organic construction of the Reich on the basis of the Länder'.

Schulenburg in particular dealt with the re-organization of the Reich. At his request proposals for a re-arrangement of frontiers were prepared in the Reichsstelle für Raumordnung (Reich Office for Territorial Planning). The official purpose of the exercise was a readjustment of agricultural marketing zones. On one occasion he represented his special section, 'The division of the Reich', in the Kreisau Circle. It was probably on the basis of this discussion that several copies of a map showing the proposed arrangements were prepared, apparently by König. The map (Countess Yorck and van Husen possess surveying copies) shows the following nineteen Länder: Schleswig-Holstein with Mecklenburg, Hannover, Westphalia with Düsseldorf and Oldenburg South, the Rhineland, Baden, Württemberg, Saarland, Hessen with Pfalz, Kurhessen with Thuringia, Brandenburg, Saxony, Frankia, Bavaria, Austria including the northern Tyrol, Pommerania, Wartheland, Silesia, Danzig and West Prussia, East Prussia. No decision was ever taken about the map: it was only discussed.

The Kreisau proposals for the structure of the Reich had certain striking features: the significance of civil or human rights, the idea of small communities or voluntary associations, of local self-government communities, the concept of basic democracy and the attitude towards political parties.

In his 1941 memorandum, *Starting point*, Moltke emphasized that freedom of the individual should be one of the essential points in any programme of political reconstruction. He did not, however, intend this freedom to be understood as an absolute right. 'The provision of freedom is, therefore, to be understood as something done for the individual which obliges him to strive for self-restraint' (see p. 320). Everybody ought to be given the opportunity to do something useful for the community. In association with such activity Moltke proposes, with more idealism than realism, that such activity should be bound up with the grant of certain political rights, e.g. active in the case of election rights, passive in holding public offices, etc. Activity of this sort should not be what an individual does in the normal course of duty but should be honorary, another proposal that did not match modern times. A drafted list of problems includes the following: 'What can be done to demonstrate our intention of protecting life and limb of the individual?'

In order to underline the differences between the new administration and the totalitarian state, the 'Basic Principles for the Reconstruction' began with general principles which gave an idea of the general objective of the new government: Legal security, the guarantee of freedom of belief and conscience, acknowledgement of the inviolable dignity of the human person as the foundation of the legal and international order that is to be aimed at, public protection of the family, encouragement of every individual's

personal political responsibility, a share for each individual in
self-government of the small and manageable communities that
were to be revived. 'Rooted and proved at this level, he must share
in the decision-making of the state and the international community through his own elected representatives. In this way he is
given a strong sense of sharing responsibility for political activity
in general.'

Moltke more than anyone else was responsible for working out
the idea of the small communities or voluntary associations. The
solution that Moltke offered to the dangers of centralization of
power in the state was the concept of the pluralist society—one in
which there are several sources of power other than the state. He
thought that he saw in the voluntary association a significant source
for a pluralism of power. These were to create active sources of
political engagement, experience and training for citizens. They
were also to generate new centres of power that could contest both
among each other and with a limited state for a basis of a democratic consensus.

Moltke realized that a mass of unorganized aggregates of individual citizens could never counter the centralized power of the
modern state. Intermediate political organization and cultural
associations that had free access to the mass of citizens and opportunity to organize them to engage in political contest or cultural
achievement, would be a guarantee of a democratic society. 'In
relation to the large community, to the state, or to even larger
communities,' he wrote in 1939, 'the only person who will have
the right sense of responsibility is the person who bears some
form of responsibility in smaller communities. Where this is
lacking, these who are only ruled will come to feel that they
have no share in events and are not responsible for what happens,
while those who only govern will come to feel that they, as the
ruling class, are responsible to no-one.' There must be a decisive
break with the authoritarian state (*Obrigkeitsstaat*); it should be
essential that the individual citizen should be intimately involved
in the life of the state. Therefore, it should be important to develop
the administrative system that gave the individual the greatest
opportunity to feel responsible. According to Moltke the worthiest
objective should be 'a social order with the greatest possible
number of the smallest possible communities'. By this he did not
mean interest groups but communities dedicated to aims of common concern, e.g. a voluntary fire service, an association founded
to keep the block of flats clean, to care for the gardens and to run a

communal *Kindergarten*, a society to purchase and maintain community institutions, an association for the preservation of natural beauty, scientific and cultural associations, etc. He wondered how the state could profit from these communities, what could be done 'from above' to advance these associations and to restrict others that created 'positions of power from which to push through their own private interests at the expense of the community as a whole'. In detail this idea was worked out and later documents also mentioned them.

To further the sense of responsibility of the citizens was an important question, but in modern times much of the work was done by qualified, paid men. How was the average man going to be able to spare the time to devote himself to this task? Only in marginal and subsidiary cases could there be talk of it. Further, the mere fact of a multiplicity of associations in a society does not necessarily provide the conditions of pluralism that alone can assure the survival of personal freedoms. The population of a society could be organized into a set of associations that merely served the interests of the state as in the times of national socialism and could be abused by the state as was the case then. What was required was a multiplicity of affiliations, wherein no one group demanded the whole lives of its members. Thus trade unions had members of various ethnic and religious groups, churches cut across class lines, and political parties drew from a heterogeneous range within the population. Such extensive cross-cutting affiliations prevented, according to a recent book by William Kornhauser, one line of social cleavage, such as class, from becoming dominant.* Moltke is proved to have been very right in seeing that an essential condition for a democratic society was the existence of a number of autonomous secondary associations which reduced the vulnerability of their members to domination by elites. Against the state, there was also the possibility that the administration could be controlled by independent administrative courts.

The principle of self-government from below, including the ideas of Freiherr von Stein, occupied an important place in the thinking of the Kreisau Circle. The reforms of Stein at the beginning of the nineteenth century aimed at bringing Prussia into line with the general liberal trends of Western Europe. Even though French and, still more, English ideas exercised an important influence on him, Stein was concerned to mould the reforms to suit conditions in Germany. He tried to preserve and revive

* *The Politics of Mass Society* (New York, 1968), p. 230.

patterns of communal public life with which he had become acquainted in Westphalia and which, though somewhat romantic, also had a clear educational function. Owing to the rise of Prussia Stein's reforms were not widely implemented. Even in 1918 the proposals for self-government were only effected in the social and economic sphere; the power of the central authorities increased during the Weimar period. Alongside the Land government offices there grew up a network of medium level and low level Reich offices. There were even Reich self-governing bodies. This led to a reaction. At the Heidelberg party conference of 1925 the S.P.D. pledged itself to decentralized self-government. From other sides the idea of self-government and generally of an organic structure of the state was preferred above the parliamentary system. A prominent lawyer like Hans Peters preferred the system of self-government for the protection of minorities to a radical democracy which in his eyes was one-sided. It was also in line with the Catholic conception of 'subsidiarity'.

In the documents of the Kreisau Circle, but not only there, the idea of self-government re-appears. Moltke wrote in detail about it. Whereas according to him the state, apart from possible financial help, ought to have no direct link with the smaller communities, by contrast the link between the small communities and the self-government bodies—rural, parish, country, town and province—ought to be very close and activity in the small communities ought to be seen as a form of practical experience and preparation for work in the self-government bodies. In the documents of the Circle the principle of self-government has been worked out in the directions about the structure of the Reich.

The history of self-government in Germany and especially that during the Weimar Republic shows, however, that the chances for such a system were no longer so bright. Intended as a counterbalance against the authoritarian monarchy, it lost much of its significance with the disappearance of the monarchy in 1918. The interest of the citizens in this system diminished also. Meant particularly as a reaction against the growing bureaucracy, only a small part of the citizens, an upper middle class, took an active part in it and instead of a fall in the number of civil servants, there emerged a new group, those of the public authorities. For the average citizen the difference between these two groups was not even clear and all together they were considered and criticized as bureaucracy.

That the men of Kreisau were serious about building from

below, can be seen from the electoral regulations for the various representatives institutions. The starting point lay in the communities that were 'within the individual's range of vision'; the parish and the subordinate divisions of the towns independent of the countries. Here everyone who was over twenty-one or who had fought in the war was to have the right to vote, and anybody who was over twenty-seven and whose candidature was agreed upon by a certain number of voters could be elected.

Members of the armed forces could be elected. The second level was formed by the counties and the towns independent of the counties. Their representative institutions were to be directly elected in accordance with the same principles governing the representative institutions of the local communities. The Land came next. The Landtag and the City Assembly in the Reich cities were to be elected by the representative bodies of the counties and towns independent of the counties or, in the case of the Reich cities, from the representative assemblies in the political subdivisions. Political civil servants as well as members of the armed services were ineligible for election at this level. At least half of those elected should not belong to one of the electing corporations. The Reichstag, at the highest level, were to be elected by the Landtags and the same special regulations applying to the Landtag elections apply here also. This system of basic democracy with their indirect elections would, it was hoped, counteract the dreaded influence of central government. It could, the men of Kreisau believed, produce a Reichstag whose members possessed the greatest expert knowledge and experience and who constituted a political elite in the true sense of the word.

The Circle's effort to establish genuine authority can be seen in the regulations covering the highest offices in both the Reich and the Land. Both the Reich Commissioner and the Land Commissioner had to guarantee continuity and, in addition, the Land Commissioner was responsible for carrying out Reich policies in the Land; both of them were to be elected by the respective electoral bodies for twelve years. The person politically responsible to the Reichstag was the Reich Chancellor who could be removed by the Regent of the Nation or by a constructive vote of no confidence in the Reichstag. At the Land level the comparable figure was the Chief Minister who was to be elected by the Landtag. These regulations were intended to prevent a conflict between the authorities and the people in their representative assemblies. In the Reich Government the only other ministers were to be departmental ministers, and the Land government privy councillors, who were to be nominated by the head of the Reich or, at the Land level, by the head of the Land on the basis of proposals from the Chancellor or Chief Minister. This fact confirms the impression that the government was intended to be a well-balanced 'team' whose harmony should not be destroyed by changes in personnel. By providing for ministers who were experts in their own departments, the Kreisau Circle also hoped to create a safeguard against bureaucratic control. Instructed by the lessons of the Weimar Republic, they wanted to avoid a 'double government'; the legislature should not have to fear legislative competition from the executive. Another important feature was the disciplinary authority of the Reich Council or Land Council over the members of the government. They were intended to exercise a judicial oversight over the individual ministers. The composition of the Reich Council was meant to safeguard the federal character of the constitution.

In the author's view only in exceptional cases in modern times can a system like 'basic democracy' be applied; the collapse of the Nazi régime was just such an opportunity. This system, however, was provisional and had to be replaced in due course by one involving direct elections on all levels. Yet there is in the documents of the Circle no evidence that their proposal bore a provisional character. The Kreisau group also underestimated the influences and the possibilities for abuse at the top and could have increased the distance between citizens and government and governed instead of diminishing it. Moltke's basic principle of educating the citizens is institutionalized here within a state structure with some doubtful features. Might it not for that reason even hamper the realization of Moltke's aim?

Finally, a study of these particular proposals reveals no mention of political parties. This is not because their existence was taken as a matter of course; on the contrary, many members of the Kreisau Circle disliked them. They identified the growing pains of parliamentarism in Germany with the system as such. Older members, like Steltzer, took a romantic anti-liberal attitude and saw political parties as breakers of the unity of the nation; they brought the political divisions into the villages, as the phrase goes. Nor, as we have already seen, were political parties any more popular with the younger members. A declared supporter of the Weimar Republic though Moltke was, he did not believe in them; thus only the negative aspects of them were stressed. We must concede, however, that the proliferation of parties during the

Weimar years made it none too easy to discover the positive features. Even many social democrats were against bringing back the political situations of Weimar, and Mierendorff included in his summons the slogan: 'Never again will the German people lose their way in party conflicts.'

On the other hand we do not find in the Kreisau documents any explicit declaration that political parties were undesirable such as occurs in other documents of the German resistance. Further, Haubach was certainly asked by Leuschner to prepare a re-organization of the S.P.D., and those men of Kreisau who survived did in fact join political parties directly after the war. Indeed the attitude taken towards the trade unions suggests that few members of the group would have objected to parties provided that they were built up from below.

CHAPTER 17

The Economy (Including Agriculture)

The economic system must not be considered as an end in itself. Neither is it the exclusive concern of the state. The discussions in the Kreisau Circle sought for a middle way between these poles. They regarded the economy as an instrument with which human beings can shape the external conditions of their life or, as Gablentz has put it, with which they can 'responsibly shape the natural world'. It is men who are the initiators in this process of organization and because they take the initiative, because they are the subjects who control the economic system rather than the objects of its control, they require a social order which allows them their true status as beings who, in the truest and noblest sense, are made in the image of God. But to describe this social order as 'free' is inadequate. Freedom can be interpreted as arbitrariness, as unfreedom for others. A better word is 'responsible', used in several Kreisau Circle documents. Responsibility assumes an obligation towards the community but it does not set freedom aside or twist it into collectivism. Every 'responsible' social order ought to develop between the two poles of freedom and obligation; it is not a case of 'either . . . or' but of 'both . . . and'. 'This approach shows the influence of Catholic ideas, as expressed in *Quadragesimo Anno* and other papal statements, as well as a reaction against the excessive claims which national socialism made for the state.'

Reacting against the liberal lack of order and the national socialist compulsion to order, the men of Kreisau demanded that the aim of social policy should be to place men once more at the centre of events and to guarantee them the opportunity to develop as individuals. Personal freedom and respect for human dignity must occupy the central position, or as Moltke himself put it: 'The object of economic activity must be to make the individual person freer by liberating him from subordination to the natural world. The object must not be to diminish his freedom by replacing his dependence upon the material world by a dependence upon men —a dependence which is just as great when it relates to an employer as to an official' (see p. 291). Delp wrote in a similar vein in his *Dritte Idee.*

Such an objective requires vigorous forms of corporate life and corporate activity covering the whole range of human affairs, personal responsibility and self-government within defined spheres of responsibility, and co-determination in both the political and economic spheres. 'In addition to the material benefits that the economy provides, we should aim at a meaningful relationship between individuals and communities and their work.' Work must be organized in such a way that it encourages personal responsibility. One aim should therefore be to guarantee each individual a real share of responsibility in the industrial undertaking. The workers' creative participation in the economy is a precondition for a successful transition from class conflict to co-operation. The social order requires material protection for all members of the nation. 'The working man is to be guaranteed the income which he requires to preserve human dignity and which is commensurate with his importance to the community.' Everybody must be enabled to earn enough from his work to keep himself and his family. 'Until very recently many countries had not succeeded in guaranteeing the general right to work. It is absolutely essential that we should overcome structural unemployment both in industrial and agricultural countries and in the colonies. Any country which does not master this problem, or which only masters it in war-time conditions, has failed. It is irrelevant whether this failure stems from incorrect organizational measures or simply from inaction—in the expectation that everything will sort itself out.'

The men of Kreisau discussed the unemployment problem frequently and thoroughly. The great economic crisis during which almost half the young men had been without work for years at a time, was a decisive experience in their lives. Using his experiences in the United States as a basis, Einsiedel made a thorough study of the possibility of eliminating unemployment. Other members of the Circle had also met the problem in practice in the work camps and later in the Labour Service. Their experiences and discussions produced concrete proposals. 'The fiasco in unemployment insurance has shown that this emergency cannot simply be met by technical insurance or financial methods. Of more relevance would be the creation of a catchment area for those who have been temporarily excluded from the competitive economy. This should not, however, lead to undercutting in the free market economy. A publicly run sector in the national economy offers one solution to the problem of creating catchment areas of this kind.'

All citizens were not only to be equal before the law; they should also have an equal opportunity to develop their powers in public life, in cultural and economic life, and to enjoy a full share of the gross national product. Education and vocational training should not depend upon the wealth of the parents. 'All those who are engaged in economic activity have the same rights, the same protection and freedom before the economic laws of the land. They also have certain minimum duties.' Schmölders' memorandum makes another point: 'Much more effective methods are needed if the desire to achieve something is to be permanently strengthened and kept alive; the counterpart of achievement must be found in a perceptible rise in the social order and an open recognition of the person who has achieved something, that satisfies him and appears to all his competitors to be worth working for. These conditions will best be met by a system in which achievement becomes the basic criterion of a person's position in society and his qualification for participating responsibly in the process of policy making.' If a person was not in a position to work because he was old or sick or an invalid, then the community would come to his aid. Increases in economic power that result in equality in working and economic life should be adjusted.

Everybody ought to be free to choose his occupation and his place of work. Compulsory measures for a planned distribution of labour, except in cases of special emergency, were only to be permitted by special laws and even then only for limited periods. Citizens should be free to carry out their profession or trade within the framework of the existing laws. 'Free choice of occupation, freedom of trade and freedom for entrepreneurial initiative are elements in the organizational structure whose incentive power cannot be dispensed with under any circumstances by those in charge of the economy.' Private ownership and in particular the ownership of land and means of production corresponding to the productive power of a family enjoy the protection of the state. This protection can be removed by law in special cases. Law is also needed to sanction the transfer of private property to public ownership. Property carries with it obligations, particularly the obligation to care for the land entrusted to the owner. Property rights must not be improperly enforced. The ownership of the capital invested in a business does not necessarily justify the claim to direct the business, particularly not when the capital has been inherited. The rights of inheritance had to be limited.

There was no Kreisau 'economic theory' as such. The Kreisau design for linking ideas as to how the economic system should be directed to the common good with the revival of personal values in economic life, was inspired more by ethics and organization than by doctrine. The Circle in fact brought a number of very different ideas to bear on their discussion of social and economic problems. Yet memories of the world-wide depression and the failures of national socialist economic policy brought both opponents and supporters of state economic management much closer together.

A memorandum on 'the Organizational Tasks of the Economy' which Einsiedel and von Trotha wrote in 1942 states in the opening paragraphs: 'It is therefore one of mankind's tasks to ensure not only that the economy provides whatever is essential, but also that it is so organized that individuals and groups can discover in it a framework for their own personal development, free of coercion.' This provided the starting point for discussion of the organization of the economic system. Schmölders agreed: 'Today, the state and socialist planned economy has reached the point where the organizational and controlling measures adopted against the acquisitive spirit have begun to bury and overgrow the source from which it originally derived its inspiration, namely the lively powers of human personality.' All organizations were therefore to be built from below rather than from above. In so far as technical and economic developments allowed, manageable spheres of responsibility were to be created in which both official and self-governing bodies were to have as much autonomy as possible. Tasks that did not need to be attended to by the state ought to be transferred to the self-governing organizations. A higher authority ought only to assume those responsibilities that cannot be discharged within a smaller sphere. The construction from below ought to begin with the individual's achievement and the ethos of his work. The erosion of achievement through compulsory labour had to be checked and personal accomplishment ought to be seen as the only qualification for political responsibilities. 'The high-minded economic ethics of the Middle Ages seem to me to provide convincing proof that genuine efficiency is feasible and compatible with human nature, not only in a system of unlimited freedom of competition but also in a system in which there are strict political and social obligations.'

Then there was the problem of the industrial undertakings. It was not simply a technical instrument in the hands of the public or of the entrepreneur designed to produce particular products, it was also a working partnership in which the greater part of the population spent the greater part of their lives. Its internal structure must therefore comply with the demand for a free society. Each worker ought to have a share in the management of the concern: the size of the share would be determined by the amount of responsibility held and by the ability of the worker to take a general view of the firm's undertakings. Hence the men of Kreisau demanded the right of co-determination for each member of a business enterprise, a right that should receive legal recognition in regard to all social and personnel questions. Workers' co-determination in the economic field was to be exercised not in the individual plant but at the higher level where decisions on economic policy were made. At the factory level, however, the worker could demand to be kept constantly informed even about economic matters. He should also have a share not only in the management of a firm but also in the firm's profits, and in particular in the increased value of the undertaking.

An increase in the competence and responsibilities of the works unions was regarded as a better way of creating industrial partnership, than the return to a unitary, ever-powerful federation of trade unions, which would naturally emphasize class distinction and the idea of conflict. The members of the group viewed large concentrations of power and central organizations with grave mistrust. They would have much preferred to have dispensed even with the 'German Trade Union'. That is why the regulations governing a 'German Trade Union' stand right at the end of the protocol on the 'economy' from the second Kreisau conference. It is true that it was 'an instrument for carrying through the economic programme', but that it would need to continue in existence once this had been done was very much doubted. By contrast the works unions are given an important place in this protocol. The results of the further discussions can be seen in the 'Basic Principles'. The section on the works unions has been somewhat shortened and it is followed immediately by a section on the 'German Trade Union' which is, therefore, given much more prominence than in the earlier document. Further, it is now described not as an 'instrument' but as 'a necesary instrument'. Nonetheless this union was not, under any circumstances, to be a central authority. Its structure was to be adjusted to the state and economic structure. The individual industrial units were to elect the members of the Land Chambers of Commerce; the latter were to be composed of an equal number of representatives of management and labour. The chambers were also responsible for the development of the different occupations and for the arrangements that this necessitated. The problem of whether trade union representatives should work at least half the time that those they represented did, was still a matter of discussion. While Moltke and Yorck opposed any increase in 'officials', Mierendorff and Haubach decisively rejected their proposal, with Trott tending to support them. White-collared workers were no longer going to be allowed to fancy themselves outside society. At the head of the system of economic self-government there was to be a Reich Economic Chamber, composed of delegates from the Land Economic Chambers. There was thus to be an economic representative system alongside the political system; in brief, the structure of the economic system was intended to be similar to the structure of the state.

Kreisau thinking about future economic developments can best be studied by examining in turn their ideas on a number of aspects of social and economic policy.

Basic Principles. 'The Reich government considers that the basis for economic reconstruction lies in orderly competition carried on within limits set by the government and, as far as its methods are concerned, subject to government inspection.' This is a key sentence from the 'Basic Principles'. The economy could never dispense with incentive; which was needed to increase individual initiative. Freedom must not, however, degenerate into lack of restraint. According to Schmölders, 'the competitive principle of the commercially orientated economy has revealed considerable defects and gaps when applied in practise in the past and these cannot be tolerated in the future'. The running of the economy could no longer be entirely left to individuals as this would be undesirable as regards social justice. The state should therefore direct the economic system. 'The state is the unlimited master of the economic system', wrote Moltke, only, however, in order that it can pursue a policy of full employment and achieve the best possible results from the general effort. 'It is the price that the economy must pay for its liberation from complete state control,' Schmölders maintained.

Yet in the course of the discussions there was a steady wane in the emphasis placed upon the need for the state to direct the economy. The state ought to manage the economy 'without destroying the efficiency of the private sector'. There were many examples of government direction of the economy—Einsiedel mentions collectivization in Russia—in which state direction led to a loss of human freedom. This was to be avoided. In particular the state ought to deal with three problems in its economic management: it should take care that the economic system is working at maximum strength, determine the direction of economic development, and finally see that economic activity is in harmony with the needs of a healthy social order. These tasks ought to be drawn together and worked out in one plan. When Einsiedel and Trotha considered in detail the advantages, dangers and possibilities of such a plan, they concluded that the state ought only to employ indirect means to guide the economy. Further, the authority issuing directives ought to be delegated as much as possible in order to avoid a concentration of power in the hands of the central authorities. The general principle ought to be upheld 'that decisions can only be taken by the person who is in a position to observe the consequences of his decision' (see *Neuordnung im Widerstand*, p. 538). Finally, all the decisions taken by the state economic administration ought to be subject to examination by the courts. 'There is a possibility of substantially reducing the dangers that accompany the consolidation of the state's power in the economic sphere, by creating a system of economic law.'

Nationalization. 'The concern of the whole community in the basic industries requires a special degree of government regulation of these sectors of industry. Key mining, iron and metal, chemical and fuel firms should be taken over by the public authorities. These publicly owned industries are to be directed and inspected on the same principles as apply generally in the economic system.' The Circle accordingly thought that those branches of industry which occupied a key and powerful position in the national economy should be taken over by the publc authorities. In most cases this had already happened. Schmölders considered the actual application of the plan, but he was even more concerned with the consequences of nationalization for the economy. He proposed a division of the economy into a public and a competitive sector. It would of course be difficult to arrive at a 'fair' distribution of labour and experience. The solution of this problem lay in ensuring that the needs of the community were taken fully into account by those responsible for managing the 'official' part of the national economy, by such means as strict control of expenditure and of wages, salaries and profits. This should be combined with an absence of controls upon earnings and profits in the remaining 'free' sector, to which the healthy and capable younger generation would turn out of preference, if they considered the prospects attractive. At the same time there ought to be some provision for selection on the basis of achievement within the public sector, so that the beneficial effects of competition could also be felt in this part of the economy as well; the competitive system ought to a certain extent to be 'imitated' here through appropriate contracting procedure, etc., so that the distribution of labour and capital investment achieve the best possible results in these branches of the economy.

Population policy. The end of the war would create an urgent need for a large number of measures. First, order would have to be restored. Then work and bread would have to be provided for the home-coming soldiers and the workers released from the armaments factories; accommodation would have to be found for the homeless and the most essential supplies guaranteed. Another important measure would be the reunion of families who had been separated by the national socialists. That is why the 'Basic Principles' included the following: 'The basic unit of peaceful communal life is the family. It is protected by the public authorities who also guarantee education and the external necessities of life: food, clothing, housing, parks and health.' The Circle's political proposals also included the provision of a second vote to all 'heads of families'.

In addition to preliminary measures such as these, the Kreisau group worked out still more plans in this sphere. 'There must be town and country planning of sufficient quality to guarantee the population a secure and healthy basis for life,' declared the protocol of the second conference. Moltke pointed out in this connection that it was precisely the state, as 'master of the economic system', that could advance non-economic objectives; by the use of economic resources it could, for example, help to promote a healthier distribution of the population by its choice of garrison towns. A major difficulty in this connection lay in the wide variety of conditions within the economy. Schmölders worked on this problem. How could the flight from the land and other migratory movements be effectively countered? It could not in his view be done with official prohibitions; immigration restrictions and residential restrictions were inadmissible. Better results would probably be achieved with the help of a good fiscal policy. 'The cost of living in the areas that need support could be brought below the national average by means of complete or partial tax exemption and this would decisively reduce the discrepancy in real wages, e.g. in relation to the higher living standards in the west.' Housing policy also offered considerable opportunities for adjustment. A state-controlled housing system could help in some respects. A decentralization of the administration along the lines that they envisaged would also have a favourable impact on the problem. 'The restoration of a socially satisfying communal life, which favoured the development of the free personality and to which the church was able to make an important contribution, would create a powerful counterweight to the flight from the land and migratory tendencies in areas where the nominal wages were low.' Frau von Trotha was the person most concerned with conditions in the large cities. There were also some relevant ideas in Rosenstock's work. Steltzer, too, had already urged that relations between town and country should be improved, not only economically but also in terms of population balance. In their memorandum Einsiedel and Trotha observed that in spite of the increase in prosperity resulting from the modern industrial economy—a development that they very much welcomed—most countries had witnessed a concentration of population in wretched industrial districts that largely deprived them of the possibility of a healthy existence. 'The state can encourage healthier industrial conditions by wage regulations, the building of houses for home ownership and the construction of "new towns" as well as by taking measures towards slum clearance' (*Neuordnung im Widerstand*, p. 524).

Industrial Development. In the transition from war economy to a peace economy the government ought at first to retain ownership or at least control of the means of production, and output would be switched to satisfy civilian needs. Volkswagens would be produced instead of tanks, merchant ships instead of warships, housing blocks instead of air-raid shelters, etc. Gradually, however, public control ought to be withdrawn in favour of free production. As there would be a general shortage of viable machines and factories, systematic measures would have to be taken, so Schmölders believed, 'to get all productive resources in the peace economy in action again as quickly as possible and to create additional employment opportunities in the shortest possible period'. He also demanded that the location of industry should be rationalized on a nation-wide basis. He believed that unrestricted competition as a method of selection was often costly to the national economy and detrimental to a systematic development of productive capacity. It threatened to alter the social structure permanently in favour of the larger concerns and industrial alliances. The alternative method of a healthy distribution and decentralization of industry would make a valuable contribution to the rationalization of the whole economy and would be completely in agreement with the ideas of the Circle.

Einsiedel and Trotha also stressed the need for a purposeful distribution of industry. In undeveloped agricultural areas, a decision would have to be taken as to how far industrialization was desirable. In addition there would have to be agreement about which industrial tasks were urgent and about how the problem of industrial location should be solved. Several measures that could be adopted within the scope of this kind of industrial development policy were considered, e.g. the preferential treatment of firms in a specific area when government contracts are being distributed, special tax privileges, special transport rates and government subsidies for house building. In exceptional circumstances it could be cheaper for the state to effect the transfer of industry by government order, e.g. when there was a considerable threat of unemployment.

Prices policy. Among the members of the Circle, Yorck was especially familiar with the practical problems of a policy on prices as a result of his official activities. Einsiedel and Trotha stressed the possibilities of prices policy in the social reconstruction. Schmölders, too, considered the problem. 'The restoration of freedom to fix prices requires some government provisions against a return of early capitalist forms of exploitation, and in particular against the passing on of wages pressure produced by competition. The system of competitive price formation starts as a matter of principle from the idea of complete mobility of prices and costs, including wages; . . . there is no doubt that this consequence of free competitive price formation cannot be permitted in the modern social welfare state; the state will have to succeed in laying down some form of wages regulation, prices regulation, etc.' What were the exceptional cases in which free price formation ought not to be allowed? In the first place, a number of goods and services that were already outside the free market, such as transport and supply, schooling and social insurance; then the absolutely essential foodstuffs such as grain, bread, potatoes and animal products; further, at least provisionally, urban dwellings and finally a group, still requiring further definition, of the more important subsidiary and raw materials required in farming and in industry, such as iron, coal, cement, fertilizers, etc. 'It must be borne in mind that the necessary adjustment between demand and supply ought, as a matter of principle, to be carried out in a way as near as possible to the free operation of these forces, through a price fixing process that determines the values of individual goods and services on the basis of urgency of demand and production costs.'

Cartels. 'Where the existing commitments and nexus of interests (monopolies, cartels, combines) make competition impossible, it is the task of the government to apply the principles of competition and to protect the interests of the community as a whole.' These words from the protocol on the economy from the second Kreisau conference state the basic principle in the Kreisau policy on cartels. Schmölders proposed a 'monopolies board' which would keep a constant watch on the market dominance of the larger combines, cartels and firms and take early measures to eliminate abuses. Einsiedel and Trotha remarked that the state had to guarantee through its oversight of cartels and monopolies that the economic efficiency of existing firms and the emergence of new undertakings were not jeopardized. At the same time the state ought to encourage the positive usefulness of the cartels and see to it that economic competition did not lead to a frittering away of resources. Changes could not be permitted in the economic structure of particular areas or branches of production simply and solely on the basis of the decisions by individual industrialists. A warning was given, however, against falling into the belief that certain measures such as the break-up of combines or nationalization were the only ones possible. 'It is precisely here that a variety of new legal solutions must be found that are appropriate to the peculiarities of individual production processes, that allow for the dangers of increasing bureaucracy and that guarantee the co-operation of all suitable persons.'

Foreign Trade. 'The organization of the international economy has proved inadequate. There has been an absence of any thorough-going measures to bring about a genuine distribution of work among the separate countries which would put an end to the present rivalry.' The question of international economic co-operation was one that the Kreisau members were deeply interested in. Their concern can be seen in the quotation from Trotha and Einsiedel above, in the discussions at the third Kreisau conference and in Moltke's lists of problems. In all these cases the problem of relations between the German economy and the European and world economies was considered from the point of view of integration. Schmölders, on the other hand, was primarily concerned with the question of how the German national economy could be restored to health; he dealt with the problem of foreign trade from this angle. In this context he stressed the necessity for direction of foreign trade, which implied restriction. The presence of exporting power and import requirements in the internal European economy created particular problems for the domestic management of the economy, especially in the field of prices. Thorough market research ought to maintain a regular supply of information about the most favourable export prices that could be obtained and the lowest import prices in the most important sectors from the point of view of the balance of trade; the profits achieved by importing goods that are lower priced on the world market than at home ought to be used to provide a subsidy, through a cartel-type organization, for the export of goods that are faced by effective foreign competition. With the help of the 'foreign trade cartels' it ought to be possible to make exports and imports independent of the domestic price structure.

AGRICULTURE

After the Nazi seizure of power the farmer was proclaimed the bearer of the national socialist state. A great four-year plan was announced; Darré, the director of the Office for Agrarian Policy, and Kerrl, the Prussian Minister of Justice, prepared a Hereditary Farm Law. This law with its marked antisemitism and its application of the Nazi ideas about 'blood and soil' has been justly censored for its 'mediaeval backwardness and manifest dependence on pre-scientific superstition'. In spite of the assistance that it offered in the removal of debts, this law deprived the farmers of their freedom. Henceforth they were kept under strong state and party control.

In a memorandum of 1933 Steltzer described the government's policies as one-sided and inadequate. He observed that the Hereditary Farm Law ran counter to the interests of the rural economy as a whole, since the protection of existing farm units of up to 300 acres gave pointless preference to the larger farmers and, as a result, discouraged settlement in farming areas, to the detriment of the younger rural population. 'It is impossible to see the urgency of this law', he wrote. In its place he advocated an investment programme and general planning. Agricultural settlement had completely broken down. 'Likewise the measures taken to organize a united peasantry can only raise doubts. Administrative centralization is everywhere repressing natural resourcefulness and self-help. The compulsory organization of agriculture from above will not create an estate so much as a bureaucracy that lacks any rapport with the real forces on the land.'

Einsiedel, in a paper dated 1941, turned first to the fashionable demands for the mechanization and rationalization of agriculture. He rejected both the industrial-capitalist and the fascist solutions. These solutions 'tend to divert popular life from organic development into organized existence' and 'denaturalize human work so that it simply becomes a partial, technical activity within a general, rational work programme'. If this were allowed to happen 'the last intact organic sector of life will have been destroyed'. As 'the roots of organic life have been much less damaged in rural areas . . . a reconstruction which is founded on the individual worth of each person and on the consciousness of community, which makes allowance for distinctive styles of individual and communal life and chooses as its foundation self-government based upon individual responsibility, ought for these very reasons to attach considerable value to a strong and tranquil rural population'.

If such a situation was to be achieved then it was essential, in the first place, for the flight from the land to be halted. The material incentives to migrate should be eliminated, the 'rhythm of rural life' maintained. Only if this were done would the rural population be able to attain their rightful importance in the nation as a whole. It was also essential that as many individuals as possible should find an independent living in the country. Agricultural questions were not simply economic in nature; the answers ought to take account of political objectives and of the social responsibilities of the rural population. Another requirement was that agriculture should be represented by independent and highly cultivated individuals. They would provide an ample counterweight to other groups in the population. This point would have to be taken into account when the distribution of land and property was being considered. The group would constitute an agrarian elite in relations with the outside world.

As far as relations between town and country were concerned, care ought to be taken to eliminate the cultural dependence of the countryside upon the large city and to make it sufficiently independent in cultural matters. If a European solution were adopted an entirely new situation would arise and a customs and currency union would create different economic circumstances. The production costs in the different European countries had become so distorted by war-time conditions that they no longer offered any firm foundation for calculation. A decline in output was to be expected. Having outlined what facts had to be reckoned with when preparing their proposals, Einsiedel concluded by outlining a plan of action. They had 'to map out the way ahead for German agricultural policy, bearing in mind the social and political responsibilities of the rural population and the economic unity of Europe. We must consider: 1. Formulating a list of production requirements that are politically essential and ways of meeting these requirements. 2. The schedule, distribution and prices of agricultural products.' Einsiedel's and Trotha's joint memorandum lays particular stress upon the responsibility of the state in this matter. 'The state can make a substantial contribution to ending the flight from the land by making adequate payment for agricultural products and thereby making it possible to raise agricultural wages, and by encouraging the building of homes for agricultural workers and cultural institutions in the countryside' (*Neuordnung im Widerstand*, p. 53).

At the Circle's conference on agriculture the participants were told about agricultural conditions and problems in the different parts of Germany so that they could form a general picture. They also expressed opinions on the problems of the day. It was difficult and laborious to prepare any kind of concrete plans, as they had no idea of what possibilities would be open to agriculture after the collapse. They discussed how the consequences of the national socialist theories of blood and soil, the Hereditary Farm Law, the regimentation of agriculture in the 'Reichsnährstand', etc. could be surmounted. Agricultural self-government was to be built up once again and attention was to be paid to the stunted progress of mechanization and the closely associated readjustment of agricultural production. The optimum size of farms was also discussed.

As progressive Silesian landowners, Moltke and Yorck were extremely interested in the outcome of these deliberations. Plans for land reform, particularly in East Germany, took up much of the discussions in the inner circle at Kreisau. At the centre of their considerations of land reform was the idea of raising agricultural production. The solution seemed to lie in a healthy mixture of large and small farms. They also talked about the value and the best organization of the peasant co-operative system which, it was hoped, would enable the rural population to master their problems by vigorous co-operation and through which they should develop a strong occupational organization. Central to their thinking were the personal responsibility and freedom of the individual farmer and the small community in relation to the larger complexes of power.

CHAPTER 18

Foreign Policy

National socialist foreign policy contained both nationalist and imperialist tendencies. The slogan 'Home to the Reich' was nationalist, but the 'Living Space Policy' had implications that went beyond nationalism. The 'urge to expand eastwards' (*Drang nach Osten*) stemmed from an expansionist policy, from a desire to seize power outside Germany as well as within it. The breach with the League of Nations meant withdrawal from international co-operation. In general, the national socialist foreign policy signified in several respects a break with tradition. It led finally to a permanent state of war.

The documents make it clear that the foreign policy proposals of the Kreisau Circle were based upon a fundamental belief in a Europe integrated into a federal state. It need hardly be said, that these ideas had nothing in common with the Nazi New Order, and were in direct opposition to the foreign policy of Hitler's Germany which was both nationalist and imperialist.

The main motive behind the emphasis on European co-operation is made quite clear in the 1941 memorandum, in which Moltke attempts to analyse post-war opportunities. The first objective is stated unequivocally to be the elimination of excessive nationalism. 'It is the historical purpose of this war', writes Moltke elsewhere, 'to overcome the antipathies and to provide once more a common foundation, at least for Europe. The necessary corollary of this hope is one sovereign State of Europe which will overcome all demands for national sovereignty.' Moltke believed that he could already detect the end of nationalism, and commented that in both France and Germany nationalist slogans had lost their appeal. The strong impression made during his journey in 1940 to France probably promoted this remark; he did not surmise at the time the excessive nationalism to which the Nazi leaders would be able to whip up so many Germans, nor that the German terror actions in the occupied countries in and after 1941 would evoke fervent nationalist reaction which became a strong stimulus for many resistance groups there. Nevertheless the theme reappears in the foreign policy memorandum of April 1942, and then in the report of the third Kreisau conference, where we read: 'The free and peaceful development of national culture is incompatible with the retention of absolute sovereignty by each individual state. Peace demands the creation of an order that spans the separate states.'

The second motive behind the stress on European co-operation was the desire to achieve a settlement of the minorities problem, not only for German minorities but for the whole central and eastern European area. Several members of the Circle had studied this problem intensively and were acquainted with it from first hand. Lukaschek and van Husen had been members of the Mixed Commission of the League of Nations for Silesia (see p. 68), the latter writing at the time: 'The knowledge and consideration of these findings will be of the greatest significance in strengthening the law of minorities, and thereby the peace of Europe.' The younger Silesian members of the Circle also had been much concerned with this problem, Moltke himself being foremost in emphasizing that it was not simply an east German problem, but concerned the whole area of central and eastern Europe. He had intended to devote his doctorate to a consideration of this subject. He had been, for example, critical of the way in which the German minority in Poland allowed themselves to be guided by Berlin as this was no answer to the problem. These early impressions can be traced in the documents of the Circle. In the report of the third conference it is asserted that respect for and protection of one's own nation 'must not become an excuse for amassing political power or for degrading, persecuting or oppressing a foreign people'. The problem is also given prominence in the 'Observations on the peace programme of the American churches'. The earlier work is referred to specifically there, and personal as well as territorial autonomy is demanded. The object of a law of minorities must be to guarantee equality in education and jurisdiction and, above all, in religious rights. One section of this memorandum finishes with these words: 'The successful fulfilment of this claim for cultural autonomy as promoting European collaboration, especially in those parts of Europe where the population largely consists of mixed nationalities, would, we are sure, help to solve one of the more vital problems concerning the question of permanent peace for Europe' (see pp. 370–71).

The third motive was the hope that European co-operation,

particularly through the intertwining of the separate national economies, would accelerate the post-war work of reconstruction and remove the threat of a new war. 'The future peace can only be durable if the economic system is organized in accordance with political needs. . . . The European countries must agree upon a distribution of work that ensures the even development of all productive forces. If this is done the distress of the post-war period can be overcome by intensive reconstruction work. . . .' There are similar comments in the foreign policy memorandums, and in the *Observations on the peace programme* the following statement appears: 'Without any limitation of the sovereign power of the states by an efficacious international organ, renewed abuse of military power is always to be feared.'

Following this exposition of the motives that led the Kreisau Circle to emphasize the need for European co-operation, we must now ask what kind of organization they envisaged. The problem, as one of the memoranda points out, was to discover a structure which would satisfy the members of the European community of nations which would at the same time be acceptable to the victors in the war. Among the Moltke papers there are three drafts of the memorandum on *Starting points, Aims and Problems*, which he wrote in the year 1941. In all of them, Europe is described as a Federal State. Its frontiers are the Atlantic, the Mediterranean, and the Black Sea. In the East they stretched from the eastern frontier of Bessarabia to the former Poland, the former Baltic states and Finland. Within the unified sovereign state, Europe had to be divided into much smaller, non-sovereign states, which would themselves be connected by arrangements of a political nature. As examples, Moltke quoted the Scandinavian states, the Baltic states, the east European states, the Mediterranean states, etc. England and Russia were not included in the European Federal State. In order to counter-balance the power of the Federal State, the smaller units were to be established as self-governing states, with a large degree of competence. The emphasis was placed upon building from below. The competence of the Federal authority was to include economic planning and the administration of the African colonies. In the first two drafts of the memorandum, other powers were also given to the central government, for example, foreign policy and defence. The Federal authorities were to be established in a small area outside the control of any of the lesser states, and in which there were no special economic interests and no damning historical associations. Moltke thought of a territory probably somewhere in Bohemia, Silesia, or Austria. This was perhaps the continuation of an idea that he had had already in his youth. When he was only 21, he wrote to his grandparents in South Africa: 'I believe that Silesia and Vienna are the two centres from which Germany and Europe can really take a serious interest in the East and the Balkans, and I believe the whole European crisis between West and East, and the agrarian crisis in the whole of Europe's East spring from the same root, and that it is our duty to work on this problem.' The states—or the historically conditioned self-governing bodies as they were called—were to be roughly equal in size in importance and number of inhabitants, but the internal constitutions could be quite different. According to van Husen, it was anticipated that in order to reach that aim Germany, France and Italy should disappear and be divided into several 'states' to exclude any predominance in the confederation. The highest legislative authority in the European state was to be answerable to the individual citizens. At the top of the executive there were to be two cabinets. One was to consist of departmental ministers, with an inner cabinet consisting of the five most important ministers (the Prime Minister, the Foreign Minister and the Ministers of Defence, Finance and the Interior). Alongside them, in a consultative role, there was to be a cabinet made up of representatives of the governments of the states. In addition there was also to be a European court, a permanent secretariat, economic planning authorities and an ambassadors' conference from all the European states.

Moltke, who was consciously trying to avoid the mistakes of the League of Nations, worked his ideas out in considerable detail, and then handed them over to others for further expansion. He did not—as we see in his 1942 letter to Lionel Curtis—regard Europe simply as an organization. 'It is no use establishing a united sovereign state, if we cannot restore the basic unity of principle that has been shattered for centuries.' A common basis, a connecting link was essential if the organization was not to become coercive. For Moltke, the fundamental sources of the European outlook on life were the Christian religion, classical education and the socialist way of thinking. 'A common awareness of these three primary sources is the presupposition of the creation and preservation of a European community with a unified sovereignty.'

The insistence of a European solution is maintained in the foreign policy memoranda, even though sometimes only in the form of general observations. The dramatic alterations in the development of the war made it essential to confine consideration to the bare essentials. Thus in the notes on the peace programme, there is only the following sentence on the subject. 'Developments, particularly in Europe, point at the inappropriateness of the sovereign nation state as the ultimate international authority and create pressure towards the formation of larger associations of individual nations.'

Two questions constantly recur in the papers and discussions on the subject: first, whether the ideal was attainable, and secondly, what the reaction of the Allies would be. Moltke commented that in his opinion the totalitarian state had destroyed all smaller communities. Men, however, still needed some kind of ties: the vacuum would have to be filled. He also believed that the end of the war would give an opportunity for penitence and contemplation such as there had not been since the year 999 when people predicted the end of the world. Even more urgent, however, was the problem of the Allies' reaction. Moltke wrote: 'If the defeated are able to convince the victors of their responsibility, which I consider possible, the victors' example could provide the impetus for a speedy development in the direction of the stated objectives.' The question was raised repeatedly. Moltke concluded with the words: 'The end of the war offers an opportunity for a beneficial reconstruction of the world such as mankind has not had since the decay of the mediaeval church.' Trott, in the notes on the American Peace Programme, spoke of 'universal repentance after the terrible experiences and the chastisement of this war and its probable consequences'.

The European co-operation described above could only be achieved if *Germany* was defeated, Moltke wrote in April 1941. A German victory would produce not peace but an armistice and would, as he added, 'deprive our study of any relevance'. How this German defeat would be brought about, could not be foreseen at that time. 'This situation could be the result of a variety of factors; the physical exhaustion of the population, the industrial exhaustion of the nation, political changes within Germany, or disturbances and rebellions in the occupied territories which, because of the extent of the occupied areas, and the way in which they had been treated, could not be stemmed and would lead eventually to an armed invasion by the Anglo-Saxon powers.' The need for a German defeat was stressed once again by Moltke at the end of 1943 in Turkey. 'The group believes that an indisputable military defeat and occupation of Germany is absolutely essential for both moral and political reasons' (see p. 373). In 1942 Moltke wrote to his English friend Curtis: 'We hope that you clearly understand that we are ready to help you to win the war and the peace.' That it was not easy for him to write these words is clear. The Kreisau group reckoned not only with the defeat, but also with an occupation of Germany, as is indicated in the 'First Instructions to the Provincial Commissioners' and in the 'special Instructions' (see p. 354). There was also detailed discussion of the matter in Moltke's conversations in Turkey at the end of 1943.

Kreisau views on the structure of post-war Germany had a strong federalist emphasis with important implications for foreign policy: there were to be several German states instead of one, and Prussia was to be partitioned. But which regions ought to belong to these German states and where ought the frontiers to lie? Moltke is said to have attached little importance to this question. The important point, as he observed, was that in the areas that were left to the Germans justice should be restored. He foresaw that large parts of Germany, including his own Silesian homeland, would be lost. He thought that Silesia would be given to either the Poles or the Czechs. He took this as part of the tragedy of war and was ready to accept the inevitable without bitterness or recrimination. Others, however, were not ready to go so far. The hope that Austria would voluntarily join with the German states was generally entertained. It would appear from Deutsch's already mentioned study of the 'Twilight War' that this hope was prompted by certain Austrian contacts and by the promises of the English government in contacts with the German opposition in Rome. The need for German unity was accepted by many Germans even if they did not agree with Hitler's solution. Within the German area it would provide an effective counterweight to Prussia—even if the latter were partitioned.

Before the war, two of the most important problems in European foreign policy had been relations with *France* and *Poland*. 'To us socialists,' wrote Haubach, 'a Franco–German and Polish–German understanding is much more than a temporary solution of certain difficulties. It is the stable and permanent foundation of the future Europe.' In his memorandum of 1941 Moltke wrote very optimistically that as a result of the division of Europe into self-governing bodies of approximately equal size, 'the absolute dominance of the former Great Powers, Germany and France, has been broken without creating resentment'. On Poland, van Husen had already written as early as 1930: 'The existence of Poland and good relations between it and Germany are a European necessity.' After all that had happened in Poland since 1939, the Kreisau

Circle was quite aware that Germany had much to make good there—a matter frequently discussed by Moltke. In several documents the restoration of a free Polish state which would belong to a European federation of states, was stressed. The Eastern frontier of Poland was described as the frontier of 'the old Poland'. If relations between Poland and Russia were for long unclear, the consequences of the Katyn affair* in 1943 clarified for Moltke a great deal. Also the restoration of a free Czech state was regarded by the Kreisau Circle as necessary and natural. The Trott memorandum of 1942 made reservations on this head, using the formula 'within the limits of their ethnographic frontiers', to cover the Sudetenland. As to the Balkan region, Moltke had been concerned with its problems since his youth (see p. 23). The well-known American diplomat George Kennan writes, on the basis of his discussions with Moltke, that people like him were urgently needed if the future of the region between the Elbe and the Bering Straits was to be happier than the past had been.†

As cultural expert at the German Embassy in Bucharest, von Haeften, too, had been able to follow developments in the Balkans closely. When he re-visited these countries at the end of 1943 he wrote a detailed report for the German Foreign Office, in which he sees only two intact and legitimate organizations left in the Balkans: Tito's movement and the orthodox church. As to Tito's movement he observed that alongside its nationalist–revolutionary tendency it had also developed Pan-Slav traits as a result of being recognized by Moscow. In a draft Foreign Office memorandum Haeften was severely critical of his country's Balkan policy: Germans had never adopted a positive attitude towards the orthodox churches of the area, and should Germany miss its chance, Russia would take over its role.

The Circle's experts discussed many times whether Britain could be a member of a future European federation and, with its reserves, advance post-war European work, or whether such a close association between Britain and Europe was impossible precisely because of Britain's commitments to the Empire. The widely travelled von Trott apparently favoured the integration of Britain into Europe, whereas Moltke took the other view. Moltke attached much more

---

* On 13 April 1943 the Germans discovered the corpses of thousands of Polish officers, prisoners since the first week of the war, and established their identity with the aid of an international committee. As a consequence of the crime the Polish exile government severed all contacts with Russia.

† *Foreign Affairs* 29 (1950–51) p. 361.

importance to the significance of the Empire than any of the others; according to him the prestige achieved by Britain and the Empire during the war might even open the prospect of Britain regaining her 'old position' in relation to the United States. Except for indirect influence through his mother, the thinking of Moltke as a landed aristocrat from east of the Elbe, was particularly European-centred and his ideas about the world beyond Europe were to a large extent dependent upon the views of other people. The influence of Lionel Curtis can perhaps be seen in his romantic picture of the British Empire. His strongly emotional attitude could not fundamentally be erased by changes in the situation; in the documents this can easily be detected. In the first draft of Moltke's 1941 memorandum Britain's anticipated position at the end of the war was described as follows: 'Britain's primary interest lies in once more outstripping the United States of America in the leadership of the world, and in reasserting its traditional spiritual title to leadership. If Britain is to exercise leadership among the Anglo-Saxons, it must have peace on the European continent at its rear. At the same time the war will have proved that the fleet is the most powerful instrument of war and that, therefore, Britain does not need a "continental sword".' The second draft of the memorandum already contained an important change: 'Great Britain, Iceland and Ireland belong to the European Federal State. Great Britain's membership, however, is of a somewhat looser nature, enabling her to remain the spiritual centre of the Anglo-Saxon world and, more especially, to maintain her position in relation to the United States of America.' The third draft stated, however, again a compromise solution: 'Great Britain, Ireland and Iceland belong to the British Empire.' This change should not, however, lead to conflict between Great Britain and Europe. The closest possible degree of co-operation ought to be achieved. Hence Moltke added: 'Political and military relations have been so arranged between these countries and the European territories that military conflict between them is impossible' (*Neuordnung im Widerstand*, p. 518). Economically, however, Britain was reckoned to be part of Europe.

The Kreisau group did not have the same personal relations with the United States as they had with Britain. Still, they were convinced of its growing importance as an economic world power. It is, however, interesting that Reichwein's assessment of conditions there after his visit in the twenties was not entirely positive. When he reviewed a book on Siberia a few years later—the crisis had already begun—he remarked in passing: 'Is it a new country of unlimited potential? America has taught us scepticism. . . .' Adam von Trott who, as a descendant of John Jay, had a very personal relationship to the country, found it difficult to understand the policy of the United States, which he hoped, in vain, was in a position to bring the belligerents together. Moltke on the basis of his romantic picture of the British Empire saw Britain as still the main point of the Anglo-Saxon world. Thus, for example, he wrote to his wife after Roosevelt's re-election in 1940: 'This election could be a milestone in the history of the world: . . . as far as the world is concerned, it could provide a really capable organizer and opponent of the dictators with freedom to act. If R. were to use this opportunity, he could go down in history as one of the greatest men of all time, who succeeded in reversing the war of Independence, in achieving the fusion of the Empire with the USA and thereby restoring the undisputed and indisputable supremacy which is the pre-requisite to a stable peace.' Similar ideas can also be seen in the memorandum of 1941. It seems, however, taking into account the succeeding drafts of this memorandum, possible to detect the beginning of a shift in Moltke's views here towards giving the USA a more independent position. Moltke's conversations with Waetjen, whose mother was American, may have played a part in this. It is probable that these changes also affected discussion in the Circle, and it is perhaps also admissible to see the comments on the American peace programme as an example of the new attitude. Beyond this the Kreisau group expressed high hopes about the share of the United States in the work of reconstruction after the war.

The question as to whether Russia belonged to the European Federal state was also frequently discussed. The Russian régime was odious to everyone. This had led Moltke to anticipate the collapse of the communist régime following the campaign in Russia and the formation of a new and free order there, but after a few weeks of war he revised this opinion. Despite all the criticisms of the communist régime the necessity of peaceful co-operation with Russia was accepted. This point was, for example, made in the Schönfeld memorandum, even though it also contained some critical comments. Trott and some others particularly thought that it was necessary in the German interest to balance the very marked western orientation in Moltke's ideas, with an emphasis upon Germany's central European position and the importance of the Great Power in the east. Mierendorff's proclamation too made an emphatic reference to co-operation with Soviet Russia. The same attitude can be seen in Moltke's discussions at the end of 1943 in Turkey, when he stressed the need for 'loyal co-operation with Russia and avoidance of all international conflict'. To advance this co-operation it would be advisable for any German government to have a very strong left wing.

Thus, the Circle believed that efforts should be made to establish new forms of co-operation and that the idea of Russia as the arch-enemy—which made peaceful co-operation impossible from the outset—had to be avoided. They believed, for the rest, that it was totally wrong to identify the people of a country with the régime or political system, because they discovered the detrimental effects of such an attitude in their own experience. They held the Russian people and Russian culture in high esteem, and expected that there would be a religious awakening in Russia similar to that in Germany during the war and that this would exercise a positive influence upon conditions in the country.

The men of Kreisau, as typical Europeans of that time, con-centrated on Europe and the Great Powers and gave only marginal attention, or none at all, to other areas. According to Moltke, the world was divided into two spheres of influence, one European, the other Anglo-Saxon. He outlined the following partition: 'The European sphere of influence includes French and Italian North Africa, Russia, the Black Sea and Turkey. The Anglo-Saxon sphere of influence should extend over India and Africa south of the Congo, South America, the Near East including Egypt, Arabia and Palestine and the Far East were according to him areas of tension lying between the two combinations, South America and the Far East towards the Anglo-Saxon world while the Near East gravitated towards Europe.' Several members such as Adam von Trott and Adolf Reichwein did have a great interest in the Far East and particularly in China.

As regards the colonial problem, a section in Moltke's memor-andum from 1941 noted that the former French and Italian Africa including the Congo should be under European rule and that the responsibility for administering these colonies was considered to be a common task of Europeans. Here too Moltke was led by his pro-English feelings; he made a firm distinction between the British and the other colonies—Egypt should remain further a British responsibility. In still another case the Biritish influence was clear in Moltke's thinking. When in the *Kommission zur Fort-bildung des Kriegsrechts* the problem of the military employment and training of coloured people was under discussion, Moltke remarked that Britain did not intend to train Africans, a view he personally shared, giving the following explanation: as countries other than in Africa were to be independent, they had to receive military training so that they could later defend themselves. There was, however, no question of granting independence to African countries, so training would simply be dangerous. That was why a distinction ought to be made between African and the other territories. That the struggle for independence in certain British territories could lead to a desire to leave the Empire would certainly have been disagreeable to Moltke, who romantically regarded the Empire as the beginning of the future world organization. With Furtwängler, for example, he disagreed about the situation in India and would not hear of independence. We may suppose that other members had a different view, but in the documents there is little said about the colonial problem. Only the Schönfeld memorandum outlines the importance of finding a real solution.

It stands to reason that the Kreisau Circle were completely persuaded of the need for an international organization after the war. They followed the discussion in the Allied countries on this matter closely and tried to make their own contributions to it. Moltke himself had already considered the problem before the war. When he visited the Secretariat of the League of Nations in Geneva in 1935 he noted with regret: 'The worst thing about it is that each person regards himself not as an official of the League of Nations, but as a representative of his country, and goes about his work in the secretariat in such a way as to ensure that his country will give him a good post when he leaves the secretariat.' However, it was not only an international spirit that was lacking; there was also no recognition of the authority of international legal principles. 'In the present situation the Permanent Court at the Hague is much more important than the League of Nations, and perhaps most important of all are the courts of arbitration.'

Moltke felt very encouraged when his English friend, Lionel Curtis, published the third volume of his *Civitas Dei*. Unlike the first two, which were deeply rooted in Christianity and which sketched the historical development, Moltke read this third volume with interest. It dealt in particular with the practical problem of creating a world commonwealth interpreted as the realization of God's kingdom on earth. Its proposals suggested to Moltke the outline of a possible international order. According to Curtis, states would have to surrender their sovereignty to an international organization, the British Empire playing an important part in this evolution. 'If an international commonwealth built from countries within the British Empire came to include countries which had never been part of that Empire, the most difficult stage in its growth to a world commonwealth, after its first foundation, would have been crossed. . . . Before a commonwealth had moved very far on the lines here rapidly sketched the danger of world wars would have become a thing of the past. Human society would have recovered at least the degree of stability reached in the nineteenth century.'

These ideas influenced the development of Moltke's own thinking. In his memorandum of April 1941 we looked upon the possibility of a new European order as a first stage towards a world order. What should be aimed at was a state of affairs in which the divisions and dissensions between the inhabitants of this world were only of secondary significance, because those who were grouped into one party were still primarily controlled by the magnet which attracts and influences all alike, and because enemies are in agreement about the most essential point. 'I cannot be more precise,' wrote Moltke, 'about these universally valid values, because it is the task of the whole of mankind to create this magnet, and because it would be presumptuous to suggest that it was already established at a specific place and that it was simply up to others to place themselves within its sphere of influence.'

In January 1943 Moltke passed on to several interested persons excerpts from a Foreign Press Report on a fourteen point programme for a new world order by the Inter-American Committee of Jurists. The programme emphasized the priority of law and morals, rejected war as an instrument of national policy and demanded that in future, differences should be settled by peaceful means. In this connection it advocated an extension of the jurisdiction of the International Court at The Hague. After the war an international community ought to be organized on the basis of the co-operation of all nations. Further demands included an effective system of collective security, the renunciation of political imperialism and exaggerated nationalism and the removal of tariff restrictions.

The international attitude of the Circle can be seen in its documents. Criminals were to be punished by an international court in order to achieve 'the restoration of a peace based upon trust between nations' (see p. 342). The International Court at The Hague was mentioned in this connection. The Protocols of the third Kreisau conference claimed that the economic organization of Europe was a prerequisite to a peaceful organization of the world economy, moreover in a somewhat romantic formulation: 'Peace demands the creation of an order that spans the separate states. As soon as the participation of the nations is assured, the authorities in this new order must have the right to demand of every individual, obedience, honour, and where necessary the sacrifice of life and property for the highest political authority in the international community.'

At the time of the third Kreisau conference in April 1943, the Federal Council of the Churches of Christ in America published 'Political Propositions for Peace'. The contents of the document probably reached the Kreisau Circle either through a Foreign Press Report or via Geneva. A reply to the American proposals was deposited at Geneva in November 1943. It has already been argued that the contents cannot stem from Trott alone. They are the Circle's ideas, written down by Trott. The reply gives an emphatic warning against a repetition of the mistakes made at the end of World War I. The basic statutes of the international organization ought not to be linked with the peace treaties again. A true collaboration of nations and federations in this organization was considered to be essential. A great deal of attention was paid to the solution of economic problems: the underlying idea in international transactions as well as national transactions was to be 'order combined with a maximum of freedom'. The document claims 'that the future international organization should be capable of fighting against national and private monopolies as definite obstacles in the way of peace'. Social justice was to be developed: the idea of law ought to be the basis of collaboration. Limitations upon the sovereign power of national states would be necessary. The answer closes with the words: 'In our opinion the most important and most direct contribution that Christianity can give towards the shaping of a lasting peace lies in the struggle against the demoniacal powers and in the solution of the mass problem by means of a truly Christian social order and the upbringing and training of a Christian elite.'

PART 5
EPILOGUE

CHAPTER 19

Kreisau and the 20th of July Attempt

At the beginning of October 1943, Claus Schenk Count von Stauffenberg, a relative of Yorck, took up his duties as Chief of Staff in the General Army Office in Berlin. His influence, however, had already begun to be felt in opposition circles as early as September. That he was not unknown to Moltke can be seen from a conversation that the latter had with Freiherr Hans Christoph von Stauffenberg in 1941 or 1942. Moltke asked: 'You have a cousin in the headquarters? Couldn't he be useful?' Stauffenberg answered that he had not seen his cousin Claus for a long time and that he would like to check on his attitude with Claus's brother Berthold before he gave an answer. A few weeks later Berthold told him: 'I have had a talk with Claus. He says that we must win the war first. While it is still going on, we cannot do anything like this, especially not in a war against the Bolsheviks. When we get home, however, then we can deal with the brown pest.' Besides this first occasion with Claus von Stauffenberg's typical response, Hans Christoph could remember another conversation with Moltke later in the war, when Moltke observed: 'Well, we've found out in the meantime that your cousin Claus can be useful.' This was presumably when Claus was already on the way to or in Berlin. After his own home had been destroyed in the heavy bombing raids, Moltke—and Gerstenmaier—lived with Yorck, and it appears that Claus visited the house on several occasions when Moltke himself was present. So it appears that there was a loose personal connection betwen Stauffenberg and Moltke; though their aims and methods would not always have been the same.

Then came—not unexpected by himself—Moltke's arrest in the middle of January 1944. His co-operator in the Ausland-Abwehr, Wengler, who was arrested two days earlier, is clearly right when he says that Moltke's arrest was in the first instance a part of the general operation of the Reich Security Office against the

Ausland-Abwehr, but also an attempt to remove the irksome Moltke from his post. When, in April 1943, the closest colleagues of General Oster, Hans von Dohnanyi and Dietrich Bonhoeffer were arrested, Moltke sought out Wilhelm Adam, the District Magistrate of Schweidnitz, whom he knew personally and in whose district the Kreisau estate stood and asked him whether he could not arrange for Moltke to be transferred to the agricultural department in Breslau. However, when it turned out that it was still possible for him to continue his work in Berlin, Moltke withdrew the request. Moltke's arrest had nothing at all to do with the work of the Kreisau Circle, of which the Gestapo appear to have had no inkling. The charge, that he had warned an acquaintance—Kiep—was not a serious one. He received permission to continue work on office papers in the concentration camp at Ravensbrück. Indeed, a few days before 20 July a senior Gestapo officer visited Moltke there and discussed with him where he should be transferred—to the front or to the occupied countries.

The arrest nevertheless put an end to Moltke's many-sided activities. This event had a decisive influence upon the development of the Kreisau Circle. It was Moltke who, together with Yorck, had held everything together, had provided the stimulus and taken the initiative. He had, as Gerstenmaier has put it, 'rescued the Circle from resignation by systematic planning and work', and although he could be strict and would allow no digression, the others had accepted his leadership. This centre was now missing. Nevertheless as Moltke's imprisonment was for a long time no more than a kind of protective custody, indirect links were still maintained. Repeated efforts to have him freed were made in the months that followed and this objective was at the centre of the thoughts and discussions of his friends, but all such attempts failed. The Kreisau work as such came to a standstill and several of the members and the contacts lost touch with the Circle.

After Moltke's arrest, Yorck indeed tried to continue the work, but a variety of circumstances made this increasingly difficult. His cousin, Count Stauffenberg, soon attempted to gain his co-operation in the plans for an assassination. When Tattenbach, at the request of his fellow Jesuit, König, went to Yorck to find out whether anything was still happening, he returned with the information that the whole work had come to a halt. Delp finally visited Stauffenberg, not because he could no longer stand the Kreisau Circle, but because nothing was happening any longer. This made Delp restless and provoked him to look for contacts elsewhere. One could, properly speaking, say that there was now no Kreisau Circle, but only Kreisau members. Moltke's arrest, therefore, brought about a big change.

When Lukaschek visited Yorck in Kauern in April 1944, he met Countess von Moltke there. She had high hopes that her husband would be released within the next few days. Yorck informed him about the general situation which, militarily, was rapidly approaching a crisis. Further he told him about Beck and, following on from this, about the appointment which his relative Count Stauffenberg had got in Berlin. He also reported on Goerdeler's activity, saying that Leuschner had completely gone over to him, but that Leber was very much in the forefront of their own Circle. About any urgent plans for an overthrow of the government he said nothing; simply that there might be 'trouble brewing'. When Steltzer was in Berlin at Whitsun 1944, he had conversations with both Yorck and with Trott, who had became the foreign policy adviser of Stauffenberg. Yorck did not seem to think that a *coup d'état* was imminent, whereas Trott, by contrast, told him that the military under Stauffenberg's leadership would soon act. His proposal for a meeting between Steltzer and Stauffenberg came to nothing because Steltzer had to leave by air. The Circle's distinctive work, Steltzer noted, had come to an end. In Norway he made preparations with the help of Brodersen and his ordnance officer, J. W. von Moltke, a younger brother of Helmuth Moltke, for the time of the German collapse there. In an attempt to impress on the other side how fatal it was for the Allied policy to refuse any political contact with German opposition circles, Steltzer, with Brodersen's help, prepared a memorandum at the beginning of July 1944. The memorandum was intended in the first instance for Moltke's friends in the 'Round Table' group. It was transmitted to this group by the future Norwegian Defence Minister, Hauge. Hauge later reported that the memorandum had arrived.

Events took a decisive turn when Leber and Reichwein were arrested in July, following conversations with communists. These discussions had been preceded by a debate as to whether contacts should be established with the communists. Opinions differed. Haubach was completely opposed, Reichwein strongly in favour. Although the latter was not himself a communist, his socialism was unambiguous and almost bitter. He laid strong emphasis on socialist solidarity. He believed that the remnants of German communism belonged to the socialist movement and that they should be won over to their plans. He had been put in touch with members of the Central Committee of the Communist Party by Fritz Berndt and Ferdinand Thomas, and preliminary discussions had been held in the house of Frau Reichwein's brother at Wannsee. Stauffenberg also seems to have approved the proposal to put out a feeler. This may have been why Leber declared himself ready to co-operate. The matter was discussed once again at Yorck's home with Leber, Lukaschek, Husen and possibly others. At the beginning they had a very fruitful discussion of cultural problems, including school policy. On schools, Leber declared that he accepted unconditionally the parents' right to decide upon what education their children should have. He then went on to say that two men who were known to be communists had approached him and told him that they knew that he belonged to a resistance movement and that they wanted to collaborate. They asked for a meeting to discuss the matter. Lukaschek and Husen were very sceptical and suggested that communists who had been released from concentration camps might well be spies. Leber thought that they were reliable since he and they had shared the same quarters in a concentration camp for five years.

The first discussion with the communists took place on the following day. Although it had been agreed that no names would be mentioned, one of them greeted Leber by name. Instead of two, Jacob and Saefkow, there were now three communists, and the third, Hermann alias Rambow, was a spy. Their restrained attitude made Leber suspicious and he refused to take part in any further discussions. Only Reichwein went to the next meeting and he was arrested along with the communists. Leber was arrested on the following morning. They were severely tortured. Their friends feared that the Gestapo would move in. They knew that however resolute the prisoners might be, information could well be forced out of them under torture. They therefore tried hard to persuade the military group of the resistance to act quickly. Stauffenberg sent a message to Frau Leber that he was aware of his obligations to her husband. Indeed the arrest of Leber, who was to hold the post of Minister of the Interior in the first government, and of Reichwein who was a candidate for Education, prompted Stauffenberg to hasten on the assassination attempt.

According to Poelchau these events were decisive for Yorck in converting him into a supporter of assassination. Other Kreisau members also, for example Haubach and Einsiedel, gave up their objections on the basis of these facts, for it seemed to them that this was now the only possible solution, even though they were mostly still unable to give up their fundamental rejection of it. It is difficult to imagine what torture this must have caused them, for to them the methods that the conspirators planned to use were offensive. Haeften said to his brother Werner, 'we cannot employ gangster methods', and yet he too saw no other way out. This colossal inner tension, which affected his health, led him, still at the beginning of July 1944, to take his friend Krimm (a military chaplain at the time, and just then on leave) to one of the final decisive discussions with Yorck, Trott and others, in order to give his Christian arguments greater weight. The effort was fruitless, however, and it only earned him the censure of his friends. In the end he, too, consented to the assassination because, like his friends, he could no longer bear the guilt of being a silent bystander. Several of the other members of the Kreisau Circle now put themselves at Stauffenberg's disposal.

In connection with the assassination attempt Adam von Trott went abroad several more times to maintain his contacts and to get new ones in order to receive help from the Allied powers. In June 1944 he had a secret meeting in Switzerland with von Schulze-Gaevernitz, the assistant of Allen Dulles, and also obtained a passport for Sweden, where he spoke with several contacts; it is not clear if he at that time had also a meeting with a representative of the Russian side. Alexander Werth had to undertake the last journey to Sweden in the following month as Trott had fallen under suspicion, but Werth's journey was also unsuccessful. However, as late as July, Trott was able to make a last visit to Holland, where he met Patijn, Von Roijen and Reinink in Goerschen's office. He reported that the assassination attempt would take place within three weeks, and tried to find out what the Dutch reaction would be. The Dutch could not give any definite reply as the government in London would have to be consulted. When Patijn asked what the prospects of success were, von Trott answered: 'Twenty-five per cent'.

In Berlin the final preparations for the attempt had meanwhile been made. Stauffenberg had received a new appointment and now belonged to the very limited group of persons who had occasionally to make reports to Hitler at the Führer Headquarters in East Prussia. This gave him the opportunity to perform the attempt himself. On 6 July he took with him a packet containing explosives to a Hitler conference, but for various reasons the attempt was not made that day, nor when opportunities presented themselves on the 11th and the 15th. Day X was then definitely fixed for the 20th, because it was not possible to wait longer. Already on the evening of the 14th, before he flew to East Prussia, Stauffenberg had gone for a short discussion to van Husen's home. Leber's arrest had necessitated changes in the planned distribution of offices, and it was decided to appoint Yorck to the post of Under State Secretary in the Reich Chancellery while van Husen was proposed for the post of Under State Secretary in the Ministry of the Interior. Contrary to their original intention of taking no office, Yorck and van Husen agreed under the pressure of circumstances. A car was to collect van Husen at mid-day on Day X and take him to 10 Prince Heinrichstrasse where the political leaders would be gathered.

On 20 July when Stauffenberg was still in the Führer Headquarters, Yorck as the liaison officer between the military and civilian conspirators was among the officers who awaited the return of Stauffenberg in his office in the Bendlerstrasse. Later in the afternoon as rumours began to spread about the failure of the attempt, Gerstenmaier was called by Yorck to come to the Bendlerstrasse. In the following hours rumour became certainty.

The civilian conspirators waited all that day in vain for hopeful reports from the military insiders. In the Foreign Office, among others were von Trott and von Haeften, who was to take over the direction and transformation of the Foreign Office and to act, just as his father had in World War I, as a liaison officer between the Foreign Office and the military authorities. Haeften had a provisional written authority in his case and he knew precisely what immediate steps he had to take and, in particular, which people he would have to arrest. When the special radio announcement of the failure of the assassination came, and there was still no word from the military side, von Haeften and von Trott tried several times to ring Haeften's brother Werner, who was adjutant to Stauffenberg, but they could not get through. When the street, which had been temporarily closed by troops as a consequence of the orders of the conspirators, was reopened, they were forced to recognize the awful truth that they could no longer expect any news. They decided immediately to separate in order to prevent any further suspicion.

CHAPTER 20

Prison and People's Court

Almost all the members of the Kreisau Circle who had taken part or become implicated in the events of the 20th of July were arrested, Yorck and Gerstenmaier in the Bendlerstrasse and late in the evening Lukaschek in Breslau. Unknown to him a telegram, which was intercepted by the Gestapo, had been sent in the after-noon from the Bendlerstrasse by the conspirators ordering the local army commander, Koch-Erpach, to place himself under the authority of Lukaschek. Von Trott and von Haeften met that same night under cover of darkness in the Grünewald. Flight seemed unthinkable because their families would be left behind as hostages. Von Haeften was arrested on the 23rd and von Trott on 25 July. A gigantic man-hunt began and according to Gestapo sources at least 7000 persons were arrested. A special apparatus was set up to interrogate the prisoners and to prepare their trials. Among the men of Kreisau, Steltzer also was ordered to Berlin. He decided not to escape to Sweden and was arrested on his arrival in Berlin. Van Husen was next and on 9 August, just as he was about to depart on a business trip that would have offered him the opportunity to hide, Haubach, who on the day of the assassination attempt had been at the home of his friend Emil Henk in the Allgau. Of the Jesuits Delp had already been arrested in Munich on 28 July. König heard from some reliable informants that the warrant for his own and Rösch's arrest had been published in the *Reichskriminalblatt*. The Gestapo had already entered the Pullach college on their way to arrest him when he succeeded in escaping from the building and disappeared into a safe hiding-place arranged by Rösch. The Gestapo never found him. Rösch himself also went underground, first in a monastery and then later with a farmer's family. On 11 January 1945, however, he was betrayed and arrested. In the train to Berlin he was able to persuade the guard to tell his friends in Munich where he was. Besides König, the third Jesuit member, only von der Gablentz, Peters, von Einsiedel, von Trotha and Poelchau among the members of the 'inner circle' were not arrested.

One can imagine Moltke's disappointment. In a long discussion with Bishop Berggrav in March 1943, he had given two reasons why he had kept himself aloof from the assassination plans. In the first place he wondered if it would be good to begin a new order with a murder; secondly the group which had to prepare the attempt had for tactical reasons to remain small, so that in case of failure other groups would not be endangered. He also stressed that he considered the reconstruction of the administration as his special task, but that he should not shirk his duty if he was needed absolutely to kill Hitler. Now after the failure of the 20 July attempt he knew that several members of the Circle had been implicated and were lost to reconstruction; another consequence was the thwarting of his own release. He had always been sceptical about the technical feasibility of an assassination attempt. 'Don't you see that we are not conspirators? We can't do it, we haven't learned how, and we ought not now to try it for the first time; it will go awry and we will do it in a dilettante manner,' he said on one occasion. Moreover, endeavours to get Allied military support for an attempt had all been in vain. Moltke was thus very negative about what was done on 20 July. It is typical of his mood that he told his wife shortly afterwards, 'If I had been free, it would not have happened.' He maintained this position in conversations with both Poelchau and Gerstenmaier in prison. Only in the course of a long conversation between Moltke and Gerstenmaier, arranged with the help of a medical assistant, in which Gerstenmaier emphasized the importance of the attempt in the eyes of the outside world, does Moltke appear to have agreed.

After interrogation all the participants of the attempt, including the insiders, were sentenced, most of them to death, by a so-called People's Court set up at Hitler's command. The trials, in which several of the accused showed signs of torture, were conducted right through to the death, described as God's judgement, of the notorious Freisler himself. He reduced the trial to 'a caricature of legal process' and to a mockery of any true concept of justice. Some of the evidence collected at the preliminary interrogations can be seen in the Kielpinski Reports. Because of their mixture of lies, truth and half-truth, however, they must be used with caution.

Among the accused at the first major trial on 7 and 8 August 1944 was Yorck. In the course of the procedings Yorck had the

Execution chamber in Plotzensee Prison, Berlin, where members of the Kreisau Circle and others were hanged after the failure of the 20th July plot

courage to say that the treatment of the Jews and national socialist legal practice had been decisive in determining his attitude towards national socialism. Yorck was able to summarize his basic attitude in the following words: 'What is fundamental, what links all these problems together, is the state's totalitarian claim upon the citizen which excludes his religious and moral obligations to God.' Before he was executed—on the same day—he managed to let his friends know, through Poelchau, that the Gestapo were not yet on the track of the Kreisau Circle.

On 15 August, Hans Bernd von Haeften and Adam von Trott stood before the People's Court. When asked by Freisler whether he saw that he had committed treason, von Haeften answered in the negative and declared that he looked upon Hitler as the instrument of evil in history. Freisler was particularly sharp in his attack on Trott. His importance to the Gestapo can be seen from the fact that he was not, like the others including Haeften, executed on the same day, but only on 26 August. From him, Stauffenberg's adviser on foreign policy, the Gestapo hoped to extract more information.

It was not until 20 October that other members of the Kreisau Circle came before Freisler: Leber, Reichwein, Maass and Dahrendorf. They had been interrogated for a long time. When Reichwein, who had not lost hope, began to give a defence of himself in a feeble voice—mistreatment in prison had almost robbed him of his voice—and Freisler saw that even in the court he was still able to grip people, he interrupted rudely and tried to drown everything he said by bellowing at him, as if he was trying to prevent him from making an impression. Leber, who had already suffered most terrible degradation during four years in prisons and concentration camps in the thirties, had been fearfully mistreated in his most recent imprisonment, being 'interrogated' for four nights at the Dragon police school. Only when his wife and children were arrested did he make a statement, and even then he limited himself to his own activities. At the trial itself he was never given a chance to speak even one complete sentence. He was dubbed the 'German Lenin' by Freisler. Dahrendorf was the first to receive only a prison sentence. The Gestapo hoped that they would get further information from Leber, who had been one of Stauffenberg's closest colleagues, and he was not executed until 5 January 1945. From his prison cell he greeted his friends who were still free with the words: 'For such a good and just cause the sacrifice of one's life is the proper price.'

G R H—T

The importance of the Kreisau Circle in the resistance movement against national socialism eventually came to light, and it was underlined by Freisler himself in the trial of 9 and 10 January 1945 of Moltke, Haubach, Gerstenmaier, Delp, Steltzer; of the Bavarian contacts of the Circle, Sperr, Reisert and Fugger, and of Gross, one of the Cologne contacts. The case against Haubach and Steltzer was later on treated separately. The accused, who had been in regular touch with one another even in prison, had co-ordinated their defence with the help of secret messages during the past weeks. In this, as in many other ways, the prison chaplain Poelchau, being a member of the Circle, had given particularly valuable help. The case against the accused was that 'they had together undertaken to change the constitution of the Reich by force, and to deprive the Führer of his constitutional power and thereby, at the same time, to give assistance at home to the enemy power during a war against the Reich'. As these were the charges, the prisoners had agreed to put their non-participation at the centre of their defence. This understanding can still be detected in several of their letters. As these letters were liable to seizure, they contained only what was legally proven, and not what had actually happened. (See also footnote † p. 385.)

Delp was the first to appear before the court. He too had been severely maltreated under interrogation. As far as Freisler was concerned, his elimination was already certain and the trial was only a charade. According to Freisler's own subsequent account, Delp's defence was 'fairly out of this world', and from this one can only conclude what a vast gulf separated the Catholic priest and Jesuit, for whom God alone was 'the supreme authority', from Hitler's servant Freisler. Although Delp was merely mocked, the difference between the two men was only too apparent and Delp was able to write afterwards: 'The way the trial was conducted has given my life a worthy motif (*Thema*), for which one could both live and die.'

The chief accusation against Gerstenmaier was that he failed to reveal Goerdeler's plans and the meetings of the Kreisau Circle when he knew about them. His presence at the Bendlerstrasse on 20 July was also a source of embarrassment. Throughout both the interrogations and the trial he acted as though he were unworldly and naïve. Because he had actively participated in the events of 20 July, he stood rather outside the defence maintained by Moltke. Even though, however, greater suspicion attached to him, he did in fact succeed in convincing the judges of his other-worldliness.

The explanatory comment on his sentence spoke of him as 'a man whose world view is entirely incomprehensible to us'. Later, in the vehicle that carried them back to prison, Moltke praised Gerstenmaier's skilful and sound defence, which indeed helped him too to escape with only a mild sentence.

While the others were being tried, their relations with Moltke and with 'the Moltke Circle' were constantly pointed out. Thus, to a certain extent, Moltke occupied a central position. He rejected the charges against him and insisted upon his own nonparticipation, maintaining that he had only 'thought'. As the Nazis could not prove anything else against him—what can be proved legally is by no means synonymous with historical reality—this line of defence was maintained throughout the trial and can be seen even in his letters. His plea was, however, rejected and the notes on his sentence stated: 'He did not only think.' Many details of the trial remain unknown. For the Nazis his thoughts were ground enough for speaking of high treason. During a long duel between Moltke and Freisler, they succeeded in establishing 'the incompatibility between Christianity and national socialism'. The two had only one thing in common and that was that they demanded 'the whole man'. Thus, in this trial too, the problem of the ultimate authority was raised and Freisler recognized the fundamental character of Moltke's resistance. 'We shall be hanged as disciples of Christ,' Moltke was able to say. Apart from Gerstenmaier, only Reisert and Fugger survived. Later on the same day, at another trial, Steltzer too was condemned to death, and later still Haubach, rather surprisingly, received the same sentence. On 23 January, Moltke, Haubach, Sperr and others were executed. Haubach, who was seriously ill, had to be carried to the gallows on a stretcher. In an attempt to make his position intelligible in his farewell letter to his sons, Moltke wrote: 'My whole life long, from my school days on, I have been fighting against a spirit of pettiness and violence, arrogance, intolerance and absolute merciless consistency that is latent in the German and that has found its expression in the national socialist state. I have also worked towards the overcoming of this spirit, along with its evil consequences, such as excessive nationalism, racial persecution, irreligion and materialism.' Delp survived until 2 February. Steltzer, on the other hand, was saved just in time through the help of his Scandinavian friends; in particular Arvid Brodersen and Bishop Bjørkvist, who persuaded Kersten, Himmler's Finnish masseur, who had great influence on his patient, to intervene on Steltzer's behalf. As Himmler attached great importance to the goodwill of the Swedes, he gave orders on 4 February that the execution should not be carried out, the day before it was due to take place. Kersten's secretary received the job of taking the order to the prison authorities; although delayed by a heavy bombing raid, she arrived at the prison in time.

Of the others, Lukaschek and van Husen were brought to trial after Freisler's death in an Allied raid; van Husen was given only a slight sentence, and Lukaschek was acquitted, as he attacked the torturing that he had undergone and retracted all that he had said during the investigations. Rösch was not brought to court and at the end of the war he managed to save both himself and others. Thus, even though his death had sometimes been predicted by Gestapo officials during earlier interrogations, he remained, miraculously, alive.

CHAPTER 21

Against the Stream

The German Resistance was the response of a minority, who, in their rejection of national socialism, were one; the ideas of the various groups of which it was composed were many. Typical, however, for the most of them, was the inward renewal that they had gone through in the course of the Nazi years. None more than the Kreisau Circle were aware that a transformation would be essential and they therefore rejected any idea of a 'Restoration' and tried to take their stand on the demands of the future. The Circle's plans—never regarded by them as definitive—were described by one of its leading members, the sociologist and Catholic Alfred Delp, in the following words: 'We must endeavour so to organize the external life of men, their social, their economic, their technical relations, that they are assured of relatively secure access to everything that they need to make life, in all its forms, livable. Men themselves are to be the measure of their own objective, and the implementation of our plan must always be judged in the light of what it is reasonable to believe possible. Is this going to lead men to God? That is the basic presupposition. We must first strive to order and shape the conditions of life in such a way that the vision of God is no more a superhuman effort.'

After the war, however, things turned out differently. A restoration of the past did in many respects take place, in spite of all good intentions. Why was this? In the first place because many who aimed at making a really fresh start had been killed by the Nazis, and this accounts for the leading members of the Kreisau Circle. Secondly the international clash between West and East made men adopt dogmatic positions, which had its effect on the evolution in Western Germany. In this connection the careers of men like Steltzer and Lukaschek are more typical than that of Gerstenmaier. Finally, history suggests that after times of great changes people dislike all further reforms and are all the more quickly ready to revert to an idealized reproduction of the past.

In trying to sum up the post-war experiences of the surviving men of Kreisau, only a few general remarks are here possible.

The Circle had always considered an occupation of Germany after the collapse of the régime to be necessary; they believed that Germans would only be ready for an inward renewal if they were compelled to understand that the national socialist leaders were alone responsible for the defeat and the chaos. Men like Moltke also had hopes that the victors would by their example further the renewal. After the collapse the survivors of the Kreisau Circle did not hesitate, therefore, to offer their services for the reconstruction of their country. The Soviet occupying authorities thus commissioned Steltzer together with his friend Hermes, to set up an office for Food and Agriculture. Lukaschek became Minister of Agriculture in Thüringen. Van Husen acted as adviser to the Americans on questions relating to constitutional and administrative law, and in this post made great efforts to reorganize the legal checks to administration. Poelchau, Einsiedel and von Trotha offered their services to the Russian authorities; Poelchau worked in the penal section of the justice in the Soviet Zone for prison reform and Einsiedel and von Trotha took over responsibility for economic planning. During the summer of 1945 Einsiedel and von Trotha often talked to American visitors to Berlin for the State Department about the Kreisau proposals for European integration. Einsiedel wrote: 'It is rightly demanded of the German people that they should undergo a profound transformation. The souls of many Germans are still full of poison but the other peoples of the world can only assist in this transformation if they themselves accept the spiritual values that are to find a home once again in Germany.' Alas, Einsiedel could no longer share in reconstructional work; after a number of cross-examinations, he was, as early as October 1945, arrested by the Russians. His ignorance of the fact that the Germans had had poison gas standing ready for use during the war was interpreted by the Soviets as evasion, his membership of the Kreisau Circle being insufficient in the eyes of the Russians to exonerate him. It appears he was taken to Russia to an institute of economic planning in Moscow, and then brought back to Germany in the spring of 1948. He died of hunger shortly afterwards in the concentration camp at Sachsenhausen.

The co-operation of the men of Kreisau with the occupying authorities did not mean, however, that they agreed to all their measures. Thus Steltzer, who after his departure from Berlin was given the post of Oberpräsident and shortly afterwards that of a

Prime Minister of Schleswig-Holstein, greatly regretted that the British authorities did not consider him a partner so much as an executive carrying out their instructions. He asked again and again for more freedom; he also tried without success to apply some of the Circle's ideas to the work of denazification. However, he and men like Lukaschek also realized how much defeated and impoverished Germany had to thank the Allies for. Lukaschek indeed made the comment that the debt to the Americans for the enormous aid that they, as the victors, had granted to the vanquished should never be forgotten; nor should their economic recovery be attributed solely to the nation's own virtues. About the attitude of many of his countrymen he remarked: 'I do not believe in collective guilt, but unlike the majority of my compatriots, I believe just as little in collective innocence.'

Hans Peters had a chance to follow up his paper on the aims of a new cultural policy given at the first large gathering in Kreisau 1942. He now proposed to add an Under Secretary of State for Culture to the functionaries mentioned in the Potsdam Treaty of 1945. Further he supported a moderate federalism, in which the central government retained those rights that practical considerations decreed it should have and advocated a considerable extension of self-government, as a method of enabling the citizen to participate in public affairs. Also in later publications he regretted that the Bonn Constitution founders were influenced too much by their reaction against Nazi times.

Lukaschek devoted himself to the seemingly insoluble problem of refugees, becoming Minister of Refugees in the first Bonn cabinet, and with the help of international experts he succeeded in legislating for those unfortunates and in enabling them to create a new life. After four years ten million men were well on the way to building a new existence for themselves. It was Lukaschek's aim to integrate these people wholly in the Federal Republic. Von Trotha prepared a paper for the Amsterdam founding conference of the World Council of Churches. Too optimistically perhaps, he regarded refugees as a group which, having lost their possessions, could help to bring about new forms of social life and a spiritual renewal. At the same time Steltzer in Schleswig-Holstein, where the population doubled in a few months, came to realize that many of them, thanks to their peculiar position, were disposed to support a policy of renewal and integration. When this dawned also on Adenauer, whose main concern was with the tactics of the domestic political battle, Lukaschek's name was not on the list of candidates in the elections of 1953. Neither was he offered a cabinet post in the second Adenauer government, the ex-Nazi Oberländer being considered more suitable.

During his time in Schleswig-Holstein Steltzer founded, with the help of von Trotha and others, a non-party organization; the aim was to apply Kreisau ideas on reconstruction by establishing links between the various social groups and working for a just social order. Several conferences were held and different social groups brought together. After retiring from Schleswig-Holstein Steltzer became Director of the 'Public Affairs Institute', designed to perform the same task as the well-known Public Administration Clearing House in Chicago. But the new structure of the Bonn State and the suspicion of many leading politicians gave this initiative too little room to flourish.

In many respects such chances for a renewal as had existed, were lost. The fundamental problem of how the Nazis had come about was evaded and new problems were dealt with in terms of restoration and tradition. Von der Gablentz sharply criticized this failure and in his opinion Konrad Adenauer was largely but by no means exclusively to blame.

Seen from Berlin the German situation in the first post-war years looked quite otherwise than from Bonn. This led several of the men of Kreisau and others, in spite of the worsening in the East–West relations, to keep in touch and remain at their posts as long as possible. Hans Peters, who was elected in 1946 a member of the first city Assembly for the whole of Berlin, when the Soviet-controlled Berlin university was re-opened in 1946 became a full Professor and was Dean for two and a half years. He was a frequent speaker on both the East Berlin and American radios and no restrictions were placed on what he said. He believed that many opportunities were lost during that period. Another example is Harald Poelchau, who was elected to the managing committee of the East German Ministry of the Justice; he was also given a teaching post in criminology and prison studies at the same legal faculty as Hans Peters. Large numbers of students attended both his lectures and seminars. Later, he maintained, that 'during that period it would have been easy to create a free democratic Berlin on a broad basis' and criticized the naïve identification of Christianity with the politics of the West German C.D.U. Party. When von Trotha tried to open the way for East Berlin professors such as Alfred Kantorowicz and Ernst Niekisch to give lectures at the 'Political University' (*Hochschule für Politik*) which he had founded under Otto Suhr, this was prevented by the West Berlin Senate.

Another important field after the war was the re-establishment of contact with the world abroad and realization of the aims of European integration. Von Trotha felt that the national restoration, such as had occurred between 1945 and 1947 in almost all European countries, could only be broken down by the establishment of a federal structure in Europe; consequently he became co-founder and president of the Europe Union in Berlin and represented Berlin and the German movement for a united Europe at Strasburg. He was enthusiastic about this work and wrote optimistically: 'In the Strasburg assembly for the first time European programmes are being discussed by Europeans with European viewpoints.' In the 'Political University' Trotha paid particular attention to the department of 'Foreign Studies and Foreign Policy' where he made European integration the main theme. He also took part in many ecumenical conferences. Steltzer was the founder and the first president of the 'Deutsche Gesellschaft für Auswärtige Politik', an independant research institute for foreign policy much like the well-known 'Chatham House' in London. This institute was founded in 1955 and until his seventy-fifth birthday Steltzer was president. The periodical *Europa-Archiv* which William von Cornidas had founded was brought under this institute. Eugen Gerstenmaier meanwhile specialized in foreign policy questions, and acted as chairman of the Foreign Affairs Committee of the West German Parliament until he was elected Speaker in 1954.

From 1962 until shortly before his death in 1967 Steltzer was back in Berlin, where he could work for a true solution of the German problem from the peculiar Berlin situation. He pleaded for an end to cold-war attitudes and advocated a West–East relaxation policy, supporting to this end the activities of the 'Evangelical Academy' in Berlin. Only a few days before his death, its work to establish the Comenius Club, which aims at improving relations between West Germany, the German Democratic Republic and Eastern Europe, was crowned with success. It is perhaps typical for Steltzer's attitude that at his funeral there was no delegation from the West German C.D.U. of which he was a co-founder, while a deputation came over from the D.D.R.

For different reasons the surviving members of the Kreisau Circle did not act after the war as a group; what they could achieve was therefore diffused. Yet in several sectors of the West German society, and beyond, their influence can be perceived—for most of them it was an influence against the stream. Only four members of the inner Circle—von der Gablentz, Poelchau, van Husen and Gerstenmaier—are still alive today (1970), when several reforms both in the foreign and in the internal sphere suggest that the tide of restoration has begun to ebb. If this is so, their resistance against reaction and totalitarianism in all their forms was not after all in vain.

PART 6
DOCUMENTS

Introduction

None of the documents which follow were written for publication, a fact to be borne in mind when assessing them. Only a part of the documentary evidence of the activity of the Kreisau Circle was, however, preserved, for many papers, naturally enough, were destroyed, either in the fatal year 1944 itself or later, during the period of imprisonments.

The author wishes to thank all those who have given permission for the publication of one or more documents. In particular he extends his thanks to Countess von Moltke for many documents from her husband's papers. She retains the copyright and any future publication requires her permission.

The German original *Neuordnung im Widerstand* contains a small number of documents not reprinted in this edition but referred to in the footnotes. The extracts from Moltke's Last Letters, and Moltke's Letter to an English Friend, which have been added, are printed with kind permission of Henssel Verlag, Berlin, which is planning a comprehensive edition of the Moltke Letters, 1930–45.

1. Moltke to Einsiedel*

Berlin, 16 June 1940†

Dear Einsiedel,

On several points we did not come to any firm conclusions, because we thought that events would come to our aid and enable us to try out in practice what we had not formulated theoretically and perhaps could not formulate. Now the situation is different. Events will not come to our aid and we will only master these difficulties if we get them straight in our own minds and sort them out by ourselves. We are still as far from a change as Voltaire was from the French Revolution when he used to practice by closing his letters: Écrasez l'Infame. How great the distance between intellectual and spiritual triumph and practical transformation must have seemed to him then, and how short it seems to us today. We can console ourselves with this and go on thinking afresh.

I have a number of questions on the organization and planning of the economy, which I would be very glad if you would answer.‡ There seems to me to be a danger that a planned economy could come to occupy a position in human affairs that had all the drawbacks of a deified state and would be considered even more strictly from a utilitarian standpoint. How can this danger be overcome?

In considering economic questions, I start out from the following basic principles, which I would like you to comment upon.

1. The economic sphere is one in which each individual must have a function to perform, so that he is in a position to prove his worth obviously and tangibly and to contribute to the physical or spiritual well-being of the community through his own effort.

2. The objective of the economic activity of the community as a whole is:

a) to provide the basic essentials of life for the individual,

b) to provide the individual with a fair share of the surplus products,

c) to provide the individual with an opportunity to devote himself to the cultivation of beauty—in the widest possible sense.

* There are typescript copies of all the letters in this part of the documentary section in the Moltke papers, file of memoranda and political letters; there are, in addition, some hand-written originals but the original copies of the remaining letters appear to have been destroyed.

† The letter was not sent until the following day, see Moltke to Einsiedel, 15 July 1940.

‡ See p. 108.

The objective of the economic activity of the community as a whole is not:

a) to provide the individual with an unfair share of the surplus products.

b) to provide individuals, groups or everybody with such considerable diversions that they are able to evade their own inadequacies and so save themselves the bother of concentrating on their own education,

c) to produce in such a way that material things dominate men,

d) to create a situation in which some men dominate other men.

3. The object of economic activity must be to make the individual person freer by liberating him from subordination to the natural world. The object must not be to diminish his freedom by replacing his dependence upon the material world by a dependence upon men—a dependence which is just as great when it relates to an employer as to an official.

4. The object of economic activity is to provide the resources with which all higher aims can be fulfilled, without, however, determining the character of these higher activities.

The highest objective of economic activity—leaving aside its educational value—can only be to contribute towards the gratification of the senses—that is, in the last resort, beauty. It must do this without coming into collision with the individual's longing for justice and without placing such limitations upon the freedom of the individual that he is not in a position to develop his body, spirit and understanding freely and fully.

May I possibly have your views on the sentences above? Are they true or false or in need of development or abbreviation? When we have agreed on these points I will ask you to discuss the implications of these principles with me. If you understand justice as I have used it in the last paragraph, then the theme that I wish to explore with you can be defined as follows: What does the manifestation of justice in the economic system mean?

Yours,

2. Moltke to Yorck*

17.6.40.

Dear Yorck,

Now that we have got to reckon with a triumph of evil and, instead of the suffering and misfortunes for which we had prepared ourselves, we will have to endure a much nastier mixture of external fortune, comfort and prosperity, it is all the more important that we clarify our minds about the foundations of a constructive political science. I want to make

* See p. 107.

a start on this process of clarification—of my mind not of yours—in this letter, by harking back to a discussion that we had with Schulenburg just under a fortnight ago.

You perhaps remember the wager that we made. Schulenburg was prepared to bet that within ten years there would be a state of which we could completely approve. I was ready to maintain the opposite. This led on to a discussion of what we meant by such a state and I proposed justice as the criterion, so that Schulenburg will have won his bet if within ten years we have a just state, allowing for the limitations imposed by human shortcomings.

We then had to define what we meant by justice and we agreed that justice could be said to exist when each individual was able to develop and express himself fully within the framework of the state as a whole.

The next stage of our discussion, and the point that I want to take up here, was reached when you said that you would want to place a heavy security against the free opportunity of each individual to express himself and I replied that for the purposes of our bet, we have given sufficient security with the reference to 'within the framework of the state as a whole'.

Our discussion ended there and I would like to start at this point, by discussing what is meant by your word 'security', since this is one of the most important and fundamental problems in a renewal of the state and we cannot leave it just as we left it at the end of our discussion.

The foundation of all political science seems to me to consist of the following fundamental principles:

1. It is not the purpose of the state to control men and to restrain them by force or by the threat of force, but rather to bring men into such a relationship with each other and to maintain that relationship that the individual can live and act in complete security without at the same time harming his neighbour.

2. It is not the purpose of the state to turn men into wild animals or machines, but rather to provide the individual with the support that enables him to develop and use his body, spirit and intelligence without hindrance.

3. It is not the purpose of the state to demand unconditional obedience and blind faith in itself or in something else, but rather to guide individual men so that they live according to the dictates of reason and exercise this reason in all activities and, at the same time, to prompt them against wasting their powers in hatred, anxiety, envy, or any other kind of unjust behaviour.

The ultimate purpose of the state is therefore to act as the protector of the freedom of the individual. If it does this it is a just state.

I am far from believing that these principles can be fully realized. I believe them, however, to be standards against which we must judge all constitution-making. Putting it bluntly, I think one could say that there are three features of the present state that one would like to see removed:

terror, power and faith that is not a product of individual citizens. None of these can be entirely eliminated: a deterrent (terror) is essential to guarantee internal security, power is essential to guarantee external peace, and faith is essential to excite the individual citizen to participation and to provide him with the necessary motivation that only a few can derive from reason. Nevertheless these are compromises that have to be made in the interests of reality; they are not permanent features that have their own inner justification.

This brings me to the central point that I want to clarify; whether or not we disagree about fundamentals. Your 'security' is a compromise of this sort, a concession to reality, which one must keep as small as possible—and which, through education, both of children and adults, one must work to reduce. The state which, at best, we can expect will have to begin with security against the freedom of the individual, and the objective must be to remove this security as quickly as possible.

I would very much like an answer from you before I go any further, since there are too many side-tracks that lead away from this fundamental problem, which one might define as: What do we mean by the manifestation of justice in the state?

Yours,

3. *Yorck to Moltke*

7.7.40.

I am following your example by writing my answer, unfortunately illegibly, since conversation too easily becomes bitty and because this discussion between us ought to serve to establish a starting point.

Before I come on to the main subject of your letter, I should like to comment on your description, at the beginning of the letter, of the German victory as the triumph of evil. I can agree with this assessment in only one respect: it holds good to the extent that these events reflect the triumph—wanted by one man—of nihilism. It does not apply to what has occurred independently of and indeed contrary to his will. Evil was intended but perhaps good has been created. My optimism really stems from a short journey through the so-called enemy territories. In the novel atmosphere one can more easily discover a new point of view and for me the great surprise was to come across people who were neither full of hatred nor dejected and whose efforts were not directed at revision or revenge. Instead I found a readiness to create a European community on the basis of accomplished facts and the belief that values that had hitherto dominated were inadequate when measured against human reality and that the young people had not been broken. The collapse of the French army must therefore it seems to me be attributed not to military and technical causes in the last resort, but much more to the spiritual condition in which the French went to war. I see this as a warning, in that with the rejection of the 'system' spiritual resources are being denied that have already attained a living power and which cannot be countered simply by negation. The real task is to set them off in the right direction. Even if—as I hope—we are witnessing the end of an epoch, we must look at the kernel from which the new life will arise among the ruins. This is by way of introduction, since it seems to me that a discussion of these questions is also appropriate in the context of a search for a common starting point for the task of discovering the basic principles of a new state. I must confess that I have long recognized the need to develop these basic principles but I have nonetheless not done so.

Previous attempts have lacked precision and consistency and above all profundity. For we are not in any way simply concerned with external and organizational problems, but with the discovery of the substance of national and state life and the form that is appropriate to this substance. This discovery assumes a knowledge of previous developments and therefore of the spiritual driving forces that have together and in conflict with one another shaped history.

Like you I am sure that one can only fulfil this responsibility through really serious study, and the question arises for me as to whether I can combine work of this sort with my everyday concerns. Unfortunately, I cannot yet give an answer to this question, but I am trying to discover what the answer is as quickly as possible.

I will, however, attempt to answer your question about the nature and scope of the 'security'.

On the basis of the three negative definitions of the function of the state, you summarize its positive functions in the proposition that it is the protector of the freedom of the individual. The idea of freedom has undergone so many changes that its meaning in this context needs to be explained. I think that I can find a definition in your own words, when you say that the individual ought to be able to live and act in full security without at the same time harming his neighbours. In this sentence freedom is subordinate to an ethical postulate which relates to the community and therefore also to the state. This obligation of the individual and towards community seems to me essential to the argument, and in it are to be found the combination of law and duty that I described in our conversation as a security against the individual. With this notion I intended to transform the freedom of an individual for himself into freedom for others, which is, to my mind, the only possible foundation of life in a state. I intended to express the idea that the period of distress which, despite external successes, will come, will confront us with the duty to act for the community to 'serve'. Nonetheless this should be understood within the context of the idea of law, according to which objective constitutional and legal order is a personal right of the individual, who must not be exposed to the arbitrary political will of the all-powerful state and towards whom the state too has a relationship governed by law and duty.

A second point that must be noted is that law and morality are inseparably linked and that even the state's will must be subordinated to morality. The real nature of the state seems to me to be manifest where it appears to men as an instrument of divine order and is accepted as such by them.

For this reason it seems to me more relevant to consider its purpose positively and not, in reaction against tyranny, negatively. I hope that I have made myself clear, even if I have limited myself to hints. If we discover a common starting point, I am quite ready to collaborate and I will try to make time. However let us first discuss the first point.

4. Moltke to Yorck

12.7.40.

Dear Yorck,

I want to begin by answering your first point about the current situation.

Throughout my adult life I have worked together with people of other countries, and since 1935 especially I have quite deliberately tried to help the 'new forces' in England to establish their position against the ruling generation, above their own. (The generation between the present rulers and the new generation was practically destroyed in World War I.) I did this because I was convinced that only the triumph of this new generation in Great Britain could prevent the war. I remain convinced that the relationship with these men must be re-established as early as possible.

This applies to the intellectual partnership between us.

I do not, however, believe that it can be applied to the political sphere. Spiritual intention and reality, understanding and external form will never coincide, because our will is not strong enough nor our understanding clear enough. However, the enormous discrepancy that there is today between intention and understanding on the one side and reality and external form on the other, is intolerable. In my opinion we would destroy the spiritual and intellectual partnership that exists between us and the best members of other nations, if we tried to reconcile them to a situation which must be altered—if they and we are to be released from the tension between understanding and external form.

My opinion is as follows: it is our task to arrive at such a degree of understanding, that we enable ourselves and others to overcome the present external form on the basis of the clarity that we have created.

We must not, however, obscure our own understanding and the

understanding of others in the interest of maintaining the present external conditions (among which are the victory and its consequences).

I hope that this is clear. I am entirely in agreement with you about the reasons for the French collapse. A facade has collapsed before the new building that has been under construction for many years was strong enough. The demolition contractor cannot, however, complete the new building, although he has made it easier by knocking down the facade—at the cost, it must be said, of enormous human suffering.

Yours,

5. *Moltke to Yorck*

15.7.40.

I come now to the second part of your letter. I am also in favour of positive definitions; the negative ones in my letter of 17.6.40 were only intended to make the positive aspect clearer, by presenting a contrast.

1. I have the impression that we are still talking about two different things; I am talking about constitutional law, while you are talking about the attitude of the individual towards the state. 'Freedom for others' is something that only the individual himself can possess; if the state forces him to it then it is no longer freedom. 'Service' in the sense that we have employed it can only be voluntary. Whether a person works for others or only for himself, whether he serves or not, depends on the individual and on his own attitude. No law is capable of improving men; the law must only keep the way open for those who, without it, are 'improved'.

We must clarify this point in discussion.

2. I'm not clear whether your thesis that the state is subordinate to a moral command is correct. I am inclined to the view that ethics are related to the individual; every individual who administers the state's power must feel himself subordinate to an ethical law, but not the state as such. I am inclined to think that the latter idea is wishful thinking. For the individual, however, Kant's words are valid: act in such a way that your action could be taken as a universal standard.

I would also like to examine this problem further.

3. I would also like to have discussed your comment that 'the state appears as an instrument of divine order'. I am of the opinion that political science belongs to the sphere of philosophy and not theology and I think that it is extraordinarily dangerous to give a religious interpretation and a religious substructure to a political order.

I would like to discuss all three points with you because they cannot be clarified in writing.

Yours,

6. *Moltke to Einsiedel*

15.7.40.

1.

In our last discussion we talked about the ideas in my letter of 17.6.40 and as far as I can remember, you disputed my points 2d and 3 and thought that point number 4 was inadequate.

You were of the opinion that in points 2 and 3, one could get the impression that I limited the dominance of men over men to the political sphere, with the intention of keeping the economy as far as possible beyond the compass of the state.

Is your objection overcome if point 2d is reformulated as follows: 'To create non-functional domination of men over others.'?

I find it rather more difficult to get hold of point number 3. For the purposes of illustration we assumed that the state's form was an aristocracy and from this we deduced the following consequences:

a) The power of decision on important economic questions belongs within the sphere of politics and, therefore, within the competence of the aristocrats;

b) The right of the individual within the 'enterprise' in which he works and the right of the employer to maintain his economic freedom are subjective rights which are beyond the discretion of any civil servant and for the maintenance of which the individual or the employer only makes use of the civil servant;

c) Between these two spheres there is the sphere of administrative discretion, in which the economic civil servant does decide creatively, and in which the individual and the employer are dependent on these civil servants. I therefore propose the following formulation of point 3: 'The object of economic activity must be to make the individual person freer by liberating him from subordination to the natural world. The object must not be to diminish his freedom by replacing his dependence upon the material world within the sphere of his economic activity by a dependence on men, either employers or civil servants.'

I propose that point 4 should remain unaltered. By doing so we leave the question 'To whom shall the resources for the higher activity be assigned—the individual, the employer, the economic bureaucracy or the political authorities?' open. To my mind the question about who should have the right to dispose of these resources is a political question and therefore does not belong here. I will only add by way by explanation that, in keeping with the whole of my attitude, I would favour assigning these resources to three groups: the individual, the self-governing corporation and the highest political authority, but never the employers or the bureaucracy.

2.

I would suggest therefore that we pursue the following programme:
a) Examine my formulations once again word by word so that we arrive
at lucid concepts. I distrust all picture language since it is usually more
of a hindrance than a help and because one can never be certain that
everybody interprets the picture in the same way. It is impossible to do
entirely without pictures if one wants to popularize something; pictures
should only be employed, however, when the framework of concepts is
clear. Hence I consider it my duty to cuarify the concepts.

What still needs to be established is whether the relationship of the
individual to the economic system, as it is presented in my formulations,
has been exhaustively treated. I should be grateful if you would check
on this.

b) Once we have agreed about the formulation of these points and are
quite clear what we mean by them, our next job, in my opinion, is to
substantiate these formulations and to indicate where they differ from
the most important theories.

c) Alongside this we must also outline the practical implications of
our ideas and indicate which economic institutions are essential, which
desirable, which harmful and which, either existing or planned, must be
eliminated in all circumstances.

If we can complete (b) and (c), we should succeed in achieving clarity
in our own minds.

Let us develop both these points in the immediate future.

Yours,

7. *Moltke to Yorck*

21.7.40.

The paper 'The image of the Western State', that I am returning with
this letter, interested me greatly. I felt like someone who sees his
reflection in the water: everything is the same and yet everything is
completely different. Assuming your permission, I have prepared a tran-
script so that I can give it rather longer consideration. Despite the
material differences between us, it was of the greatest interest to me
and I can only congratulate its author on this clear and convincing pre-
sentation of what, to my mind, is an extremely obscure subject.

Nonetheless, the paper doesn't convince me. Perhaps it is good
theology, but it is not political science. It is too romantic for my taste
and tries to establish a state of affairs that may have been possible before
the Reformation and the Age of Enlightenment. The truths which are
enshrined in it are eternal—for the individual, but anachronistic if
applied to a community possessed of sovereignty.

I am the last person to claim that I myself have achieved any clarity on this and I will try to analyse the paper even more thoroughly within the next weeks.

What I have to say now, therefore, must be understood as the product of my own uncertainty and as an effort to achieve clarity for myself. I only put it down in writing, because I want very much to draw your attention to a point in which perhaps we start from different basic principles. I had always looked upon my opinion in this matter as beyond discussion, and you evidently felt the same about yours.

For me there is, on the one side, religion, revelation through Christ and the prophets, faith and obedience, and on the other, philosophy, wisdom which is achieved by the use of reason, understanding. Both lines meet in ethics since, in my opinion, Christian moral doctrines agree with what can be deduced by reason.

Since, however, revelation is a grace that cannot be enjoyed by all citizens and since there are no generally valid rules for the life of the community set down in Holy Writ, but only special regulations for the Jewish state, revelation cannot form the basis of constitutional law and every attempt to make it do so must, in my opinion, result in fruitless discussions.

Because of this, the paper 'The image of the Western State' appeals to Christian moral teaching as well as revelation for help. If, however, revelation contains no constitutional law, it cannot say anything about the relationship between moral teaching and constitutional law either. If revelation is irrelevant, therefore, we are left, as far as this paper is concerned, with unlimited speculation or conclusions based on reason and with this choice I opt for the conclusions based on reason. In my view, constitutional law is entirely based on rational conclusions, without any support from revelation, so that for me there is no choice.

I once heard Nawiaski describe a particular constitutional idea put forward by Carl Schmitt as a floating ball of lightning that was entirely self-sufficient and appeared to have neither a beginning nor an end. It seems to me that the constitutional ideas in this paper have precisely the same quality, as soon as one abstracts the theology from them, which cannot form the basis of the constitution. That is why primitive Christianity did not create a state and that is why the disciples and apostles never formed a group adapted to self-government.

This is all rather confused and it is only intended to indicate my ideas. I will try to give them rather more definite and coherent shape before the year is over and then perhaps we can discuss the matter again.

8. *Gablentz to Moltke*

9.8.40.

Dear Moltke,

Your thesis is correct: actions that cannot be defended ethically cannot be pardoned by an appeal to the interests of the state. However, to sustain this thesis we must, I believe, go somewhat deeper.

In contrast to you I believe that political science can *only* be established on the basis of theology. Without this foundation, one finds oneself helpless in face of the dilemma between the ethics of ultimate ends and the ethics of responsibility, described by Max Weber in his lecture, 'Politics as a Vocation'. Either the aim of ethics is personal salvation or, to put it in secular terms, self-esteem; in which case I remain caught in the abstract freedom of the ethics of ultimate ends, which are indeed autonomous but which are exhausted before they achieve any concrete form; or the object of ethics is something objective, either an action or a community. In this case the state, as the permanent expression of a community, very quickly pushes its way to the fore as an end in itself and one finds oneself in the plight of the ethics of responsibility. Here there is a concrete objective, but it is external and beyond the individual's control (heteronomous) and therefore undermines his human dignity.

The fallacy that lies behind both the ethics of ultimate ends and the ethics of responsibility is that both are directed towards self-preservation rather than surrender. 'What does it profit a man if he should win the whole world and lose his soul?' or in Latin *'Propter vitam vivendi perdere causas.'* The question about the *Causae vitae* can only be answered if I believe that the world is meaningful and that the humble individual can grasp this meaning and shape his life on the basis of this understanding. True ethics have to be 'theonomous' (Tillich).

As far as political science is concerned this implies: the state has a purpose in so far as it aligns itself with the standard of the kingdom of God, and that is to develop a just order through men who are free. The statesman who is aware of this standard ceases to feel any tension between personal and political ethics. It is his political duty to act on the basis of love and respect and not hatred: even where he must be harsh, it is his duty to refrain from abusing men as means for his own ends: even where he has temporarily to cut things down, it is his duty to remember the enduring order of things.

In the service of the Reich he will have with great severity to make his authority prevail; but at the same time he will not forget that there must still be opportunities left open and men available who can either be enlisted for his own work later, or, when his own work proves inadequate, correct errors. We need a political law of sanctuary. Even forces that we need at first to remove from political life must not be destroyed because they will be needed again at some time or other if the state is to be durable and not simply constructed on the basis of our own subjective attitude.

All this is of necessity abstract. One can only formulate more substantial objectives for a particular state at a particular time. The genuine state community exists where the grasp of the substantial tasks is so strong and steady that reference to moral science is only necessary as a corrective. The only person who can lead a state is the one who can be enthusiastic about these substantial tasks. If the moralist is incapable of doing so then he should keep out of politics.

To what extent I have answered your question I with the above must be seen in the course of conversation.

II. Christian moral teaching is entirely irrelevant. There is one equal, authentic, abstract and 'humanist' morality that is valid for all men, and which is as evident to the Stoic as it is to the Christian and the Confucian. For us the most accessible definition of it is Goethe's reverence for what is beneath us, what is equal to us and what is above us. If the church is worth anything, if, that is, she has a real spiritual substance, a 'magical' power, then her members will take this morality seriously. If the church loses her magical power and becomes simply an organization for moral propaganda, then she ceases to have any use even as an educational instrument. The church exists through the sacrament, through prayer, through meditation, but not through moral instruction.

The state must take some risks in its relationship with the church. It must allow full freedom for worship and preaching, that is for the Christian interpretation of Nature and History. It not only can, it must prevent the church from adopting attitudes and doctrines that it would not allow its ordinary citizens to hold,—that is any attitude or doctrines that are irreverent and malicious; in acting against these it is not acting against the church but against the subjective utterances of confused Christians.

The state can and ought to secure itself, even by using the law, against any form of state church, including church taxes. The best that the church can hope for is that the long-since obsolete church taxes will be gradually removed and that there might perhaps be negotiations about the restoration of church property that has been secularized in the past. If the state allows the church to live in this way and does not intervene in her very distinctive life, then it will derive the satisfaction of being able to find its best servants amongst the members of the church, since they are more discerning and more selfless than others, not because of a special morality but because they are more open to grace.

9. Moltke to Gablentz

31.8.40.

The conclusions of our discussion of 23 August, which made the first sections of both our letters redundant, I would summarize as follows:

I. Theory of the State

1. Theology and Political Science are separate disciplines; there is no such thing as a Christian state.*

* There is no theological doctrine directly relating to the state, only to men within the state; there is, thus, no such thing as a Christian state. (Correction made later by Moltke, cf. Gablentz's letter of 7.9.40.)

2. If we are trying to formulate the first principles of the state today, we proceed from the basic principles of ethics, by which we mean 'humanist' ethics, independent of the content of the Christian or any other religious revelation.

3. The purpose of the state is to provide men with the freedom that enables them to perceive the natural order and to contribute to its realization.

4. There are, however, no ethical precepts that cover the state: neither in its relationships with its own citizens, nor with other states, nor with citizens of other states: the state is amoral.*

II. *Theory of the Statesman*

1. The statesman's task is to fulfil the purpose of the state, as it is formulated in I, 3 above.

2. In order to fulfil this task, he must

a) feel himself committed to ethical precepts from whatever sources he may derive them;

b) be able to perceive the order in the nature of things and to act in accordance with it.

3. This task demands of a man understanding, self-denial and self-assurance which, in your opinion, can only be derived from the Christian revelation; anyone who has these qualities you claim as a Christian even if he does not profess himself to be one. It is in this sense that you speak of the 'Christian statesman'.

4. We agree that the formation and sustenance of a Christian states-man are functions of education.

Please examine these formulations and see whether you can approve of them. There are some points that need to be discussed further, especially I, 3 with its tension between 'freedom' and 'natural order'. I should be grateful if you would give me help on this.

Yours,

10. *Moltke to Yorck*

1.9.40.

Our discussion of faith, and with it of revelation and state, led us away from our original theme. I am at present doing some work on the problem of religion and state and I will prepare, in time, a note on my conclusions. I am not yet, however, ready to discuss these ideas and I would be very grateful if we could return to the original theme which was the relationship between the individual and the state. I have looked through our earlier letters again and I am convinced of the inadequacy of my first formulations.

* The state is amoral because it is abstract. When we concern ourselves with man we are dealing with the concrete statesman. (Later correction by Moltke.)

One more comment by way of introduction: the question of the relationship between the economic system and the state should, in the first instance, remain outside our discussions. I am not blind to the importance of this question, but it is essential to draw distinctions between topics and to discuss first one and then the other. I therefore propose that we assume that the relationship between the economic system and the state is fundamentally one of restraint, and with this we set the problem on one side. What is left for us to discuss at the moment is the relationship between the state and the individual who has already been fed and clothed, who has a house and who is in possession of the means not only of satisfying his basic needs, but also of his higher requirements. It follows also that the role of the individual as debtor to the state is excluded from our discussion.

This brings me back to my main thesis which is that the characteristic of the just state is the freedom of the individual and by that I mean every individual. This thesis still appears to me to be important.

This brings us to the problem of the opposite pole to freedom—the restraint upon the individual—which is just as important as freedom. You once described this as the 'security against freedom' and on another occasion as 'the duty to serve' the community as a whole, and 'the obligation towards the community'. These descriptions do not satisfy me; I have already told you some of the reasons for my dissatisfaction. What I want to ask is whether you could make a start with the idea of 'natural order' or the 'order in the nature of things'. The opposite poles could then be defined as: freedom within the framework of natural order. This is what constitutional law would have to attempt to realize.

I can see that it is impossible to define either idea and that all that one can do is illustrate them. It is also true that it is impossible to prove either the existence of freedom or of the natural order and that each must be perceived intuitively.

I would maintain, however, that most people are able to recognize a state of unfreedom and of defective natural order. I would also maintain that my formulation has the advantage over yours in that 'the duty to serve' and the 'obligation towards the community', are demands of an ethical nature made upon the individual which, therefore, belong to the sphere of education, including self-education, and which do not belong to constitutional law or to the theory of the first principles of the state.

In addition, I have the following observations to make: freedom never exists as an absolute, but only within the framework of natural order; outside order there is no freedom; it is also true, however, that natural order assumes freedom, because an order without freedom is not natural; this can be seen in the natural urge and right to self-preservation both of the individual and of the species. To conclude, I get the feeling that we have made an advance with this definition and that my freedom and your security have now been combined into an intelligible definition.

Simply by way of illustration I point at what must be considered when defining the relationship of the individual to the state within the framework of 'natural order'; age, sex, family circumstances, profession, service to the community, origins, residence, position in a community.

I should be grateful if you would consider these ideas, and I would only ask that you leave aside the questions of religion and the economy, assuming the first to be subject to the principle of absolute freedom and the second to be subject to the principle of restraint.

Yours,

11. *Gablentz to Moltke*

7.9.40.

I have only a few qualifications to make on your letter of 31.8.

I. 1. There is no theological doctrine directly relating to the state, only to men within the state; there is, thus, no such thing as a Christian state.

I. 4. The state is amoral because it is abstract. When we concern ourselves with man we are dealing with the actual statesman.

II. 3 and 4. I would not insist on the Christian statesman, but only on the just statesman. I am indeed convinced that Christ works in every good man, but I do not lay claim to every such person for the Christian community if he does not himself recognize or desire his membership.

It is very much more difficult to say anything about the memorandum, 'The image of the western state'. The argument is so beautifully concise that one is in danger of either simply agreeing with it or, if one cannot accept certain specific aspects, of laying the whole thing on one side with an uncomfortable feeling. I think that the best approach to this piece is to ask what is lacking in it. There is hardly any mention of just those matters that concern us in economic policy and in foreign policy. I am troubled by section 6, the state and the economic system and section 7 the state and humanity. The statement in paragraph 3 on page 2 is incorrect; 'this interrelationship between the person and the state is the foundation of western culture'; it is in fact the *basic question*; the foundation, on the contrary, is a mixture of, in the first place, a world picture derived from Christianity and Antiquity, secondly the Germanic attitude towards men and material things in which the two extremes of submission and organization receive equal emphasis, and finally the physical influence of the European terrain and, in particular, chance factors such as its geographical situation and its climate, etc.

This leads us on to things, i.e. to the economic system, and to the distinction between human groups, i.e. to foreign policy. What is said about the person and his unconditional worth is both fine and correct. One can agree that the state exists 'to perfect the human being'. Man is not, however, perfected through the abstract development of general qualities, but through the concrete formation of environment and society.

Justice does not simply mean: to provide men with a sphere of freedom, but to provide men who have been trained in freedom with the possibility of creating a just social and economic life. This is what gives substance to such a fine and correct statement as that at the end of 1). For the same reason, it is wrong to write that 'earthly power aims at exclusiveness, and as a perversion of the divine example it belongs to the principle of Evil'. Power is equated with sin. This is absolutely untrue. Following Jacob Burckhardt an ascetic attitude towards power has developed which is just as exaggerated as the ascetic monastic attitude towards sex. Just as a genuinely celibate order is essential to the national community, so it is essential that certain men and groups refrain, as a matter of principle, from exercising political power. (Here lies the purpose of a separated church; and it is from this that, for example, the Quakers derive their strength.) However just as it is wrong to declare sex, which is dangerous, sinful because of the danger of sexuality, it is also wrong to reckon power, which is tempting, corrupt because the majority of those who occupy positions of power succumb to temptation. It also seems to me to be incorrect to maintain 'that the individual requires an organized communal life, so that he can live in accordance with his innate desire for justice'. The individual needs communal life so that he can fulfil his task of shaping the world.

All that he says about justice is correct but remains formal because the basic matter by which justice is tested is not considered. It is impossible to ask whether the law of a state is 'either law or is already in itself power'. It will always be both if it is in order. It will be state-less, i.e. ineffectual Law, if power is lacking and it will be naked, i.e. evil power if it is only power.

What is to be said about other nations' right to existence can be more clearly developed from our position than from the author's.

On the last paragraph in section 2: justice and love do indeed form a unity in the Divine Being. The principle of justice among men, however, cannot be love itself but only the conversion to love. This is so because justice does not deal with men who are free and loving, but rather with men who are unfree and hate one another.

The remarks on state and church are historically correct. It is also true that the church cannot withdraw from any sphere of life. The state must suffer the proclamation of the church. The church is in a sense the natural censor of the state, and it is precisely the authoritarian state that requires such an objective independent authority, if it will not or cannot submit any longer to criticism by its subjects in the style of the nineteenth century. The Pope must be the father confessor of the Kaiser. Only the church can possess the objectivity and the sense of responsibility which enables the state to submit to it. The contemporary church, however, is just as inadequate in these respects as the contemporary state. The education of the 'Christian Statesman' and the education of priests aware of their secular responsibility must, accordingly, go hand in hand. In the first instance, this task will probably be beyond the capacity of either organization, and it will therefore have to be undertaken by individuals who achieve and maintain a priestly attitude in the middle of secular life.

The section on state and society is all right.

The section on the state and education over-values, in my opinion, the importance of the communication of knowledge. Some relevant points are made, by way of contrast, about education in a craft. 'The educated person is one who knows that he satisfies independent judgements within his own sphere of life.' Corresponding to these different spheres of life, there are in fact different and equally valuable forms of education. The basic requirement of all forms of education is that they should always lead to an experience of the three 'reverences'. Reverence for what is equal to us leads every type of education to an acknowledgement of the communal nature of the state. The state itself, however, cannot be the source of education. It can only make room for education. The source of education must lie in an autonomous educational community, i.e. if she appreciates her responsibilities correctly, the church. Everything of value that we have gained from a humanistic education has only been preserved by the power of the Christian understanding, which is now gradually diminishing. We have, in other words, experienced a form of secularized Christianity. Education comes once more within the province of Christianity when the limits of secular perception are reached in philosophy, natural science and historical interpretation. If the official churches do not recognize this in time they will be pushed to one side by the new education which, although not Christian in its starting point is—to the astonishment of its own supporters—Christian in its results. This education and the church that is renewed with it are no longer limited to the experiences of western civilization; it does not orientate the life of the nation and with it of the state directly towards the task of humanity, but it does reveal the west as only an intermediary between the nation and humanity.

12. *Moltke to Yorck*

16.11.40

In connection with our last discussion, I would like to say the following about your criticism of my memorandum:*

1. On the question of the incongruity of the three relationships. You maintain that the individual, the economic system and faith are on three quite separate levels. I will allow you that but that does not in itself deny the thesis that the entire substance of the state must be derived from its relations to these three elements.

You might certainly say: the individual is everything and the state acts

* Compare p. 310.

only upon and through the individual, and for this reason only the state and the individual stand in relation to one another. Faith is the faith of the individual, while the economy is directed to the maintenance of the individual. You might go on to say: faith exists before the state and the state preserves its substance, its character and its position in the world order on the basis of the faith of the individual. This too is correct within its own limits, but it is nonetheless not a denial of the fact that there is a special relationship between the state and faith.

You want to set the economic system on a lower level; your brother's notes do the same and this is one of the points at which I am completely at odds with you. The economy is today an object of the state's concern in its own right, and it belongs to the perfecting of the state and of the individual just as much as education, spiritual training in its narrowest sense and the preparation of devout men. I am convinced that the economic system and its organization is no less an aid to understanding the divine order of the world than spiritual education. I take this to be a very early idea that was only destroyed in the course of the nineteenth century, and in its medieval form found expression in the idea of the three fundamental estates: Producers, Teachers and Soldiers. I should be very grateful if you would re-examine your ideas, therefore, in this respect.

2. As to the question of the importance of faith, of history and of spiritual education for understanding the state, I share your view that the individual's conception of the state is determined by his basic attitude and that this attitude is itself decisively influenced by his faith, his understanding of history, and his spiritual education. I agree with you that we cannot conceive of a state apart from our idea of World Order and that has been shaped among Europeans by Christianity and classical intellectual and historical education. I will give due attention to these ideas in my new draft.

3. On the question of whether the personality of the state demands an independent state ethic, I fear that I disagree with you. I cannot see any ethical principles that are valid for anything more than the behaviour of man. If we maintain that the state is a moral personality, we are, I believe, on the way that leads via Hegel to a deification of the state. If you agree let us discuss this point once again. I get the impression that in fact the differences between us here are not substantial but formal. With kindest wishes,

Yours,

13. *Moltke to Gablentz*

16.11.40.

In connection with our last discussion, I would like to set down a few ideas which should help to clarify our positions.

1. You say that the triple distinction between Soldiers, Teachers, and

Producers is so self-evident to you that it requires no justification. As I have deliberately left the Soldiers outside the scope of my remarks, there remain only the Teachers and Producers. Why are you unwilling to include the Teachers within the relationship between the state and the individual, since the whole relationship between state and the individual is founded on education, the provision of the preconditions of self-education and character formation? You can say what you will but it does seem to me that spirit and faith are essentially different and do not belong together. Faith may be—and perhaps here you are right—a precondition for education; is it, because of this, any less a precondition for the true statesman, the true economist and the true soldier? The educationalist has not got a lease on faith. I should be very grateful therefore if you would consider whether you could not agree with me in saying that faith does not appear to be a fully integrated part of the substance of the state, but rather one of its predeterminants.

2. Your second suggestion that the relationship between the state and the economic system should be replaced by the relationship between the state and things seems to me to be rather too subtle and not entirely in accordance with the facts. The economic system is: things plus men plus immaterial qualities of the most varied character.

3. This leads us on to the main point which is the relation between the state and faith. At the moment, I think the following points are correct:

a) In deciding what is the substance of the state, each individual starts off from a firm foundation in which all the elements that distinguish the individual himself are woven together; for the Europeans however, there are four elements in particular: the Christian religion, classical education, socialist ideas and historical ties. I believe that these four elements are characteristic and determinative for every European today. It is only within the scope of these fundamental assumptions that we can form any ideas and these elements are therefore essential preconditions of our understanding and our will.

b) Faith cannot be considered as an essential element of the state; it is not an objective of the state and one must, in my opinion, say that.

c) Faith is of essential significance in the formation of the just statesman, in whom understanding and will are one. You go as far as to say that no non-believer can be a just statesman and you get out of the difficulties that arise in connection with this thesis by claiming that everybody who qualifies as a just statesman is a believer whether he himself says so or not. I will gladly go with you on this, since we are virtually in complete agreement.

d) We are similarly agreed on the question of the importance of faith for criticism.

On looking at these three points I cannot see any serious material difference between us. You place the law more in the foreground when talking about the relation between the state and the individual, while I emphasize the promotion of understanding = education, and the encouragement of the will to act in accordance with the understanding —again = education. I agree with you that there are such things as minimum human rights but they mainly belong to the sphere of the economy and the others I regard simply as a prerequisite to education.

Please consider these points again. I will send you a revised draft in a little while in which I will try to take account of these viewpoints. With warm wishes,

Yours,

1. The Foundations of Political Science†

I.

In trying to form a picture of the state that is to be created we shall have to begin again from the beginning. Everything that stood firm and was securely established has now been called into question.

We must first be clear about what the substance of the state is—what it is from which the state derives its life and what distinguishes it from a large, organized group. If this substance is clearly perceived, it can be developed under any form of constitution. The problem of the state's organization, therefore, only arises when the question about the state's substance has been clearly answered. As it is secondary we have not dealt with it here. I do not consider organization inessential—on the contrary, it is extremely important—but I believe that the substance must first be established.

II.

The substance of the state can be understood in three relationships: in the relationship between the state and the individual, in the relationship between the state and the economic system, and in the relationship between the state and faith. In addition there is foreign policy, which concerns the relationships between the state whose substance and form are settled and other states and their citizens. Here we are only concerned with the substance of the state and therefore with the three relationships.

The substance of the state is fully exhausted in these three relationships, for every activity of the state affects one of these three. If we enumerate the existing government departments and envisage any new ones that might be created, we discover—excluding foreign affairs and defence matters which are concerned with external relations—that there are no functions of government that are not comprehended in one or more of these relationships. In their original sense civil and criminal law come within the sphere of the state's relationship with the individual; other parts of the law belong to the realm of the state's relation-

---

* Typescript copy in the Moltke papers, file of memoranda and political letters. In the top right-hand corner of the first page there is a 'No. 5' in Moltke's handwriting. Another note in the left-hand corner also indicates that there were five copies of the document: the first was intended for Y (=Yorck), the second for G (=Gablentz), the third for E (=Einsiedel), the fourth for T (=Trotha), and the fifth for Moltke himself. After the G there is a W, possibly this refers to Waetjen.

† See p. 109.

ship with the economic system; education comes within the relationship between the state and faith and the state and the individual.

At the same time these three relationships cover the whole substance of the state. It is impossible to dispense with any of them. If the relationship between the state and faith is omitted then education could not be contemplated, the economy and the glorification or oppression of the individual could exceed all limits and there would be no standard by which these developments could be judged. The idea that there is no relation between the state and the economy is absurd.

Finally these three relationships exist independently alongside one another. Each has its own independent significance; the substance of the state that can be deduced from the relationship between the state and the individual cannot be discovered in its relations with the economy and faith; the relationship between the state and faith cannot be replaced by the relationship between the state and the individual. These relationships exist in a state of tension and, to a limited degree, of conflict, with the result that they constantly need to be harmonized. The practical solution of each individual problem will simply have to be regularly assessed in the light of these relationships.

III.

I believe that the relationship between the state and the individual can be expressed in a single sentence:

The purpose of the state is to provide men with the freedom that enables them to perceive the natural order* and to contribute to its realization.

This thesis only replaces an unformulated riddle by a formulated one and it requires further clarification. The formulation of the riddle nonetheless marks an advance.

1. To provide the individual with freedom is an essential function of the state. It means protecting him against oppression by others and giving him the opportunity to provide himself, through his own activity, with the economic commodities that allow him to master the natural world and which thereby remove any ground for hatred and fear. This part of the thesis is obvious and does not require any further explanation: the unfree man is an animal or a machine.

2. To provide one person with the freedom that another will not allow him entails the use of force by the state and encroachment upon the freedom of the other. This use of force by the state seems to contradict its function of providing the other person with freedom. This apparent contradiction is removed by the second part of the thesis where the 'natural order' is introduced as a limitation upon freedom.

3. Before I turn to consider the perception of the natural order in more detail I would like to interpose a comment on the relation between freedom, law and power. When the law (in the true sense of the word)

* Just order (note in the margin).

sets a limit upon my freedom, it does not encroach upon my freedom so much as set a check upon my arbitrary action in the realm of freedom. I recognize the force that is used to keep my arbitrary power in check as legitimate. However, I only regard those restrictive measures as legal in this sense, that do not arise out of the arbitrary will of others who, overstepping the bounds of their own freedom, try to encroach upon mine. This applies above all to the arbitrariness of the legislator. Law in the true sense of the word cannot stem from the arbitrary will of the individual but must arise from the nature of things or, as I have described it above, from the natural order. The use of force that is not backed by law of this kind is arbitrariness; law without the backing of force is useless against lawbreaking arbitrariness. This brings me to the conclusion that the use of force aimed at establishing the natural order is legitimate and places a limit only upon arbitrary action and not upon freedom.

4. The natural order cannot be defined but it can be perceived, and certain of its characteristics can be described. Thus the natural order includes the spiritual and physical inviolability of men, respect for all other men and for their physical and spiritual existence, and respect for animate and inanimate nature. It also includes the recognition that the degree of freedom allowed to each person must vary according to the degree of responsibility that he exercises: a child must, for his own good, have less freedom than an adult. All these are points that are beyond dispute and require no proof.*

The degree of understanding and the capacity to act in accordance with this understanding varies. As defective understanding must be remedied by the use of force the statesman's own degree of understanding is of decisive significance. This problem will be discussed under the heading of the relation of the state to faith.

5. The freedom of the individual is part of the natural order. It does not stand above this order but within it, and it is established and limited by it. An order that does not include human liberty will not be recognized by us as 'natural order'. This order is called natural because it arises from the nature of things, and contains its own sanctions within itself. Every breach of the natural order will be remedied by a slow and painful natural process. The legitimate use of force,† which aims at rectifying the breach of the natural order with human instruments, is not itself a part of the natural order but stands outside it, and only serves to remove the natural sanction and to maintain the natural order through its own human sanctions, thereby rendering the natural sanction unnecessary.

6. It follows from this that the use of force would be superfluous if each individual completely understood the natural order and realized it. As the use of force has limits, as its effects are always questionable and as it ties down resources it is desirable that each individual should be

* Minimum rights unavoidable (note in the margin).
† No contradiction of the above (note in the margin).

enabled to perceive the natural order. The more each individual understands the natural order the less the need to have recourse to force to uphold this order and individual freedom. The less recourse there is to force, the easier it is for the individual to perceive the natural order as it stands out all the more clearly and obviously. The use of force and individual understanding are thus related in the following way: greater understanding diminishes the need for force, while a lesser amount of force increases understanding. The order of these statements is important, as an inversion would suggest that we are attempting to discover the natural order by renouncing all order. Force can only be replaced by an understanding that already exists. If the state renounces force before the necessary understanding exists, then the vacuum will be filled by individuals or groups using force against the state. In practical terms the best path lies somewhere between the two poles of excessive and insufficient use of force.

7. To increase the understanding of the natural order is a function of both youth and adult education. The state too has a responsibility for advancing this understanding. It must give the individual the opportunity of demonstrating his understanding by participating in the realization of the natural order. Understanding that lacks an opportunity to work itself out in practice is both fruitless and uncontrollable. The activity of creating order itself increases understanding. That is the meaning of the last part of the thesis—i.e. that it is part of the purpose of the state to enable the individual to contribute to the realization of the natural order.

IV.

I define the relationship between the state and the economy as follows:

A. The state is the unlimited master of the economic system. The question of whether the economic objectives are to be reached by economic freedom or economic restraint is irrelevant. It is not a question of principle but of means.

B. In the distribution of the economic output it is the task of the state:

a) to enable each individual to provide himself with the essentials of life.

b) to prevent individuals from acquiring an unjust share of the surplus products and one, many, or all persons from abusing the possibilities created by the economic system purely for their own distraction or to set up economic controls over others.

c) to advance the non-economic objectives of the state, e.g. education of young people and adults, the creation of viable administrative units, the widest possible distribution of the population over the whole territory.

d) to provide the resources with which all higher aims can be fulfilled without allowing the economic system to define the content of these higher objectives.

C. It is the function of the state to ensure that the independence of the natural world that has been achieved through economic activity is not purchased at the cost of an increase in purely economic dependence upon other men.

1. What comes within the sphere of the state is not free but bound. The economic system has been transferred during the course of the last hundred years from the sphere of the individual to the sphere of the state. By this process the original freedom of the economic system has been replaced by restraint. Today, it is the stateman who decides, from the standpoint of utility, which types of economic activity he will allow to continue in freedom and which not. It is idle to establish any general rules about which activities ought to be free and which might be free, or to distinguish between levels of economic freedom or control. Each new situation requires new decisions.

2. Of more importance are the principles that must be observed in the distribution of the economic output. In the first place, it is essential that each individual should receive the provisions that he needs to live. Whether the state does this through standard wages, old age and sickness insurance, or through taxation and the direct provision of these essentials, is fundamentally immaterial and can only be decided by reference to the general economic objectives and the functions of the state in its relationship with the individual. Within this sphere, the full responsibility falls on the state today.

The function of the state with regard to superfluous products is restrictive: it must protect against an abuse of these goods. By doing this it also achieves the positive objective of a just distribution of them.

The advancement of the non-economic objectives of the state with the help of economic resources is of decisive importance. Each statesman must prove his worth by advancing these objectives and by carrying out the responsibilities associated with them. Good planning will make it possible to fulfil some of these tasks without it being obviously a distributive process; the government, for example, could help to promote a healthier distribution of the population by its choice of garrison towns.

All the resources needed to fulfil the higher objectives must be taken from the economy without any strings attached. They must be at the disposal of individuals or groups who have proved themselves, free from any explicit or implicit demands or expectations. This applies to all research, especially in the Arts and to all institutions established for the cultivation of the Arts.

3. In addition, the economic system is important to the individual because it gives him the opportunity to prove his worth in an obvious and tangible way. The state must give every individual the opportunity to prove himself in this sphere; success must make a difference to the development of the individual's life. Education in the understanding of

the natural order will only be possible for many if they have the opportunity to prove themselves in the economic sphere and to retain the fruits of their success. It is difficult to appreciate the natural order if one has oneself become a victim of the unnatural order, in that one is either not allowed to prove oneself or one derives benefits from an unnatural order. It follows that it is a function of the state to guide the economy in such a way that it gives the individual an opportunity to develop his abilities and to participate in the economic process.

4. By the application of its laws to the economic system, the state must prevent the creation of purely economic controls by some men over others. This does not affect the necessary relationships of authority and dependence that arise out of the work process itself; neither ought it to affect the relationships that result from government control over the economy. Both these types of control are functional; they arise from the relationship of partners to one another and do not overstep the sphere of essential relationships. A responsibility covers both those in authority and those in a state of dependence. The dependence that the state must prevent is the purely economic dependence in which the controlling section bears no responsibility and succeeds at best in establishing economic values.

V.

I define the relationship between state and faith in the following theses:

A) There is no such thing as a theological doctrine of the state, only a doctrine of man in the state; there is, therefore, no Christian state.

B) In formulating the basic principles of the state we proceed from the binding principles of the individual's ethics seen as 'humanist' ethics, and independent of the content of the Christian or any other religious revelation.

C) The state, however, is amoral because it is abstract.

D) If the state is to perform the tasks that it is intended to, the statesman must feel himself committed to ethical precepts, from whatever source he may derive them, and be capable of perceiving the order in the nature of things and acting in accordance with this understanding. Most men will only be able to accomplish this task through faith. The formation and education of the just statesman is thus in practice equivalent to the education of the Christian statesman.

E) It is part of the function of the state to advance the understanding of the natural order in each individual; to fulfil this it requires the faith of the individual, since it is only given to a few to perceive this order without, and apart from revelation.

1. The state does not appear in Christian revelation. In the Old Testament only the Jewish state appears, and it is organized as a theocracy. This hardly belongs to Old Testament revelation, and has become utterly meaningless to us. The Christian revelation is concerned

with the individual and not with the state. No state can claim to be a Christian state. Thus, it is impossible to deduce the substance and purpose or organization of the state from Christian revelation.

2. The same is true of moral philosophy. The state is abstract and, therefore, stands outside the sphere of moral philosophy. Any attempt to censure a state for its actions, or to prohibit this or that action on the grounds of morality, is doomed to failure; the laws that have allegedly been breached do not exist for the state; such reproaches can achieve nothing.

3. It follows from these two basic theses that the demands of faith and ethics apply only to the actions of the individual. Just as there is no moral guilt on the part of the state, there is also no special moral justification for the actions of the state. If the state is deprived of a possible moral justification for its actions, the ethical responsibility of the individual remains entirely unaffected. There are only actions by individuals acting as agents for the state, for which they are fully responsible; they therefore cannot excuse what they have done by claiming that reasons of state made it essential: the state can provide no cover for the actions of an individual. This fact must be made quite clear, so that no-one tries to hide behind the state.

4. It is only possible to formulate a basic theory of the state on the basis of an ethical idea. Precisely because the state is amoral and the individual who acts for the state is fully responsible for what he does, the basic theory of the state must proceed from the basis of the ethical precepts that are binding upon the individuals acting on its behalf; if this does not happen, the individual finds himself in a standing conflict between his duties as a servant of the state and as an ethically responsible individual.

5. The ethical principles from which we proceed are 'humanist'. There are certain binding moral doctrines that are valid for all within Western civilization, and which are independent of the Christian revelation even though for the Christian these principles find their clearest expression in Christian moral teachings. Because this is so, it is possible to formulate a basic theory of the state which is binding on all and understood by all, without at the same time requiring an acceptance of either the Christian or any other religious revelation.

This first section establishing the theses shows how far faith and the state are separated. Faith is important at the moment at which the individual, whether as statesman or as a citizen, comes into relationship with the state.

6. Statesmen are those who are entrusted with the tast of fulfilling the purpose of the state. They guide an amoral machine, the activity of which derives its purpose from them. If one is to avoid a catastrophe one must place high ethical requirements upon the responsible group of statesmen. They must understand the 'natural order' and act in accordance with this understanding. Precisely because the state machine is

amoral and does not place any limitation upon itself of its own accord, the demands made on the leading group are extraordinarily large. Very few can discover the enormous strength that is needed to fulfil these demands on the basis of simple understanding. Normally this strength can only be derived from revelation, that is from faith. For this reason the just statesman is normally the Christian statesman. He uses the Christian faith as the source from which he derives the strength to apply the precepts of morality to his actions as an agent of the state.

7. The state requires lively and effective faith to fulfil its function of advancing the understanding of the 'natural order'. All human passions are hindrances in the way of understanding the 'natural order'. A state that tries to advance this understanding through reason alone or through arguments of enlightened self-interest, will never get very far: its citizens' understanding will be small. This understanding, which can never be fully achieved, is primarily promoted through faith: faith is the most important source from which the individual can derive his understanding and by which he can be moved to act in accordance with his understanding. What has been said already about the statesman applies here also.

8. Finally faith is an essential factor in the criticism of the state and of the actions of its agents. A broad body of faithful men will judge statemen by the ethical precepts that they derive from their faith, and the consciousness of this criticism is likely to keep the statesman on the right path. Any statesman can corrupt a faithless mass, but he cannot corrupt a body of devout men.

Those who act as agents of the state in accordance with directives and general instructions, stand between the statesman and the citizen. In view of their responsibility what has been said about the significance of faith for the statesman or the citizen applies to them even more.

9. I would summarize the significance of faith for the state as follows: the state requires faith in the training of the just statesman, in the education of the citizen in the understanding of the natural order and in the maintenance of an effective criticism of the actions of the agents of the state.

Berlin, 20.10.1940.

2. Starting Point—Objectives—Problems*

24.4.41

I. Starting point†

The analysis of the situation in which we find ourselves can easily be endangered and falsified by the objectives at which we are aiming. The actual, objective state of affairs is difficult to establish. In the following I have tried to give a broad outline of the position from which we start, as it appears to me.

* Typescript copy in the Moltke papers, file of memoranda and political letters, with date and corrections in Moltke's handwriting. † See p. 256.

1. The individual is unbound but unfree.

The obligations by which the individual is bound have changed. In some form or other all the possible variations, stretching from simple herd instinct and unity with the soil through to the fully developed society based upon a profound religious foundation, have already appeared. The early Middle Ages can be taken as the period in which these obligations reached their highest point, when every individual felt himself bound to the church and by comparison with this obligation all other relations were secondary. It is possible to represent it thus: the individuals are small pieces of metal distributed over the whole of the then-known world. In the centre there is a powerful magnet towards which all are orientated regardless of whether or not special links or separatist tendencies exist among them: both friendship and enmity are dominated and regulated by the shared orientation.

As this magnet weakens the European world begins to disintegrate into smaller groups until finally the Reformation makes the magnet's neutralization quite obvious. The former, universally binding obligation was replaced by a host of different ties, a development that led finally to the emergence of the sovereign states as fully equal and supreme foci for limited objectives. At first certain relations that cut across these lines were tolerated and allowed to continue: the common European experience of the Renaissance or of Romanticism created bonds, of varying strength, that crossed national frontiers and the international labour movement has tried to create a new obligation that, in the minds of its creators, is intended to establish itself against the state. None of these other ties, however, has had sufficient coherence to make a claim on the whole man in the way that the state finally did and has done in this century.

As, however, the state is 'of this world' its claim upon the whole man has been manifestly an abuse of secular power and this abuse has led to the dissipation of the sense of obligation in the same way as, perhaps, the abuse of secular power by the church led to the disintegration of her function as a binding force. The sense of inner commitment to the state has been replaced on the one hand by something similar to the herd instinct to associate together for security and, on the other hand, by control and coercion of the individual. This process has deprived the individual, who has lost his sense of obligation, of his freedom. This is true of the whole of continental Europe, and perhaps also of Russia.

2. Individual responsibility has also been affected by this process of disintegration.

All the small social groups in which the individual still bears responsibility have been caught up in the process. All the functions of such small autonomous social groups are being gradually taken over by state organizations. This holds true of the old self-governing bodies, of cultural, charitable and other societies of all kinds. It is a method by which the state frees the energies bound up in these small societies for its own purposes.*

A feeling of responsibility for the development of the whole of mankind hardly exists any longer. It is also difficult to see at the moment how any such feeling of responsibility ought to express itself.

Equally there is no longer any individual responsibility for the state as such. The state today can only exist through its organization; the individual's place in the organization is such that he cannot break through to a feeling of responsibility towards the whole. The state machine consists only of technicians and specialists who work in isolation.

3. The means of expression have been destroyed.

Words have lost their unequivocal meaning, symbols no longer arouse a unified response, while works of art have been deprived of their absolute significance and, like all educational values, have been subordinated to expediency. They serve the state and in doing so they have lost their absolute significance and have become relative. It is indeed no exaggeration to say that everything that ought to be absolute has become relative, that the means by which alone we can express absolute values, namely words and symbols including works of art, have been abused and have lost their unambiguous content and have thereby ceased to be the transmitters of absolute values. As a result those things like the state, race and power that are entirely lacking in absolute value have become absolute.

II. Objectives

The objectives that we are aiming at seem to me to be quite clear: the individual must be reawakened to an awareness of his inner commitment to values that are not of this world. Only on the basis of this awareness can freedom be restored to him.† In this way the individual will recover a sense of responsibility which will lead to the blossoming of a true community, but this development, and the educational work that will arise from it, will only be possible if the means of expression, which are all that we have at our disposal, are once again universally valid and universally intelligible.

Before asking the question: Are these objectives attainable? we must ask ourselves whether we have rightly understood the objectives. It is important to make this distinction between the two questions, since otherwise there would be a temptation to confuse objectives that are the only ones considered obtainable with the correct objectives. This leads to the forfeiture of a large number of allies, since each person can justifiably be of a different opinion about the question of attainability, which is a purely speculative question, even when there is a fundamental

---

* This certainly also applies to industry and to a certain extent to the family (note by Yorck).

† The values of this world should also be without reciprocity (note by Yorck).

agreement about principles. There must, however, be agreement among all those who can possibly be considered as allies over the question as to whether the stated objectives, independent of their attainability, have been correctly defined.

1. Are these objectives correct? The heart of the matter lies in the sense of commitment to values that are not of this world. The objective is imprecise, I admit, and I would be grateful for any improvement. What I am trying to describe is the feeling that everybody is committed to the *same* values. This excludes, therefore, nationalism and racialism.* What should be aimed at is a state of affairs in which the divisions and dissensions between the inhabitants of this world are only of secondary significance, because those who are grouped into one party are still primarily controlled by the magnet which attracts and influences all alike, and because even enemies are in agreement about the most essential point. I cannot be more precise about these universally valid values because it is the task of the whole of mankind to create this magnet, and because it would be presumptuous to suggest that it was already established at a specific place and that it was simply up to others to place themselves within its sphere of influence.

The second important point is the establishment of freedom. Freedom is the counterpart of commitment; they both belong together. Freedom is the touchstone of obligation, and commitment is a part of freedom. Thus they both belong together.

The third point is the sense of responsibility. That is a consequence of the certainty of obligation. A sense of responsibility is the outward sign of the existence of obligation. A sense of responsibility assumes both freedom and obligation. All actions that affect the community—and that means every conceivable action—must be performed on the basis of this sense of responsibility. Immediately this occurs human societies will once more blossom out, from the family, as the smallest community, through the prosecution of common interests of any kind and the administration of public affairs, to the International Community. Nothing that is done in the world or that sometimes must be done would be destructive of the community, if it was obvious to all that it was done on the basis of a sense of responsibility and that, in the last resort, it stood under the precept, 'love thy neighbour as thyself'—even if thou art obliged to cause him suffering.

The fourth point is the restoration of the means of expression. All that has been said hitherto can only be achieved in association with the restoration of the means of expression and this restoration itself is a consequence of the achievement of the first three objectives. Yes must again be yes, and no, no. Good must once more be an absolute, and Evil likewise. It is hardly to be expected that a co-operative effort will produce any beneficial results if those involved are incapable of making themselves understood.

* A must (*absoluta*) (note by Yorck).

2. Before I move on to the question of the attainability of these objectives, I have to consider, as a supplementary question, whether these objectives are complete and comprehensive. As far as I am concerned everything is contained within these objectives. If that is not plain enough, then I must clarify further. There are, to my mind, three elements: the inner disposition (obligation in freedom), the outward action (the sense of responsibility within the community) and the means of transmission (word, symbol and work of art). I am not aware of anything that is not included within these three elements.

3. The question as to whether and to what extent these objectives are attainable is inevitably controversial and open to debate. These objectives are always attainable by individuals but never by all men. It could only be said that they have been attained if such a considerable section of mankind had attained them, that human affairs were decisively influenced by the consequent disposition of this group. The question of attainability may, therefore, be defined as follows: can the disposition that corresponds to any one of these objectives be achieved by so many men that human affairs are decisively influenced by its achievement? I am ready to answer in the affirmative. In support I would adduce the following spiritual and intellectual trends that are, in my opinion, discernible:

a) The end of power politics,
b) The end of nationalism,
c) The end of racialism,
d) The end of the power of the state over the individual.

This war will demonstrate the inadequacy of these four connecting links in communal action. They will be driven *ad adsurdum*; indeed they already have been to some extent. The greatest extension of power will not bring peace. Nationalism has already been seen to have lost its attractions in both France and Germany. Racialism is absurd if the country that is supposedly protecting and upholding the race associates with its declared enemies, while the tolerant country protects racialist interests. If the most colossal powers of the state over the individual do not bring about peace, there will be a revolution against these powers.

The following positive points also support the view that the objectives can be attained:

a) The complete destruction of all communities that are smaller than the state will create a vacuum that cries out to be filled once the state idol itself has been destroyed. It is possible that it will not be filled and that mankind, or at least Europeans, will disintegrate like an amorphous crumbling mass. The innate need of human beings for some kind of ties, however, means that it is quite possible that the vacuum will be filled in a manner compatible with our objectives.

b) The end of the war will see a readiness for contemplation and penitence that has not existed since the year 999, when the end of the world was expected.

c) If the defeated are able to convince the victors of their responsibility—which I consider possible—the victors' example could provide the impetus for a speedy development in the direction of the stated objectives. Summing up, it is my opinion that the end of the war offers an opportunity for a beneficial reconstruction of the world such as mankind has not had since the collapse of the medieval church.

The section on the problems that arise from the starting point and objectives must now follow. These objectives must, however, be set against a probable political and military situation after the end of the war, in order to be both flexible and concrete. What is expected, therefore, must first be stated.

III. Expected political and military situation at the end of the war

A) *External Relations*

1. Germany has been defeated, i.e. she is no longer in a position to continue the war.

This situation could be the result of a variety of factors: the physical exhaustion of the population, the industrial exhaustion of the nation, political changes within Germany, or disturbances and rebellions in the occupied territories which, because of the extent of the occupied areas and the way it which they have been treated, could not be stemmed and would lead eventually to an armed invasion by the Anglo-Saxon powers. There are several variants but in my opinion they are without special significance.

Note: A German victory would produce an armistice but not peace, since it would be followed by a struggle for the mastery of the seas, which decades of fleet-building have made inevitable. For our purposes, the possibility of a German victory is of little interest since it would defer the conditions on which the fulfilment of our objectives depends to a much later period. A German victory would deprive our study of any relevance and would necessitate an entirely different programme.

2. Peace brings with it a united European sovereign state, which extends from Portugal to a point as far east as possible. Within this united Europe there are a number of smaller non-sovereign states that are meshed together by various political arrangements. They would share at least the following: customs frontiers, currency, foreign policy including defence, constitutional authority and, if possible, economic administration.

3. Peace brings with it an Anglo-Saxon Union whose economic centre of power lies in the American continent. Great Britain and the British Empire, in particular the Navy, have achieved a prestige which they do not need to share with a continental power and which offers them the prospect of regaining their old position in relation to the United States. Britain's primary interest therefore lies in once more outstripping the USA in the leadership of the world empire and in re-

asserting its traditional spiritual title to leadership. If Britain is to be free to exercise leadership among the Anglo-Saxons it must have peace on the European continent at its rear. At the same time the war will have proved that the Navy is the most powerful instrument of war and that, therefore, Britain does not need a 'continental sword'.

4. The European sphere of influence includes French and Italian North Africa, Russia, the Black Sea and Turkey. The Anglo-Saxon sphere of influence extends over India and Africa, south of the Congo. South America, the Near East including Egypt, Arabia and Palestine and the Far East are areas of tension lying between the two combinations. South America and the Far East tend towards the Anglo-Saxon world while the Near East gravitates towards Europe.

5. This prospect not only offers the possibility of a relatively speedy restoration of the shattered economic regions but also provides starting points for co-operation between the European and the Anglo-Saxon world, as long as the domestic political preconditions for this exist.

6. The military situation is indicated by the fact that the Anglo-Saxon Navy is substantially stronger than the Navies of Europe, the Far Eastern states, Russia and South America put together.

B) *Domestic Politics*

1. The European demobilization has led to the creation of a large common economic organization, directed by an inter-European economic bureaucracy and by economic self-governing bodies. Economic policy has been unequivocally subordinated to the rest of domestic policy.

2. Europe is divided into self-governing administrative units, formed in accordance with historical traditions. They are somewhat similar in size and have special relations with each other within groups. In this way the absolute dominance of the former Great Powers, Germany and France, has been broken without creating resentment.

3. The administration of cultural affairs is de-centralized, but the possibility for regular exchanges between the regions remains. The confessional communities are disestablished, but they still have strong claims to be supplied with resources.

4. The constitutions of the individual states are entirely different. They all agree, however, in fostering the growth of all small communities. These latter enjoy certain rights in public law and they have an acknowledged claim to a share of public resources.

5. The highest legislative body in the European state is responsible to the individual citizens and not to the self-governing bodies. As a matter of principle, eligibility for both active and passive electoral rights will not be attained on the basis of age, but rather on the basis of specific constructive activities for the community. Whether universal suffrage ought to follow from this or whether the highest legislative body ought to be formed otherwise are questions of technique rather than principles.

6. Life and limb are to be protected by a legal process that allows no opportunity for the employment of police methods. Economic activity is to be assured by conferring on certain occupations a status similar to that enjoyed by property. A private sector in housing and consumer goods is to be safeguarded.

7. Non-functional rights over the means of production are to be further restricted, without removing the pleasure that can be derived from responsibility and initiative.*

8. The highest executive power is exercised by a cabinet of five persons: the Prime Minister, Foreign Minister, Defence Minister, Minister of the Interior and Minister of Economics. In addition there will be a number of junior ministerial posts which will be represented at Cabinet level by one of the five senior ministers.

In addition to this cabinet of departmental ministers, there will be a cabinet drawn from the Länder, which will consist of representatives from the Land Governments. It will have a permanent consultative function.

IV. Problems that must be considered

1. The spiritual objectives are as follows:
a) The inward commitment of the individual;
b) The freedom of the individual;
c) An individual sense of responsibility;
d) The expression of a sense of responsibility in small communities;
e) The restoration of the means of expression.

a) The inward commitment of an individual cannot be fostered by a third person. The problem that arises at the end of the war, therefore, can be defined as follows: how can the individual be made aware of an inward obligation? It seems to me that it is the responsibility of the church to arouse this feeling; all that the state can do is to provide room for the church to do her work. This can be done by providing for pastoral care among the troops that are to be demobilized, by keeping Sunday as a day of rest and by prohibiting all sporting and other activities during the hours of Church services.

b) The freedom of the individual must be one of the essential points in any programme of political reconstruction. This freedom, however, cannot be presented as an absolute right, but simply as a counterpart of the inward obligation and its outward expression.

The provision of freedom is, therefore, to be understood as something done for the individual which obliges him to strive for self-restraint. Given this framework, the objective must be complete freedom of speech, freedom to print, subject to a control which is self-administered, and freedom of movement. The only limitations upon this freedom should be those imposed by the criminal and civil law, and not by police

* Socialization (note by Yorck).

measures. At first, the freedom of association and assembly should be restricted to the small communities.

c) The individual sense of responsibility and its expression in small communities. This is one of the most important starting points for advancing all our objectives. Everyone must have the possibility of doing something useful for the community. He must be provided with an opportunity for this. Certain political rights, for example, active and passive electoral rights, eligibility for public office, etc., should also be linked with constructive work on behalf of the community. It is open to discussion which activities should be recognized as constructive contributions to the community and rewarded with political privileges. As a matter of principle, activity of this sort should not be what an individual does in the normal course of duty. I have the following activities in mind in this connection: voluntary work in work camps—decisions about political privileges should rest with the camp leader, who would be excluded from such rewards because he works as camp leader in a professional capacity—local government, the administration of welfare institutions, honorary church administration, participation in the honorary leadership of co-operative societies, housing associations, student groups, university and school associations, etc.

d) The restoration of the means of expression. Symbols and works of art can only be created by the talented. Every statesman, however, needs words and actions to make himself intelligible. Words have been deprived of their meaning and actions have become ambiguous. Actions today have been replaced by words, which themselves are followed by contradictory actions for which no word of explanation is given. It is essential that words and actions should be in harmony with each other. Actions must be above suspicion, while words, once the actions have made an impact and have been accepted as straightforward, must be modest and gentle.

The opportunity to restore the means of expression exists from the very beginning of the new era. Indeed, the stability of the new era will essentially depend on whether this happens or not at the earliest moment. The opportunity presents itself with the formation of the first cabinet; the manner of demobilization is also fundamentally linked with it. Thus, for example, an internal decree which lays down the following order for release: first, independent farmers, craftsmen and businessmen with less than ten employees, then all employees in craft, agricultural or business concerns with less than ten employees, and then all who intend to settle on the land as craftsmen—would have a greater effect in restoring the means of expresssion than a Government Law for the Protection of Small Concerns announced on all propaganda media. The restoration of a metallic currency based on the real worth of the metal is another aspect of this process.

2. Further problems arise from the anticipated external situation.

a) What must a United European State look like if it is to satisfy the members of the European community of nations, and be acceptable to the victors? What are its communal, spiritual foundations?

b) The minimum strategic and military requirements of the European State.

c) What organizational proposals can be made for a planned economy? To what extent can such proposals be effected in individual branches of industry through self-government even before a unitary sovereign authority has been established? To what extent can demobilization throughout Europe, understood as a communal activity, become the foundation stone of co-operation: employment of troops in the restoration of destroyed units of production; gradual take-over of this work by European work camps and a corresponding release of troops, etc.

d) In the general confusion, how can the capacity for action of the most important cabinets and their co-operation be assured. The use of military authority and its gradual replacement by civilian authorities, if possible from the very beginning a standing assembly of ambassadors from all the European States, the avoidance of the bottleneck of armistice commissions and of the juxtaposition of different co-ordinating systems.

3. It seems to me that several quite distinct groups of problems emerge from this survey and that the solution of the problems under 1. and the closely associated need for the formulation of principles for the new era are the most important. These principles are essential to provide the first stable cabinet with the inner warrant that it needs to exercise its authority as well as credibility domestically and trustworthiness and legality in its external relations. Unless this is achieved and maintained, the most splendid proposals dealing with the problems outlined above will be, politically speaking, waste paper.

V. List of Problems

1. What responsibilities can the churches take over and what demands do they make?

a) Pastoral care among the forces;

b) The release of priests, training of new priests, exchange of priests between the various states;

c) Consecration of holidays: service and work, press, radio, sporting, artistic and social events;

d) The formulation of coherent themes for specific days; e.g. especially days of penitence and prayer;

e) Education of young people in religion;

f) Avoidance of doctrinal controversy.

2. What can be done to make it clear that we intend to protect life and limb?

a) The abolition of police powers to arrest without judicial warrant, even if the arrested person has been caught in the act;

b) Regular investigation of all arrests;

c) The setting up of a special court to protect the individual against arbitrary arrests;

d) What measures must be adopted to prevent abuse of the fundamental freedom to print?

e) To what extent must the freedom of movement be limited in the interests of a planned economy?

3. What types of communities are to be recognized and provided with political privileges?

a) Which official body is to sanction a community?

b) What rights can be granted to the community?

aa) Self-government;

bb) Tax exemption;

cc) Police and supervisory functions;

dd) Compulsory powers over members;

ee) The right to concede political privileges to members;

ff) Claims to financial support from the state.

c) What political privileges can be conceded to members of such communities?

aa) Active and passive electoral rights;

bb) Admission to public political offices;

cc) Other special advantages in influencing the decisions of the higher administrative organs.

d) Who decides about the rights that are to be conceded to a community or its members?

aa) A general government office for conferment?

bb) The community's superior regional corporation?

cc) The community's leader?

4. What measures can be adopted immediately to give the New Course adequate means of expression?

a) The publication of all laws and decrees by one office;

b) Reduction of the number of official statements of intention;

c) The abolition of the ministry of propaganda;

d) Centralization of the few important functions, and the decentralization of all others.

5. The constitution of the European State?

a) Communal ideology;

b) Communal responsibilities;

c) Internal constitution of the individual States;

d) The size of the individual States;

e) Special relationships within specific groups of individual States (the Scandinavian States, the Baltic States, the East European States, the German States, the Balkan States, the West European States, and the States of the Mediterranean, etc.).

6. The strategic and military requirements of the European State;

a) Defence of the coasts or a mobile fleet?

b) Defence of the internal lines of communication;

c) Defence of the entrances to the Mediterranean;
d) Defence of the Dardanelles and the Baltic Sea;
e) Defence of North Africa;
f) Defence of all frontiers up to the Urals;
g) Internal disarmament;
h) Qualitative disarmament;
i) Strength of the fleet;
k) The Air Force.

7. Setting up of Pan-European offices for economic planning.

a) The development of European Cartels into organs of the whole economy;

b) The development of Pan-European labour organizations;

c) The creation of a European office responsible for the reconstruction of the devastated areas, with powers to distribute the burden;

d) The creation of a European office responsible for important community economic problems;

e) The organization of demobilization;

f) The creation of a European economic co-ordinating body;

g) The creation of a European currency and investigation of the possibility of a return to metallic money.

8. The creation of European political co-ordinating bodies.

a) The replacement of military authorities by civilian authorities;

b) The prevention of the setting up of frontiers;

c) The establishment of an assembly of ambassadors from all the European States;

d) The establishment of a Pan-European permanent Secretariat;

e) The establishment of a Pan-European Supreme Court.

1. *The First Kreisau Conference, 22–25 May 1942**

I. Fundamental Statements†

1. Church and State

We see in Christianity the most valuable source of strength for the religious–ethical renewal of the nation, for the conquest of hatred and deception, for the construction of the western world and for the peaceful co-operation of nations. We welcome and acknowledge the integration that has already been achieved by two bishops, each representing one of the great Christian confessions, with the object of establishing a common position on the aspects of the Christian world view that affect the structure of public life.

Freedom of belief and conscience and the public practise of the Christian religion are guaranteed. All clergy and laity who have been unjustly imprisoned for their Christian convictions or on spurious charges are to be set free. All restrictions on residence are lifted. Freedom is to be restored to church organizations such as youth, social and occupational associations. The publication of religious literature is again made possible. The Christian heritage is to be granted to its proper place in the whole of education as well as in films and broadcasting. Parents are to have their natural right to educate their children in accordance with the principles of the Christian faith and the dictates of their own conscience. The state itself will help to overcome the inward and outward disruption of the family. Sundays are to be free of compulsory state occasions.

The German Evangelical Church and the Roman Catholic Church are guaranteed autonomy and self-government. The state's supervisory role is to be adjusted to correspond with the altered circumstances, both in a material and personal sense, on the basis of historical developments and established law.

More precise directions for the future legal status of the other religious and ideological communities will follow negotiations with them.

2. School

The educational work that the school, the family and the church have to carry out determines the subsequent attitude of the individual towards God and his active membership of the living and natural communities of family, profession and nation, parish, state and church. The

* Typescript copy, as with all the basic Kreisau documents, in the Moltke papers, file of basic texts.
† See p. 145.

329

school ought to satisfy the right of every child to receive an education that is suitable for him. It ought to arouse and strengthen his moral powers. Active learning shapes the character for life. The child ought to acquire the amount of knowledge and skill appropriate to what is required of his age group.

Character training produces an upright man of religious conviction who is able to adopt as the guide-lines of his behaviour good morals and lawfulness, truth and sincerity, love for his neighbour and loyalty to his own conscience. The man educated in this way will be mature enough to take responsible decisions. Learning helps towards the moral formation of personality and prepares for practical life.

Technical schools and colleges of further education that build upon the foundations laid by the elementary schools or by their own lower levels, develop an organically structured knowledge and skill by increasing the share of responsibility given to the pupil.

The state school is a Christian school in which religious instruction by both confessions is a compulsory subject. The lessons are the responsibility of the churches and, where possible, will be taken by clergymen.

The universities that have existed hitherto are to be reorganized as colleges of further education and Reich universities. The colleges are responsible for providing specialist training for those professions that require a completed course of studies at a college and a thorough academic education. The Reich universities are centres of general research and teaching. They are the highest seats of learning and presuppose specially selected students and intellectually distinguished researchers and teachers. The teaching function of the university is to provide academic instruction and education for those who will hold public office and to whom the highest powers and, therefore, the greatest responsibilities will be given.

II. The General Guide-lines

Universities and Colleges of Further Education

The Reich universities are centres of universal scholarship. They develop the specialist research carried out at the colleges and secure its relationship with the rest of scholarship. This responsibility rests upon the teachers as a community. The teaching body must be composed of researchers who combine specialist competence with a universal vision. Specialization dictates the form of all scholarship; the notion of scholarship as a unified entity presupposes the common endeavour of leading members of all the traditional faculties.

The traditional faculties and their basic disciplines are to be represented at every Reich university. Too much specialization would destroy the inner unity; this has its place in colleges. In addition to research, the Reich university ought to endeavour to provide the highest education.

The character of the Reich university as the highest centre of scholarly research and teaching presupposes specially trained and approved students and limits the numbers of those admitted. The essential qualification for admittance to a Reich university is a certificate of maturity from the classical gymnasium and a completed period of studies at a college of further education.

The university's function as a researching, teaching and learning community demands the greatest possible integration of living and working conditions, with places of work and living quarters close together. The medium sized town offers the most favourable conditions. The university town ought to be at the centre of a lively and historically interesting district.

The constitution of the Reich university is based upon extensive autonomy and self-government. The first rector is to be appointed by the state; the first teachers are to be nominated by the state on the recommendation of the rector. The Reich university confers the Master's degree as proof of a successful period of study. The Master's degree is normally an essential qualification for appointment to leading positions in public service, demanding the greatest responsibility.

The colleges are to be responsible for providing specialist training for those professions that require a completed course of study at a college and a thorough grounding in scholarship. The churches are to be responsible for training theologians. The colleges are to include the following disciplines: law, economics, medicine, the arts subjects, natural sciences, education, agriculture, veterinary studies, forestry, engineering and mining.

In order to protect specialist research and teaching against over-specialization and to guarantee it easy integration into the totality of scholarship every teacher must have the Master's degree.

III. Observations

1. The question as to whether teacher training belongs in colleges or in technical schools is left open. The details of college courses must anyway be finalized.

2. Certain guide-lines for the preparation of new textbooks have been agreed. A new and uniform history book is considered feasible. The present textbooks must, however, be banned, even before the new ones are ready.

3. The representative of the state responsible for negotiations with the two bishops is the Reich Chancellor. The remaining administrative work in the sphere of church–state relations comes under the competence of the Minister of the Interior.

4. The possibility of 'a German Christian Community' to which all Christians regardless of their confession would belong, is put forward for consideration. With government protection, it would ensure that the Christian standpoint was taken into account in all, even local, affairs.

This version which corresponds verbally to the corrected draft is the original copy. The preliminary drafts and the corrections made of them have been destroyed.

Kreisau, 27 May 1942
Moltke

2. *The Second Kreisau Conference (finally agreed text of 18.10.42)**

a. The structure of the State

The Reich is the highest authority among the German people. In its political form it is essential to develop genuine authority and real co-operation and participation by the people. It rests upon the natural divisions of the nation: family, local community and region. The structure of the Reich is based on the principles of self-government. The latter unites the moral values of freedom and personal responsibility with the requirements of order and leadership.

This structure will assure the unity and concerted leadership of the Reich and will enable it to be integrated into the community of European nations.

The political will of the nation is to be exercised within limits that are still open to the inspection of the individual. Physically, economically and culturally integrated Länder are to be formed on the foundation of the natural divisions of parish and county. In order to make the self-government really effective, the Länder ought to have between 3 and 5 million inhabitants.

The distribution of responsibility is to be made according to the principle that every corporation is responsible for performing all the tasks that it can most sensibly carry out itself.

I. The Parish (*Gemeinde*)

The representative institutions of the parish are to be elected by all who are qualified to vote in secret and direct ballots.

The principles of electoral organization: everybody who is over 21 or who has fought in the war has the right to vote; heads of families have an additional vote for each child not entitled to vote; anybody can be elected who is over 27 and whose candidature is agreed upon by a number of voters—the number depending on the size of the parish—members of the armed forces cannot be elected.

II. The County†

The representative institutions in the counties and in the towns that are independent of the counties are to be elected in accordance with the same principles as those that govern the representative institutions of the parish. The same applies to the subordinate divisions of the Reich

* Hand-written comment by Moltke.
† *Kreis*: the equivalent in size of the smaller American county rather than a county of average English size.

cities. Electoral districts that are too large for the individual voter to survey are to be subdivided.

III. The Land

1. The Landtag and the city assembly in the Reich cities are to be chosen by the representative bodies of the counties and towns independent of the counties or, in the case of the Reich cities, by the representative assemblies in the political subdivisions. Any male citizen who has completed his 27th year can be elected. Political civil servants and members of the armed forces cannot be elected. The electoral arrangements should ensure that at least half of those who are elected do not belong to one of the electing corporations.

The Landtag has the following responsibilities:

Determination of the budget, taxes and Land laws; the right to question the chief minister of the Land and the right to pass resolutions on all matters relevant to the politics of the Land and its administration; election of the Land governor on the basis of a proposal by the Land Council.

2. The *Land government* consists of the chief minister and the requisite number of privy councillors. The chief minister is to be chosen by the Landtag on the basis of a proposal by the Land Commissioner; the privy councillors are to be nominated by the Land Commissioner on the basis of a proposal by the chief minister. Members of the Land government must be citizens of the Land.

The Land government is responsible for the government of the Land and the execution of the Reich's functions within the territory of the Land.

3. The *Land Council* has the following responsibilities:

To propose candidates for the post of Land Commissioner for election by the Landtag;

To send recommendations to the Landtag;

To exercise disciplinary authority over the members of the Land government.

4. The *Land Commissioner (Landesverweser)* is to be elected every 12 years by the Landtag on the basis of a proposal by the Land Council, and his appointment is to be confirmed by the Reich Commissioner.

The Land Commissioner has the following responsibilities:

Oversight over the whole administration of the Land and the appointment of civil servants;

He bears responsibility for carrying out Reich policies in the land;

He is president of the Land Council.

IV. The Reich

1. The *Reichstag* is to be elected by the Landtags. Any male citizen of the Reich over 27 can be elected. Political civil servants and members

of the armed forces cannot be elected. The electoral arrangements should ensure that at least half of those elected do not belong to one of the electoral bodies.

The Reichstag has the following responsibilities:

Determination of the Reich budget, Reich taxes and Reich laws.

The right of questioning the Reich Chancellor and the right to pass resolutions on all matters relevant to the policies of the Reich and its administration.

The right to elect the Reich Commissioner on the basis of proposals by the Reich council.

2. The *Reich government* consists of the Reich Chancellor and departmental ministers. The Reich Chancellor is to be appointed by the Reich Commissioner with the agreement of the Reichstag, and the ministers are to be nominated by the Reich Commissioner on the basis of proposals by the Reich Chancellor.

The Reich Commissioner can dismiss the Reich Chancellor; the dismissal will become effective with the appointment of a new Reich Chancellor. The Reichstag has the right to demand the dismissal of the Reich Chancellor with a qualified majority, as long as it makes a proposal at the same time to the Reich Commissioner for a new Reich Chancellor.

3. The *Reich Council* consists of the Land commissioners, the presidents of the Reichstag and the Reich economic chamber and Reich councillors appointed for 8 years by the Reich Commissioner with the agreement of the Reich government.

The Reich council has the following responsibilities:

To propose candidates for the office of Reich Commissioner for election by the Reichstag;

To establish principles governing the transfer of civil servants from one Land to another and from the service of Land to the Reich service;

To send recommendations to the Reichstag;

To act as a disciplinary authority over the Reich government and the Land Commissioners.

4. The Regent of the nation (*Reichsverweser*)* is to be elected for 12 years by the Reichstag on the basis of proposals by the Reich council.

The Reich Commissioner has the following responsibilities:

Supreme command of the Armed Forces.

Presidency of the Reich Council.

With the countersignature of the Reich Chancellor:

Appointment and dismissal of Reich ministers and Reich civil servants.

Representation of the Reich in relations with the outside world.

Execution of the Reich laws.

* The historic word *Verweser* was used in the Austrian–Hungarian Empire for the Regent of Hungary. It was also associated with the attempted liberal revolution of 1848 when the Habsburg Archduke John was named as *Reichsverweser* of Germany.

*Final Agreed Text of 18.10.42.**

The Economy

1. Preamble

The economy serves both the community and the individual. It must not only provide sufficient food, clothing, housing and other material goods, it must also create an opportunity for a social order to emerge in which the individual and his family have the chance to develop. In addition to the material benefits that the economy confers, the aim should be to create a sensible relationship between individuals and communities and their work. There must also be town and country planning of sufficient quality to guarantee the population a secure and healthy basis for life.

The system of economic self-government based on the Länder ought to provide those engaged in industry with the opportunity of contributing to the realization of these social objectives of the economic system. The Reich economic leadership should advance the economic policies of the Länder through their influence upon markets and basic industries and provide for as trouble-free development of the economy as is possible.

All those who are engaged in economic activity have the same rights, the same protection and the same freedom before the economic Law of the Land.

They also have certain minimum duties. These include fairness and propriety in economic management, and the honouring of agreements and continuance in work where agreements have been concluded.

The working man is to be guaranteed the income that he requires to preserve human dignity and that is commensurate with his importance to the community. This basic insurance, which will be borne by the individual, the firm, the economic self-governing corporations, the German Trade Union and the state will also cover the worker's dependants.

II. Basic Principle of the Economic System

1. The basic principle of the economic system is orderly competition carried on within limits set by the government and, as far as its methods are concerned, subject to government inspection.

2. Where the existing commitments and nexus of interests (monopolies, cartels, combines) make competition impossible, it is the task of the government to apply the principles of competition and to protect the interests of the community as a whole.

3. The concern of the whole community in the basic industries entails a special degree of government regulation of these sectors of industry. Key mining, iron and metal, chemical and fuel firms should be taken

---

* Only the Preamble was in fact finally considered (note by Moltke). The rest was considered at the third Kreisau conference (author's note).

over by the public authorities. These publicly owned industries are to be directed and inspected on the same principles as apply generally in the economic system.

III. The Industrial Undertaking

1. The industrial undertaking should be understood as the economic partnership of those who work in it.

2. This partnership is expressed in the works union to which both the owners and the entire labour force belong.

3. The works union carries on its economic activity as a partnership. Management responsibilities lie with the director who keeps representatives of the labour force regularly informed and is advised by them. The rights and duties of the members of the works union, and in particular the share of the labour force in the profits and increased value of the concern, will be the subject of a contract agreed between the owners and the employees' representatives. The agreement is subject to the approval of the economic self-governing corporation of the Land.

IV. The Organization of Economic Self-Government

1. Economic self-government is organized on the basis of the Länder.

2. By law all industrial, commercial and craft concerns are members of the Chambers of Commerce and all agricultural and forestry concerns belong to the Chambers of Agriculture. The Chambers of Commerce and Agriculture are linked in the Land Economic Chamber.

3. The Chambers of Commerce and Agriculture are to be composed of an equal number of elected representatives of management and labour. In the elections each voter has to choose one employer and one representative of the labour force. The Land Economic Chamber will consist of representatives nominated by the Chambers of Commerce and Agriculture.

The Chambers issue their own ordinances subject to the approval of the Land Commissioner. The presidents of the Chambers and their deputies are to be elected by the Chambers, but they must receive the assent of the Land Commissioner.

4. The Chambers are responsible for the self-government of the economic system; they can also be entrusted with Reich or Land responsibilities by the relevant economic authority in the Land (Land Economic Office, etc.). The responsibilities of these bodies include in particular the supervision of vocational training, which will follow nine years of schooling and which ought to fit in with the needs of the economy as a whole. It will normally last for two years. The Chambers are also responsible for providing for professional advancement by means of suitable technical and material arrangements.

5. The Reich Economic Chamber, at the head of the system of economic self-government, is to be composed of delegates from the Land Economic Chambers. The Reich Chamber issues its own ordinances

subject to the approval of the Reich Economic Minister. The president is to be elected and his election must be approved by the minister. The Reich Chamber is responsible for giving regular advice to the minister; it has the right to table motions in the Reichstag. At the same time it is responsible for ensuring a united effort by the Land Economic Chambers.

V. Government Economic Administration

1. The Reich Economic Ministry is responsible for government economic management. Its sphere of competence covers all sections of the economy including agriculture, transport, labour, etc.

2. The Reich Economic Minister is advised by the Reich Economic Chamber and employs the Land Economic Offices, the highest economic authorities in the Länder, to carry out his policies.

3. The Land Economic Authorities (Land Economic Offices and their subordinate bodies) are responsible for the same sections of the economy as the Reich Minister.

The economic administration is part of the general government structure. The Reich Economic Ministry deals with the regional self-governing organizations and with individual concerns through the Land offices.

4. The Reich and Land economic administrative authorities are assisted by Reich specialist offices, which are responsible for assembling and assessing material on all that is going on in industry. These offices can also be used by individual concerns in carrying out projects for the community.

They have the right to receive information.

They are administered by a director and an advisory committee. The director and his assistants are officials of the Reich economic administration.

The Advisory Committee is elected by the industrial undertakings. The committee advises the director and takes decisions on matters that come within the sphere of economic self-government.

The regulation of contributions lies with the advisory committee subject to the approval of the Reich Economic Minister.

VI. The German Trade Union

1. The German Trade Union is an instrument for carrying through the policy outlined in I to IV and for constructing the state that this economic programme presupposes. It finds its fulfilment in the execution of this programme and in transferring projects to which it has attended to the organs of the state and the economic self-government.

2. If the projects that the trades union ought to attend to require its continuance, it should be so constructed as to fit in with the governmental and economic structure.*

* Moltke wanted this Section, or at least (2), to be omitted if possible.

3. The Third Kreisau Conference

a. Foundations of a foreign policy for the postwar period

Kreisau, 14.6.43.*

A just and durable peace cannot be based on force. It can only be discovered through human sensitivity to the divine order which upholds man's inward and outward existence. This sensitivity is imperative. Only when it is possible to make the divine order the test of relationships between men and nations will we be able to overcome the moral and material disorder of our time and establish a genuine peace.

Situated in the midst of the collapse of power structures that have lost all sanction and that are founded exclusively on technical mastery, Europeans more than any other group of men face this problem. The path to a solution lies open—through the determined and energetic exploitation of the Christian heritage. The responsibility for our own cultural group that arises from this excludes any attempt to intervene forcefully in the cultural sphere of others because it decisively rejects the use of force. If this responsibility is to be discharged there are certain irreducible domestic and external requirements:

1. Destruction of the totalitarian hold upon the free exercise of conscience and acknowledgement of the inviolable dignity of the human person as the foundation of the legal and international order that is to be aimed at. Everyone has a full share of responsibility in social, political and international affairs. The right of everybody to work and property, regardless of race, nation or creed is upheld by the public authorities.

2. The basic unit of peaceful communal life is the family. It is protected by the public authorities, who ought also to guarantee education and the external necessities of life: food, clothing, housing, parks and health.

3. Work must be so organized that it encourages rather than stunts personal responsibility. This entails attention to working conditions and the provision of advanced professional schools. It also requires that each person should have a real share of responsibility in the individual firm, and beyond that in the general economic sphere to which his own work contributes. The economic authorities must guarantee these basic requirements.

4. The political responsibility of each individual requires that he should share in the self-government of the small and manageable communities that are to be revived. Rooted and proved at this level he must share in the decision-making of the state and international community through his own elected representatives. In this way he is given a strong sense of sharing responsibility for all political events.

5. The special responsibility and loyalty that everyone owes to his nation of origin, his language and the intellectual and historical traditions of his people must be respected and protected. However, this must

* See p. 147.

not become an excuse for amassing political power and for degrading, persecuting or oppressing a foreign race. The free and peaceful development of national culture is incompatible with the retention of absolute sovereignty by each individual state. Peace demands the creation of an order that spans the separate states. As soon as the participation of the nations is assured, the authorities in this new order must have the right to demand of every individual obedience, honour, and where necessary, the sacrifice of life and property for the highest political authority in the international community.

6. The law which has been trampled upon must be restored and given authority over all orders of human existence. Under the protection of scrupulous, independent and fearless judges it is the keystone of any future peace.

b. Questions on the relationship between economic and foreign policy

Kreisau, 14.6.43.*

The future peace can only be durable if the economic system is organized in accordance with political needs.

The economic organization of Europe is the prerequisite to a peaceful organization of the world economy, of which Europe is a part through its share in world trade.†

The European countries must agree upon a distribution of work that ensures the even development of all productive forces. If this is done the distress of the postwar period can be overcome by intensive reconstruction work, and the inhabitants of Europe can be permanently provided with sufficient food, clothing, housing and other material goods and, at the same time, with opportunities of employment. There should also be support for a distribution of population which assures the separate national groups a secure and healthy basis for their life in their traditional territories.

The European economic system must be freed from the restrictions inherited from the nation states. The basic principle is orderly competition under the supervision of the European economic authorities. The broader function of the European authorities is to induce the separate national economies to grow together into an organic and well-organized entity. This can be achieved through control of heavy industry, through the supervision of European cartels and through other indirect measures, particularly fiscal, credit and transport policies.

Assuming the above, the following questions arise:

1. Uniform intra-European currency and abolition of customs restrictions.

a) What consequences does the European currency and customs union

* See p. 147.
† Europe including England without Russia, Turkey, and the Asian and African shore bordering on the Mediterranean.

have for the individual European states? What adjustments of either a permanent or transitional nature are necessary to prevent any undesirable developments?

b) On what basis can the European currency union be established?

c) Can the internal tariffs be abolished immediately? What functions do they have in a transitional period?

d) What special measures may be necessary in a transitional period? (e.g. prohibitions against the squandering of certain commodities in order to prevent the spoliation of national economies that are still relatively well equipped.)

2. Regulation of currency relations between Europe and the world. What is the attitude to the Keynes and White Plan?

What counter-proposals should be made?

3. Work distribution within the European economy.

a) What is the impact of competition on the existing distribution of labour in Europe?

aa) In agricultural areas?

bb) In industrial areas?

b) What consequences of competition within Europe are considered undesirable? What measures should be taken to protect against undesirable consequences?

4. Economic relations between the European economy and the world economy.

a) What is the probable extent of European trade relations with the rest of the world?

b) What groups of products and in what quantities will Europe export and import on grounds of expediency, and what is th ebalance of interests amongst the commercial partners in the rest of the world?

c) What parallel institutions to an international bank—Keynes–White Plan—appear requisite in the sphere of the exchange of goods and the movement of capital?

5. Report on enemy* plans for the organization of the European and world economy.

To what extent is there agreement amongst the enemies and where do their differences lie?

c. German participation in the punishment of War Criminals (first draft)

Kreisau 14.6.43. (Rewrittten 23.7.43. (Note by Moltke))

The Punishment of Criminals

In the course of the war many offences have been committed against the law. In character, extent and intention they are both serious and detestable. It is absolutely essential for the restoration of the rule of law

* Gegnerisch, i.e. of the Allies.

and with it of peace in Germany and in the community of nations that they should be punished. If law is to be helped to victory, however, then it can only be by measures that are themselves legal, and that are not determined by political considerations or passions.

After the 1914–18 war the restoration of a peace based upon trust between the nations was prejudiced by inadequate attention to and treatment of similar problems. In Germany itself serious domestic conflicts arose which contributed to the origins of the present war.

It is therefore essential on grounds of law and political expediency that the matter should be settled in an honourable and dignified manner.

The German people themselves have the greatest interest in seeing that the appropriate punishment is given for violation of the law. It is therefore necessary to establish a retrospective German law which renders lawbreakers liable to imprisonment or death according to the normal processes of the law.

The criminals who are to be punished are those who have offended against the essential principles of divine or natural law, or international law or the generally agreed positive law of the international community, in such a way as to have clearly demonstrated outrageous contempt for the obligations contained in these legal principles.

The person who orders a criminal action, or who, in a responsible position, instigates a crime, or who spreads general doctrines or instructions of a criminal nature is also a criminal.

Those who are accessories to, abet or incite to a crime are to be judged according to the general criminal law.

In the case of a crime committed under orders, the orders do not provide a ground for suspension of punishment even if an immediate threat to the body or life of the person who performed the deed, or some other coercion, appears to make compliance with the commandment not blatantly immoral in the circumstances. This is especially true if the person who committed the offence has shown either before or at the time of or after the deed that he approved of the command.

The interest of the international community in the punishment of these crimes takes precedence over the domestic punishment of them.

The demand for the extradition of criminals for punishment by the courts of either one or all the victorious powers offends against the natural dignity of the statesman who will personally have to surrender the criminals and the nation itself. It is an essential precondition for the successful formation of an international community in the future that every action should be consistent with personal dignity. Historical experience indicates that submission of a government to any such demands for extradition would immediately deprive that government of political authority among its own people, and would provoke passions, insinuations and mischief and destroy the foundation of the peace that had been attained. An extradition of this kind would be an act of force, and would carry force into a future that ought to be governed by law.

G R H—Z

Punishment by a universal international court and the surrender of the criminals to this judicial authority would offend against neither law nor dignity. Instead it would make a positive contribution by providing a foundation for and a test of the future co-operation of the international community.

Only a universal court composed of representatives of all who took part in the war, regardless of which side they were on, or even of all the nations of the world, could have the necessary moral and legal authority to pronounce, in a really just sentence, the necessary moral and legal condemnation of the crimes. A sham judgement issued by a body that had not been legally constituted would not advance the restoration of the law, but would instead have the opposite effect.

Historically and practically speaking the obvious court for these purposes is the international court at the Hague. A number of legal doubts have been raised about entrusting it with a penal role, but in the present situation there can be no really substantial objections to doing this. Non-membership of the League of Nations is not an obstacle to involvement in the court according to article 35 of its Statute. The assembly of the League of Nations would have to alter article 4 relating to the composition of the courts, under the headings, reduction in the number of judges and regulations governing the composition of the court. Benches of six judges (three from the victorious powers, two neutrals, and one from the defeated nations) would seem to be expedient, with the deciding vote resting with the president, as in article 55 of the Statute. The right of demanding a particular sentence would, in accordance with article 34, lie with the injured party. Defence counsels would be engaged by the accused and their governments, and there would also be the possibility of an official defence counsel. The details of the proceedings would be regulated according to the rules of the court. The remarks about the facts of the case already made in connection with sentences in national courts would form the basis of sentencing in the international court. Any more precise definitions or any widening in the scope of the law would have to be established by the court with due judicial discretion and preferably in imitation of the law of the offender's own country.

The responsibility for guarding the accused who are handed over to the court by their governments would have to rest, on the basis of special agreements, with the Dutch government.

Punishment would be carried out by states specified by the court, but excluding the one against which the offence had been committed, under the supervision and in accordance with the rules of the court.

If this attempt to arrive at a just solution of what is a serious hindrance to peace for all concerned succeeds, a further step will have been taken towards establishing the rule of law between the nations, and evil will have brought forth good. If, however, a solution is adopted on purely political grounds, outside a court that can be recognized as just, then evil will be answered by evil, and force will once again stand threateningly at the beginning of the path into the future.

4. The Punishment of War Criminals (Second Draft)
23.7.43.* (Note by Moltke)

The criminals who are to be punished are those who have offended against the essential principles of divine or natural law, or international law or the generally agreed positive law of the international community, in such a way as to have clearly demonstrated outrageous contempt for the obligations contained in these legal principles.

The person who orders a criminal action or who, in a responsible position, instigates the crime, or who spreads general doctrines or instructions of a criminal character is also a criminal. Those who are accessories to, abet or incite to a crime are to be judged according to the general criminal law.

In the case of a crime committed under orders, the orders do not provide a ground for suspension of punishment, even if an immediate threat to the body or life of the person who performed the deed, or some other form of coercion, appears to make compliance with the command not blatantly immoral in the circumstances. This is especially true if the person who committed the offence has shown either before, at the time of, or after the deed, that he approved of the command.

If crimes have been committed before the publication of this law, the proceedings should be concluded with a judgement that establishes that the accused is guilty of the crime.

Whoever is highly suspect can be proscribed by the court, the public prosecutor's office or the higher administrative authorities. The person so proscribed may be arrested by anybody. He should be handed over to the police, and at the earliest opportunity brought by them before the competent court. All other protective measures applying to preliminary arrest and remand do not apply to a person who has been proscribed. The proscription comes to an end with the conviction or acquittal of the person concerned, or when proceedings are dropped.

Substantiation of the above

1. Numerous breaches of the law have been committed under national socialist rule. In character, extent and intention they are both serious and detestable. It is absolutely essential for the restoration of the rule of law and with it of internal and external peace, that they should be punished. If law is to be helped to victory, however, then it can only be by measures that are themselves legal, and that are not determined by political considerations or passions.

It is therefore essential on grounds of law and political expediency

* See p. 149.

that the matter should be settled in an honourable and dignified manner.

2. The proposed paragraph of the penal code, which is utterly clear in its condemnation of crimes, establishes a special category of punishable offence for which the offender is liable to either imprisonment or death. Prosecution will be according to the normal processes of the law. In order to make arrest easier, the possibility of proscribing the criminals is provided for.

In addition to the measures proposed, consideration ought to be given to further paragraphs directed against those who harbour a proscribed person or help him to evade capture or conceal him.

3. The retrospective application of the new category of crime contradicts the basic principle of *nulla poena sine lege*. The purely procedural provisions about proscription are not affected by these objections. The basic principle of *nulla poena* has been a common feature of European criminal law since the 18th century. Historically, it emerged as a defence against arbitrary actions by absolutist governments. It does not correspond to a basic ethical requirement, regardless of which legal method one adopts. The old criminal law which did not contain any firm penal provisions (before the Bamberg Criminal Court order and the CC Carolina) did not recognize this principle and it is still unknown in some Swiss cantons even today. It is also worth noticing that the Circles to which the offenders belong have disowned and abolished this principle. However, the return to settled legal usage and the reawakening of legal security and confidence in the law, require that we abide by the basic principle even in the case of these criminals, and that we refrain therefore from applying this category retrospectively.

It follows from the above that crimes committed before the publication of this law cannot be punished on the basis of this new paragraph of the penal code. A punishment can only be carried out, therefore, when the accused has also committed offences that were already punishable under the provisions in operation at the time of the offence. The principle of *nulla poena* does not, however, stand in the way of a purely declaratory assertion by the court that a crime has been committed, even where the category is being retrospectively applied. This application of the new provision as a *lex imperfecta* is a valuable contribution towards the reawakening of awareness of the law and will be understood as a kind of expiation. The majority of the Third Reich's criminals are also guilty of ordinary offences, especially of being accomplices to the fact, so that even now the requisite punishments for their crimes can be meted out.

4. Alongside this legal retribution special action is necessary to provide compensation for those who have been injured and discriminated against through arbitrary and coercive actions against life and limb, property, honour and civil rights. (Concentration camps, unjust sentences, loss of civil rights, confiscations, dismissal of public servants.) Legal provisions will be published that simplify the conduct of such

proceedings against those who have been declared criminals, and which generally increase the liability upon the criminals and their property.

5. The reduction of civil and political rights when a person is declared a criminal is likewise reserved for a special ruling.

5. Briefing for Negotiations Concerning the Punishment of Criminals by the International Community (Second Draft)

23.7.43.* (Note by Moltke)

Numerous breaches of the law have been committed under national socialist rule. In character, extent and intention they are both serious and detestable. It is absolutely essential for the restoration of the rule of law, and with it of internal and external peace, that they should be punished. If law is to be helped to victory, however, then it can only be by measures that are themselves legal and that are not determined by political considerations or passions.

The German people have the greatest interest in seeing that the appropriate punishment is given for violation of the law. This is a matter which is very much the Germans' own. However, the right of the International Community to demand that these offences be punished is not to be disputed.

After the 1914–18 war the restoration of a peace based upon trust between the nations was prejudiced by inadequate attention to, and treatment of, 'war criminals'. In Germany itself serious domestic conflicts arose which contributed to the origins of the present war. It should not be forgotten that the character of the problem after the First World War was quite different. Nonetheless it is interesting, in the light of renewed demands for the international punishment of 'war criminals' for 'systematic atrocities', to take a retrospective glance at the provisions of the Versailles Treaty.

In article 227 the Kaiser was charged with a 'supreme offence against international morality and the sanctity of treaties', and was ordered to appear before five judges drawn from the victorious powers. The judgement was to be based upon 'the highest motives of international policy', with the general objective of 'vindicating the solemn obligations of international undertakings and the validity of international morality'. The punishment was left to the discretion of the court.

According to article 228 the allied governments could bring individuals—whom the Germans were bound to surrender—before their military courts for 'acts in violation of the laws and customs of war', and they would be sentenced 'to punishments laid down by law' without any reference to German domestic punishments.

Article 229 laid down that criminals guilty of offences against citizens of one of the victorious powers would be tried in the military tribunals

* See p. 149.

of the power concerned, while those guilty of offences against citizens of various powers would be tried in tribunals composed of members of the powers concerned.

These were not, therefore, courts of the international community, but organs of the victorious powers. This time we must avoid the error of 1919, when German co-operation was made practically impossible, and strive after a solution which is both honourable and dignified and which is consistent with the purpose of the law. Only a solution of this nature can become a cornerstone of peace, rather than a threat to it.

The demand for the extradition of criminals for punishment by the courts of either one or all the victorious powers offends against the natural dignity of the statesman who will personally have to surrender the criminals and the nation itself. It is an essential precondition for the successful formation of an international community in the future that every action should be consistent with personal dignity.

Punishment by a universal international court and the surrender of the criminals to this judicial authority would offend against neither law nor dignity. Instead it would make a positive contribution by providing a foundation for and a test of the future co-operation of the international community.

Only a universal court composed of representatives of all who took part in the war, regardless of which side they were on, or even of all the nations of the world, could have the necessary moral and legal authority to pronounce the necessary moral and legal condemnation of the crimes. A sham judgement passed by a body that had not been legally constituted, would not advance the restoration of law, but would instead have the opposite effect.

Historically and practically speaking the obvious court for these purposes is the International Court at the Hague. A number of legal doubts have been raised about entrusting it with a penal role but in the present situation there can be no really substantial objections to doing this.

Non-membership of the League of Nations is not an obstacle to involvement in the Court according to article 35 of its Statute. The Assembly of the League of Nations would have to alter article 4 relating to the composition of the Court. Benches of six judges (3 from the victorious powers, 2 neutrals, and 1 from the defeated nations) would seem to be expedient, with the deciding vote resting with the President as in article 55 of the Statute. The right of demanding a particular sentence would, in accordance with article 34, lie with the injured party. Defence counsels would be engaged by the state of which the accused is a citizen, and there would also be the possibility of an official defence counsel. The details of the proceedings would be regulated according to the rules of the Court. The points made in the appended law, under the heading, 'Grounds for the conviction of criminals in the national courts', would, it is proposed, form the basis of sentencing in the International Court.

The basic principles of *nulla poena sine lege* would have to be binding upon the International Court in the light of the emphasis that has been placed upon it internationally in recent years in relation to the actions of German governments. Thus, as in the enclosed proposals for procedure within Germany, the courts would have to make a declaratory assertion that a crime has been committed, and find a punishment for it in the law operating at the time of the offence in the country of which the offender was a citizen. As far as crimes in occupied territories are concerned, it can be left to the discretion of the court to decide when there are discrepancies between the laws.

In connection with the number of those who ought to be charged, it is interesting to note a practical rule that Macaulay deduced from English history before 1689 (*History of England*, Vol. I, ch. 10, p. 312, London 1864):

'The rule by which a prince ought after a rebellion to be guided in selecting rebels for punishments is perfectly obvious. The ringleaders, the men of rank, fortune and education, whose power and whose artifices have led the multitude into error, are the proper objects of severity. The deluded population when once the slaughter on the field of battle is over, can scarcely be treated too leniently.'

The responsibility for guarding the accused who are handed over to the courts by their governments would have to rest, on the basis of special agreements, with the Dutch government.

Punishment would be carried out by states specified by the Court, but excluding the one against which the offence has been committed, under the supervision of, and in accordance with, the rules of the Court.

If this attempt to arrive at a just solution of what is a serious hindrance to peace for all concerned succeeds, a further step will have been taken towards establishing the rule of law between nations, and evil will have brought forth good. If, however, a solution is adopted on purely political grounds, outside a Court that can be recognized as just, then evil will be answered by evil, and force which as a source of law must be broken, will be reinstated as the ultimate arbiter.

6. Basic Principles of the Reconstruction

draft of 9.8.43.* (note by Moltke)

The government of the German Reich sees in Christianity the foundation for the moral and religious renewal of our nation, for the conquest of hatred and deception and for the reconstruction of the European community of nations.

The point of departure lies in human sensitivity to the divine order which upholds man's inward and outward existence. This sensitivity is

* See p. 149.

imperative. Only when it is possible to make the divine order the test of relationships between men and nations will we be able to overcome the moral and material disorder of our time and establish a genuine peace.

The internal reconstruction of the Reich is the basis for the achievement of a just and durable peace.

Situated in the midst of the collapse of a power structure that has lost all sanction and that is founded exclusively on technical mastery, Europeans more than any other group of men face this problem. The path to a solution lies open—through the determined and energetic exploitation of the Christian heritage. The Reich government is therefore resolved to fulfil the following irreducible domestic and external demands with all the means at its disposal:

1. The law which has been trampled upon must be restored and given authority over all orders of human existence. Under the protection of scrupulous, independent and fearless judges it is the keystone of any future peace.

2. Freedom of belief and conscience are guaranteed. Existing laws and regulations that infringe these principles are to be repealed immediately.

3. Destruction of the totalitarian constraint upon conscience and acknowledgement of the inviolable dignity of the human person as the foundation of the legal and international order that is to be aimed at. Everyone has a full share of responsibility in social, political and international affairs. The right of everybody to work and property, regardless of race, nation or creed is upheld by the public authorities.

4. The basic unit of peaceful communal life is the family. It is protected by the public authorities, who ought also to guarantee education and the external necessities of life; food, clothing, housing, parks and health.

5. Work must be so organized that it encourages rather than stunts personal responsibility. This entails attention to working conditions and the provision of advanced professional schools. It also requires that each person should have a real share of responsibility in the individual firm, and beyond that in the general economic sphere to which his own work contributes. By this means he is to co-operate in the development of a healthy and secure social order in which the individual, his family and the communities can develop organically within co-ordinated spheres of activity. The economic authorities must guarantee these basic requirements.

6. The personal political responsibility of each individual requires that he should share in the self-government of the small and manageable communities that are to be revived. Rooted and proved at this level, he must share in the decision-making of the state and the international community through his own elected representatives. In this way he is given a strong sense of sharing responsibility for political activity in general.

7. The special responsibility and loyalty that everyone owes to his

nation of origin, his language and the intellectual and historical tradition of his people must be respected and protected. However, this must not become an excuse for amassing political power, or for degrading, persecuting or oppressing a foreign race. The free and peaceful development of national culture is incompatible with the retention of absolute sovereignty by each individual state. Peace demands the creation of an order that spans the separate states. As soon as the free consent of all nations involved is assured, the authorities in this new order must have the right to demand of every individual obedience, honour, and in case of need the pledge (Einsatz) of life and property for the highest political authority in the international community.

The Structure of the Reich

The Reich remains the highest authority of the German people. Its political constitution ought to be characterized by genuine authority, and real co-operation and participation by the people. It rests upon the natural divisions of the nation: family, parish and Land. The structure of the Reich is based on the principles of self-government. The latter unites freedom and personal responsibility with the requirements of order and leadership.

This structure ought to assure the unity and concerted leadership of the Reich and ought to enable it to be integrated into the community of European nations.

The political will of the nation is to be exercised within limits that are still open to the inspection of the individual. Physically, economically and culturally integrated Länder are to be formed on the foundation of the natural divisions of parish and county. In order to make the self-government really effective the Länder ought to have between three and five million inhabitants.

The distribution of responsibility is to be made according to the principle that every corporation is responsible for performing all the tasks that it can most sensibly carry out itself.

Even today it is the responsibility of all public authorities to see to it that each measure and statement is in character with the ultimate objective of a legal constitutional state of affairs. The removal of the disorders and abuses that are the result of the national socialist war and collapse and that menace the life of the German nation must be accompanied as soon as possible by a determined effort, employing all available resources, to create a constitutional Reich structure on the following principles.

I. The Parish

The representative institutions of the parish are to be elected by all who are qualified to vote in secret and direct ballots.

Everybody who is over 21 or who has fought in the war has the right to vote; heads of family have an additional vote for each child not entitled to vote; anybody can be elected who is over 27 and whose candidature is agreed upon by a number of voters—the number depending on the size of the local community; members of the Armed Forces cannot be elected.

II. The County (*Kries*)

The representative institutions in the counties and in the towns that are independent of the counties are to be elected in accordance with the same principle as those that govern the representative institutions of the parishes. The same applies to the subordinate divisions of the towns that are independent of the counties. Electoral districts that are too large for the individual voter to survey are to be subdivided.

III. The Land

1. The Landtag in the Länder and the city assembly in the cities outside the counties are to be chosen by the representative bodies of the counties and cities or, in the case of the cities outside the counties, by the representative assemblies in the political sub-divisions. Any male citizen who has completed his 27th year can be elected. Political civil servants and members of the armed forces cannot be elected. The electoral arrangements should ensure that at least half of those who are elected do not belong to one of the electing corporations.

The Landtag has the following responsibilities:

Determination of the Budget, taxes and Land laws; the right to question the chief minister of the Land and the right to pass resolutions on all matters relevant to the politics of the Land and its administration; election of the Land governor on the basis of a proposal by the Land council.

2. The Land government consists of the chief minister and the requisite number of privy councillors. The chief minister is to be chosen by the Landtag on the basis of a proposal by the Land Commissioner; the privy councillors are to be nominated by the Land Commissioner on the basis of a proposal by the chief minister. Members of the Land government must have their hereditary home in the Land.

The Land government is responsible for the government of the Land and the execution of the Reich's functions within the territory of the Land.

3. The Land council has the following responsibilities:

To propose candidates for the post of Land Commissioner for election by the Landtag;

To send recommendations to the Landtag;

To exercise disciplinary authority over the members of the Land government.

4. The Land Commissioner is to be elected every 12 years by the Landtag on the basis of a proposal by the Land Council, and his appointment is to be confirmed by the Reich Commissioner.

The Land Commissioner has the following responsibilities:

Oversight over the whole administration of the Land and the appointment of civil servants;

He bears responsibility for carrying out Reich policies in the Land;

He is president of the Land Council.

IV. The Reich

1. The Reichstag is to be elected by the Landtags. Any male citizen of the Reich over 27 can be elected. Political civil servants and members of the Armed Forces cannot be elected. For the time being the electoral arrangements should ensure that at least half of those elected do not belong to one of the electoral bodies.

The Reichstag has the following responsibilities:

Determination of the Reich budget, Reich taxes and Reich laws.

The right of questioning the Reich Chancellor and the right to pass resolutions on all questions of Reich policy.

Election of the Reich Commissioner on the basis of proposals by the Reich Council.

2. The Reich government consists of the Reich Chancellor and the departmental ministers. The Reich Chancellor is to be appointed by the Reich Commissioner with the agreement of the Reichstag; the ministers are to be nominated by the Reich Commissioner on the basis of proposals by the Reich Chancellor.

The Reich Commissioner can dismiss the Reich Chancellor; the dismissal will become effective with the appointment of a new Reich Chancellor. The Reichstag has the right to demand the dismissal of the Reich Chancellor with a qualified majority, as long as it makes a proposal at the same time to the Reich Commissioner for a new Reich Chancellor.

3. The Reich Council consists of the Land Commissioners, the President of the Reichstag and the Reich Economic Chamber and Reich councillors appointed for 8 years by the Reich Commissioner with the agreement of the Reich Government. The Reich Council has the following responsibilities:

To propose candidates for the office of Regent of the nation for election by the Reichstag;

To establish principles governing the transfer of civil servants from one Land to another and from the service of the Land to the Reich service;

To send recommendations to the Reichstag;

To act as a disciplinary authority over the Reich Government and the Land Commissioners.

4. The Reich Commissioner is to be elected for 12 years by the Reichstag on the basis of proposals by the Reich Council.

The Reich Commissioner is the Supreme Commander of the Armed Forces, and president of the Reich Council.

With the countersignature of the Reich Chancellor, he represents the Reich in relations with the outside world.

He executes the Reich laws, appoints and dismisses the Reich ministers and Reich civil servants.

Church, Culture, Education

The Reich government welcomes the energetic co-operation of both major Christian churches in shaping public life.

The public exercise of the worshipping, pastoral and educational functions of both the Christian churches is not to be hindered and is placed under the protection of the Reich government. The publication of religious literature is once again made possible. The Christian heritage is to be granted its proper place in the whole of education as well as in films and broadcasting.

The legal relations between the German Reich and the German Evangelical Church and the Roman Catholic Church are to be freshly defined in accordance with these principles and with the friendly agreement of both churches. The agreements in the concordat remain unaffected by this.

More precise definitions of the future legal status of the other religious and ideological communities will follow negotiations with them.

Parents are to have their natural right to educate their children in accordance with the principles of Christian faith and the dictates of their own conscience. The state itself has to help to overcome the inward and outward disruption of the family. Sundays are to be free of compulsory state occasions.

The family, church and school perform the work of education together. A school ought to satisfy the right of every child to receive an education that is suitable for him. It ought to arouse and strengthen his moral powers and give him the amount of knowledge and skill appropriate to what is required of his age group.

Character training produces an upright man of religious conviction who is able to adopt as the guide-lines of his life, good morals and lawfulness, truth and sincerity, love for his neighbour and loyalty to his own conscience. The man educated in this way will be mature enough to take responsible decisions. Learning helps towards the moral formation of personality and prepares for practical life.

Technical schools and colleges of further education that build upon the foundations laid by the elementary schools or by their own lower levels, develop an organically structured knowledge and skill by increasing the share of responsibility given to the individual.

The state school is a Christian school in which religious instruction by both confessions is a compulsory subject. The lessons are the responsibility of the churches and, where possible, will be taken by clergymen.

The Economy

All those engaged in economic activity have the same minimum duties. These include fairness and propriety in economic management, and the honouring of agreements and continuance in work where agreements have been concluded.

The basic insurance that the workers need to preserve their human dignity is to be provided by the management. At the same time every effort is to be made to bring about as early as possible a general rise in the minimum wage which has been reduced by the severe damage to the economic system caused by the war. The contributions required to bring this about are to be made by the individual, the firm, the economic self-governing corporations, the German trade union and the state and they must allow for the insurance of the workers' dependents.

2. The Reich government considers that the basis for economic reconstruction lies in orderly competition carried on within limits set by the government and, as far as its methods are concerned, subject to government inspection.

Where the existing commitments and nexus of interests (monopolies, cartels, combines) make this competition impossible, it is the task of the government to apply the principles of competition and to protect the interests of the community as a whole.

The concern of the whole community in the basic industries entails a special degree of government regulation of these sectors of industry. Key mining, iron and metal, chemical and fuel firms will be taken over by the public authorities. These publicly owned industries are to be directed and inspected on the same principles as apply generally in the economic system.

The Reich economic authorities will advance the economic policies of the Länder through their influence upon markets and basic industries and provide for as trouble-free development of the economy as is possible. The Reich government encourages the development of the industrial undertaking into a partnership of those who work in it. In a partnership of this kind—called a works union—the share of the labour force in the profits and particularly in the increased value of the concern will be agreed upon between the owners of the concern and the representatives of the labour force. The agreement is subject to the approval of the economic self-governing corporation of the Land.

3. The 'German Trade Union' is an essential instrument for accomplishing the economic programme described above and the state structure that it presupposes. Its purpose is to carry out this programme and transfer tasks to which it has attended to the agencies of the state and the economic self-government. If the tasks that the trade union ought to attend to require its continued existence, its constitution must be adapted to the structures of the state and economic system.

4. In the system of economic self-government based on the Länder,

industrial, commercial and craft concerns are members of the Chambers of Commerce. Agricultural concerns are members of the Chambers of Agriculture. The Chambers of Commerce and Agriculture are linked in the Land Economic Chamber. The Chambers of Commerce and Agriculture are to be composed of an equal number of elected representatives of management and labour. The Land Economic Chamber will consist of representatives nominated by the Chambers of Commerce and Agriculture.

The Chambers issue their own ordinances, subject to the approval of the Land Commissioner. The presidents of the Chambers and their deputies are to be elected by the Chambers, but they must receive the assent of the Land Commissioner.

The Chambers are responsible for the self-government of the economic system; they can also be entrusted with Reich or Land responsibilities by the relevant economic authority in the Land (Land Economic Office, etc.). The special responsibilities of these bodies include the supervision of vocational training which will follow nine years of schooling and which ought to be adapted to the needs of the economy as a whole. It will normally last for 2 years. The Chambers are also responsible for providing for professional advancement by means of suitable technical and material arrangements.

The Reich Economic Chamber, at the head of the system of economic self-government, is composed of delegates from the Land Economic Chambers.

The economic administration is part of the general administration of the state. The Reich Economic Ministry deals with the regional self-governing organizations run by the individual concerns and with the individual concerns themselves through the Land Economic Authorities.

7. First Instructions to the Provincial Commissioners

draft of 9.8.43.* (note by Moltke)

If the inward and outward distress of the German people is to be mitigated and their lot decisively altered then it can only be on the basis of a clear and coherent conception of the German future. Such a firmly defined conception is all the more essential as military and political developments could create a situation in which individual parts of the country were militarily occupied or isolated, or in which there was no Reich government, or at least no government that could issue binding orders.

It is of the utmost importance that in such circumstances responsible leaders in the different Länder and parts of the country should act harmoniously and in agreement on basic matters, even when there is no opportunity for consultation and contact, and thus preserve and confirm

* See p. 149.

the inner solidarity of the German Länder as part of one civilized nation.

The principles set out below, which in view of the variety of ways in which the situation could develop have been confined to fundamentals, ought to guarantee that, in the event of possible unfavourable military developments, the German people present a united will in their dealings with the other nations.

I

The liberally inclined German workers and the Christian churches together represent and lead those forces in the nation that can embark upon the work of reconstruction. They alone, with their ever-powerful spiritual traditions, can guarantee at this moment of time that the substance of the German nation as a civilized nation is preserved and its cohesion as a political entity rescued from its present peril. Supported by these forces, we commission you with the heavy responsibility of assuming the office of Provincial Commissioner in the region assigned to you, the territorial limits of which are marked on the accompanying map, and of taking possession of the instruments of power that are necessary to exercise your authority. The military authorities in the area are under instructions to obey your orders.

The Provincial Commissioner is responsible to the Reich for organizing the political, cultural and economic resources of the Land;

1. He is to provide legal security, personal freedom and a genuine share in responsibility for all the inhabitants of the Land and so encourage the natural expression of the Land's political will and afford an opportunity for the special character of the regions to develop through the proposed self-government.

In order to provide the constructive forces in the Land with opportunities for responsible co-operation you must ensure without delay that well-known and trustworthy people are commissioned with these tasks in both town and country.

2. The Commissioner, in close association with the recognized upholders of civilization in the Land, is to facilitate the reconstruction of Christian education, and consequently a genuine renewal of spiritual and intellectual life. If this is to be achieved, what is required more than anything else is immediate co-operation between Land and Church, founded upon mutual trust.

You must therefore make immediate contact with representatives of the Church in your Land.

3. It is particularly important that the Provincial Commissioner should enlist the responsible co-operation of the workers in administration and industry.

You must therefore establish immediate contact with the Commissioner of the German trade union, which should be recognized as the only legitimate representative of the working man.

These principles are explained in more detail in appendix 1.

In performing your duties you ought to follow the guide-lines set out below:

I*

1. In the appointment of personnel you have an entirely free hand to take any measures that you regard as requisite to maintain an orderly administration and to preserve peace and order. All prominent national socialists are to be kept out of important positions as a matter of principle.

Once you have chosen your closest colleagues you must first fill the key positions with absolutely reliable people. You also have the right to appoint personnel in the Reich agencies and regional corporations in your Land.

Appointments to official positions can only become effective after they have been ratified by you as Provincial Commissioner.

2. In the event of the declaration of martial law (a state of emergency) the military holder of executive power remains subject to your general political instructions.

3. The standard applied in the necessary arrests should be that of personal guilt and particular note should be taken of the regulations about law-breakers in appendix 2. The guilt is to be tested and decided upon by the normal legal processes as early as possible. In addition all persons should be arrested of whom it is suspected that they could hinder the state in carrying out the necessary measures.

Steps are to be taken immediately to liberate those who have been unjustly deprived of their freedom.

You are enjoined to take all requisite measures without waiting for instructions from superior offices.

4. The boundary corrections that have become necessary as a result of the new delimitation of frontiers must be carried out immediately in co-operation with the Provincial Commissioners of the neighbouring Länder. Regular contact with all the neighbouring Provincial Commissioners should be established as a matter of priority. The former regional boundaries remain in force in the first instance for the administration of the post and railways as well as for the Armed Forces.

II

1. All laws and decrees that discriminate against individuals because of their membership of a particular nation, race or religion are not to be enforced; discriminatory measures based upon them are to be abrogated forthwith. With these exceptions the existing laws and administrative decrees are as a general principle to remain in force in the first instance.

2. a) All measures that maintain the fighting power of the German

* Numbering as in original draft.

Armed Forces or, at a later date, help towards orderly demobilization, are to be carried out as Reich functions with precedence over all other relevant tasks; actions required to perform these tasks are to be taken regardless of any resistance.

b) Any interruption of the orderly continuation of the existing system of procurement and distribution in the economy must be avoided in any circumstances. Interference in the flow of provisions and relaxation of the rationing system are the most serious menace.

3. Alongside the maintenance of the integrity of your Land and of order and security in your Land your most important task is to build up self-government along the lines indicated in the principles set out in appendix 1. In doing this you ought to integrate the economic interests and political forces in your Land as fully as possible into this system of self-government, and you ought to reduce bureaucratic administration and consolidate your own authority from below.

4. You must do all that is necessary to enable the economy to carry through the essential measures of readjustment as far as possible without help from outside and while maintaining an adequate level of production. In order to restore permanent conditions the migration of non-resident labour should be encouraged. Restrictions on immigration and residence cannot be imposed upon Germans.

5. In order to cover the inevitable expenses you are empowered, on the basis of the *Reichsleistungsgesetz* to demand the finances that you require.

1. *Memorandum for the English Government**
(strictly private and confidential)

(end of April 1942)†

I

The development of recent weeks and months has not brought us nearer to answering the question, who will be the so-called 'victor' in the present struggle. And yet it has become more and more obvious to all thinking people that western civilization as such is dangerously threatened in its spiritual and material fundaments. The following features which characterize the present European situation should be kept in mind as they may shortly determine conditions in the entire world.

1. *Intensified mass destruction of life and economic substance.* Economic losses, inescapably bound up with the war, are bringing about such general impoverishment that even victor nations will be grievously affected by them for many decades.

Human losses will be of a magnitude which threatens the very continuance of civilized society for years after the war. This pertains not only to the powers at war, but to all nations which, although not directly involved in the struggle, suffer from its manifold repercussions (famine, epidemics, etc.).

2. *Increasingly totalitarian control of national life everywhere.* The absorption of all national reserves and resources, economic as well as human, by total warfare is becoming unavoidable even in countries which by temperament and on principle are opposed to totalitarianism. Restrictions necessary during such a war are bound to thwart the realm of personal freedom, its cultural and economic productiveness to the point of suffocation.

3. *Trend toward anarchical dissolution.* The gradual breakdown of personal security and civil life has already created an extremely vulnerable state of affairs all over Europe. It is impossible to ignore the danger of a complete breakdown of the framework of civilized existence. The military and diplomatic achievements of the Soviet Union are giving a strong impetus to illegal cells of the Third International everywhere in Europe. And Soviet methods in Finland, in the Baltic, Poland and Roumania as applied in 1939–1940 do not justify the belief that bolshevism has as yet changed into a form of government adapted to western standards.

* Printed with kind permission of Hans Rothfels and the Munich Institute for Contemporary History.
† See p. 183.

II

In view of this situation and its potentialities of catastrophe we consider it necessary to address ourselves to all those on this side of the Atlantic and beyond it who can still realize the scope of this danger. We consider it an irrefutable fact that in spite of all differences between individual countries there is as yet such similarity of conditions and community of spiritual heritage between ourselves and the West that all attempts to discuss certain vital dangers which threaten the essence of our common future should be made under all circumstances.

We do not intend to justify our own position, we are ready to accept our due share of responsibility and of guilt. But we feel justified to appeal to the solidarity and fairness which some responsible groups in the West are extending to those forces in Germany which have consistently fought against Nihilism and its national socialist manifestations. The consciousness of this solidarity in thoughts and in deeds seems to us an indispensable condition for continuing this exchange of views. Such solidarity should first express itself in the fact that appeals like this are not flaunted and discredited by wrong use in the press as it has happened in the past. We would particularly ask our friends to do everything in their power to prevent this in the future.

Matters which may appear as sensational news on your side of the frontier are often of such a precarious character on ours that a minimum of sympathetic imagination should prevent giving publicity to them. Deliberate attempts to discredit the forces standing behind a message like the present one have been noticeable even in the Christian periodical press. In this respect we can only appeal to your conscience.

III

The most urgent and immediate task to stave off catastrophe in Europe is the earliest possible overthrow of the Regime in Germany. The change can take place either by way of anarchical dissolution or by the establishment of a Government which would return to the standards of civilized Europe.

The first possibility would be tantamount to a wholesale European catastrophe. It would be inevitably linked up with Soviet military success and form the first step towards world revolution by military means.

A success of the second possibility is only conceivable if it is also linked up outside Germany with the final overcoming of European nationalism particularly in its military expression.

The forces in Germany striving for the latter possibility are inspired by the ideas and the circles of the Christian opposition which has crystallized in years of struggle against national socialism. Militant Christianism in its widest sense is the only unbroken core of resistance within the Nazi state, and it has now formed powerful contacts with groups hitherto indifferent to Church and Religion. The key to their common efforts is a desperate attempt to rescue the substance of personal human integrity, equally threatened by Nazism and anarchic Bolshevism. Restitution of the unalienable right, divine and natural, of the human person forms their basic aim. The political and constitutional reconstruction, for which they are working, is conceived in terms of a practical application of the Christian European tradition to modern human needs in the social, political, economic and international sphere.

Seizure of power by these forces in Germany is hindered by the following obstacles:

a) The dire necessity of national defence against the Soviet Union and against anarchical developments on the eastern frontier of Germany as well as in the Balkans.

b) Existing control of the entire national life by police (Gestapo) and the anticipated difficulty of dealing with Nazi remnants and anarchical outbreaks after the Nazi overthrow.

c) The complete uncertainty of the British and American attitude towards a change of government in Germany.

d) The movements of indiscriminate hatred anticipated in the event of a sudden relaxation of German control in the occupied parts of Europe.

The last two problems cannot be overcome without international co-operation even at this stage.

IV

Without, for obvious reasons, giving further details of names, dates and programme, it can be said here that our support is drawn from the following groups:

1. Substantial parts of the working class.

2. Influential circles in the army and bureaucracy.

3. The militant groups in the Churches.

These groups agree on the following lines and principles of reconstruction:

a) Self-government and decentralization within Germany.

The structure of the State thus achieved, would be characterized as follows: Breaking up of the masses by the creation of smaller and greater units of local self-administration. Application of modern socialist principles in all sectors of political and economic life.

b) Self-government and federalism within Germany should be organically connected with federalism within Europe (including Britain) and close international co-operation with the other Continents.

This European Federalism within Germany would have the following results: Re-establishments of the rights of self-determination within the frame of the European Federation for all nations, particularly those actually under Nazi rule.

We believe in the necessity to reconstitute a free Polish and a free Czech state within the limits of their ethnographic frontiers.

Progressive achievement of general disarmament which we consider to be an economic and social problem as much as a problem of national policy.

c) Renunciation of economic autarchy in exchange for free access to raw materials overseas.

d) The political and economic reorganization of Europe must be free of concepts such as 'status quo' and 'status quo ante'. The main emphasis must lie on social and political security.

e) The New Germany would be willing to co-operate in any international solution of the Jewish problem.

f) Germany would be willing to co-operate with all other nations in order to overcome the misery existing in the Countries now under Nazi rule.

V

We consider these points a first basis for talks on a wider and more detailed scale and are ready to join in with all those who are determined to halt this tremendous destruction of all human values. An exchange of ideas seems to us hopeless only as long as we are faced with a one-sided tendency to blame and to judge. There is a definite difference between active crime and criminal negligence. But, whatever the responsibilities are, there should be a common recognition of our failure to deal in a Christian manner with the historical, geographic, economic and psychological factors which have brought the world to the present situation.

We sincerely hope that our still unadequate attempt to do so will be met with frank co-operation in the practical task to face a common future beyond the catastrophe now confronting us all.

2. *Schönfeld Memorandum**
(Statement by a German pastor at Stockholm)†

(31st May 1942)

I

The many opposition circles in Germany who had beforehand no real contact with each other have crystallized during the last winter into active opposition groups working now closely together as centres of a strong opposition movement to the whole Nazi régime on the European Continent.

There are three main groups of action preparing to overthrow the Nazi régime and to bring about a complete change of power.

1. Essential parts of the leadership in the Army and in the central State administration.

* Printed with kind permission of Rev. E. Bethge and Chr. Kaiser Verlag, Munich.
† See p. 149.

(In the Army they include key men in the Highest Command O.K.W. for the front troops, Navy and Air forces as well as in the Central Command of the Home Military forces; also in the State administration the liaison men to the State Police forces largely in opposition to the Gestapo.)

2. The leaders of the former Trade Unions and other active liaison men to large parts of the workers.

(Through a network of key men systematically developed during the last six months they control now key positions in the main industrial centres as well as in the big cities like Berlin, Hamburg, Cologne, and throughout the whole country.)

3. The leaders of the Evangelical Churches (under Bishop Wurm) and of the Roman Catholic Church (the Fulda Bishop Conference) acting together as great corporations and as centres of resistance and reconstruction.

By their close co-operation these three key groups of action have formed the strong opposition movement which, in the given situation, would have sufficient power to overthrow the present régime because of their control over large masses having now arms in their hands, and, as regards the workers, at their disposal.

II

The leaders of these key groups are now prepared to take the next chance for the elimination of Hitler, Goering, Goebbels, Ley and Co., together with whom the central leaders of the Gestapo, the S.S. and the S.A. would be destroyed at the same time, especially also in the occupied countries.

This change of power would not lead to the establishment of a military clique controlling the whole situation but to the coming into power of a government composed by strong representatives of the three key groups which is able and definitely prepared to bring about a complete change of the present system of lawlessness and social injustice.

Their programme is determined by the following main aims:

1. A German nation governed by law and social justice with a large degree of responsible self-administration throughout the different main provinces.

2. Reconstruction of the economic order according to truly socialistic lines, instead of self-sufficient autarchy a close co-operation between free nations; their economic interdependence becoming the strongest possible guarantee against self-reactionary European militarism.

3. A European Federation of free States or Nations including Great Britain which would co-operate in a close way with other federations of nations.

This Federation of Free European Nations to which would belong a Free Polish and a Free Czech Nation should have a common executive, under the authority of which a European Army would be created for the permanent ordering of European security.

The foundations principles of national and social life within this Federation of Free European Nations should be oriented or reorientated towards the fundamental principles of Christian Faith and life.

III

The internal circumstances are becoming now peculiarly favourable to a *coup d'état* by the Army and the other combined forces of the Opposition. It would help and quicken this process towards the change of power along the lines mentioned above (see II) if the Allies would make it clear whether they are prepared for a European peace settlement along the lines indicated.

If otherwise the Allies insist on a fight to the finish the German Opposition with the German Army is ready to go on with the war to the bitter end in spite of its wish to end the Nazi régime.

In the case of agreement for a European peace settlement as indicated the Opposition Government would, after a *coup d'état*, withdraw gradually all its forces from the occupied and invaded countries.

It would announce at once that it would restitute the Jewish part of the population at once to a decent status, give back the stolen property and co-operate with all other nations for a comprehensive solution of the Jewish problem.

It would be prepared to take its full share in the common efforts for the rebuilding of the areas destroyed or damaged by the war.

It would declare itself at once disinterested in any further co-operation with the Japanese Government and its war aims, being prepared on the contrary to give at disposal its forces and war material for finishing the war in the Far East.

It would be prepared to co-operate for a real solution of the Colonial problem along the lines of a true mandate system in which all member nations of the European Federation should participate together with the other nations or federations of nations concerned.

It is to be expected that representatives of the S.S. will offer the elimination of Hitler in order to secure for themselves power and a negotiated peace.

It would be a real support for the start of the whole process towards the change of power as indicated if they would be encouraged in any way to go on.

It would help the opposition leaders to mobilize and to lead all the other forces of the Army and the nation against Himmler and the S.S. leaders against whom the bitterness and hatred is greater than against any one else.

In regard to the Russian Problem

1. The opposition groups have no aims to conquer or to get for Germany parts of Russia as a colonial area.

2. They hope that it may be in the future possible to co-operate in a really peaceful way with Russia, especially in the economic and cultural field.

3. But they are not convinced that the totalitarian methods of revolutionary brutal warfare would be changed without very effective guarantees, even when the totalitarian régime in Central Europe would have been abolished.

4. They would regard the building up of an Orthodox Russian Church by the renewal of Christian faith in Russian as a real common basis which could further more than anything else the co-operation between Russia and the European Federation.

3. Memorandum by a Traveller from Stockholm handed to the Bishop of Chichester and the Bishop's covering letter to Curtis

a. A Memorandum Handed to the Bishop of Chichester by a Traveller from Stockholm, August 30th, 1943*

Recent information from a leader of the opposition movement in Germany indicated, first, it is much more difficult for the opposition to organise in Germany than it is in the occupied countries. In the occupied countries the entire population is opposed to the occupying force, while in Germany the opposition must oppose its own government, and it is difficult to tell who can be depended on.

Two major lacks are found:

1. (a). *the lack of unity,* due to three factors—
    (i) the highly organized Party, and its many dependants who must depend upon the Party for their jobs, creates a group of people who will not take part in the opposition.
    (ii) because there is no assurance from either Russia or Great Britain and the United States that Germany will have a future in case it is defeated, the great mass of people cling to the only force they know, namely, the national force, which at present is in the hands of the Party.
    (iii) because of (ii) there is a growing conviction that Germany will be destroyed: therefore we must cling to our own government.
(b) *the lack of men*: practically all men between 18 and the class of 1899, namely, the age of 44, are in the army and on the fighting fronts. Those who remain are either members of the Party or not

---

* Typescript copy in the Curtis files (Round Table archives). The original 4,000 word letter from which this memorandum was compiled has since been published (1970) in *Vierteljahrshefte für Zeitgeschichte.* The text of this important, recently discovered document came to our notice too late to be reproduced here.

able to participate effectively in the opposition. Women are so fully occupied, either in war work or absorbed in the struggle to provide a living, they have not the time or the energy to take an active part in the opposition movement. It is believed that the worse the economic situation becomes the less likelihood there is of a revolution, as human energy will not be sufficient to do other than struggle to keep alive. There is not even time for the average women to even think of war.

2. *Lack of communication*: there remains practically no means of communication through which the opposition can form and organize effectively. Telephones are impossible: posts are inadvisable: messengers cannot travel due to the restrictions on the trains: conversations are extremely dangerous: the result is that the 'whispering campaign', while it may be effective in the city, does not extend beyond the border of the city in which the campaign is carried on. The chief means through which the opposition is held together is by *authentic* information which comes from the B.B.C.: on the other hand the B.B.C. is not well-informed about what to say to strengthen the opposition movement.

Other difficulties.
(a) The upper class keep the army out of touch with civilian life. There is no group today in Germany so secluded and shut off from civilian life as the army. An illustration was given when hundreds of letters from German prisoners of war in Russia were destroyed by the government so that their families would not be informed with regard to conditions in Russia.
(b) The civilians are uninformed. For example, the average civilian is not aware of the extent of the persecution of the Jews. He is led to believe that when a Jew is sent to the East he goes there not only to be protected but to live a more 'secluded' life. If members of the opposition are killed it is either unknown, or they are represented as criminals.

The weakness of the opposition and its limited method.
The opposition is described as those 'of whom one hears so much and notices so little'. The effective opposition are those who are not heard of. When they disappear they are thought of as 'nameless deaths'. Because nameless their deaths are often thought of as useless. On the other hand there is considerable 'throwing sand in the machinery'.

Any weakness in the opposition is the effort to save individual lives rather than to be a co-ordinated force. There has been too much trust in generals. There is a tendency now to de-centralize life in Germany and this tends to make the work of the opposition ineffective.

Summary.
I feel that my notes were somewhat sketchy in that I have not been able to add much to my recent conversation with you. The whole purpose of this letter, however, was the suggestion which I passed on to you, through which one of the leaders of the opposition believed that continuous information could reach the proper authorities in Great Britain so that the B.B.C. could more effectively aid the opposition.

b. Covering letter of Bishop Bell to Curtis*
Copy
Private

> The Palace,
> Chichester.
> 14th September 1943.

Dear Mr. Curtis,

Private

A few days ago I had a visit from an American friend just after his return from Stockholm. I saw him before he went to Stockholm on Y.C.M.A. Prisoners of War business and again after his return. While there he was given a letter by a Swede called Johannson† of Sigtuna, which was written to you by a German friend. It was five pages and unsigned, though the name Johannson said begins with 'M'‡ and he is known to be a prominent leader of the Opposition and he had left the letter on his way back to Germany from Norway. At the end of the letter he refers to Michael§ and Julian,‖ the implication being that they were friends of yours whom you would recognize.

The letter was very secret and it was realized that it was quite impossible to bring it over to England. I know Johannson and when I was in Stockholm myself last year¶ I saw a lot of him and from time to time he sees German churchmen. My friend was asked to memorize as much as he could of the contents of the letter and these contents were passed on to me by word of mouth and subsequently written in a memorandum, a copy of which I enclose. In sending it he says 'I fear that my notes were not adequately taken to give you a full content of the letter'. As he was only two or three days in London before flying back to U.S.A. and he did not know how he could get into touch with you personally he was asked by Johannson to give any information that he had obtained to William Paton** and to me. William Paton had died and I was the only person who could be reached. The typed memorandum does not give one the full impression that conversation gives, but you will gather something from it. The particular desire which this German voiced was that a

---

* Typescript copy in the Curtis files.   † See p. 184.
‡ Moltke.   § Michael Balfour.
‖ Julian Frisby.   ¶ See p. 192.
** See p. 43.

thoroughly trusted Britisher should if at all possible be placed in Stockholm in connection with the British Embassy, someone sensitive to the opposition with whom the opposition could establish contact. It would never do to have such an arrangement as part of the Secret Service; on both sides information is often got from the same sources and betrayal would be certain, in their view. In the letter, though not in the memorandum, the suggestion was made that if only somebody like Michael or Julian could be in Stockholm for this purpose it would make the whole difference. You, it was thought, would be sure to recognize who Michael and Julian are.

There is a great inert mass in Germany now which (it was put to me) has gradually lost all confidence of a peace which would give Germany any chance. Those who are against Hitler are nevertheless thrown back upon their own people as they distrust Britain and distrust Russia for different reasons, and are terribly handicapped when thrown back to their own people because they do not know there what individuals they can trust. Still, in spite of Himmler, the soul of Germany such men feel is not lost.

I was authorized to use my own discretion in letting the 'right persons' have the information, though my friend was most anxious not to be mixed up with it himself as he is engaged in purely philanthropic work. I have, therefore, let Sir Robert Bruce-Lockhart have a copy of the memorandum. If you would like to see me one day when we are both in Town I should of course be very happy to see you and talk it over.

Yours sincerely,

(Sgd) George Chichester

4. *Observations on the peace programme of the American Churches**

November 1943†

However much we welcome a statement on the basic principles of a peace today, we feel nevertheless that we must point out that we are not yet in a position to form any clear idea of the conditions under which peace negotiations will be carried out. Further, there are, we believe—without particular national experiences in mind—certain additional points that need to be made alongside the six points.

---

* A German version of this document has been published *VfZ* 12 (1964) pp. 300 ff. with an introduction by Prof. Hans Rothfels. The archives of the World Council of Churches in Geneva (Study Department), contain a document by a 'Christian study group' (No. 19 E/43–International Order) which is, with the exception of a lengthy introduction and a few minor omissions and additions, a translation of the German document published by Prof. Rothfels. The translators have used this translation because it was almost certainly the text that went to the USA. Where it has omitted paragraphs and sentences in the original German document, they have supplied translations of their own.

† See pp. 189, 268.

I

Everything should be done to prevent the recurrence of any connection between the peace treaties and the fundamental statutes of the future international organization. While peace treaties are known to reflect to a great extent the constellation of power prevailing at the close of the war, the statutes of the future international organization should really be founded on the moral and objective requirements of a true collaboration of nations and federations, all of whom enjoy equality of rights. In the statutes the idea of might should be definitely subordinated to the idea of rights. This signifies, among other things, that exclusion from this organization must not be allowed to be pronounced in consequence of opinions and desires expressed by certain powers, as, for instance, on account of suspicions or the like, but only on account of defences that have been clearly proved. If, for instance, the nations that suffered defeat in the present war were to be excluded from the international organization, even temporarily, in spite of having established a legal and responsible government at the close of the war, this would be an offence against the conception of right on which the international organization is to be based, in favour of considerations of political might which, if they were allowed to penetrate the organization, would again poison it at its very roots. For this reason the words 'in due course' and 'as quickly as possible' in reference to the collaboration of neutrals at present in enemy countries seem to us to imply the danger that the principle of arbitrary power politics is substituted for supreme principle of objective right.

We agree as to the necessity for federations within the framework of the general international organization, especially for Europe, as is emphasized in the American document. In our opinion, however, the legal and political construction of such federations must, if it is to be durable, be based on the fundamental principle of self-government. No European federation could possibly be lasting, that was created from without by means of direct or indirect force and coercion. The European federation must be created by the parties concerned even though the tremendous difficulties of the period of transition may render support from outside, given in agreement with the representatives of such self-government, necessary for the restoration and preservation of peace in Europe. Interference from outside would otherwise put a veiled system of coercion in the place of self rule. This would very soon give rise to the same defects and abuses as the so-called 'New Order' of national socialism has done.

II

We, too, consider the solution of certain economic problems as of utmost importance for the restoration of peace. Christians everywhere will agree in principle and without reservation with the aim of delivering the masses from economic need and obtaining for them a higher standard of living on the broadest lines. Nor can we doubt that it would be impossible to obtain the same without economic and financial agreement between the different states. On the other hand it is doubtful whether free trade is feasible or even desirable for this purpose. It seems to us that the underlying idea concerning national and international transactions in goods should be that of order combined with a maximum of freedom. True order and freedom in international trade are chiefly endangered by the existence of monopolies. We would agree with the British reply to this point when it emphasizes that, in order to establish durable economic peace, the states concerned should co-operate in giving up their own monopolies and in putting an end to private monopolies.

With regard to State Monopolies it must be made quite clear that it is by no means sufficient to give up the monopoly formally but not virtually. It would, for instance, by no means suffice that a wealthy country should formally offer the treasures of its soil for sale to all other countries on the same conditions. The others (i.e. also the poorer countries) must practically be in a position to buy them. This, however, will only be the case if they can pay for such imports by exports to the countries concerned and if they are not put at a disadvantage in an indirect manner, e.g. by financial manipulations. Otherwise the poorer countries might find themselves in a position similar to that of a workman on the labour market who, although allowed to make a formal 'free' contract, is in reality obliged to work for wages that very often do not give him his just share of the wealth of the nation. This kind of situation is bound to have disastrous consequences internationally, just as it does domestically.

The imperial monopolies of certain territories must also receive urgent attention, on the grounds of population policy, if there is to be a just and durable peace. The colonization of under-populated areas could do a great deal to relieve the pressure of population internationally, for example, in Eastern Asia.

We therefore believe that the future international organization should be capable of fighting against national and private monopolies as definite obstacles in the way of peace.

III

It is a matter of the greatest importance, if peace is to be assured in the future, that measures should be taken which provide for the possibility of adapting existing treaties to changing circumstances. The crucial question seems to us to concern the identity of the authority that will make the necessary modification of treaties. An organization that possesses the authority to sanction treaty modifications cannot be constituted without substantial and universal limitations on the sovereign powers of national governments. At this juncture nothing definite can be said on this problem, except to point out that recent developments, particularly in Europe, have demonstrated the inadequacy of the nation state as the ultimate authority in international affairs and increased the pressure for a greater co-ordination of individual states.

IV

As we have already emphasized above, we believe that the restoration of genuine self-government is a fundamental prerequisite to national and international recovery.

In Central and Eastern Europe, more particularly, the problem of self-rule cannot be solved without limitation of sovereign power. Such limitation was provided for in the Minorities treaties of 1918. With regard to minorities the establishment of a disinterested legal organization does not appear impracticable. Its authority would have to be founded on clearly defined 'minorities laws', i.e. the legal rights of 'national groups'. In this sphere a certain amount of preliminary work was done by the League of Nations in spite of certain failures in the experiments made. The great mistake in this attempt at solution was its rationalistic abstraction which did not take into account the complex sociological realities of 'national groups'. Thus the autonomy of 'national minorities', i.e. of national groups characterized by common language and culture, does not only concern groups living together in special districts, but also those which consist of scattered individuals and communities who are united by common culture and customs. In addition to territorial autonomy there must also be personal autonomy, founded on the personal legal rights of the members of the 'national groups'. Such 'Minorities Statutes' should, in our view, aim at complete equality for these 'national groups' in the way of education and jurisdiction and above all, in religious rights. The successful fulfilment of this claim for cultural autonomy as promoting European collaboration, especially in those parts of Europe where the population largely consists of mixed nationalities, would, we are sure, help to solve one of the most vital problems concerning the question of permanent peace for Europe.

V

An international organ for controlling armaments, that depends only on the moral support of humanity, can hardly be imagined after our experiences in the twentieth century, unless universal repentance after the terrible experiences and chastisement of this war and its probable consequences represses the worship of political power, and thus the actual limitation of sovereign power becomes the aim of a large majority or of leading groups of mankind. Without any limitation of the sovereign power of states by an efficacious international organ, renewed abuse of military power is always to be feared.

The question as to whether the defeated nations are to be effectively disarmed or not must above all be looked upon as belonging to the peace treaties and not to the statutes of the future international body. Nevertheless, the unilateral disarmament of a defeated nation in the peace treaties would seriously jeopardize the proper functioning of this international body. This would result in the creation of second-class nations, whose equality in at least one important branch of international collaboration would practically be out of the question. If all military establishments were to be internationalized they would have no share in the new military order and the statutes relating thereto would not apply to them. This would bring the legal character of the organization into disrepute in the eyes of the nations that were thus wronged, and would further destroy the moral fellowship so essential for the future international order. International collaboration that is burdened from the very beginning with distrust against entire nations can never be permanent and would be wanting in happy and constructive collaboration.

We feel obliged to emphasize the fact that the negative methods of attempting to achieve peace by means of police power and limitation of armaments should not be over-estimated. Their value for preserving peace is far smaller than that of the positive methods by which continued practical and constructive collaboration of all nations is assured.

VI

Christians in all countries will support the claim to religious and intellectual freedom. It ought to be pointed out in addition, however, that the measure of freedom is all the greater the more personal and public life is truly Christian in spirit and practice. The danger by which this freedom is menaced is that the spiritual dynamic of Christendom is not equal to the modern obstacles with which Christian life is faced. As present day events have proved, freedom is not assured by simply proclaiming it or by education in idealism and rationalism. The striking discrepancy between fundamental Christian demands and their actual implementation on earth should be constantly borne in mind as a warning and an inspiration, in the international collaboration of the future and the gradual, step-by-step implementation of these demands. Only those who take these discrepancies seriously can effectively ensure that Christian arguments are not abused to advance other objectives (e.g. imperialism).

A purely idealistic approach to affairs runs the risk of ignoring and suppressing national, historical, geographical, cultural and confessional realities. We must not start from a dream. We must try to perform the difficult duties that confront our generation, with humility and with a genuine attempt to achieve real Christian impartiality. Rationalistic education has often led men to have a Utopian conception of human nature and to ignore the social fact of mass disintegration and of the demoniacal forces that have gained power through this fact.

In our opinion the most important and most direct contribution that

Christianity can give towards the shaping of a lasting peace lies in the struggle against these demoniacal powers and in the solution of the mass problem by means of a truly Christian social order and the upbringing and training of a Christian elite.

5. *Exposé*
on the readiness of a powerful German group to prepare and assist Allied military operations against Nazi Germany.*

(December 1943)†

Note: This exposé defines the attitude and plans of an extremely influential group of the German opposition inside Germany on the subject of hastening the victory of the Allies and the abolition of Nazism. It has been prepared on the basis of frequent and searching conversations and discussions with a leading representative of this group about the political future of a free democratic Germany, cleansed radically of Nazism, and about the maximum contribution that can be made immediately by determined German patriots towards making this Germany a secure reality.

The exposé is to reproduce clearly and concisely the views and intentions of this group of responsible democratic Germans within Germany.

Background and standing of the German oppositional group

Apart from the Nazi Party hierarchy and its subordinate organs and functionaries, there are left in Germany two elements vested with political power: the officers corps of the Wehrmacht, and the upper ranks of the Civil Service, which, in their ministerial grades at least, represent a fairly closely-knit network of officials interconnected by personal acquaintance, official association, often long-standing friendship.

Within the overlapping spheres of high officialdom and professional army circles, three categories of people can be distinguished:

1. Politically non-descript specialists who are absorbed altogether in their service duties, being either too vague or too cautious to express their views or engage in political activity. They constitute the majority, especially among the professional officers.

2. Confirmed national socialists.

3. Decided and conscious opponents of Nazism.

---

* This document has not been written by Moltke, but on the basis of talks with Moltke. In the German edition a German translation made in 1943 has been published. The above is a copy of the original English version that went to the USA, printed by kind permission of Alexander Rüstow.

† See p. 199.

The third category is again divided in two wings, of which one favours an 'Eastern', pro-Russian orientation, the other a 'Western', pro-Anglo-Saxon trend. The former is considerably stronger than the latter, particularly in the Wehrmacht; in Luftwaffe circles it rules supreme. The driving force behind the Eastern wing is the strong and traditional conviction of a community of interests between the two mutually complementary powers, Germany and Russia, which led to the historical cooperation between Prussia and the Russian monarchy, and between the Germany Republic and Soviet Russia in the Rapallo period (1924), when the Reichswehr and the Red Army concluded a far-reaching understanding regarding military collaboration and reciprocal training facilities. Historical bonds of this character are reinforced by the deep impression wrought by the power and resilience of the Red Army and the competence of its command. Among the Eastern wing the foundation of the German Officers' League at Moscow has evoked a powerful echo, the more so, as the leaders of the League are recognized in the Wehrmacht as officers of outstanding ability and personal integrity (by the standards of their caste). This group has for a long time been in direct communication, including regular wireless contact, with the Soviet Government, until a breach of security on the Russian side led to the arrest and execution of many high-placed officers and civil servants early in 1943.

The Western group of the opposition, though numerically weaker, is represented by many key men in the military and civil service hierarchy, including officers of all ranks, and key members of the OKW. Furthermore, it is in close touch with the Catholic bishops, the Protestant Confessional Church, leading circles of the former labour unions and workmen's organizations, as well as influential men of industry and intellectuals. It is this group which is seeking to establish a practical basis for effectual collaboration with the Anglo-Saxon Allies.

Conditions of collaboration with the Allies

The following are the future material factors and present political arguments which form the logical prerequisites of a successful collaboration between this Western Group of the German democratic opposition, and the Allies.

1. Unequivocal military defeat and occupation of Germany is regarded by the members of the group as a moral and political necessity for the future of the nation.

2. The Group is convinced of the justification of the Allied demand for unconditional surrender, and realizes the untimeliness of any discussion of peace terms before this surrender has been accomplished. Their Anglo-Saxon sympathies result from a conviction of the fundamental unity of aims regarding the future organization of human relations which exists between them and the responsible statesmen on the Allied side, and the realization that in view of the natural convergence

G R H—BB

of interests between post-Nazi Germany and the other democratic nations there must of necessity result a fruitful collaboration between them. The democratic Germans see in this unity of purpose a far safer guarantee of a status of equality and dignity after the War than any formal assurance by the Allies at the present time could give them, provided any such assurances were forthcoming.

3. An important condition for the success of the plan outlined in the following points is the continuance of an unbroken Eastern front, and simultaneously its approach to within a menacing proximity of the German borders, such as the line from TILSIT to LEMBERG. Such a situation would justify before the national consciousness radical decisions in the West as the only means of forestalling the overpowering threat from the East.

4. The Group is ready to realize a planned military co-operation with the Allies on the largest possible scale, provided that exploitation of the military information, resources, and authority at the Group's disposal is combined with an all-out military effort by the Allies in such a manner as to make prompt and decisive success on a broad front a practical certainty.

This victory over Hitler, followed by Allied occupation of all Germany in the shortest possible time, would at one stroke so transform the political situation as to set free the real voice of Germany, which would acclaim the action of the Group as a bold act of true patriotism, comparable to the Tauroggen Convention concluded by the Prussian General Yorck with the Russians in 1812.

5. Should, however, the invasion of Western Europe be embarked upon in the same style as the attack upon the Italian mainland, any assistance by the Group would not only fail to settle the issue of the War, but would in addition help to create a new 'stab-in-the-back' legend, as well as compromise before the nation, and render ineffectual for the future the patriots who made the attempt. There is no doubt that half-measures would damage the cause rather than promote it, and the Group is not prepared to lend a hand in any collaboration with limited aims.

6. If it is decided to create the second front in the West by an unsparing all-out effort, and follow it up with overwhelming force to the goal of total occupation of Germany, the Group is ready to support the Allied effort with all its strength and all the important resources at its disposal. To this end it would after proper agreement and preparations be ready to despatch a high officer to a specified Allied territory by plane as their fully empowered, informed, and equipped plenipotentiary charged with co-ordinating the plans of collaboration with the Allied High Command.

7. The readiness of a sufficient number of intact units of the Wehrmacht to follow up the orders given under the Group's operational plan, and co-operate with the Allies, could only be counted upon with a sufficient degree of certainty if the above conditions are fulfilled. Other-

wise there would be a grave danger that the orders and operations agreed upon by the commanders and staffs belonging to the Group would at the decisive moment fail to materialize for lack of support, or be executed only with great friction.

8. The Group would see to it that simultaneously with the Allied landing a provisional anti-Nazi government would be formed which would take over all non-military tasks resulting from the collaboration with the Allies and the political upheaval that would accompany it. The composition of this provisional Government would be determined in advance.

9. The Group, which comprises personages belonging to the most diverse liberal and democratic parties and schools of thought, regards the possibility of a bolshevization of Germany through the rise of national communism as the deadliest imminent danger to Germany and the European family of nations. It is determined to counter this threat by all possible means, and to prevent, in particular, the conclusion of the War through the victory of the Red Army, followed by a Russian occupation of Germany before the arrival of the Anglo-Saxon armies. On the other hand no cleft must be allowed to develop between the future democratic Government and the masses of German labour. A non-communist democratic home policy will only be possible in conjunction with a whole-hearted policy of collaboration with Russia, designed to eliminate all hostility or friction with that power. In this way it should be sought not to antagonize the strong pro-Russian circles in Germany but to rally them in a common constructive effort and win them over. Finally, what must be avoided at all cost is the development of a situation which would lay a democratic Government open to the reproach of placing foreign interests above national concerns, and unify against this Government the forces of nationalism, communism and Russophily.

10. The envisaged democratic Government, in order to steal the thunder of left radicalism, should operate at home with a very strong left wing, and lean heavily on the social democrats and organized labour, even, if necessary, seek the co-operation of personally unimpeachable independent communists.

11. The initial HQ of the democratic counter-Government would under the postulated circumstances best be Southern Germany, perhaps Austria. It would be advisable not to subject the civilian population of this territorial basis to indiscriminate air attack, since experience teaches that bombed-out populations are so exhausted and absorbed by the effort of providing for their bare survival and subsistence that they are out of play as far as revolutionary action is concerned.

1. *Letter in English from Moltke to an English friend (Lionel Curtis) in 1942**

I will try to get this letter through to you, giving you a picture of the state of affairs on our side.

Things are worse and better than anybody outside Germany can believe them to be. They are worse, because the tyranny, the terror, the loss of values of all kinds, is greater than I could have believed a short time ago. The number of Germans killed by legal process in November was 25 a day through judgements of the civil courts and at least 75 a day by judgements of the courts martial, numbers running into hundreds are killed daily in concentration camps and by simple shooting without any pretence of a trial. The constant danger in which we live is formidable. At the same time the greater part of the population has been uprooted and has been conscribed to forced labour of some kind and has been spread all over the continent untying all bonds of nature and surrounding and thereby loosening the beast in man, which is reigning. The few really good people who try to stem the tide are isolated as far as they have to work in these unnatural surroundings, because they cannot trust their comrades, and they are in danger from the hatred of the oppressed people even when they succeed in saving some from the worst. Thousands of Germans who will survive will be dead mentally, will be useless for normal work.

But things are also better than you can believe, and that in many ways. The most important is the spiritual awakening, which is starting up, coupled as it is with the preparedness to be killed, if need be. The backbone of this movement is to be found in both the Christian confessions, protestant as well as catholic. The catholic churches are crowded every Sunday, the protestant churches not yet, but the movement is discernible. We are trying to build on this foundation, and I hope that in a few months more tangible proof of this will be apparent outside. Many hundreds of our people will have to die before this will be strong enough, but today they are prepared to do so. This is true also of the young generation. I know of two cases where a whole class of schoolboys, the one in a protestant part of the country, the other in a catholic part, decided to follow the calling of priests, something which would have been quite impossible six months ago. But today it is beginning to dawn on a not too numerous but active part of the population not that they have been misled, not that they are in for a hard time, not that they might lose the war, but that what is done is sinful, and that they are

* The original text is in the Curtis files in the Round Table Archives.

personally responsible for every savage act that has been done, not of course in a mortal way, but as Christians. Perhaps you will remember that, in discussions before the war,* I maintained that belief in God was not essential for coming to the results you arrive at. Today I know I was wrong, completely wrong. You know that I have fought the Nazis from the first day, but the amount of risk and readiness for sacrifice which is asked from us now, and that which may be asked from us tomorrow require more than right ethical principles, especially as we know that the success of our fight will probably mean a total collapse as a national unit. But we are ready to face this. The second great asset which we are slowly but steadily acquiring is this; the great dangers which confront us as soon as we get rid of the NS force us to visualize Europe after the war. We can only expect to get our people to overthrow this reign of terror and horror if we are able to show a picture beyond the terrifying and hopeless immediate future. A picture which will make it worthwhile for the disillusioned people to strive for, to work for, to start again and to believe in. For us Europe after the war is less a problem of frontiers and soldiers, of top-heavy organizations or grand plans, but Europe after the war is a question of how the picture of man can be re-established in the breasts of our fellow citizens. This is a question of religion and education, of ties to work and family, of the proper relation of responsibility and rights. I must say, that under the incredible pressure under which we have to labour we have made progress, which will be visible one day. Can you imagine what it means to work as a group when you cannot use the telephone, when you are unable to post letters, when you cannot tell the names of your closest friends for fear that one of them might be caught and might divulge the names under the pressure?

We are, after considerable difficulties, in communication with the Christian groups in the various occupied territories with the exception of France, where, as far as we can find out, there is no really effective opposition on a fundamental basis, but only the basis of casual activity. These people are simply splendid and are a great accession of strength to us giving trust to many others. Of course their position is easier than ours; moral and national duties are congruous even to the simple-minded, while with us there is an apparent clash of duties.

Happily I have been able to follow the activities of my English friends, and I hope they all keep their spirits up. The hardest bit of the way is still to come, but nothing is worse than to slack on the way. Please do not forget, that we trust that you will stand it through without flinching as we are prepared to do our bit, and don't forget that for us a very bitter end is in sight when you have seen matters through. We hope that you will realize that we are ready to help you win war and peace.

Yours ever,

* Original version: '. . . that in discussing your book *Civitas Dei* I maintained . . .'.

2. *Mierendorff's Proclamation*

Berlin 14.6.43.

Today, Whit Monday 1943, the undersigned have solemnly decided to confirm their joint activity as Socialist Action by drawing up the following programme of action.*

Socialist Action is a non-partisan national movement dedicated to the deliverance of Germany.

It is fighting for the liberation of the German people from the Hitler dictatorship, for the restoration of the nation's honour trampled underfoot by Nazi crimes, and for the freedom of the nation within a socialist order.

The Action Committee is composed of representatives of the Christian churches, the socialist movement, the communist movement and the liberal forces, and its composition is an expression of its determination and its unity.

The struggle will be conducted under the banner of Socialist Action, the red flag with the symbol of freedom upon it: the socialist ring linked with the Cross as a token of the unbreakable unity of the working nation.

In this difficult hour Socialist Action calls the working population in town and country and our brave soldiers to join in the struggle, in the conviction that the deliverance of our common Fatherland from political, moral and economic disintegration is only possible through:

1. The restoration of Law and Justice.

2. The removal of all restraints upon conscience and the introduction of absolute toleration in matters of belief, race and nationality.

3. Respect for the foundations of our civilization, which is inconceivable without Christianity.

4. Socialist organization of the economy, to uphold human dignity and political freedom and to guarantee the security of the salaried employee and worker in industry and agriculture as well as the farmer on his land. This is the prerequisite of social Justice and Freedom.

5. Expropriation of the key firms in heavy industry for the benefit of the German people and as the foundation of the socialist organization of the economic system, aimed at putting an end for good to the pernicious abuse of political power by high finance.

6. Self-government in the economic system with equal partnership for the working population as a basic element in the socialist order.

7. Protection of agriculture against the danger of becoming a plaything of capitalist interests.

8. Dismantling of bureaucratic centralization and the organic construction of the Reich on the basis of the Länder.

9. Wholehearted co-operation with all nations, and particularly in Europe with Great Britain and Soviet Russia.

The German people still have no opportunity to raise their voices.

* See p. 152.

That is why the ruins and the graves call all the more loudly to unity, to action! It is up to us to act before our homes are destroyed and the collapse is complete. Only the united front of all opponents of National Socialism can accomplish this task.

Bearing in mind the war dead and the martyrs of freedom who have been murdered by the power madness of Fascism and the suffering of our soldiers, we vow:

Never again will the German people lose their way in party conflict! Never again can the working class destroy itself in fratricidal struggle! Never again dictatorship and slavery!

A new Germany must emerge in which the working population orders its own life in the spirit of real freedom.

National Socialism and its lies must be destroyed root and branch, so that we can regain self-respect and the German name can be once again honourable in the world. The demand of the hour is: Away with Hitler! Fight for Justice and Freedom!

Difficult years stand before us. It is almost beyond human power to re-establish what Hitler's power madness and the war have destroyed.

Nevertheless! Socialist Action embarks on the work with determination. We summon all upright Germans to honourable co-operation. We will commit all our powers, all our ability, all our self confidence: and by these means we shall prove to history that we are still stronger than our destiny, by mastering it.

3. *Letter from Moltke to Alexander Kirk*

(Istanbul, 1943)*

Dear Mr. Kirk,

May I in this way send you my best greetings and wishes and my most sincere compliments. Perhaps it would be best to explain first, why I have stated quite definitely that I would be unable to see anybody before having seen you. You will realize that any discussion on the ways and means to end this war and to begin peace require an enormous amount of confidence on the part of both participants; on your side because the credentials I could produce would necessarily be incomplete as they can only receive their value from and through action; on my side for reasons of security as well as of policy. From my point of view any partner to such discussions must be able to visualize what life in my country is like, and he must have the discretion required to use anything I might say in a manner which will not be harmful to myself and to fundamental, permanent interests of peace. Therefore I must be sure of talking to somebody whose personal loyalty is beyond doubt and whose political judgement is up to the complex and tangled situation prevailing in my country and in several other countries of continental Europe. Obviously such qualifications demand at least personal acquaintance between those who are

* See p. 199.

responsible for the conduct of the discussion and personally I do not know of any American in this part of the world who would fulfil these qualifications but for you. I trust that you will understand this position and that you will excuse any inconvenience to which you may have been put in consequence.

Any discussion would have to start with an appreciation of the military and political situation. I am under the impression that all exhortations by the President and Mr. Churchill to the contrary notwithstanding, some people expect an early termination of the war in Europe.

I would be interested to get your opinion on this point, which is fundamental to the possibilities of co-operation: if a speedy end were in sight co-operation would become much easier technically and much more difficult politically.

On the other hand I might be able to give you an account of the German political scene. You, who know Central Europe and totalitarian states in general would thereby be enabled to gauge the value of my credentials, although nobody can be exact on this point before the event. Such a report would furthermore show you the possibilities and limits of any military or political assistance we can render to our common cause. I am afraid that to somebody who has never lived in a totalitarian country the limits of such assistance are not understandable while he will have great difficulties in even recognizing its chances.

The political-post-armistice world would have to be touched as far at least as it constitutes part of the diagnosis of the present situation. You will understand that the example of Italy has had the most damping effect on all thought of internal change and it would have to be made clear by what means a repetition will be prevented.

Once these questions of the diagnosis of the present situation have been disposed of, the main point of co-operation arises. This must be followed into its military and its political possibilities. You will realize that some unity of purpose on the political side is a conditon of effective military co-operation. As to the military co-operation, I am of the opinion that for military as well as political reasons only such co-operation is feasible as will turn the tables with one stroke. This will require the patience to wait and wait and wait until effective military power on a very considerable scale can be employed, such in fact, as will undoubtedly prove overwhelming once our assistance is added.

As I see it that would be the ground to be covered and I suppose that we would agree fairly quickly. The remainder is not a question of policy but of technique and is therefore beyond my competence. But we would have to agree on ways and means to contact the technicians on both sides.

The place for any discussions can be arranged by you. I can leave Istanbul next time I come for 48 hours. I am completely in your hands as to this point, relying on you to see that the arrangements made will keep the risk down. As to the time; I believe that, if I hurry up with my work at home, I will be able to come here at the earliest by the middle of February, at the latest middle of April.

Please accept my best wishes for Xmas and the New Year.

4. *Letter from Moltke to his wife after his trial (Extracts)**

Berlin, Jan. 10th, 1945†

My dear,

What a stroke of luck! I have been brought back here to Tegel once again, so that the dice, although it is already determined how they shall fall, are once more balancing on edge, so to speak. So I can still write a report in peace and quiet.

To take the end first; at about 3 o'clock Schulze,‡ who did not make an unfavourable impression, read out the proposed sentences: in the case of Moltke, death and confiscation of property; Delp the same; Gerstenmaier, death; Reisert and Sperr, the same; Fugger, 3 years' penal servitude; Steltzer and Haubach to be dealt with separately. Next came counsel for the defence, all of them really very decent, no monkey-tricks. Then the last statements of the accused, when I was the only one to refrain from speaking. I noticed from Eugen's§ statement, that he was getting a bit rattled.

Now for the course of the trial. All these details are, naturally, official secrets.

It took place in a small hall, which was full to bursting. Looked as though it had once been a schoolroom. After a long introduction from Freisler concerned with formalities—that the trial was secret, veto on reporting it, etc.—Schulze read out the indictment, and again only the short text, as in the warrant for arrest. Then they called on Delp, whose two policemen stepped up alongside him. The procedure was as follows: Freisler,¶ whom Hercher** has very accurately described as talented, with some genius in him, and unintelligent, and all three in the highest degree, outlined one's career, one confirmed or supplemented what he said, and then he got down to the facts which interested him. Here he picked out just those that suited his book, and left out whole sections. In Delp's case he started off by asking how he got to know Peter†† and me, what the first conversations in Berlin had been about, and so came to the Kreisau meeting of autumn '42. Here again a lecture by Freisler, into which one might insert answers, objections, or even fresh facts; however, if this looked like breaking the thread of his argument, he got impatient, made out that he didn't believe it, or bellowed at one. The build-up for Kreisau as follows: first there had been general discussions

<hr>

* This and two other 'Last Letters' of Moltke were first published by Curtis in *The Round Table* xxxvi, pp. 213–31 (1945–46). In gratitude, Hans Peters was sent by Cologne University to confer an honorary degree on him.

† See pp. 278, 279.	‡ Public prosecutor.
§ Eugen Gerstenmaier.	¶ President of the People's Court.
** Moltke's counsel.	†† Peter Count Yorck von Wartenburg.

more on matters of principle, then what was to be done in the case of defeat had been discussed, and finally the choice of Regional Commissioners. The first phase might have been tolerable, though it was considered surprising that all these conversations should have taken place without the participation of a single national socialist, but instead with ecclesiastics, and only people who subsequently were implicated in the 20 July affair. The second phase, however, was in itself utter defeatism of the very blackest kind. And the third, open preparation for high treason. Then came the conversations at Munich. These were all made out to be much less serious than the indictment suggested, but a hail of brickbats assailed the Catholic clergy and the Jesuits: assent to tyrannicide—Mariano—illegitimate children, anti-German attitude, etc., etc. All this bawled out but only with moderate violence. Even the fact that Delp had absented himself from the discussions held at his quarters was thrown in his teeth as being 'typically Jesuitical'. 'By that action you yourself showed that you know perfectly well that high treason was afoot, out of which such a holy, consecrated fellow would naturally be only too anxious to keep his tonsured pate. So off he goes to church, to pray the while, that the plot may develop along lines pleasing to God.' Next came Delp's visit to Stauffenberg. And finally Sperr's statement, on 21 July, that Stauffenberg had made overtures to him about a *coup d'état*. These two last points passed off quietly. It was noticeable, however, throughout the hearing that my name was brought in by Freisler in every other sentence like 'the Moltke circle', 'Moltke's plans', 'also belonging to Moltke', etc.

The following were laid down as fundamental principles of the law: 'That the People's Court regards as being already tantamount to treason any failure to report defeatist utterances such as Moltke's, especially when emanating from a man of his consequence and position.—As being already tantamount to preparation for high treason to broach matters of high policy with people who are in no way competent to deal with them, particularly when they do not even belong, in any active capacity, to the Party.—As being already tantamount to preparation for high treason for anyone to presume to form an opinion about a matter that it is the Führer's business to decide.—As being tantamount to preparation for high treason for anyone, even while himself holding aloof from all violent action, to prepare measures for the event when a third party, namely the enemy, shall have overthrown the Government by force, for by so doing he is counting on the force of the enemy.' And so on and so forth. The only conclusion to be drawn from it all being, that it is tantamount to high treason if one does not suit Herr Freisler.

Next it was Sperr's turn. He more or less got out of the Kreisau business—it must be admitted somewhat at my expense. However, he was reproached as follows. 'Why didn't you report it? Don't you see how important that would have been? The Moltke circle was, up to a point, the moving spirit of the "Counts' group", which in turn had charge of the political preparation for the 20 July plot: for the real motive power behind 20 July lay in these young men and not at all in Herr Gördeler!' Taking it by and large, Sperr's treatment was friendly.

Next Reisert. He was treated in a very friendly fashion. He had three conversations with me, and it was chiefly held against him that he had not immediately noticed after the first that I was an arch-traitor and rank defeatist, but had gone on and had two further talks with me. Above all he was charged with not having denounced me.

Finally Fugger. He made an excellent impression. For some time he had been under the weather, but had now pulled himself together, was discreet, sure of himself, did not incriminate any of us, spoke good, broad Bavarian, and never pleased me so well as yesterday; not a trace of nerves, although he had been scared stiff all the time he was here. He at once admitted that, after what had been said to him that day in Court, he realized he ought to have reported matters, and was dismissed with such good grace that yesterday evening I really thought he would be acquitted.

However, the name of Moltke kept cropping up all through the other examinations. It ran through everything like a scarlet thread, and, in view of the aforementioned 'legal principles' of the People's Court, it was clear that I was to be done away with.

(Short section showing layout of court here omitted)

And now for the second day. That was where my turn came. We started off quite mildly but very fast, practically break-neck. Thank goodness I'm quick on the uptake and could take Freisler's pace in my stride; which, incidentally, pleased us both. But if he carried on like that with someone not particularly quick-witted, the victim would have been condemned before he so much as noticed that Freisler had passed beyond the preliminary account of his career. Up to and including the conversation with Gördeler and my position with regard to it, everything went quite smoothly and without much fuss.

At this point I objected that the police and the security authorities had known all about it. This gave Freisler paroxysm No. 1. Everything that Delp had previously experienced was mere child's play by comparison. A hurricane was let loose, he banged on the table, went the colour of his robe, and roared out, 'I won't stand that; I won't listen to that sort of thing'. And so it went on the whole time. As I knew in any case how it would turn out, it all made no odds to me; I looked him icily straight in his eyes, which he obviously didn't care about, and all of a sudden could not keep myself from smiling. This spread to the officials sitting to the right of Freisler, and to Schulze. I wish you could have seen Schulze's expression. If a man were to jump off the bridge over the crocodiles' pond at the Zoo, I don't think the uproar could be greater. Well, anyhow, that exhausted the subject.

Next, however, came Kreisau. And there he did not waste much time over the preliminaries, but made a beeline for two things: a) defeatism, and b) the selection of Regional Commissioners. Both gave rise to a fresh paroxysm as violent as before, and, when I submitted in defence that it all had come about as an offshot of my official duties, a third paroxysm. 'All Adolf Hitler's officials set about their work on the assumption of victory, and that applies just as much in the High Command as anywhere else. I simply won't listen to that kind of thing—and even were it not the case, it's clearly the duty of every single man for his own part to promote confidence in victory.' And so on in long tirades.

But now came the crux of the whole thing. 'And who was present? a Jesuit father! Of all people, a Jesuit father! And a protestant minister, and three others, who were later condemned to death for complicity in the 20 July plot! And not a single national socialist! no, not one! Well, all I can say is, now the cat is out of the bag! A Jesuit father, and with him, of all people, you discuss the question of civil disobedience! And the Provincial Head of the Jesuits, you know him too! He even came to Kreisau once! A Provincial of the Jesuits, one of the highest officials of Germany's most dangerous enemies, he visits Graf Moltke in Kreisau! And you're not ashamed of it, even though no decent German would touch a Jesuit with a barge-pole! People who have been excluded from all military service, because of their attitude! If I know there's a Provincial of the Jesuits in a town, it's almost enough to keep me out of that town altogether. And the other reverend gentleman—what was he after there? Such people should confine their attentions to the hereafter, and leave us here in peace! And you went visiting Bishops! Looking for something you'd lost, I suppose! Where do you get your orders from? You get your orders from the Führer, and the National Socialist Party! That goes for you as much as for any other German, and anyone who takes his orders, no matter under what camouflage, from the guardian of the other world, is taking them from the enemy and will be dealt with accordingly!' And so it went on, but in a key which made the earlier paroxysms appear as the gentle rustling of a breeze.

The upshot of the examination 'against me'—since it would be absurd to talk of 'my examination'—the whole Kreisau meeting, and all subsidiary discussions arising therefrom, constituted preparation for high treason.

Really, after this climax, the only thing I need tell you is that the end came in about five minutes. What we did in Fulda and Munich was, on the whole, passed over, Freisler being of the opinion that we could make what we liked of that. And then he asked, 'Have you anything more to say?' To which, unfortunately, after some hesitation, I replied, 'No', and so was through.

To sum up the effect of all this, I rather think that if the others, whose names have come to light—though not during the trial because, when we saw how matters were going, we all took care not to mention any other names—have not yet been arrested, they are probably regarded as a negligible quantity. However, should they be arrested later, and then prove to have had knowledge amounting to more than mere social chatter on these matters, especially on anything connecting them with a possible defeat, then they must expect the death penalty.

Taking it all in all, this emphasis on the religious aspect of the case corresponds with the real inwardness of the matter, and shows that Freisler is, after all, a good judge from the political angle. This gives us the inestimable advantage of being killed for something which a) we really have done, and which b) is worth while. But that I should die as a martyr for St. Ignatius Loyola—which is, what it ultimately amounts to, since all the rest was a side-issue by comparison—really is comical, and I already tremble at the thought of Papi's paternal indignation, since he was always so anti-Catholic. The rest he will approve, but that! Even Mami won't be wholly in agreement.

(Short section omitted)

The best thing about a judgement on such lines is this. It is established that we did not wish to use force; it is further established that we did not take a single step towards setting up any sort of organization, nor question anyone as to his readiness to take over any particular post; though the indictment stated otherwise. We merely thought,* and really it was only Delp, Gerstenmaier and I, since the others counted as associates, and Peter and Adam† as maintaining connection with Schulenburg, etc. And in face of the thoughts of these three isolated men, their mere thoughts, national socialism gets in such a panic that it wants to root out everything they may have infected. There's a compliment for you! This trial sets us poles apart from the Gördeler stuff,‡ right apart from all practical activity; we are to be hanged for thinking together. Freisler is right, a thousand times right, and if we are to die, I am all in favour of our dying on this issue.

(Short section omitted)

It is only a question of men's thoughts without even the intention to resort to violence. The submissions we all made in our defence, that the police knew, that the whole thing arose out of official business, that Eugen didn't catch on, that Delp was never actually present, these must

* See pp. 278–79.
† Adam von Trott zu Solz.
‡ Countess von Moltke points out that although her husband and his more radical friends never approved of Gördeler's active plans and would have nothing to do with his hazardous method of conspiracy, the expression in the text is certainly not intended to impugn the integrity of Gördeler's aims or his untiring, upright, brave, and able personality. It should also be added that this letter which could have fallen into the wrong hands, consistently upholds the policy of the defence in court. In fact the Kreisau Circle was deeply involved in political organization, and after Moltke's arrest his closest friends were actively involved in the 20 July plot.

G R H—CC

be brushed aside, as Freisler rightly brushed them aside. So then all that is left is a single idea: how Christianity can prove a sheet-anchor in time of chaos. And just for this idea five heads (and later it may well be Steltzer's, Haubach's and even possibly Husen's as well) look like being forfeited tomorrow. But for various reasons—because the emphasis during the trial lay on the trio Delp, Eugen, Moltke, and the others were only involved through having been 'infected', because no member of any other faction was involved, no representative of the working class, no one having the care of any worldly interest—because he made it clear that I was opposed in principle to large estates, that I had no class interests at heart, no personal interests at all, not even those of my war-time job, but stood for the cause of all mankind—for all these reasons Freisler has unwittingly done us great service, in so far as it may prove possible to spread this story and make full use of it. And indeed, in my view, this should be done both at home and abroad. For our case-histories provide documentary proof that it is neither plots nor plans but the very spirit of man that is to be hunted down. Long live Freisler!

Since Dr. van Roon completed his research for this book, several new collections of material relevant to the foreign relations of the Kreisau Circle have come to light. Two are particularly important:

(a) *The Berggrav Papers, Oslo.* Among the private papers of the late Bishop Berggrav of Oslo, there are a number of diary jottings and memoranda describing his conversations with members of the German opposition during World War II. They include notes on meetings with Steltzer and Moltke on 8 January and 18 March 1943. Their discussions ranged over a variety of topics including, inevitably, the composition and plans of the German opposition and the possibility of influencing Allied propaganda. At their second meeting Moltke raised the question of the ethical and theological justification for an attempt on Hitler's life. Berggrav, who later described it as the most difficult matter on which he had ever been asked to give his advice, replied that in certain circumstances the murder of a tyrant was justified, but that in his opinion it was already too late to murder Hitler. Those who were contemplating removing the tyrant needed not only the means to assassinate him, but also, and still more important, the ability to form a new government which could secure peace. By this stage in the war Berggrav did not believe that any new German government could do this.

(b) *The archives of the Ecumenical Institute, Sigtuna, Sweden.* These archives contain a large number of documents which throw new light on the activities of Trott, Gerstenmaier, Schönfeld, Steltzer and Moltke. Some of these documents have recently been published by Mr. H. Lindgren in the *Vierteljahrshefte für Zeitgeschichte*, 3 Heft, 1970, and include the 4000-word letter of Moltke to Curtis (see p. 364), and Adam von Trott's Memorandum for the Allies, written in Stockholm in June 1944.

Ed.

Selected Bibliography

(English language publications)

I

GERMAN HISTORY

BALFOUR, M. *West Germany* (London, 1968)

BARRACLOUGH, G. *The Origins of Modern Germany* (Oxford, 1957)

CARR, W. *German History, 1815–1945* (London, 1968)

CARSTEN, F. L. *The Reichswehr and Politics 1918 to 1933* (Oxford, 1966)

CHALMERS, D. A. *The Social Democratic Party of Germany* (Yale, 1964)

CRAIG, G. A. *From Bismarck to Adenauer. Aspects of German Statecraft* (Baltimore, 1958)

DEHIO, L. *Germany and World Politics in the Twentieth Century* (London, 1959)

KLEMPERER, K. V. *Germany's New Conservatism* (Princeton, 1957)

KRIEGER, L. *The German Idea of Freedom* (Boston, 1957)

LAQUEUR, W. Z. *Young Germany. A History of the German Youth Movement* (New York–London, 1962)

MEINECKE, F. *The German Catastrophe* (Harvard, 1950)

MOSSE, G. *The Crisis of German Ideology* (New York, 1964)

NICHOLLS, A. *Weimar and the Rise of Hitler* (London, 1968)

ROSENBAUM, K. *Community of Fate: German–Soviet Diplomatic Relations 1922–1928* (Syracuse, 1965)

SIMON, W. M. *Germany, a Brief History* (New York, 1966)

STERN, F. *The Politics of Cultural Despair* (New York, 1963)

STOLPER, G., et al. *The German Economy 1870 to the present*, 2nd edn (New York, 1967)

WHEELER-BENNETT, J. W. *The Nemesis of Power. The German Army in Politics*, 2nd edn (London, 1964)

II

NATIONAL SOCIALISM

ALLEN, W. S. *The Nazi Seizure of Power* (Chicago, 1965)

ARENDT, H. *The Origins of Totalitarianism* (New York, 1951)

BAUMONT, M. (Ed.) *The Third Reich* (London, 1955)

BELOFF, M. (Ed.) *On the Track of Tyranny* (London, 1960)

BRAMSTED, E. K. *Goebbels and National Socialist Propaganda* (London, 1965)

BULLOCK, A.   *Hitler: A Study in Tyranny* (New York, 1952)
BULLOCK, A.   *Hitler and the Origins of the Second World War* (Oxford, 1967)
CONWAY, J. S.   *The Nazi Persecution of the Churches 1933–1945* (London, 1968)
DALLIN, A.   *German Rule in Russia 1941–1945* (New York, 1957)
Documents on German Foreign Policy, Series C and D (London and Washington, 1950 ff.)
HILBERG, R.   *The Destruction of the European Jews* (Chicago, 1961)
JARMAN, T. L.   *The Rise and Fall of Nazi Germany* (London, 1955)
KOGON, E.   *The Theory and Practice of Hell* (London, 1950)
KRAUSNICK, H. (and others).   *The SS State* (London, 1968)
LEBOVICS, H.   *A Socialism for the German Middle Classes* (Princeton, 1969)
LEWY, G.   *The Catholic Church and Nazi Germany* (New York and Toronto, 1964)
O'NEIL, R.   *The German Army and the Nazi Party 1933–1939* (London, 1966)
RAUSCHNING, H.   *The Revolution of Nihilism* (New York, 1939)
REITLINGER, G.   *The SS* (London, 1956)
ROBERTSON, E. M.   *Hitler's Pre-war Policy and Military Plans* (London, 1963)
SCHOENBAUM, D.   *Hitler's Social Revolution* (Oxford, 1965)
SCHWEITZER, A.   *Big Business in the Third Reich* (London, 1964)
SEABURY, P.   *The Wilhelmstrasse* (Berkeley, 1954)
SHIRER, W.   *The Rise and Fall of the Third Reich* (London, 1960)
TAYLOR, A. J. P.   *The Origins of the Second World War* (London, 1961)
TOYNBEE, A. (Ed.)   *Hitler's Europe* (London, 1955)
TREVOR-ROPER, H. R.   *The Last Days of Hitler* (New York, 1947)
TREVOR-ROPER, H. R. (Ed.)   *Hitler's Table Talk* (London, 1953)
WARNBRUNN, W.   *The Dutch under German Occupation 1940–1945* (Stanford, 1963)
WHEATON, E. B.   *Prelude to Calamity. The Nazi Revolution 1933–1935* (New York, 1968)
WRIGHT, G.   *The Ordeal of Total War: 1939–1945* London, 1968)
ZAHN, G. C.   *German Catholics and Hitler's Wars* (New York, 1962)

III

GERMAN OPPOSITION

ABSHAGEN, K.   *Canaris* (London, 1956) (tr.)
BETHGE, E.   *Dietrich Bonhoeffer* (London, 1970) (tr.)
BIELENBERG, CHRISTABEL.   *The Past is Myself* (London, 1968)
BOEHM, E.   *We Survived* (New Haven, 1949)
BRYANS, J. L.   *Blind Victory* (London, 1951)

DEUTSCH, H. C. *The Conspiracy against Hitler in the Twilight War* (Minneapolis–London, 1968)

DONOHOE, J. *Hitler's Conservative Opponents in Bavaria* (Leyden, 1961)

DULLES, A. W. *Germany's Underground* (New York, 1947)

FITZGIBBON, C. *The Shirt of Nessus*, 2nd edn (London, 1956)

FRAENKEL, H. and MANVELL, R. *The July Plot* (London, 1965); *The Canaris Conspiracy* (London, 1969)

GALLIN, O. S. U., MOTHER M. A. *Ethical and Religious Factors in the German Resistance to Hitler* (Washington, 1953)

GISEVIOUS, H. B. *To the Bitter End* (London, 1948) (tr.)

GRAML, H. etc. *The German Resistance to Hitler* (London, 1970) (tr.) *The Hassell Diaries* (London, 1948) (tr.)

KRAMARZ, J. *Stauffenberg, the Man Who Nearly Killed Hitler* (Introd. by H. Trevor-Roper.) (London, 1967) Paperback 1970.

LEBER, A. *Conscience in Revolt* (London, 1957) (tr.)

LOCHNER, L. P. *What about Germany?* (New York, 1942)

MOLTKE, COUNT H. J. *A German of the Resistance. Last Letters*, 2nd edn (Berlin, 1964)

PRITTIE, T. *Germans against Hitler* (London, 1964)

Resistance in Germany 1933–1945. A bibliography (Bonn, 1964)

RITTER, G. *The German Resistance: Carl Goerdeler's Struggle against Tyranny* (New York, 1958) (tr.)

ROTHFELS, H. *The German Opposition to Hitler* (London, 1961) (tr.)

SCHLABRENDORFF, F. v. *The Secret War Against Hitler* (1966) (tr.)

SCHMITTHENER, W. and BUCHHEIM, H. *The German Resistance to Hitler* (London, 1969 (Eds tr.)

SCHRAMM, W. v. *Conspiracy among Generals* (New York, 1958) (tr.)

SYKES, CHRISTOPHER. *Troubled loyalty. A Biography of Adam von Trott* (London, 1968)

IV

MISCELLANEOUS

ALSOP, S. and BRADEN, TH. *Sub Rosa: The OSS and American Espionage* (New York, 1946)

BAILEY, TH. A. *Woodrow Wilson and the Lost Peace* (New York, 1944)

BLACKWELL, L. v. *Murder, Mystery and the Law* (Cape Town, 1963)

BUTLER, J. R. M. *Lord Lothian (Philip Kerr)* (London, 1960)

BUTTERFIELD, H. *Christianity and History* (London, 1949)

CHURCHILL, W. S. *The Second World War*, 6 vols (London, 1948)

COLVIN, I. *Vansittart in Office* (London, 1965)

CURTIS, L. *Civitas Dei*, Vol. 3 (London, 1937)

DEANE, J. R. *The Strange Alliance* (New York, 1946)

Documents on British Foreign Policy 1919–1939, Third Series (London, (1947 ff.)

FEILING, K.   *The Life of Neville Chamberlain* (London, 1946)

FLEMING, D. F.   *The Cold War and Its Origins* (New York, 1961)

GILBERT, M.   *The Roots of Appeasement* (London, 1966)

GILBERT, M. and GOTT, R.   *The Appeasers* (London, 1963)

GOODSPEAD, D. J.   *The Conspirators, a study of the Coup d'Etat* (London, 1961)

JASPER, R. C. D.   *George Bell, Bishop of Chichester* (London, 1967)

KENNAN, G. F.   *American Diplomacy 1900–1950* (New York, 1952)

KOHN, H.   *The Idea of Nationalism*, 2nd edn (New York, 1945)

MAISKY, I.   *Who helped Hitler?* (London, 1964) (tr.)

MORSE, A. D.   *While Six Million Died* (New York, 1968)

MOWRER, E.   *Germany Puts the Clock Back* (New York, 1933)

ROSE-INNES, J.   *Autobiography* (London–New York–Cape Town, 1949)

ROWSE, A. L.   *All Souls and Appeasement* (London, 1961)

SMITH, G.   *American Diplomacy during the Second World War* (New York, 1965)

SNELL, J. L.   *Wartime Origins of the East-West Dilemma over Germany* (New Orleans, 1959)

THOMPSON, D.   *Listen Hans* (Boston, 1942)

TIMES (Ed.)   *The History of the Times* (London, 1952)

Index